We, the King

We, the King challenges the dominant top-down interpretation of the Spanish Empire and its monarchs' decrees in the New World, revealing how ordinary subjects had much more say in government and lawmaking than previously acknowledged. During the viceregal period spanning the post-1492 conquest until 1598, the King signed more than 110,000 pages of decrees concerning state policies, minutiae, and everything in between. Through careful analysis of these decrees, Adrian Masters illustrates how lawmaking was aided and abetted by subjects from various backgrounds, including powerful court women, Indigenous commoners, Afro-descendant raftsmen, secret saboteurs, pirates, sovereign Chiriguano Indians, and secretaries' wives. Subjects' innumerable petitions and labor prompted – and even phrased – a complex body of legislation and legal categories demonstrating the degree to which this empire was created from the "bottom up." Innovative and unique, *We, the King* reimagines our understandings of kingship, imperial rule, colonialism, and the origins of racial categories.

Adrian Masters is Director of the University of Trier's *GloVib: Global Entanglements Project.* Raised in rural Costa Rica, he has written several award-winning articles on Spanish imperial history.

CAMBRIDGE LATIN AMERICAN STUDIES

General Editors

KRIS LANE, Tulane University
MATTHEW RESTALL, Pennsylvania State University

Editor Emeritus

HERBERT S. KLEIN
Gouverneur Morris Emeritus Professor of History, Columbia University and Hoover Research Fellow, Stanford University

Other Books in the Series

127. *We, the King: Creating Royal Legislation in the Sixteenth-Century Spanish New World*, Adrian Masters
126. *A History of Chile 1808–2018, 2nd edition*, William F. Sater and Simon Collier
125. *The Dread Plague and the Cow Killers: The Politics of Animal Disease in Mexico and the World*, Thomas Rath
124. *Islands in the Lake: Environment and Ethnohistory in Xochimilco, New Spain*, Richard M. Conway
123. *Journey to Indo-América: APRA and the Transnational Politics of Exile, Persecution, and Solidarity, 1918–1945*, Geneviève Dorais
122. *Nationalizing Nature: Iguaza Falls and National Parks at the Brazil-Argentina Border*, Frederico Freitas
121. *Islanders and Empire: Smuggling and Political Defiance in Hispaniola, 1580–1690*, Juan José Ponce-Vázquez
120. *Our Time is Now: Race and Modernity in Postcolonial Guatemala*, Julie Gibbings
119. *The Sexual Question: A History of Prostitution in Peru, 1850s-1950s*, Paulo Drinot
118. *A Silver River in a Silver World: Dutch Trade in the Rio de la Plata, 1648–1678*, David Freeman
117. *Laboring for the State: Women, Family, and Work in Revolutionary Cuba, 1959–1971*, Rachel Hynson
116. *Violence and The Caste War of Yucatán*, Wolfgang Gabbert
115. *For Christ and Country: Militant Catholic Youth in Post-Revolutionary Mexico*, Robert Weis

(*Continued after the Index*)

We, the King

Creating Royal Legislation in the Sixteenth-Century Spanish New World

ADRIAN MASTERS

University of Trier

CAMBRIDGE
UNIVERSITY PRESS

CAMBRIDGE
UNIVERSITY PRESS

Shaftesbury Road, Cambridge CB2 8EA, United Kingdom

One Liberty Plaza, 20th Floor, New York, NY 10006, USA

477 Williamstown Road, Port Melbourne, VIC 3207, Australia

314–321, 3rd Floor, Plot 3, Splendor Forum, Jasola District Centre, New Delhi – 110025, India

103 Penang Road, #05–06/07, Visioncrest Commercial, Singapore 238467

Cambridge University Press is part of Cambridge University Press & Assessment, a department of the University of Cambridge.

We share the University's mission to contribute to society through the pursuit of education, learning and research at the highest international levels of excellence.

www.cambridge.org
Information on this title: www.cambridge.org/9781009315401

DOI: 10.1017/9781009315425

First published 2023
First paperback edition 2025

A catalogue record for this publication is available from the British Library

ISBN 978-1-009-31541-8 Hardback
ISBN 978-1-009-31540-1 Paperback

In loving memory of Ilir Hoti, Burhan Hoti, Ahmet Zhabjaku, Graciela Valverde, and Félix David Huertas Salazar.

Contents

Figures

Tables

Acknowledgments

In Italo Calvino's 1979 novel *If on a Winter's Night a Traveler*, a Reader seeks to reveal the identity of the author of a mysterious manuscript. He approaches a publisher, Mr. Cavedagna, who recounts how a client once swindled him by misrepresenting a manuscript for publication. "What does the name of an author on the jacket matter?" the fraudster had objected (p. 101). The Reader, initially uneasy with this answer, soon begins to ponder if the swindler was somehow right. Surely, what we claim as "our" writing is never fully ours. That, if nothing else, is the argument of *We, the King*: underneath a misleading jacket sleeve, which claims a single person responsible, hides many others' hard work – many authorships.

I begin listing these debts where the story begins. I would like to thank Monteverde for teaching me that the world is a rich, tangled network of people and things, each of which count. I thank my twin, Cameron, and my parents, Alan and Karen Masters. To the maids who raised me as a child, who are family: Sandra Brenes, Marleny Ugalde, Chavela Loría, and Donay Rojas. From the *Creativa*, my long-suffering teachers, including Linda Darcy, María Auxiliadora Sánchez Beltrán, and Beth Quinn. My many friends in Monteverde: Ernesto Arévalo, Pablo and Paola Castaing, Ana Gabriela Castro, Yacdany Chavarría, Andrés Corrales Mora, Ana Rita Cruz Obando and her family, Diego González Gudiel, Hector Benjamín González, Juan Gabriel González Leitón, Jim and Phebe Richards, Nicole Rockwell, Sybil Terres Gilmar, Kim Ugalde, among many others. To Félix David Huertas Salazar (†), alias Feluco, who left us far too soon. Love to Ilmet Balje, Kyle Chao, Greg Greifeld, and Erling Thompson and Keunhyung Choi 최근형. Sincerest thanks, also, to my advisers at Bard College, Susan Aberth and Pierre Ostiguy.

To the families I have become part of along the way: first and foremost my wife, Altina Hoti, who made writing this book possible through thick and thin. My thanks also go to Burhan (†), Ilir (†), Dhurata, Vegim, Eda, Rubin, and Ambla Hoti, as well as Zamir, Merita, Jerina, and Arlind Hoxha, and Ahmet (†) and Safete Zhabjaku. To Andrea, Marino, Spencer, and Montana Serra, as well as Anne, Ivo, Max, and Rike Schwierzina, I miss all of you terribly – *Danke tausendmal.*

At the University of Texas at Austin, the almost mythical generosity and friendship of Jorge Cañizares-Esguerra crafted this work and my career along every step. Many thanks also to Lina del Castillo, Alison Frazier, Judith Hogan, Marilyn Lehman, Philippa Levine, and José Carlos de la Puente Luna, among others. For their important feedback on my dissertation, my appreciation also goes to Arndt Brendecke, Judy Coffin, Susan Deans-Smith, Tamar Herzog, and Bianca Premo. As a postdoc at the Institute for Historical Studies, I benefited deeply from Miriam Bodian, and Courtney Meador's impeccable assistance carried this project. My friends and *compinches* Brett Anderson, María Cristina Cigarroa, Miguel Felipe Daza, Ahmed Deidán de la Torre, Bradley Dixon, Kristie Flannery, Christine Foster, Diana Granda, Mike Hatch, Chloe Ireton, Robert Kilgore, Jack Loveridge, Kat Marcil, James Lee, Tania Lizeth García Piña, Julie Puma, Juan Carlos de Orellana Sánchez, Nikki Osborne, Nick Roland, Chris Rose, Samantha Rubino, Eddie Shore, Graciela Valverde (†), and Henry Wiencek – you made those eight years the most fun I have ever had.

Many generous institutions helped make this book a reality. With the help of the University of Texas History Department and a Harvard-Cambridge Economic History Project Grant, I was able to conduct research in the Vatican and Spain. In Seville, I had the good fortune of spending time with many remarkable scholars and friends: among many others, James Almeida, Berta Ares Queija, Ernesto Bassi, Samantha Billing, Ros Costelo, Marc Eagle, Chloe Ireton, Michael Francis, Luis Miguel Glave Testino, Kris Lane, Leonardo Moreno Álvarez, Esther González, Nelson Fernando González Martínez, Nicolás Alejandro González Quintero, Helen Miney, Jeremy Mikecz, Carlos Murgueitio, Juan Carlos de Orellana, Lilyam Padrón Reyes, Jesus Ruiz, Guillermo Ruiz Stovel, Andrew Rutlege, Masaki Sato (佐藤 正樹), Robert Schwaller, Ana María Silva, Werner Stangl, Flavia Tudini, Miguel Valerio, Daniel Velásquez, Christina Villarreal, Andrew Walker, David Wheat, and Bartolomé Yun

Casalilla. Through the support of a US Student Fulbright-García Robles grant I was able to work in Mexico City, where I incurred great debts to Alejandro Amedore, Linda Arnold, Aranzazú Ayala Martínez, Iván Escamilla, Tracy Goode, Martha Lifshitz, David Merchant, Anthony Palacios, Javier Eduardo Ramírez López, and Jackal Tanelorn.

I also received invaluable feedback at the Geschichte der Frühen Neuzeit Seminar, through the generous support of Arndt Brendecke and the Ludwig-Maximilians-Universität München. The Southwest Seminar and its members, especially Alcira Dueñas and José Carlos de la Puente Luna, also provided important insights and ongoing assistance. Many thanks for the support of the John Carter Brown Foundation, to Neil Safier, and to the organizers and participants of LAGLOBAL and FLACSO Ecuador – Miruna Achim, Mercedes Prieto, Alessandra Russo, and Mark Thurner, as well as to Ahmed Deidán de la Torre and his family. I also incurred great debts to Chris Albi, Edward and Carla Collins, Caroline Cunill, Sally Hayes, Felipe Ruan, and Nancy van Deusen. Much love also to Sophie Chen and Norma Chen-Iverson. In Germany, I would like to especially thank Renate Dürr and Philip Hahn, who placed great trust in me and helped pilot this project to completion through the pandemic, as well as to acknowledge the exceptionally generous funding of the German Research Foundation's SFB-923, Bedrohte Ordnungen, and the support of coordinators Heike Bäder, Andrea Kirstein, and Thorsten Zachary. Sincere appreciation also to Adolfo Polo y la Borda and Kristie Flannery for their crucial work at the SFB, as well as to Tübingen friends Daniel Becker, Herta Gehr, Max and Verena Steinacher, and Ursel Wieland. Many thanks to the various editors and reviewers who have provided essential feedback and polish: at Cambridge University Press, Cecelia Cancellaro, Matthew Restahl, Kris Lane, Bharathan Sankar, and Stephanie Taylor; from the *Hispanic American Historical Review*, Sean Mannion; from the *Renaissance Quarterly*, Jessica Wolfe and Colin MacDonald; and of course, the anonymous reviewers who greatly strengthened the final product. A heartfelt round of thanks to the many archivists, scholars, janitors, secretaries, tech and transportation workers, and others who made this book possible behind the scenes.

It is not an exaggeration to say that without all these people's work and friendship the book could not have existed. And, rather sadly, it is also because of this work that I have very often been unable to enjoy the company of the same people to whom I owe so much. To all of you who helped write this, this book is for you.

Prelude: A Peruvian *Mestizo* at the Spanish Court

Early morning, on the 26th of January 1588, a porter walked through the southeast courtyard of the royal palace of Madrid. Fumbling with a set of large keys, he unlocked the large doors of the king's foremost institution of lawmaking, privilege-distribution, and adjudication: the Council of the Indies. This handyman – his name was Juan de Cendejas – checked if the council had enough candles, paper, ink, and string. He inspected the chamber pots, and adjusted and wound the clock.[1] Damiana, a black woman, soon joined him, sweeping the floor, and kindling a fire in the hearth.[2]

Business was about to begin, and the cold, dingy offices took on some life. Juan and Damiana were joined by the council president, six ministers, a secretary, two scribes, a court reporter, a royal attorney, and various young assistants. These paper-pushers shuffled in from the cold past a small but growing group of impatient vassals seeking news about their cases. The secretary curtly promised these subjects he would see to their business, before pulling the doors closed to keep the fire's warmth in – and prying eyes out.

Inside, the secretary's assistants laid out a stack of papers on the desk. The fireplace was slowly thawing the room. Ministers began reading by candlelight to the ticking of the clock. Mercifully, it had been a slow week. Work usually flooded in during the fall, when the Armadas brought not

[1] AGI, Indiferente 1395, April 27, 1583; AGI, Indiferente 1403, "Yo Juan," no page, no date [1588]. AGI, Indiferente 1395, "Pedro Romero," April 27, 1583.

[2] AGI, Indiferente 1403, no date [1588], "Yo Juan de Cendejas"; AGI, Indiferente 426, L.27, 174r–v and 149r.

only treasure but hundreds of justice-seeking vassals. By January, most of them would have left Madrid. As the paper tide ebbed during the winter, council officials could finally whittle away at their backlog.

The day's tasks: a few court cases, travel requests, privilege petitions, and suggestions for new policies. As the hours passed, a few legal agents working for Indies individuals and groups also knocked on the door and added their requests to the pile: an agent for the cities of Popayán seeking a tithing reform; the agent of Mexico's Dominicans pursuing royal support for a monastery; others looking for the same for New Granada and Michoacán.[3] The biggest of the backlogged papers on ministers' desks was a petition that stood out among many thousands. It was unusually complex – at 224 pages long, it featured many dozens of notarized documents. The dossier's contents were also extraordinary – one of its cover letters stated that it collected the volition of "all the persons, men and women, who have been born in the provinces of Peru, of Spaniards and Indians, whom are called *mestizos*."[4] Another cover letter declared that this text contained the "power of attorney and voice" of the entire "family of the *mestizos*."[5] Never before, and never again, would council officials encounter such a large and complex effort by these sons of Indigenous women and Spanish conqueror-settlers petitioning – and even "speaking" – in unison.

These cover letters outlined the efforts of this "family" to overturn a royal decree which ordered a near-ban on *mestizos*' ordination into the priesthood. On November 7, 1578, Friar Rodrigo de Loaysa, an agent of the Augustinian Order of Peru, had petitioned ministers against mestizo ordination.[6] The council had agreed with Loaysa and thought the policy appropriate for the entire Indies, not just Peru. Scribal subalterns excerpted his petition's phraseology and transplanted parts of it into a decree. A secretary's assistant relayed the draft edict to the king's desk. With the stroke of a quill, the king then ratified this admonition against *mestizo* ordination (Figure 0.1).[7]

Beginning in 1582, some 150 would-be priests with Indigenous mothers and Spanish fathers joined forces to persuade the council that this 1578 decree was unjust. This network was socially and geographically diverse. Some of these part-Indian signatories were elites; others were barely literate. Some were from Lima and Cuzco, some from Arequipa

[3] AGI, Indiferente 1089, L.14, 121r–122v. [4] AGI, Lima 126, n/p.
[5] AGI, Lima 126, 115r–v. [6] AGI, Indiferente 1588, "El presentado."
[7] AGI, Indiferente 427, L.30, 298r–v.

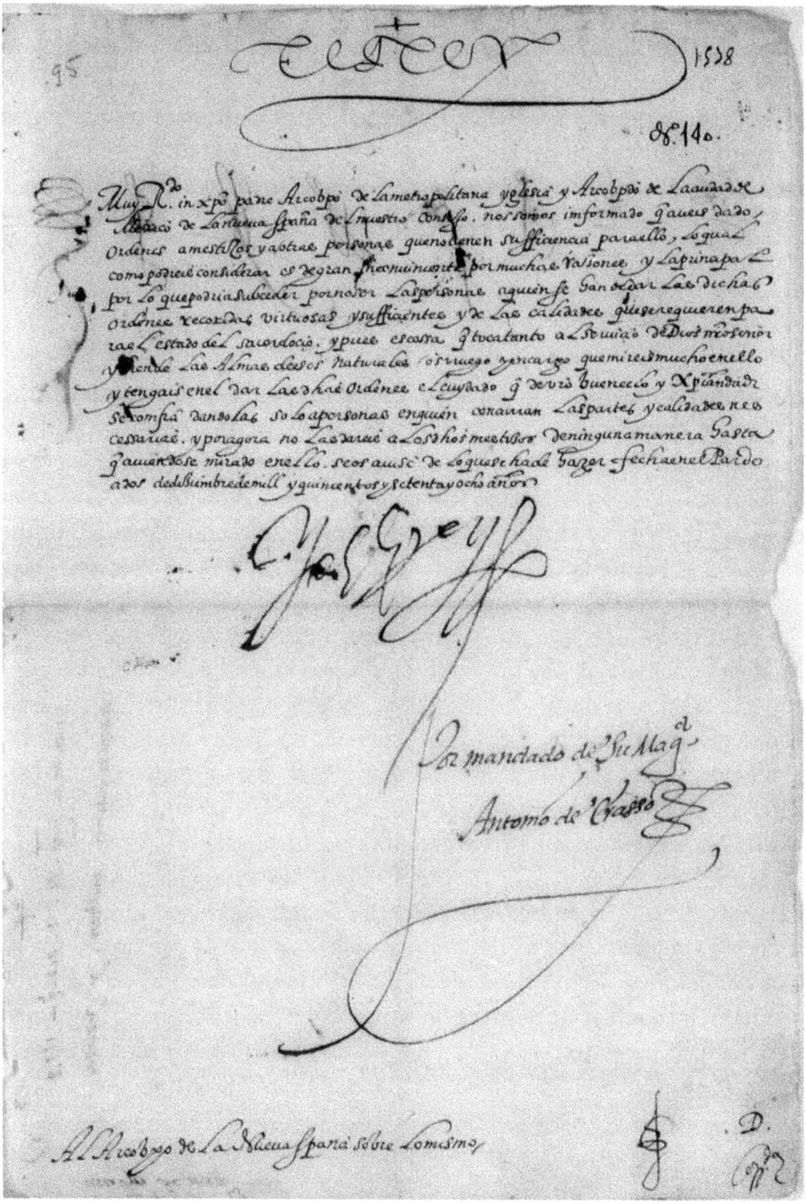

FIGURE 0.1 A 1578 royal decree barring *mestizos* from the priesthood, dispatched by the council to each Indies bishop (pictured is the decree for Mexico).

and Oropesa, others from remote Loja. This motley group coordinated with allies throughout Peru, collecting testimonies from local elites, educators, and Peruvian bishops.

Local legal agents for the case handed the final dossier to one Pedro Rengifo, who was to personally travel to the court and see the case to fruition. Pedro, perhaps born in 1541 during a lull between Peru's various civil wars, seems never to have identified his Indigenous mother's name in writing.[8] His father was conquistador Francisco Rengifo from the village of Santa Olalla, Toledo.[9] Francisco had traveled broadly and had administrative acumen: as a city councilman serving in Guatemala, La Paz, and Asunción he had often petitioned the king.[10] Pedro was a man of the Andes, never having left Peru, but did inherit from his globetrotting father a talent with paperwork. Now his horizons were about to expand dramatically. On the armada sailing across the Atlantic, Pedro eluded several calamities – disease, hurricane season, and British, French, and Moroccan pirates. He arrived in Spain in late 1584 and submitted his petition to the council by February 1585; sometime afterward, the royal secretary granted him a personal audience with the king.

Pedro's sense of awe must have been dulled by years of paperwork drudgery and delays. The monarch's gout was one such problem. Perhaps council subalterns misplaced his file, or more likely Pedro fell ill; the case was delayed for months, then years. He once again insisted in early 1588. Surely, he was eager to escape Madrid, which would welcome another wave of New World vassals with the Armadas in several months, and would once again become crowded, filthy, and expensive.

At last, on January 26, 1588, ministers jotted marginal comments on his case. Scribal assistants searched the council archives for the 1578 decree. Damiana brought the council ministers warm cinnamon tea as they deliberated.[11] They soon reached a unanimous decision, and a scribe produced a rough draft to place on King Philip II's desk. A courier passed this one-page text to the monarch's personal secretary. On August 31,

[8] Ruan, "Andean activism," 211 and "Probanza"; Duve, "El concilio."

[9] AGI, Indiferente 2082, N.75, n/p. This document is housed in the BFZ, and I have not been able to consult the original. See doc.VIII in *Colección*, 138. The sequence of documents suggests its author was Julián de Bastida in 1563; AGI, Patronato 110, R.15, n/p. In a 1562 statement in the same document, he calculated his age to be approximately fifty.

[10] AGI, Guatemala 41, N.1, 1bis., 1r–1v. Quevedo, Durán, and Duarte, *Actas*, 34–40; Freyles, 233, 368–369, 453, 555.

[11] AGI, Indiferente 1086, L.7, 310v.

1588, Philip's signature "I, the King" (*yo, el Rey*) transformed an ordinary cloth-and-ink rectangle into a text imbued with his lawmaking volition.

A council subaltern, perhaps a secretarial assistant, eventually handed Pedro the decision. The new policy established *mestizos*' and *mestizas*' full equality with Spanish men and women. Pedro had achieved his clients' reform – and had prompted a piece of royal legislation which would have a complex history but would greatly influence the next two centuries of Indies social events.

The king's signature – "I, the King" – on the decree was unmistakable. Yet so too were elements of Pedro's own cover letter – ministers had added his phraseology directly into the edict.[12] He had shaped a major, if still emerging and ambiguous, legal category of human difference. But others had helped him achieve this. Concealed under the sovereign's signature was a world of actants and laborers: not just Pedro, but part-Indigenous signatories, witnesses, notaries, procurators, the council's archives and subalterns, couriers and doormen, the assistance of Damiana, a vast system of miners and mules, the sailors and dockworkers who made the Armadas possible, the ocean winds. Behind the royal "I," there was a "we" – *We, the King*.

[12] AGI, Lima 126: 115r and AGI, Lima 580, L.9, 8v–10r; see also Ruan, "Andean activism," 221.

Introduction

The Collective Making of an Empire

Who created Spanish imperial royal decrees for the New World, and how? These are the central questions which *We, the King* seeks to answer. Getting to the heart of this problem for the early modern period in general, and specifically for the sixteenth-century Spanish Empire's dominions in the Indies, promises to reframe historians' understandings of early modern and contemporary absolutist power, lawgiving, legal categories, racialization, and society. The Spanish Empire has attracted extensive scholarly attention, in considerable part due to its conquests, its logistical challenges, its monarchs' penchant for issuing abundant decrees, its array of racial categories, and its subjects' considerable ethnic and linguistic heterogeneity. Departing from exclusively top-down or "negotiated-authoritarian" approaches, this work argues that royal decrees did not originate in the chambers of rulers and ministers alone. It centers human and nonhuman action in creating decrees, exploring how humble, middling, and elite groups cocreated a system of lawmaking and shaped (and phrased) these documents. In the process, it also explores the rise of the sixteenth-century New World's infamous legal categories of human difference (including so-called "caste" or "racial" categories).[1]

Vassals' petitions, I argue, were the origins of virtually all royal decrees. Ministers frequently even transplanted successful letters' phraseologies directly into edicts, often verbatim. This explains in large part the origin of many novel New World legal categories of human difference, like

[1] For cocreation, see Ostrom, "Crossing."

mulato, *mestizo*, and others. Of course, in an empire characterized by enormous expanses of land and sea, linguistic and ethnic diversity, and uneven literacy, these petitions did not merely glide to the court. The petition-and-response system, while generally voluminous and inclusive of free Christian vassals regardless of their status, was a complex (if often inequitable) collective undertaking. Tracing petitions' creations, their movement to the court, their fate under ministers' scrutiny, and successful proposals' transformation into royal decrees, this book also draws attention to the nitty-gritty details of early modern institutional and archival practices. All participants in this process worked to create a single, highly complex "communicative transaction," sustained by the labor of many vassals both within and far beyond the formal domain of lawmaking.[2]

This petition-and-response system involved hefty conceptual, symbolic, and written work. Some contributed muscle and sweat, as did countless Indigenous trail-sweepers, couriers, canoeists, Afro-descendant laborers (free and enslaved), sailors and port workers, doormen, and justice enforcers. Others' assistance came in the form of long hours of writing, reading, annotating, and organizing: notaries, informal assistants, legal agents, secretaries' wives, court reporters, nearly anonymous subalterns. Those involved also provided different pieces of symbolic work by cocreating the collective make-believe that all vassals had the ruler's ear, a conversation not adulterated by the fraught creation, transport, and reading of these supplications. Those who attempted to subterfuge this real-and-fictional ruler–ruled dialogue, be they internal Indies saboteurs, sovereign Afro-descendant slaves, British pirates, Chiriguano combatants, or women in the council ministers' social circles in the royal court, all profoundly transformed petition-and-response system – and risked consequences for tainting this communication.

The fiction of ruled–ruler exchange was a cornerstone of vassals' trust in the monarchy. It was from this epistolary dialogue and trust-building that communication across the world emerged – and even flourished.[3] Indeed, this back-and-forth did not merely prompt many of its laws, it shaped Indies society profoundly and itself constituted a fundamental element of a collective imperial project.

[2] Kaufer and Carley, *Communication*, 205; Puente Luna, *Andean Cosmopolitans*, 12, 50; Díaz Ceballos, "Poder compartido," 80, 291.

[3] Puente Luna, *Andean Cosmopolitans*, 50.

DIALOGUE-BUILDING AND OVERSEAS EMPIRE

Scholars of early modern governance are increasingly rejecting "extremely state-centered" models of early modern state formation, and proposing that "popular claims and initiatives could force public authorities in Europe to develop new institutional structures."[4] Some within this "empowering interactions" school have called for more bottom-up, actor-oriented models of subject–ruler dialogue, which acknowledge that such negotiations simultaneously centralized and reinforced reigning administrations while allowing a wide range of individuals and groups to design fundamental aspects of these polities.[5] In this view, states and state formation are not simply the products of coercive apparatuses which impose themselves upon passive communities, but "the outcome of communicative processes" that rendered "both parties … more powerful."[6]

Subjects could shape their states through violence or threats, through formal parliamentary gatherings, or by appealing to the arbitration of higher authorities – and often pursued many approaches simultaneously.[7] Moreover, in many of these European polities, individuals and groups could petition authorities for specific pieces of legislation.[8] A considerable body of work which extends beyond early modern Europe to the wider world, and to global Antiquity, the Middle Ages, has increasingly begun to trace similar patterns – indeed, many of liberal modernity's still-treasured myths of oriental despotisms and fatalistic peasantries may be in the process of crumbling thanks to these advances.[9] Historians have not

[4] Blockmans, Holenstein, and Mathieu, *Empowering Interactions*, preface.

[5] I follow the definition of "bottom-up" employed by Anastasopoulos, in *Political Initiatives*, 6, taking "bottom" to mean anyone outside of the legislative process, and "top" to refer to legislators.

[6] Blockmans, Holenstein, and Mathieu, *Empowering Interactions*, xxxiv–xxv.

[7] Holenstein, "Introduction: Empowering Interactions," in *Empowering Interactions*, 19.

[8] Van Hoss notes that "Legislative power, considered to be an exclusively princely prerogative in absolutist doctrine, appears to have been strongly influenced by the common practice of petitioning. The preambles of many laws and ordinances mention that the legislation responded to popular complaints," "Introduction," 30. Blickle, "Concepts and Approaches," 294; Würgler, "'Silent Masses," 16; Blockmans et al., *Empowering Interactions*; Brakensiek, "New Perspectives," 31–41; Nubola and Würgler, eds., *Forme*; Shaw, "Writing to the Prince"; Fosi, *Papal Justice*, especially 208, 212, 223; Rigaudière, "Issues at Stake," 74–101; Lasala and Rabikauskas, *Documento* 54, 95, 241–249; Pratesi, *Genesi* 37, 74; Nubola, *Supplications*, 41; Kumin and Würgler, "Petitions," 39; Holder, "Doléances," 23–67; Hengerer, "Wer Regiert," 87–140; Hespanha, *História*, 350–364.

[9] Darling, *Circle of Justice*, 7; Westbrook, *Law from the Tigris*, 30; Vernus, "Royal Command," 259–340; Feissel, "Petitions aux Empereurs," 33–49; Bagnall, "Women's Petitions," 54–55; Connolly, *Lives*; Millar, *Emperor*, 240–272; Corcoran, *Tetrarchs*;

rigorously extended this burgeoning subfield's insights to one of the early modern era's most crucial arenas of social change: the sixteenth century Spanish Empire, where Iberian warriors and their Indigenous allies toppled New World societies and sowed upheaval without precedent (see Figure 0.2). If subjects in Europe and elsewhere indelibly shaped their governments by petitioning for legislation, how might vassals in overseas territories undergoing profound social, legal, and conceptual upheaval and flexibility have used petitioning to shape emergent administrations' institutions and laws?[10]

PETITIONERS AND THE CREATION OF HUMAN DIFFERENCE IN THE INDIES

For many decades, researchers have expressed substantial interest in one set of social features which emerged in the sixteenth-century Spanish New World: the appearance of categories and institutions of human difference. Historian Juan Olaechea Labayen noted that the "discovery of America" unchained "a revolution ... of the linguistic order."[11] This transformation included new or transubstantiated words for individuals born of genealogical crosses to parents which vassals considered to be Spaniards, Indians, and Africans.[12] Many of these terms appeared in royal decrees and other documents, and it was partly from this legislation that they achieved great social significance. Scholars often call this array of endemic discriminatory social and legal categories the "caste system."[13] Interest in these terms and the so-called "caste system" occupy a central place in the literature; as Stuart Schwarz notes, "There may be no topic in early Latin American history that has generated more interest and debate than the issue of race and racial identity – including that identity's characteristics, terminology, effects, history, and hierarchies."[14]

I first stumbled upon Rengifo's case, and the overall question of how decrees were made, during several years in the Archive of the Indies, while

Faroqhi, "Political Activity," 1–39; Ursinus, *Grievance Administration*, 7–8; Römer, "Zu Formular," 167–83; Matuz, "Zur Sprache," 285–297.

[10] For a definition of institutions, see Crawford and Ostrom, "Grammar."

[11] Olaechea Labayen, "El vocabulario," 121.

[12] Olaechea Labayen, "El vocabulario," 122.

[13] It is important to note that sixteenth-century vassals did not use the term "caste' or "race' often. I will use the terms in an etic sense, in reference to today's scholarship. See Rappaport, *Disappearing*; Gonzalbo Aizpuru, "La trampa," 11–191.

[14] Schwartz, *Blood and Boundaries*, 5.

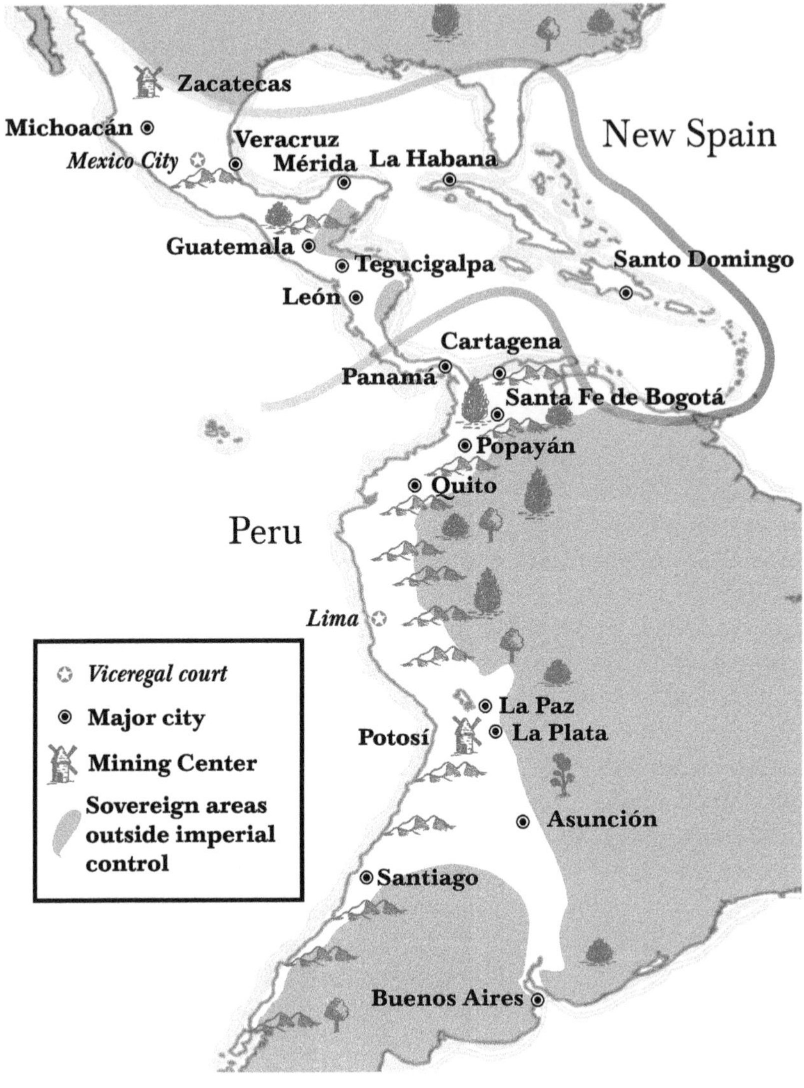

FIGURE 0.2 A map of the Spanish Indies, ca. 1570

I had been attempting to explain the sixteenth-century legal origins of the term *mestizo*. This category of human difference gradually came to mean "part-Indian, part-Spaniard" and today occupies a central part of Latin American nationalism and scholarship. My archival findings linked thousands of vassals' petitions to hundreds of royal decrees, including many featuring *mestizo*. Unfortunately, the existing literature could not accurately explain how this petitioning process worked, nor could it account for the emergence of the royal decrees which gave the *mestizo* category legal heft. Might the system of petitioning and monarchical response have something to add to this central topic of scholarly inquiry? Could many of these categories have been the by-products of these empire-wide empowering interactions?

Most scholars have explained the emergence of so-called "caste" categories as the top-down designs of powerful people or forces. Many attribute the rise of Indies caste categories to elites or rulers – the monarchy's ruling circle or local Spaniards. Others single out socioeconomics and/or mechanistic cultural processes of colonial domination and exploitation as the culprits.[15] Yet none have proven a direct, absolute, causal connection between these phenomena and the rise of caste legislation. As Yanna Yannakakis notes, "The exact origins of the caste system remain shadowy."[16] Moreover, these laws seem to lack a consistent structure across time and space. Recently, Joanne Rappaport has critiqued scholars' "propensity to envision caste as part of a coherent 'system' that subsists across the entire colonial period."[17] Karen Graubart has also described laws on *mestizos*, *mulatos*, and *zambaigos* (a term for African-Indian subjects) as "piecemeal."[18] Rengifo's case, and scholars' doubts about the nature of colonial categories, make evident that current models of Indies "racial formation" are somehow awry.[19]

The 1580s Peru debates about ordination show, on the one hand, that vassals played a direct part in defining what *mestizo* meant, and how the priesthood and convents were to operate. The council did not express a clear preference for the anti-*mestizo* Augustinians' perspective, and perhaps allowed Pedro Rengifo to triumph because of the impressive dossier. Whatever their reasons, ministers here were passive, responsive, and hardly invested in engineering a system of human difference to facilitate imperial domination. Petitioners dominated their agenda, and the empire's. Moreover, Pedro's travels highlight the fragility of this dialogue,

[15] Loveman, *National Colors*, 43–44; Mörner, *La Corona*; Cope, *Limits*, 24. Sue, *Cosmic Race*, 11; Quijano, "Colonialidad," 342. See also Quijano and Wallerstein, "Americanity," 549–57; Carrera, *Imagining Identity*, 21; Hering Torres, "Purity of Blood," 25; Bonfíl Batalla, "Sobre la ideología," no page; Lomnitz, *Exits*, 20.

[16] Yannakakis, *Native Intermediaries*, 15.

[17] Rappaport, *Disappearing*, 4–5.

[18] Graubart, "Hybrid Thinking," 222.

[19] Rather ironically, the influential and otherwise stridently top-down Mörner very nearly anticipated this argument about petitions influencing decrees in his "La afortunada"; see also *La Corona*, 124. However, these insights did not change his overall top-down model.

and the multiplicity of causal forces which could have either sped the case to completion or destroyed it. The regime of human difference in the New World that emerged in the sixteenth century was far from a consistent, systematic, top-down effort; instead, it was a complex, cocreated array of categories and policies riven with polyvalence, contradiction, and contingency.

ROYAL DECREES

This is a book about the creation of royal decrees – but what were they? Decrees – or *cédulas reales* – were brief documents, rarely longer than a page or two, bearing royal signatures. They included many themes, from privileges of individuals, families, and towns, to local, middling, and major policies. They were the Habsburgs' preferred vehicle of policy-making, and shared an equal status with another key type of text: the longer, more complex, but far less-common ordinances.

We may never even know the exact number of individual edicts which the monarchs ratified, but they certainly ratified very many. Council of the Indies officials and subalterns periodically attempted to provide rough guesses as to this number. By the time of King Philip II's 1598 death, the council had issued well over 110,000 pages of decrees on sweeping state policies, personal minutiae, and everything in between, copying them by hand into 300 to 500 massive hide-bound tomes.[20] In 1624, legal scholar don Rodrigo de Aguiar de Acuña counted some 300,000 individual decrees.[21] Five years later, his successor Antonio de León Pinelo increased the estimate to 600 books, 150,000 pages, and 400,000 individual rulings.[22]

Most of these concerned minor privileges. Many others, however, had administrative consequences across a broad spectrum, from the minor to the general. They consisted of virtually all of the bedrock laws which applied to Indies-specific affairs. One rather rough list from the late 1560s included between 17,000 and 18,000 policies for matters big and

[20] I have made this very rough calculation by adding each *registro*'s folios for 1492–1598, using Rubio y Moreno's *Inventario General*, 103–160. Fifteen massive registers (*registros*) of laws are missing, so this count is quite likely several thousand pages too low; see ibid., 43–44. In 1597, council scribes possessed at least 300 register books, according to a notary's inventory; AGI, Contaduría 7A and 7B. Diego de Encinas counted 500; see AGI, Indiferente 1416, "Diego de Encinas," May 28, 1598.

[21] Santos, "Proyectos," 57 and 60. [22] Santos, "Proyectos," 63.

small.[23] According to one official count, by 1618 these included many tens of thousands relating to privileges and minor administrative-executive orders, but also included 11,000 fundamental policy decrees; by 1635, the tally had risen to 12,000.[24] In 1681, the council published its first printed compilation, the *Recopilación*, which featured 6,385 laws, of which all but 0.51 percent dated before 1636.[25] The *Recopilación* did not replace the legal status of royal decrees, however; New World policies remained up for debate. In any case, this volume could not replace the status of royal decrees, for rulers never abandoned their claim that their will constituted *lex animata* – that is, the living law itself – and continued to imbue decrees with their legislative volition.[26]

THE LIBERAL MYTH OF HABSBURG TOTALITARIANISM

For many authors, royal decrees incarnate state-mandated racialization and authoritarianism. As with the scholarship on the top-down origins of racial categories, liberal writers have long depicted Spanish imperial lawmaking and administration as "absolutist, interventionist, centralist, statist, [and] bureaucratic."[27] The Crown has appeared frequently in the literature as an effective regime of repression which constituted a highly evolved predecessor of twentieth-century horrors: it oversaw Gestapo-like informant networks who enforced ideological purity, sponsored programs of genocide and racial apartheid, erected the first concentration camps, and cultivated the world's first cutthroat capitalist order.[28] In one author's words, the Habsburgs' (successful) quest for "absolute political control" would culminate in the horrors of the twentieth century.[29]

An even more common view is that the monarchy was an ineffective authoritarian state whose aspirations of domination – embodied in their constant production of futile laws by *motu propio* – were frustrated by the creole cunning of Spanish and Indian *pícaros*. In contemporary Latin America, many observers argue, this vision of absolutist *fiat* thwarted

[23] La Peña Cámara, "Manuscrito," 52. [24] AGI, Indiferente 1651, N.4, October 3, 1637.

[25] García-Gallo, "Legislación," 100; Sánchez Bella, *Nuevos estudios*, 103. Sánchez Bella has shown that only 0.51% of the *Recopilación*'s decrees date from after 1636.

[26] De Dios, *Poder*, 26, 71–73.

[27] Irigoin and Grafe, "Bargaining for Absolutism," 173–174; See also Zaret, *Origins*, 18; Paquette, "British impressions," 231–242.

[28] Silverblatt, *Modern Inquisitions*, 3, 95; Lomnitz, *Death*, 63–97; Quijano and Wallerstein, "Americanity," 549–557; Daniel Nemser, *Infrastructures of Race*; Mignolo, *Darker Side*.

[29] Irene Silverblatt, "Black Legend," 100.

by defiant local ingenuity characterized the region's "cultures of transgression."[30] Overall, such interpretations, by neglecting to consider the rich culture of vassal–ruler communication, have distorted not just scholars' accounts of racial formation, but have snarled our overall model of Indies society and governance.

This misunderstanding has political roots. During the liberal era, various mythological genealogies have emerged to explain Latin America's woes, especially focusing on the sixteenth century.[31] For many reformists, sixteenth-century Spanish imperial authoritarianism and the sui generis legal control of rulers over vassals primed Indies soil for its misshapen harvest. The Austrian dynasty crushed Castilian and Aragonese traditions of municipal democracy on the battlefield in the revolts of 1520–1521, sowed salt upon the budding democratic traditions of the New World, and crushed Indigenous traditions of egalitarianism.

In the liberal imagination, royal decrees in particular incarnated tyrannical government. Simón Bolívar declared these laws to be the "abysmal relics of all the despotisms, ancient and modern."[32] In 1835, the President of Ecuador declared them the "sign of the monarchic regime, the most absurd and corrupt of all those which exist among modern peoples."[33] One Panama jurist called them a "monstrous legislation ... a labyrinth with no exit."[34]

Many of Latin America's liberal reformers pointed to the sheer volume of decrees as a sure sign of this monarchical perversity. Bolivian president Andrés de Santa Cruz despaired in 1830 that Indies law had been "confused, indeterminate, contradictory, and dispersed across a thousand different volumes."[35] President Braulio Carrillo of Costa Rica described these laws as an incoherent, contradictory, "deformed and heterogeneous mass."[36] In 1831, Chile's Chamber of Deputies complained about "thirty-six thousand compiled laws and millions dispersed, without beginning, without unity ... they cannot be learned, nor can they be known."[37]

30 Araujo, "Introducción," 12.

31 Here, I define mythological thinking as a form of adult make-believe in which mythic protagonists are not embedded within their actual social structures and circumstances, and thus subject to limitations such as exhaustion and decay, but rather, exist ethereally in a disembodied manner. This vision can be comprised by pastiches of limitation-concealing fictions, including legal ones, and is not necessarily false, but rather consists of a deliberate or inadvertent causal belief that for one reason or another exists in a parallel domain from strict truth-telling. I loosely follow Segal, *Myth*, 138–142.

32 Guzmán Brito, "Crítica póstuma," 853.

33 Guzmán Brito, "Crítica póstuma," 855.

34 Guzmán Brito, "Crítica póstuma," 856.

35 Guzmán Brito, "Crítica póstuma," 851.

36 Guzmán Brito, "Crítica póstuma," 851.

37 Guzmán Brito, "Crítica póstuma," 854.

The issue of how and why so many decrees emerged in the sixteenth century, then, cuts directly through the field of politics: the long-vanished Habsburg myths of the dynasty's own power, and the even more powerful and ongoing liberal-era narratives about monarchical authoritarianism.

Scholars today largely share this view of decrees and other legal texts as Habsburg instruments to control their distant realms – and to intrude into vassals' every affair. The historiography of racial formation has frequently made this claim, but this perspective extends far beyond the so-called caste system. Carlos Fuentes does not mince words: "[I]n Spain an authoritarian order imposed itself on the movement toward a democratic order. An in the New World, the vertical structures of the Aztec and Inca empires were simply superseded by the vertical, authoritarian structure of the Hapsburgs."[38]

Felipe Fernández-Armesto has similarly stated that Spanish monarchs "aspired to regulate the most minute details of the lives of its subjects in Manila and Michoacán, down to the weight of the burdens that native labourers were allowed to carry and the identity of individuals allowed to wear swords in the street."[39] In his words, the law was a "whip" – echoing José Luis de las Heras Santos's metaphor of "absolutist" Habsburg justice as a "knife" which the Crown used to force subjects to do its bidding.[40] To avoid being lacerated by the state, vassals could only resort to foot-dragging and the invocation of the shrewd legal phrase "we obey, but do not comply." For others, decrees cast a shadow to the present. Latin American corruption itself can be explained by these edicts, which broke from the venerable Anglo tradition of judge-dominated common law and thus enabled state kleptocracy, impunity, and, ultimately, social disorder and widespread poverty.[41]

Not all scholarly depictions of this authoritarianism are quite so sanguine. To the contrary, a very large group of scholars now question whether law acted merely as "an ordering tool by the state."[42] Many refer to the dynamic between monarchs and subjects in terms of "negotiation," suggesting that vassals could skirt orders from Madrid or mute their

[38] Fuentes, *Buried Mirror*, 154. For a discussion of these views, Espinosa, *Empire* 3, especially footnote 11; See also Rodríguez, *La independencia*, 67.

[39] Fernández-Armesto, "Improbable Empire," 126; Anderson, *Estado absolutista*, 61–62; and Pietschmann, "Burocracia," 11. For similar views, see Rama, *La ciudad letrada*, 43–47.

[40] Las Heras Santos, *Justicia penal*, 31.

[41] For one particularly pointed liberal argument blaming royal legislation for Colombia's woes, see Fajardo, "Corrupción heredada."

[42] Albi, *Gamboa's World*, 3.

effects through local resistance, forcing imperial compromise. Works on "racial passing," for instance, tend to emphasize a coherent imperial legal order thwarted by local maneuvering. This tradition tacitly preserves the "command theory" of royal decrees, albeit without explicitly caricaturing Crown actions as either purely authoritarian or farcical. As the literature on racial formations shows, however, both this top-down, statist interpretation and its subtler variants remain powerful if sometimes latent currents in the historiography.

LEGAL HISTORIANS ON THE CREATION OF ROYAL DECREES

Legal studies – including those on human difference – constitute one of colonial Spanish history's biggest subfields.[43] Experts working specifically within this discipline have tended to depict imperial normativity in far subtler terms. That being said, few have attempted to elucidate the exact origin of royal decrees. Twentieth- and twenty-first-century specialists have expressed astonishment (and not a little dismay) at the sheer number of the council's "superabundant" legislative documents.[44] Alfonso García-Gallo described the Spanish Empire's legal system as "without parallel" in the history of European colonialism, singling out the Crown's "minutious ... horde of concrete and casuistic dispositions," as "one of the basic pillars, and the constitution and structure, of the Hispanic American peoples (*pueblos*)."[45] Similarly, Alfredo Jiménez Núñez has called these decrees and the "political apparatus" that produced them "one of the most interesting and controversial" elements in the Empire's history.[46]

Indeed, scholars regard these edicts, and the normative structures within which they operated, as central to this "Empire of Law." Brian Owensby has noted that "perhaps no other conquest and colonization, certainly none in modern European history, made such a point of its laws and judicial institutions as did Spain in America during and after the sixteenth century."[47] Whether or not one accepts that the Spanish Empire was truly unique in its adherence to legalism, surely its denizens' investment in legal thinking was considerable, even endemic.[48]

[43] McAlister, *Spain and Portugal*, 526. [44] Haring, *Spanish Empire*, 102.
[45] García-Gallo, "Presentación," 16. [46] Jiménez Núñez, "Sistema político," 138.
[47] Owensby, *Empire of Law*; Ross, "Legal Communications."
[48] Many thanks to Tamar Herzog for reminding me of this important wider context. McKinley, *Fractional Freedoms*, 13.

One might expect from this considerable scholarly attention to Spanish imperial law, and the importance and sheer volume of royal decrees, an extensive body of research which would explain how these and their categories emerged. Within the specialized subfield of Spanish colonial legal studies, or *derecho indiano*, there are three main approaches to explaining the creation of royal decrees, all of which fail to place their production within a concrete, flesh-and-blood universe extending far beyond the council and the narrow domain of the legal. The first *derecho* approach has been to assign them to the sole initiative of the Crown, in keeping with the contemporary mythologization of the Habsburgs. For example, Ismael Sánchez Bella declared that subjects could "not intervene in the government of the society they form[ed] a part of" and that laws were "elaborated without their intervention."[49] A second tradition, arguably the most common, mentions these documents without explaining their origins at all.

An important third *derecho* approach, innovative if sometimes rather confused, has suggested that casuistry of "incredible" dimensions produced these "minutious and copious" documents.[50] In this vision, the king and his ministers were not tyrannical authoritarians but casuists, discovering laws through dialectics aimed at resolving matters of conscience; local Indies magistrates would then reapply these dialectics when choosing whether to enforce a given law. To make a long story short, however, the petition-and-response procedure through which Crown officials made decrees was very rarely *casuistic* in the strictest sense.[51] Nor was this decision-making process primarily structured by an overarching casuistic spirit or outcome (although the acquittal of the royal conscience, always the focus of casuistic reasoning, was always a major collective concern).

In the Habsburg era, jurists and theologians produced an abundant genre of legal writings which contemporaries generally called *casos morales* and which we now call "casuistry." These works were collections of moral conundrums, each case followed by a resolution which would clarify the problem. A case might read something like "Peter is a friar but before taking vows he committed murder and subsequently escaped prison – if he leaves his Order, can authorities jail him? Or was Peter the

49 Sánchez Bella, *Nuevos estudios*, 147.

50 Jiménez, "Sistema politico," 151 and 159; see also Ots Capdequi, *Manual*; Tao Anzoátegui, *Casuismo y systema*; Owensby, "Theater of Conscience," 128.

51 For an outline of casuistry as a method, Jonsen and Toulmin, *Abuse of Casuistry*, incl. 31; Ginzburg and Biasiori, "Preface," xi–xix

Friar's oath valid, and he therefore cannot be arrested due to having acquired ecclesiastical immunity?" The author would explain over several pages how one could untangle this knot. Methodologically, a theologian or jurist would reach a conclusion through specific tactics: scrutinizing a problem quite rigorously, reading many normative sources, considering counterarguments, and unraveling the solution. The author would do so dialectically, showing readers his train of thought by citing analogies, common sense, written and unwritten law, royal decrees, other legal literature, the Bible, scholastic authorities, and other sources. He would intellectual finally "crack" the case's algebra and show future readers how he solved the moral conundrum.[52]

Strictly speaking, the council's methods for dealing with legislative-administrative *gobierno* petitions did not have the same textual format nor the same methodology as theologian-jurists did when computing the *casos morales*. Petitions did not necessarily take this paradox-dialectics-solution style, nor did decrees resemble the *casos*' conclusions. A single petition might have 150 proposals, and decrees were almost always between 1 to 2 pages long (although some could be as long as 15 pages if they excerpted entire petitions or decrees). Ministers and monarchs were far too busy and uninformed to treat all or even most incoming petitions in such casuistic detail. The themes of petitions and casuistic works also frequently differed. Moral cases like that of Peter the Friar did not seek to solve a concrete, real situation, but to discover and illuminate a type of paradigmatic problem and the legal maxim within.[53] *Gobierno* paperwork, on the other hand, could feature far more varied topics. Many petitions and decrees involved specific people in specific cases. Others concerned major issues: Was Indigenous testimony valid throughout the Indies? Should all Indians speak Nahuatl in Mexico? Should merchants establish a consulate in Mexico City? Should there be a high court in Panama? Could officials marry local women? Should a fortress be built in Havana? Both petitioners and vassals were seeking solutions variously particular and general, big and small, local and diffuse, concrete and abstract, moral and practical – meaning many supplications and decrees did not often match cases like that of Peter. Most were insufficiently "maxim-oriented" to count even loosely as casuistic texts.[54]

[52] AUST-ASPR, Consultas v.1, 359r–359v, 1614; Jonsen, "Casuistry"; Keenan, "*Moral Theology*," 163.

[53] Jonsen, "Casuistry, Situationism, and Laxism."

[54] Jonsen, "Casuistry," 12–14.

Suppose, however, that we depart from an understanding of *casos morales* in a narrow formal, methodological, and thematic sense, and ask whether *gobierno* paperwork and casuistry had some deeper resemblances. Some important scholars, including Tamar Herzog, view kings practicing casuistry, acting as jurists or theologians searching for preexisting principles. Decrees would be mere judicial "discoveries," applications of law to circumstance.[55] Did contemporaries accept that the prince's authority fell on the side of mere legal discovery, and that the ruler had no ability to *create* law? Jurists sometimes squabbled about the fine print.[56] None truly accepted that rulers could issue purely creative laws, for after all God created all men and all law, while also giving kings ample power to shape society.

Nonetheless, contemporaries believed that, within the constraints of God's creation, monarchs had the power to create human positive law. Learned scholars explicitly framed the king's decree-making as an act of *legislatio* (legislation), described sovereigns' *making*, *giving*, and *changing* of law, and often called decrees not just *decretos* but *leyes* or laws.[57] For instance, Friar Miguel Agia followed a centuries-long Iberian tradition

[55] None of this is to say that readers should understand early modern monarchical decree-production as identical with legislation in the early twenty-first-century liberal democratic sense. For the mostly incorrect view that petitions could not produce legislative decrees, see Herzog, "Immemorial," 7; *Upholding Justice*, 20; Herzog, *A Short History*, 6; "Colonial Law," where she writes, "kings were judges, not legislators," 114; see also 113.

[56] For some opponents of broad royal legislative power, see, for example, Hevia Bolaños, *Curia Philipica*, Book 1, Part 2, ¶2, 104–105, although it is worth cautioning that the author was writing for an audience mainly of lawyers and judges. For a similar view, which nonetheless allows for kings to legislate against divine and natural law in error, Agia, *Tres Pareceres*, 37, 76–78. Other sources expressed ambivalence without denying the king's major role as a legislator. While there was a general aversion to "novel" law (*novedad*), just and good laws could be "new" – not only the famous 1542 New Laws but also decrees in general. See don Diego de Torres, AGI, Patronato 196, R.16, 229r, "ley nueva y ordenanza"; see also 230r, 231r.

[57] These verbs include *hazer*, *dar*, and *mudar*. Ministers used this language of lawmaking often. For instance, in 1545 the former president of the Council of the Indies stated "I begged your Majesty not to make that law," and even referred to the Emperor's promulgation of the New Laws as the "establishment" of norms in LOC, HKR 127. Council of Castile officials spoke of making (*hazer*, *hazerla*), remaking (*hazerla de nuevo*) and changing (*mudar*); see García-Badell Arias, "La frustración," 315, 326–327. Tellingly, Council President Ovando and the king declared in the first 1571 "Book of Laws" (*Libro de las leyes*) that the monarch acted to ensure the "the governing, protection, and succor of the Christian Republic" (1r) and to this end had "gradually given laws ... dispatching decrees and provisions for each part and place, for general and particular cases," 2v. The *Libro* reunited all decrees and ordinances of general application, which had already had "force of law" (3r) in specific regions, which would thenceforth have universal application (3v). Nonetheless, likely due to the difficulty of completing this register's other six

when he wrote in the late 1500s that the king was "supreme Legislator and Monarch" and could "establish, declare, and abrogate laws."[58] That the New World lacked adequate human positive law for countless issues only made the need for decree-making more acute.[59] This is likely why petitioners and ministers did not often use the term *discovery*, or a cognate, such as *explicatio*.[60] Of course, this was not a denial that God remained the only true architect of His creation; the ruler had to placate Him by engineering and maintaining a just social order in the terrestrial realm, in the inseparable roles of law-keeper and law-maker.

A final issue concerning casuistry is implementation – a topic which, due to reasons of space, I do not address in this book.[61] For scholars today, casuistry is not only a scholar's search for maxims of justice via the consideration of concrete cases, but also the judge's adjustment of law to social circumstances. For example, perhaps Peter the Friar was guilty of murder and jailbreaking, but he had killed in self-defense and escaped prison to save children from a natural disaster. In this case, a judge using a casuistic method might forgive Peter or moderate his punishment despite royal decrees to the contrary. Here, a judge deviates from a rule-governed *system* to flexibly meet the moral specifics of the *case*.

To be sure, decrees were reflections of the royal will, and were therefore not set in stone. A monarch could easily overturn his own decree, modify it, temporarily suspend it. He could also allow (via a *gracia* privilege) for a specific individual or corporation to ignore it. Moreover, Indies officials and vassals often claimed (not without controversy) that they could temporarily soften and appeal a monarch's decree because it had

volumes, the Crown never promulgated this collection. See also Agia, *Tres Pareceres*, 37, 75–77.

[58] Agia, *Tres Pareceres*, 79 and 37. This had ancient precedent: the *Siete Partidas* explicitly depicted the king as a lawmaker; Iglesias Ferreiros, "La labor," 368, the king "*fazer ley*," (to make law), and was "*fazedor de las leyes*," (maker of the laws) 341, 344, 367–368. While there was a general early modern aversion to "novel" law (*novedad*), laws could be "new" – not only the famous 1542 New Laws but also decrees in general. See don Diego de Torres, AGI, Patronato 196, R.16, 229r, "ley nueva y ordenanza"; see also 230r, 231r. For more on the vocabulary surrounding this legislation, see Nieto Soria, *Fundamentos*, esp. 137–138, 235–236.

[59] This point about the legislative nature of decrees and the limited applicability of the discovery thesis to these documents has been well demonstrated by Mariluz Urquijo, "El concepto." For perspectives supporting decrees as legislation, see Tau Anzoátegui, "La noción," esp. 5–8, 28–37; de Dios, *El poder*, 16–28, 675–679.

[60] Herzog, "Immemorial," 4.

[61] What follows is a nonexhaustive list of works on implementation; see Gómez Gómez, "Escribir"; Tau Anzoátegui, "La noción," 67–144; Leddy Phelan, "Authority."

not been the ruler's *intention* to cause harm. We should not juxtapose *case* versus *system*, however, when considering kings' own decree-ratification; the monarch's ability to overturn his own determinations and to bend the field of legality via *gracia* renders that binary highly murky, and often irrelevant.[62] That local Indies magistrates could in a very loose sense use flexible, context-specific approach to reach decisions (especially in *justicia* litigation) is, however, quite accurate. So too is legal scholars' common observation that decrees did not always constitute the final word. Regarding how decrees arose in the petition-and-response process, however, casuistry, either as a form of decision-making or as a spirit, is an obtuse and often outright incorrect conceptual tool. In most cases, the *gobierno* petition-and-response system was formally and often in spirit a distinct format and method during the sixteenth century, and its concerns lay not with hypothetical Peters but with the flesh-and-blood Pedro Rengifo and countless others, and with these petitioners' concrete and abstract proposals. It is this petition-and-response system which I describe in the pages that follow.

EXPLORING THE GOBIERNO CHANNEL (THE VÍA DE GOBIERNO)

The vast literature on the Spanish Indies' legal culture has therefore largely not accounted for the actual process through which decrees arose. There are some works – including important recent articles by Felipe Ruan and Caroline Cunill – which give considerable attention to the specifics of how council officials assembled decrees.[63] Nevertheless, a work devoted to reflecting upon the holistic process of legislative decree-making has not yet been undertaken, leaving the overall picture of how these texts arose obscure.

At the root of much scholarly confusions lies authors' tendency to indiscriminately blur three very different types of imperial paperwork: *justicia*, *gracia*, and *gobierno*.[64] Vassals' litigation before judges, or

[62] For the case–system binary, see Anzoátegui, *Casuismo*.

[63] Some works do, in the process of illuminating another problem, mention fragments of this process; see, for instance, Muro Orejón, "La igualdad"; Real Díaz, *Estudio*; Mörner, "La afortunada gestión." For two studies which devote attention to this issue from a literary studies perspective, see Ruan, "Andean activism"; "Probanza." For a historical perspective, see Cunill, "Margins"; "Philip II"; for a hybrid case of litigation and *gobierno* petitioning for a later period, see the excellent Díaz, *The Virgin*, 15.

[64] Garriga, "Jurisdicción"; Arrieta Alberdi, "Justicia."

negocios de justicia, constituted council ministers' lowest priority (this route was also the most casuistic).[65] This remains the best-understood branch of royal justice, perhaps because it fits rather well with many liberal models of adjudication and because so many lawyers-cum-legal historians appreciate *justicia*'s familiar structure.[66] The second paperwork branch was *gracia* – decrees and petitions dealing with exceptions, such as concessions of aristocratic privileges, royal offices, patents, and pardons.[67] That our popular conception of kings associates their faculties with nobility and privilege-granting has predisposed scholars to explore this *gracia* dimension rather well.

The historiography has almost entirely ignored the workings of the third bureaucratic channel: *gobierno*.[68] This branch determined specific acts of government administration or laid out legal principles. These policies could concern miniscule, titanic, or middling issues. Unlike *justicia*, it featured no formal litigation between feuding parties before a judge. Unlike *gracia*, its decrees did not offer vassals privileges or rewards. And unlike both *gracia* and *justicia,* Indies vassals could submit *gobierno* petitions directly to the Crown without first passing through the gauntlet of local authorities.

All categories of council paperwork – especially *gracia* and *gobierno* – nonetheless overlapped in complex and often messy ways.[69] Both *gracia* and *gobierno* decrees were valid in perpetuity unless replaced by a more recent decree (unlike more casuistic and one-off *justicia* determinations or *sentencias*).[70] The council's massive handwritten volumes of Indies

[65] For three copies of the 1542 New Laws, see AGI, Patronato 170, R.47, AGI, Indiferente 423, L.20, 606v–615r, and AGS, Cámara de Castilla: Diversos de Castilla 6, N.61. For the 1571 Ordinances, see Consejo, *Ordenanzas*.

[66] Scardaville, "Justice by Paperwork," 991.

[67] For three key introductions, see the excellent de Dios, *Gracia*; Hespanha, *Gracia*; Martínez Millán and Morales, "Administración"; for grants of "citizenship" (*vecindad*) in the empire, see Herzog, *Defining Nations*; for the Habsburg practice of granting towns special prerogatives in exchange for fees, see Nader, *Liberty*; Grace also had strong connections with what scholars today refer to as "race"; see Schwaller, *Géneros*; Martínez, *Genealogical Fictions*; Cunill, "Uso indígena." See also Twinam, *Public Lives* and *Purchasing Whiteness*.

[68] What in the 1380s was the *via de expediente* became by the 1470s the *gobierno* channel, which pertained to "preparations of laws" and "acts of government" in matters administrative, military, and economic. Porras Arboledas, Ramírez Vaquero, and Sabaté i Currul, *Época medieval*, 104–107.

[69] Garriga, "Jurisdicción," 65.

[70] Moreover, vassals could allege that kings had ratified decrees due to petitioners' false claims, or that decrees were just but did not fit a new social context; nonetheless, they needed to demonstrate this and could not merely ignore decrees.

legislation also indiscriminately mixed *gracia* and *gobierno* decrees. Moreover, both differed from *justicia* court cases, in which lawyers and others often agonistically invoked volleys of theory and scholarship. In the 1500s, ministers decided upon *gracia* and *gobierno* petitions without *justicia*'s more rigorous exegeses – the latter often looked to current and centuries-bygone normative literature, and to the classics of divine or natural law.[71]

The *derecho indiano* historiography has acknowledged that *gracia* decrees arose from privilege-seekers' petitions, but has not explicitly tied *gobierno* legislation to vassals' petitions. This lack of specificity has created a muddle of these three council branches, such that experts cannot distinguish meaningfully between a court case's outcome or a new piece of administrative policy, let alone identify specific actors involved. Without singling out *gobierno* as a distinct channel, and without acknowledging a wide range of vassals' initiatives in prompting *gobierno* royal decrees, it is not possible to untangle how royal officials' policy-making process functioned, nor can one look behind past and present myths of Spanish imperial rule and find its many actants at work.

BEYOND RULER AND RULED, BEYOND THE CLOSED DOMAIN OF THE "LAW"

Delineating the *gobierno* petition-and-response process's functioning within the council is only one step toward a larger understanding of how actors created royal decrees. For some time, I was persuaded that the empowering interactions model was fully suited for the task, for it revealed subjects in action. Continual research persuaded me, however, that a model of vassal–ruler dialogue was too simple for explaining how and why the Spanish kings issued decrees. By adhering to the ruler–ruled dichotomy, ubiquitous in the historiography of empowering interactions, were we really pulling back the curtain on the sociological processes which created so many polities' decrees? Or were we promising a demystification and exposing a new and almost as reductive fiction?

Exploring cases such as Rengifo's, my files accumulated with more and more inane details about the world within and beyond the Council of the Indies. The twists and turns of this institution's bureaucratic channels

[71] Only in exceptional cases did 1500s officials (including magistrates) seek to commission the genuinely casuistic *casos morales* from outside theologians and jurists; the *casos* were not a type of document produced by monarchs or council ministers.

were becoming clearer with time, but from obscure corners of Seville's General Archive of the Indies (AGI) and other repositories, an outside universe of historical actors began to interrupt the vassal–ruler conversation. Here, an enslaved black woman cleaning the council and bringing their ministers cinnamon tea. There, a petitioner's ship delayed for months by a hurricane and pirates. A river which ran dry during rainy season isolating all of Paraguay from Peru. Secret gambling. Women influencing decision-making in the court in exchange for stunning Indigenous artworks. A legal agent secretly distorting a petition. A descendant of the Inca dynasty in Seville forging an edict (royal signature and all) with gruesome consequences. Eyebrow-raising as these outside elements were, this story would not be complete without attention to other rather gray but equally important humdrum rituals and tasks.[72] Paper, ink, marginal scribbles, a new shelf for secretaries to store royal decrees, a secretary in bed with facial paralysis. Was it even possible to write a book about sixteenth-century decree-production without incorporating as many as possible of these forces into a great causal chain?

The book whose spirit of inquiry struck me as most useful for harmonizing the council's formal work and its greater social milieu was Bruno Latour's 2002 *The Making of the Law*. The anthropologist's ethnography of the twenty-first-century French Conseil d'État or Council of State sought to understand this body's "passage of law" and relish the many twists and turns through which "humble practices of interaction metamorphose" into authoritative legal statements.[73] Latour called for a more humanized vision of how this council proceeded as an organic whole within society, critiquing scholarship's mythologized vision of law as a "neoclassical temple hovering above an astounded citizenry."[74] Law was little more than the process of lawmaking, and lawmaking was a gigantic series of procedural "winding paths" of collective, self-referential practices, including not only officials' deliberations but a far greater universe of participants.[75] Instead of envisioning the law as "a sphere apart and self-maintained within society," Latour underscored the contribution of many "extra-legal" actors, including litigants, lawyers, female secretaries, security guards, files, paper-clips, archives, furniture, "walls, corridors, frescoes, a body of members, texts, careers, publications,

[72] Knorr-Cetina, "Introduction," 7. [73] Latour, *Making*, 170, 196.
[74] Latour, *Making*, 5; see also 69, 151–152, 197. [75] Latour, *Making*, 152.

controversies."[76] His analysis revealed some of lawmaking's "materiality, its colours, its textures and its opulence, but also its fragility."[77]

The Making of the Law implicitly drew from decades of Latour's work on Actor-Network Theory, which provides a useful methodology for tracing causal processes within decree-production, the creation of legal categories, and the role of nonelites in creating imperial policy, all at once. This methodology aimed to "rebuild social theory out of networks" and thus allow us to rethink pervasive sociological concepts like "institutions, organizations, states and nations" – or, one might add, constructs like "the law," "science," or "religion."[78] This approach foregrounds the complexities of countless overlaid network chains instead of attempting to impose the universal upon the particular.[79] Following these networks' operations up close also often reveals the artificiality of many sociological and conceptual binaries pervasive in research.[80] For example, dualities between human and nonhuman actors fade – Latour instead calls for exploring anything which influences the network as an *actant*.[81]

By expanding the scope of analysis beyond the era's own mythical accounts of vassal–Crown relations, one can better appreciate the roles of actants and vassals with less symbolic capital who nonetheless made the decree-making process possible. These contributors include humans elite – from kings to ministers to archbishops; humans middling – legal agents, postal workers, ship captains; and humans humble – Indigenous runners, Afro-descendant raftsmen, maids, and enslaved custodians (among many others). The petition-and-response process also was shaped by nonhuman flora and fauna, such as mules, horses, mosquitos, cloth, and rainforests, as well as nonliving actants like paper, ocean winds, archives, and Indigenous goldwork. Ideas played a crucial part: ruler–vassal reciprocity, legal representation-by-agent, the defeminization of officialdom, the legitimacy of conquest, and the binding power of the phrase "I, the King." In fact, these spheres of ideas and materials, human and nonhuman, rulers and ruled, were not opposite at all, for they intrinsically merged and mutually shaped one another at every moment.[82] Countless actants formed part of a causal ecology far greater than the past mythologization of ruler–ruled dialogue and today's predominant idea of the law would allow.

[76] Latour, *Making*, 263, 264. See also 68, 77, 79, 83–84, and 168.
[77] Latour, *Making*, 5. [78] Latour, "Actor-network," 369.
[79] Latour, "Actor-network," 370. [80] Latour, "Actor-network," 372.
[81] Latour, "Actor-network," 373. [82] Latour, "Powers," 277.

THE LEGAL FICTIONS OF HABSBURGS AND LIBERALS

Latour notes that strong networks do not simply surrender the myths of their own construction. Actors creating networks often symbolically and conceptually cordon them off from wider connections, so that artificial domains such as "law," "science," and "religion" appear as spheres discrete from other ones (at least in our imaginations). Latour notes that after a researcher has traced a network, and has revealed the actual causal unity of spheres many once held to be distinct, he or she must go further still, devoting attention to why its participants did not understand this network as a wider process but rather as a distinct domain.[83] Though he does not belabor the point, he suggests that actants sometimes create "cutting points" – artificial truncations of networks' true organic extensions into the societies inside which ostensibly separate spheres actually operate.[84] I will refer to the outcomes of this "cutting" as *mythologizations*, for those thinking within them not only imagine certain interlinked networks as separate from one another, but implicitly model them as devoid of actors and their terrestrial constraints.

Scholarly writing on both law and legal history have tended to mythologize law, as Latour noted. Early modern actors were not so much concerned with re-enforcing a domain of "the legal" as they were with sustaining the image of a great vassal–ruler dialogue which was largely untrammeled by earthly challenges. The empire's participants expressed a collective self-image of a consenting community. Their communications network could not have existed without legal fictions. Indeed, just as there "would be no game without belief in the game and without the wills, intentions, and aspirations which actuate the agents," there could hardly be an empire built without vassals' volition, on violence alone.[85]

This widespread belief in dialogue required the constant cocreation of many vassals. One end result was an actant-created fiction of vassal–ruler contact.[86] This book relies particularly heavily on Karen Petroski's definition of legal fiction, a domain of nonactual "collective consensual 'pretending'" and disciplined role-play, with its own internally cohesive

[83] Latour, "Actor-network," 369–381, here 380. Latour refers to the "process that makes the joint production of factors and artifacts entirely opaque" as "blackboxing"; Latour, "Technical," 36.

[84] Latour, "Actor-network," 369–381, here 379.

[85] Bourdieu, "Men," 308.

[86] Fiction, etymologically derived from *fingere*, to form or contrive; Zemon Davis, *Fiction*, 4.

logic.[87] Petroski lists among legal fictions the "linguistic depictions of nonactual people" as individuals – for instance, today's widespread tendency to legally identify corporations as human beings.[88] She also mentions lawyers' and judges' claims to understand the innermost emotions and intentions of specific actors, though they "do not have direct access to these states in others" – a fiction which legal norms often require for judges' determinations. Role-play and make-believe are not aberrances in an otherwise sober legal discipline. They are endemic to normative systems, and are necessary for trust-building, sustaining community life, and enabling law to shape society.[89] It is only with these fictions that complex, imperfect processes can function – and, in the process, sustain society.[90]

The overlapping views of liberals and specialist scholars have shared a tendency to mythologize Spanish monarchs' lawmaking practices, in a sense echoing the legal fictions of the past. That is to say, these authors have approached lawmaking as an act aloof from its social and material context, and have depicted lawmakers as unmoored from their human limitations. The early modern Habsburgs might have been very flattered by twentieth- and twenty-first century scholars' overestimation of their capabilities and designs. Certainly, the Austrian ruling family did not object when courtier-historians proclaimed their descent from supernaturally capable mythological and Biblical figures.[91] In this way, in today's historiography, as well as in sixteenth-century thought, royal decree-making appears as a top-down process of Crown authorship divorced almost entirely from bottom-up contributions, and is sharply separated from a wider "extra-legal" society.[92]

How sixteenth-century vassals and rulers imagined the petition-and-response system as involving a minimum of actors, with the king playing the predominant role, also required substantial effort from all parties. The Trastámaras and Habsburgs themselves did not invest their personal time in proclaiming the divine origin of their rule, nor did they explicitly proclaim that their decrees emerged sui generis. Most decrees bearing their

[87] Petroski, *Fiction*, 28, 35. My understanding of fiction departs somewhat from that of Zemon Davis; I use fiction here to mean an utterance individuals make within a domain of semi-autonomous make-believe statements, as opposed to in the domain of truth-statements; see *Fiction*, 3.

[88] Petroski, *Fiction*, 92. [89] Petroski, *Fiction*, 59. [90] Luhmann, *Legitimation*, 4, 23.

[91] Tanner, *Last Descendant*; see also Nieto Soria, *Fundamentos ideológicos*, 38–56, 157; de Dios, *El poder*, 678.

[92] Reinhardt, *Voices*, 28 and 77; Owensby, "Pacto."

signatures acknowledged that certain vassals had requested monarchical intervention in a particular or general matter. However, these rulers did jealously defend the divine origin of their lawgiving powers. Downplaying the process of decree-making, they framed their edicts as the expression of their royal volition. They and their vassals also framed their relationship as one of a dialogue of volitions. Some sociologists today have made an argument for societies as the products of voluntarism – the gathering of many actors' "scattered wills [which] are recapitulated in the person of the sovereign."[93] Sixteenth-century vassals would have intuitively agreed with, and its intellectuals strongly approved of, this vision.[94] Francisco Suárez's masterful 1612 *A Treatise on Laws and God the Lawgiver* provided a recapitulation of scholastic works on the nature of lawmaking and, in the process, laid out many jurists' mythology of how earthly rulers created law (or, more precisely, how they ratified princely decrees or positive human law).[95] In some ways, today's historiography would agree with Suárez, who viewed law as a sui generis, top-down *obligation*, or a rope (*ligation*) with which a superior binds his inferiors.[96] Suárez's myth insisted that this chain of command did not rest with the monarch, but with God, who by His volition, or *voluntad*, delegated earthly rulers with lawmaking authority or *potestad*. The Lord thus enabled monarchs to apply their divinely commissioned intent to concrete or general problems in the form of human positive law. In this way, written or spoken laws were merely an effect or sign of a king's will.[97] The more recent the decree, the fresher and weightier the royal *voluntad*.

Vassals, too, constantly downplayed the coproduced nature of decrees, even as their writings and actions betrayed that they knew otherwise. Virtually all insisted on certain scholastic and monarchical fictions. They broadly agreed, for instance, that decrees constituted manifestations of the royal volition. As the Viceroy of Peru reported in 1596 after facing ambiguities executing certain land reforms, "all of the theologians and jurists' recommendations seek to interpret the intention and volition of what your Majesty orders and sends through his royal decrees," and his

[93] Callon and Latour, "Unscrewing," 296. For a curious Francoist vision of twentieth-century law as an "entanglement of wills through and by the vehicle of the word," see Ruiz-Giménez Cortés, "Derecho," 26.

[94] Reinhardt, *Voices*, 28 and 77; Owensby, "Pacto."

[95] Suárez, *Tratado*, ch. 3, t.10, 61.

[96] Suárez, *Tratado*, ch.1, t.1, 19; ch.3, t.10, 65; ch.5, t.3, 89–90.

[97] Suárez, *Tratado*, ch.5, tit.2-tit.6, 89–93. See also Pugliese La Valle, "Fuentes," 1402. See also AGI, Indiferente 1412, "Alonso Ramos," November 3, 1595.

own approach was to favor Indigenous communities.[98] It was through this process of seeking to discern the royal intention that "we executed the will of your Majesty."[99]

However, subjects' constant communications with the king and council also reveal certain different strains of myths from those embraced by scholastic jurists. According to petitioners, lawmakers may have derived their authority from God, but the rulers' obligation to dialogue with and listen to subjects complemented the top-down flow of authority. Petitioners insisted constantly upon the essential role of dialogue. One Miguel de Villanueva reminded the monarch from Charcas that "if the words of council are good, they must be heeded without regarding who offers them."[100] Many statements confirm vassals' convictions that the king was obliged to attend to lowly petitions. Friar Pedro Suárez de Escobar reminded the council that "it is not too much that the mortal princes, though they have their high estate, allow themselves to be pleaded by the poor who bear the lowlier place."[101] The Indians of Mexico City wrote that "we have understood that the clemency and justice abounds in Your royal breast," particularly for "us, your vassals, the natives of New Spain and especially the City of Mexico."[102] Similarly, Chongo Indian leaders wrote from Peru that the king's duty was to "maintain us in Justice."[103] The widow doña María de Aguilar boldly stated that she dared to write the king because he would not "permit, nor does he benefit from, that we widows be mistreated."[104]

But which force obliged the monarchs to heed these humble petitioners? This was the royal conscience (*real conciencia*) which impelled the king to hear the claims of all his flock, regardless of nation, ethnicity, age, or gender.[105] Indeed, the monarch was perpetually on trial before God, and his mandate depended on his careful attention to the republic's most marginal vassals.[106] Petitioners invoked this principle extremely often. Around 1527 the procurators of the City of Mexico traveled to the court and demanded that the council provide them with a bishop, saying "we

[98] AGI, Lima 33, N.11, "Hazienda. Aquí va el duplicado," April 12, 1596, 1r.
[99] AGI, Lima 33, N.11, "Hazienda. Aquí va el duplicado," April 12, 1596, 1r.
[100] AGI, Lima 270, "Algunas vezes," April 15, 1564.
[101] AGI, México 282, April 1, 1574, "Pax nobis" 648r–648v, Fray Pedro Suárez de Escobar.
[102] AGI, México 168, N.53, "Entendido tenemos," December 18 1554, 156r–v.
[103] AGI, Lima 121, "Los caçiques," January 8 1566.
[104] AGI, Santa Fe 187, 163r, "Sin que," February 5, 1574.
[105] See, for instance, Keen, *Aztec Image*, 71; Owensby, "Theater," 126.
[106] Reinhardt, *Voices*; Braun, "Conscience."

plea, and above that, we commend this to your conscience."[107] Bishop Luis Zapata and President don Lope Diez de Armendariz wrote from New Granada, "we sustain ourselves and persevere with nothing but the hope that Your Majesty will solve [this issue] as suits the tranquility of your vassals and the acquittal (*descargo*) of your royal conscience."[108] Others made similar arguments. Pedro de Ahumada wrote in 1559 that the state of affairs in Mexico put the royal conscience at risk, and that he must embrace certain reforms to "acquit your royal conscience well and [provide] the conservation of these Indians, your vassals."[109]

This principle was not a merely rhetorical ploy. Monarchs took the matter of divine judgment seriously. In their private correspondences, Spain's rulers made this explicit. Emperor Charles V would instruct his son Prince Philip in 1548 to watch over his "conscience" with "great account and consideration" about the Indies' most pressing crises.[110] As king, Philip took these concerns to his deathbed.[111]

Denizens of the empire viewed communication itself as a safeguard not only of the monarch's conscience but of their own. The prominent New Granada official Tomás López Medel stated in 1557 that he wrote the council because "I am obligated for the discharge of my conscience."[112] Luis de Salazar wrote in 1573, "It seems to me, Your Majesty, that I would always accuse my conscience, saying 'woe is me,' for I fall silent and do not say the many things that I could" if he did not petition.[113] One conquistador wrote the king from Santa Fe de Bogotá in 1583 that "if the aggrieved of these parts of the Indies" did not have "the sea of clemency and justice that glistens in . . . your Catholic breast, it would cause us such desperation so as to lose not only our bodies, but our very souls."[114] Communication was deliverance both personal and collective – and this stirred, as a secondary effect, the royal volition which created law. Dialogue was essential for the emergence of a more Christian society, a process through which all could achieve redemption.[115]

[107] AGI, Patronato 180, R.18, 349r.

[108] AGI, Santa Fe 226, N.32, "Aunque no," April 18, 1580.

[109] AGI, México 367, "E visto," December 31, 1559. Similarly, AGI, Santa Fe 187, "Justa cosa," April 15, 1573; AGI, México 107, "La experiencia," October 15, 1584.

[110] BNE, Mss.6665, 62v–66r.

[111] On his deathbed, as in life, he remained concerned about the "matters of his soul and conscience." See the "Relación," 153r–160v, BNE, Mss.5972.

[112] NYPL, ORMC, Reel 4, "Carta," 143r, December 20, 1557.

[113] AGI, Santa Fe 83, N.7, 142r.

[114] AGI, Patronato 27, R.32, 41v, "Si de los agraviados," March 24, 1583.

[115] Brendecke, *Empirical Empire*, 21 and 26.

Subjects almost always framed their petitions as personal communications with a king who would give careful attention to each one of their problems. In practice, subjects' *voluntad*, not the will of the ruler alone, was also an essential ingredient here – despite scholastics' insistence that volition flowed downward from heaven. But could a lifeless petition contain the *voluntad* of a human subject? The reality was that many vassals could not easily express problems on paper, due to challenges in accurately describing the Indies, illiteracy, language, and logistics. All petitioners had to surrender to the reality that their writings would need intermediaries of all sorts – and these middlemen had their own volitions which could adulterate dialogue. From beginning to end, *voluntad* coursed through social and logistical channels fraught with frictions of all sorts – from petition-making to ministers' final decisions.[116]

Vassals and royal officials thus constantly sought to reinforce various fictions of pure vassal–lord dialogue at weak points in the petition-and-response pipeline. A considerable part of *We, the King* explores how Crown officials and subjects created and patrolled the fiction of local intermediaries' and royal ministers' impartiality. Royal secretaries, the council, and its ministers acted similarly as intermediaries. Though it was the king's volition (expressed via his signature) which created human positive law, petitions first had to pass before the prudent eyes of royal ministers and the hands of secretaries. Ministers, however, were all too human – each brought his own *voluntad* to the vassal–lord dialogue.[117] Furio Cerol's 1559 *El Consejo, y consejeros del Príncipe* ("The Council, and Counselors of the Prince") urged that while a good minister acted as a doctor to an ailing republic, a biased one endangered all.[118]

There exists today a powerful if not completely dominant tendency among scholars to depict the Spanish royal administration as inept, corrupt, uniquely nonbureaucratic – or all three. Many historians have described the council's operations as a pure patrimonial system, characterized by "mass domination by one individual" and his or her untrammeled family interests, clientelist obligations, or personal whims.[119] Others have even described the Spanish Empire as the "epicenter of corruption" in Europe – and, perhaps, the world.[120]

[116] Vismann, *Files*, 88. [117] Erasmus of Rotterdam, *Education*, 57.
[118] Ceriol, *El Consejo*, prologue, n/p.
[119] For instance, Sarfatti Larson, *Spanish Bureaucratic-Patrimonialism*, 14.
[120] Vicens Vives, "Estructura," 148; Quiroz, *Corrupt Circles*, 148.

And yet the system of petition-and-response was not entirely or even mostly dominated by acts which we, or they, would call corrupt or patrimonial. In sixteenth-century officials' views, corrupt acts included "nepotism, traffic of influences, bribery, distortion of legislation, cash payments in quantities that range from 'gifts' with the finality of 'accelerating paperwork,' to the pay of sums that change the direction of affairs … confiscation of papers, false notarial certificates, extortive methods of all types, etc."[121]

Today's understandings of the empire's officialdom tend to emphasize venality and clientelist networks, underestimating the extent to which Habsburg monarchs attempted to shape ministers into diligent, prudent, disinterested, selfless servants who acted solely as vessels to channel rulers' decision-making, not as agents with their own blind spots and personal interests.[122] Ministers' good praxes, after all, were essential to ensure that vassals' *voluntad* reached the king's eyes and ears, for the validity of the ruler's determinations was dependent on his having received morally pure recommendations from subjects and especially from ministers.[123] As Nicole Reinhardt has noted, many contemporaries believed that both "royal will as well as councilors' competent counselling" were necessary to create not merely a *policy* but a *just* policy.[124] Erasmus of Rotterdam laid this out in his 1516 *Education of a Christian* to the young Prince Charles V. The ruler was to welcome the counsel of "wise men" as his "hands and eyes," and to take great care in defending poor and middling subjects by listening to their pleas.[125]

In the course of the sixteenth century, council officials and Crown administrators developed an anticorruption ethos, including substantial efforts to prevent powerful Indies vassals from usurping the petition-and-response system. And, as this book shows, the emerging ethos of dispassionate prudence arose in part through the intentional and inadvertent actions of women, and accrued increasingly gendered overtones due to widespread fears in the court that female subjects, pleasure, and emotion might corrupt ministers and jeopardize the vassal–lord exchange of *voluntad*. The resulting gendered supervision of all sorts of officials, both from top-down and bottom-up initiatives, played a crucial role in the Habsburg myth of an untainted vassal–ruler dialogue.

[121] Pietschmann, "Corrupción," 349.
[122] Rivero Rodríguez, "De todo," 268 footnote 5.
[123] Brendecke, *Empirical Empire*, 24, 29, 53. [124] Reinhardt, *Voices*, 28.
[125] Erasmus of Rotterdam, *Education*, 28.

CENTERING THE LABOR OF THE LAW

We, the King is a book about the labor of decree-production – more precisely, the many diverse work practices which actants contributed to the great chain of communicative transactions necessary for decree-making. As Latour noted, actants are nothing if not workers, and their net*works* nothing if not *work*nets.[126] Latour may not have stated this in uncertain terms in *The Making of the Law*, but lawmaking *is* labor, and all labor related to decree-production is part of the lawmaking process.

By viewing the petition-and-response system's diverse labor types from a richly bottom-up perspective, and by considering its great and highly diverse chain of actants from laborers to hurricanes to kings, we collide with the concept of labor itself. On the one hand, global labor history has recently sought to rethink "labor" as a concept, but continues to limit its focus to traditional topics and agents – peasants, factory workers, unions, socialist political parties, and the like.[127] But sociologically speaking, why should kings, letter-writers, secretarial assistants, legal agents, mules, notaries, or whistle-blowing wives of ministers not count as participant workers within a great network of global toil?[128] Indeed, this artificial division of labor types is a major component of the mythologization of the phrase "I, the King," and likely the root of many other sociological misunderstandings about where agency lies within countless societies' production of normative orders.

Studies of the Council of the Indies have rarely considered the issue of labor head on.[129] Beyond a wealth of biographical and prosopographical works on its members, scholarship on the council is lacking in general.[130]

[126] Latour, "Network Theory," 802.

[127] Global labor history has taken limited steps to broaden labor typologies, but largely remains focused on forms of hard labor alone; see van der Linden, *Workers*, 17–35; De Vito, "New Perspectives," 28; Hofmeester, Lucassen, Lucassen, Stapel, and Zijdeman, "Global Collaboratory," 6–10; Lucassen, "Working Together," 67–69.

[128] For innovative steps toward understanding intellectuals as laborers, see Roche, "L'intellectuel," 465–480; Sapiro, "Les professions," 3–18; Ribard, "Travail intellectuel," 715–742; Williams, "Unfolding," 508.

[129] For institutional and proposographical studies of the council, all of which sidestep the specifics of its document production, see Schäfer, *Consejo Real*; Dworkoski, "Council of the Indies"; Suárez Fernández, ed., *El Consejo*; Muro Orejón, "Real y Supremo"; García-Gallo, "Consejo y los secretarios"; Villarreal Brasca, "Consejero de Felipe III"; Antón Infante, "Consejo de Indias"; Amadori and Díaz Blanco, "Consejo de Indias"; Bernard, *Le Secrétariat*; García Pérez, *Consejo de Indias*; Burkholder, "Council of the Indies"; Burgos Lejonagoitia, *Gobernar*; López Valencia, "Royal and Supreme."

[130] Among others, see Poole, *Juan de Ovando* and *Pedro*; Gaudin, *El imperio*; Keniston, *Francisco*.

For instance, few have studied its document-producing procedures.[131] The same is true for studies of documentary genres, which have nonetheless greatly downplayed the production process itself while focusing almost exclusively on describing decrees' formal contents.[132]

Expanding our focus from institutional guidelines to actual labor portrays lawmaking in a new light. The most visionary historian to date on labor within this institution has been Margarita Gómez Gómez, who has forcefully called for studying council subalterns – an important step toward recognizing the wide net of actants who participated in the decree-production process.[133] Guillaume Gaudin and Caroline Cunill also have pressed forward in this direction.[134]

Scholars are also beginning to look beyond the confines of the council's offices. Two recent books in particular point the way forward for a bottom-up, communication-centric rethinking of imperial administration rooted in the New World. Óscar Mazín's *Agents of Royal Justice* delves deep into the social and bureaucratic worlds of Mexican cathedrals' agents at the court.[135] José Carlos de la Puente Luna's *Andean Cosmopolitans* provides an even more dramatic study, tracing how Peru's Indigenous privilege and justice-seeking communities engaged with imperial justice systems in Lima and Madrid.[136] Puente Luna's work shows the massive chains of hard communal labor, legal mediation, patronage and charity, royal bureaucracy, and ideas which enabled trans-Atlantic communities of advocacy to arise.

While none of the aforementioned works focus holistically on the petition-and-response system per se, they do testify to the windfalls which might come from studying petitioning and Crown praxes from a bottom-up perspective. Without incorporating these various labor forms into a single vision of a complex communication network, the lawmaking process will remain disconnected from human efforts, and our sociological models will remain divested of the capacity to appreciate who, beyond the myth of the king and the state, created royal decrees.

[131] Manzano, "Documento inédito"; Muro Orejón, "Igualdad"; Barrero García, "Vía ordinaria"; Díaz Blanco, "Régimen"; Gómez Gómez, "Secretaría" and "Nueva tramitación"; Cunill, "Philip II," and "Margins"; Manzorro Guerrero, "Prácticas."

[132] Real Díaz, *Estudio diplomático*; Heredia Herrera, *Catálogo*, vols. 1 and 2, and "Cedularios"; Lorenzo Cadarso, *El documento*.

[133] Gómez Gómez, *Actores*, *Sello*, "Producción."

[134] Gaudin, "Démesure," esp. 88.

[135] Mazín, *Gestores*.

[136] Puente Luna, *Andean Cosmopolitans*; Ruan, "Andean Activism"; Duve, "El concilio"; Cunill, "Philip II."

If we insist on understanding "the state" as partly magical, bereft of real, limited, fallible actants, then Latour's observation that we were never really modern holds.[137]

"POLYPHONY" AND DECREE PHRASEOLOGY

Tracing how petitions traveled to the court and worked their way through the sinews of council praxes sometimes reveals the extent to which vassals' initiatives were mediated by their legal agents, by subaltern officials, by ministers, and by the king. However, petitioners seeking *gobierno* measures also often did exert a fairly direct influence on royal decrees – and not only by acting as the primary initiators of each edict. A careful analysis of the *gobierno* process reveals that ministers almost always transplanted successful petitions' phraseologies – including vassals' proposed legal categories – into the final decree. While ministers and their subalterns did not always include all of the petition in the final product, and sometimes tweaked or rearranged elements, the expository text within each decree was virtually always a reflection of the petition itself. It was generally that case that Council officials would only diverge from this phraseological approach if its subalterns could locate precedent in their archives, and these repositories were often difficult for officials to use before the 1570s.

Council officials' practice of petition-to-decree phraseological transplantation greatly complicates the prevalent scholarly view of Crown authorship of its laws. Historians often find it impossible not to refer to royal decrees as documents which the king and the council created – and for good reason, since the sovereign certainly claimed authorship by signing "I, the King." However, the very categories and phrases which constituted this enormous body of law originated from a ruler–ruled muddle at best, and generally sprung directly from the phrases of subjects. The Crown did not speak in one voice; royal decrees featured a "polyphony" of perspectives which ministers did not rigorously attempt to tame.[138] This insight echoes several findings from other Old World eras and polities, suggesting that this avenue of textual analysis may stand to

[137] For a seminal but oft-ignored critique of this mythification of the state, see Abrams, "Notes," esp. 68.

[138] Here I am appropriating Renzo Honores' use of legal polyphony; he uses it to mean a plurality of creative legal argumentation, whereas I use it to describe the phraseologies of royal decrees themselves. See Honores, *Colonial*, 10–11; Puente Luna, *Andean Cosmopolitans*, 12.

transform our understanding of many other nonliberal regimes.[139] Indeed, the argument for an empowering interactions approach must not only increasingly attend to countless intermediary actants which made dialogue possible, but must push its analysis into the documents which these encounters themselves produced.

This insight turns many other historiographical assumptions on their heads. Was the Crown invested in creating "racial" categories by *fiat*, or did officials simply consent to using those terms proposed successfully by vassals in an almost entirely passive manner? If the latter is true, the literature's near-universal postulate that racial categories originated within the state as a coordinated effort of the Crown cannot hold. Indeed, the very taxonomic and "epistemological master pattern" which postcolonialist scholars assert emerged from imperial administrations and resulted in the "colonization [of] the imagination of … Amerindians and Europeans" must be reformulated in the light of the existence of largely bottom-up creations of categories, meaning, and law.[140] Just as imperial agents often pressed royal and ecclesiastical frameworks of thinking upon subjects, so too did monarchs and officials often accept those of their vassals.

ARCHIVES AND COMMUNICATION: RETHINKING EARLY MODERN KNOWLEDGE AND POWER

So far, I have offered a bottom-up model for royal officials' creation of decrees, in which vassals' petitions prompted and phrased royal policies (albeit only after a fraught, multiactant dialogue). For monarchs the issue was not primarily a matter of "seeing like a state" but listening like a lord.[141] This invites a rebuttal: did the monarchs and their ministers simply assent to any incoming petitions which reached their desks? The historiography has often suggested precisely the opposite: the Crown had clear ideas about the Indies, and imposed their vision through a flurry of policies. On the other hand, Arndt Brendecke's seminal exploration of knowledge production within the sixteenth-century Spanish court argues the opposite. He notes that while the postcolonial historiography has often asserted that colonial knowledge equals colonial power, this relationship is in reality far from clear. Brendecke argues

[139] For Antiquity see, for example, Lichtheim, *Ancient Egyptian Literature*, 22; Muhs, *Ancient Egyptian Economy*, 55; Feissel, "Petitions," 40.

[140] Mignolo, *Darker Side*, 141; Branche, *Colonialism*, 90.

[141] Scott, *Seeing*.

that postcolonial methodologies simultaneously promise the "unmasking [of] imperialist power structures" and bestow early modern rule with a new mask, by greatly oversimplifying the relationship between rule and information.[142]

Brendecke set out to challenge the knowledge-is-power postulate by tracing officials' production of "knowledge at court *in actu*" – that is, by conceiving of council ministers, the king, and others as flesh-and-blood actors who operated within, not beyond, their society.[143] Moreover, he emphasized how the more the empire expanded, the less and less its lawgivers knew – royal officials' rare efforts to collect systematic knowledge largely failed in the face of this titanic challenge. The council was therefore largely a passive institution, waiting for and inviting the petitions of vassals – which were always loaded with interests – in an attempt to maintain constant bottom-up communication and eke out a degree of post-facto control over Indies events.[144]

Brendecke's aim – to trouble the historiography's understanding of knowledge – did not, however, engage with the specifics of the council's decree-making process. As we shall see, his affirmation that the Crown "did not essentially collect information so that it could actively shape policy" is often true.[145] Nonetheless, by the final three decades of the sixteenth century royal decision-makers increasingly did manage to achieve some factual mastery over certain Indies affairs – particularly in limited issues of finance and war – thanks to new archival technologies and information-gathering practices. And despite Brendecke's view that council ministers were almost entirely driven by social circumstances at the expense of efficient knowledge-gathering, royal officials also moved quite aggressively against ministers' illicit social connections – a process rife with gendered overtones. Ministers did also assemble a massive and moderately well-organized archive of petitions and decrees which came to constitute their "legal truths." We should not push too far the argument about the Crown as merely a bundle of social relations which collected information as a secondary concern.[146]

This insight about the sixteenth-century council, in turn, helps clarify the relationship between early modern archives and power. Critical archival studies scholars have largely taken for granted that archives and

142 Brendecke, *Empirical Empire*, 9. 143 Brendecke, *Empirical Empire*, 253, see also 6.
144 Brendecke, *Empirical Empire*, 285–286. 145 Brendecke, *Empirical Empire*, 286.
146 Luhmann brilliantly explored the fraught connections between fact and process in *Legitimation*, esp. 5, 17, 23.

power are intertwined, but they do not clarify how heaps of documents translate into concrete benefits for administrations.[147] This mystery becomes all the more pressing in the Spanish imperial case, as sixteenth-century Habsburgs simultaneously pioneered some of the world's most centralized and sophisticated archival systems and the expansion of Europe's largest overseas dominions.[148] Even if knowledge does not quite equal power unless actants can make information useful, by the 1580s royal officials' decision-making process had managed to make something of its papers. Ministers were powerfully aided by archives of more consistent and orderly legal facts, as well as by new descriptive facts that helped ministers triumph over local interests and rationalize resources within the fields of finance and defense, affording the empire limited but significant breakthroughs.

The labor-intensive process through which the council developed these archival technologies transformed decision-making but paradoxically also diluted the agency of its ministers.[149] As paperwork technologies became increasingly central in decision-making, these "little paper tools" and reference books became actants in lawmaking in their own right.[150] So too did the custodians of these papers – primarily the powerful council secretaries, but also their wives and subaltern officials, whose influence over the now-powerful archives increasingly rendered them "gatekeepers" of great importance.[151] Officials' growing knowledge regarding financial and military spheres, bolstered by the growing contributions of their archive-savvy subalterns, also weakened some petitioners' ability to influence royal policies.

While the "gray power of files" never came close to doing away with the monarchs' need for communication with vassals, by 1598, the year of King Philip II's death, looming canyons of papers did constrain many of the flows of petitioning into channels increasingly favorable to the integrity of the empire and the interests of the Habsburgs.[152] By the early 1600s, the rise of archive-wielding secretaries, royal attorneys, and high-aristocratic prime ministers transformed this landscape once more, somewhat marginalizing council ministers and altering petitioners'

147 Yale, "The History," 333; Schwartz and Cook, "Archives" 2–14; Schwartz, "New Eyes"; Ketelaar, "Archival Temples"; McEwan, "Building"; Rao, "Affect'; Trundle and Kaplonski, "Tracing," 408–409; Caswell, "Hannah"; Lowry and MacNeil, "Archival Thinking," 3; Dueñas, "Indian," among others.

148 Vismann, *Files*, 99; Delsalle, *A History*, 108.

149 Brendecke, *Empirical Empire*, 52.

150 Klein, *Experiments*, 1–3; Blair, *Too Much*; Gardey, *Schreiben*.

151 Vismann, *Files*, 19, see also 35; Walsham, "Social History."

152 Vismann, *Files*, 91.

experiences; it is at this crucial juncture that my research ends and another chapter of the story of imperial lawmaking begins.[153]

VIOLENCE AND ENTRAPMENT

We, the King argues for understanding decree-production as a complex causal ecology comprised of many actants' muscle, effort, and legal fictions. Yet, as this book also argues, this domain of legal make-believe was not merely labor-intensive: It was also collectively patrolled and guarded by the bearers of violence, who periodically lashed out against perpetrators who maliciously sought to appropriate these fictions' properties without permission. The threat of grievous bodily injury lurked just beyond the high-minded domains of vassal–lord communication, as imperial subjects' and officials efforts to suppress sovereign Indigenous, Afro-descendant, and European attacks against those transporting mail. Harm also might befall anyone who tampered with legal make-believe, by forging or distorting ritual elements of this dialogue.

Moreover, while this book also underscores that while the petition-and-response system allowed vassals to cocreate many imperial policies and categories, this dialogue also generated subtle forms of intellectual coercion. Even if the Crown did not always impose its categories, taxonomies, and epistemological frameworks as many have argued, the very act of vassals' engagement within this communications channel enticed and obligated its participants to seek a (strongly Castilian, Catholic) common ground of statements and beliefs which was never neutral.[154] Petitioning was both a tool and a snare, trapping many subjects' status and forms of argumentation within an eerie "papereality" of legal fictions – as Pedro's clients knew all too well, as they reluctantly became *mestizos* and adopted the legal category they sought to contest.[155] This world of legal reasoning – which was far more than the ruling monarchical cabal but a nearly inescapable veritable meta-system of thought and communication – lured all into a web of legal fictions.

[153] Reinhardt, *Voices*, 30. Pérez Ramos cautions against some visions of the *validos* as all-powerful, and views them instead as aristocratic secretaries' see "Valido," 156. Another interesting development was the appearance of many more ministers with direct Indies eyewitness experience; Ponce Leiva, "Argamasa," 466. For the transition period of 1598–1603, see Williams, "Philip III."

[154] Puente Luna, *Andean Cosmopolitans*, 12.

[155] Dery, "Papereality"; Van Deusen, *Global Indios*, 128.

And yet Pedro was not merely drawn into a snare of others' making; he was cocreating the snare even as it entrapped him.

SOURCES, SILENCES, AND WRONGDOING IN CONTEXT

How can researchers working within the mythological frameworks of Habsburg and liberal-era narratives overcome intentional and unintentional camouflagings of the circumstances of decree-making? Archival work along the grain is one answer.[156] The lion's share of this documentation on the lawmaking process was produced by the Council of the Indies. While the early modern Spanish Empire's archival practices were generally superb for the era, the court's constant movement before the 1560s dispersed and destroyed many petitions, decrees, and other documents.[157] Beginning in the 1580s, high-ranking officials and royal committees increasingly borrowed council writings for specific ends, never to return them.[158] In the 1600s, kings' prime ministers (*privados*) also pillaged Madrid's archives at will for their projects of imperial reform.[159]

Many of these papers were reunited beginning in the final third of the 1700s in the Archive of the Indies (AGI), today the primary repository of the council's paperwork.[160] Virtually all surviving petitions sit in the AGI's massive *Gobierno* section, others in the *Patronato* papers; unfortunately, decrees and petitions are separate and can only be reunited through painstaking work.[161] Much of the present book is based on my attempt to reconstruct the *gobierno* petition-and-response system within the AGI. I consulted roughly 100,000 pages of royal decrees, as well as the lion's share of petitions, for every Indies region from 1492 to around 1600. This included considerable work in the legendarily opaque

[156] Stoler, *Archival Grain*. [157] BNE, Mss.10558, 12r.

[158] For cosmographers, see RAH, CJBM, A-120, 171r-230; for secretaries and *fiscales*, AGI, Indiferente 744, N.16 and Indiferente 1383A, "Memorial de las escrituras," 1567; for a secretary overseeing a Junta, AGI, Indiferente 741, N.248; for presidents' validos,' (uppermost advisers) and the King's confiscations of council documents, Campos y Fernández, *Catálogo* i.e 60–64, 373–377.

[159] BNE, Mss.10558, 19r.

[160] Lázaro de la Escosura and Ceballos Aragón, *Archivo*, 12; Cañizares-Esguerra, *How to Write*, 170–196.

[161] For a brief explanation of the Patronato section, see Aiton and Mecham, "Archivo General de Indias," 558. Gobierno petitions are also dispersed throughout other AGI sections. Additionally, hundreds are scattered in various archives, including the AGS, the AHNM, and the NLBLC.

"General Indifferent" section, where the majority of the council's internal administrative information is haphazardly dispersed.

While Council of the Indies' papers do occasionally provide rich information on the mechanical breakdowns of the petition-and-response system, their repositories have their silences as well. Ministers' illicit behaviors and social ties to petitioners are virtually nowhere to be found. Tracing their crises of integrity and the council's subsequent reforms requires consulting another sphere of paperwork: royal secretaries' and investigators' secret correspondences and audits. Some of these documents are found in the Royal Library of El Escorial.[162] Most others once belonged to a single collection, the Altamira dynasty's archives, until the family went bankrupt and auctioned its papers. Those relating to the Indies are now in New York's Hispanic Society of America, London's British Library, and Madrid's Instituto Valencia de don Juan and Biblioteca Francisco de Zabálburu. Read together, these archives reveal the rich if fragmentary social contexts of ministers' wrongdoing and of the council's major reforms. They include four council audits which royal officials conducted in 1541–1543, 1567–1571, 1586–1587, and 1587–1589, which offer glimpses into how this institution's 1542 and 1571 *gobierno*, *gracia*, and *justicia* guidelines came about, as well as the labors of reform which royal insiders undertook to ensure the preservation of the vassal–monarch bond. These archives thus reveal a dense webs of actants operating beyond the official, formal, licit domain – from powerful women to part-Indian agents to pearl necklaces and Indigenous goldwork – which contributed to collective restructurings of the petition-and-response system.

Reading along the grain, we discover the council's everyday inputs, decision-making praxes, and outputs. Reading against it, and through observers' outside perspectives on the council, the hidden frictions of the petition-and-response system sometimes manifest themselves. These two reading strategies together not only make possible a study of the Crown's failures or successes, but also often reveal the legal fictions which rescued the empire from a total breakdown of vassal–lord trust. It is from this back-and-forth that we experience surprise encounters with some of the contingent, intricate, and fragile objects, labor, ideas, and people which made up the great network of imperial lawmaking.[163]

[162] BSLE, &-II-7, 459r–462v. [163] Latour, "Network," 797–808 and "Technical," 43.

CHAPTER OVERVIEWS

Chapter 1 explores how Indies vassals created *gobierno* petitions. It traces how subjects transubstantiated their innermost volitions into material form, and made their thoughts into written words, through a series of legal fictions which enabled all involved to conceive of globe-spanning, paper-based vassal–ruler communication as a possible and legitimate substitute for face-to-face encounters. Vassals either directly wrote their proposals or did so through the labor of intermediaries such as procurators and translators. Official and unofficial middlemen were extremely numerous, assuaging authorities' consciences that they had made efforts to give all subjects access to petitioning. However, transfers of *voluntad* onto paper were fraught with problems of authenticity, especially when Indigenous vassals formulated proposals. Many observers also complained about legal agents' shortcomings and volition-contaminating undertakings. To project and fix vassals' volitions to paper, subjects turned to several signs and rituals, including the *rúbrica* (signature), the *poder* (power of attorney), and translation (*traducción*). Despite numerous challenges, Crown officials' and vassals' dedication to enabling petitioners' access to writing did yield concrete results, making *gobierno* supplications quite affordable and accessible to most, and creating the widespread belief in the possibility that ruler and ruled could indeed have an intimate dialogue of wills – even through cocreated papers which traveled thousands of leagues across time and space.

The troubled, often multiactor conversion of will into matter was only the first of the petition-and-response system's many challenges in transmitting *voluntad* to the court. Logistical obstacles constituted the greatest challenge to the fiction of ruled–ruler dialogue; these are the subject of **Chapter 2**. The myth of globe-spanning paper encounters between subjects and monarchs was a powerful and necessary fiction, but in the context of the Indies this was even more strained than in Europe. To sustain the fiction of an empire of intimate communication, many types of labor, contributed by as many types of vassals, were necessary. The royal mailing system was extremely limited. The maintenance of most communications in the face of adverse weather and topography required sailors, informal couriers, relay-runners, free and enslaved mule drivers and raftsmen, Indigenous communities, and vigilant vassals and officials. Subjects were forced to rely on travelers, especially merchants, and backwater regions without vigorous trade often struggled to fulfill the basic obligation of communicating with the monarch. The deliberate actions of saboteurs, sovereign peoples' resistance, and, especially, pirates also played a major role in interrupting the flow of petitions. Logistics were, no doubt, the empire's weakest link; subjects and officials could only maintain the fiction and reality of communication through enormous amounts of labor and perseverance.

Chapter 3 asks: how could monarchs and upright ministers uphold a fiction of acting as instruments for vassals' communication with the ruler, when they themselves had their own interests and biases? Crown officials' difficulties in resolving this question stemmed from a major paradox within imperial governance: the simultaneously patrimonial and bureaucratic nature of royal administration. Both ruler and ruled understood the monarch's duties within the patrimonial language of the family network.[164] However, when ministers imitated this lordly model, they usurped their masters' patrimonial faculties, and thus adulterated vassal–ruler dialogue with their own designs and volitions. As busy monarchs became increasingly distant from vassals, and ministers' power increased, problems concerning these officials' biases came to a head.

During the Trastámara and early Habsburg dynasties, officials' broad and informal influence over ruler–ruled dialogue had been common. The New World's monarchs did not endorse this, but also did not explicitly forbid it. After a series of 1520s revolts in Castile against Charles V's courtier-counselors, monarchs became increasingly irritated by ministers' tendency to put the personal above the public good. Since the 1524 foundation of the Council of the Indies, Habsburg monarchs and their closest counselors repeatedly sought to ensure ministers' legal and ethical distance from vassals – indeed, what we today would recognize as considerably "bureaucratic" stances.

Two milestones in ministers' departure from pure patrimonial rule came in 1542 and 1571, when the council received foundational administrative guidelines forbidding them from involving family and friends in decision-making. These ordinances did not mechanistically emerge; these rules instead owed to the efforts of Indies vassals, and especially women at the court, to shape ministers' decision-making. The might of conquistadors and the circulation of exotic Indies goods at the court initially gave female subjects new avenues to sway ministers. Subsequent crises of ministers' integrity were in large part responsible for three royal audits of the council, in the early 1540s, late 1560s, and mid-to-late 1580s. The resulting reforms curbed patrimonialism and protected even the humblest

[164] Premo, *Children of the Father King*.

vassal's ability to receive Crown officials' attention. Royal decision-making thus became almost exclusively male, and ministerial work heavily gendered, as ministers and other officials sought to exclude powerful interlopers, and especially women, from adulterating vassal–lord dialogue. These fundamental changes in the decree-making process, however, had been brought about by powerful female subjects.

Once petitions sat on council ministers' desks, these officials needed not only to listen to vassals but also to discern which proposals should become decrees. They also had to discern what was beneficial and what was deleterious for the common good. **Chapters 4** and **5** explore ministers' decision-making processes, asking: what was the relationship between knowledge and power? Early on, ministers began to develop a series of decision-making technologies, largely seeking to acquit the royal conscience. **Chapter 4** explores the peripatetic council's meager decision-making technologies, especially its gradual accumulation of legal facts. Crown officials succeeded wildly at encouraging communication with vassals, but in their excessively passive stance created a substantial number of contradictory decrees which complicated the monarch's promise of justice.

Chapter 5 explores how decision-making transformed substantially from 1561, when King Philip II fixed the seat of the court in Madrid. Ministers who now had permanent offices came to increasingly value and rely on compilations of legal facts, and developed ever-greater collections of descriptive facts as well. Ministers developed certain strategies to supplement information-poor petitions with additional perspectives and (limited) cross-referencing, and thus could sometimes detect interest-laden claims. By the 1570s and 1580s, council officials working in special juntas became much more assertive in three main fields: issues relating to Franciscans, military affairs, and financial matters. Part of this owed to officials' improving archives, which paradoxically shifted the burdens of both labor and influence away from ministers and toward secretaries and bureaucratic subalterns. This meant council ministers lost some power, even as archives and their custodians – including workers and secretaries' wives – began to exert subtle but important influence over decision-making.

Chapter 6 explores how ministers phrased decrees. Royal officials, having collectively satisficed the royal conscience through this series of decision-making technologies, now had to transform petitions into royal decrees. A close textual analysis of petitions and royal decrees reveals that ministers' and their subalterns' phraseology of decrees lifted entire phrases, often verbatim, from vassals' petitions. Indeed, subjects of many backgrounds were thus able to propose policies, and could even introduce new institutions and legal categories. The king's signature was the final fiction in the process of decree-making: a stroke of ink that concreted his authorship over the text and invested it with his law-creating volition. The birth of a royal decree was thus the culmination not only of a massive labor chain, but also of the merging of segments of subjects' petitions with the royal will. This imbued the empire's towering legislative output with a highly polyphonic character – and a highly inconsistent one at that.

CONCLUSION

This overall picture of the Council's *gobierno* praxis reveals a great deal about our misunderstandings of the era. I would hazard that understanding this long labor chain through which petitions formed and (if successful) became decrees offers an opportunity to rethink the entire empire – suddenly not a society of serfs and officials subject to passively obey, negotiate, or thwart state directives, but a world permeated by a great communicative process in which legislation was not always a foreign or imposed element. Needless to say, this petition-and-response system was avowedly undemocratic and hierarchical, and was the origin of many decrees which featured categories of human difference. We must not tear down one mythology only to erect another.

Certainly, however, vassals achieved a profound influence over the empire both through direct petitions and in their shaping of petitioning more generally. After all, *gobierno* royal decrees were often definitive commands for issues of governance, finance, policing, taxation, the parameters of privilege, judicial procedures, military operations – a full list would be almost never-ending. The empire's policies – some of them highly consequential and broad – often hung on the subtlest string of words in a decree, as Rengifo's case shows. This recalls Arlette Farge's comment that "lives are at stake in some phrases, and odds of success and failure hang upon a few words" – in the Indies, this reality played out on an imperial scale.[165] And these locutions were virtually always born in petitions which a single ocean wave or disease-carrying mosquito might have thwarted en route. A universe of discriminatory practices against *mestizos* and countless other groups hung on the most delicate semantic

[165] Farge, *La atracción*, 26.

chains within cloth-and-ink petitions, chains in turn held together by tenuous institutional and logistical webs which an even greater universe of actants influenced with every repetition of the petition-and-response cycle. This system, so fundamental for maintaining the Indies within the Spanish monarchy, was simultaneously as evanescent as an idea, as frail as a sheet of paper, as fluid as a waterway, as defiantly enduring as a Caribbean fortress.

1

Paper Ceremonies for a Global Empire

Gobierno Petitions and the Collective Work of *Voluntad*

In Lima, an elaborate act of legal alchemy was underway. An ecclesiastical notary was stitching together the proposals, proofs, and volitions of hundreds of subjects into one 224-folio dossier. He unified dozens of texts endorsed with 149 part-Indigenous petitioners' signatures from Lima, Cuzco, Oropesa, Arequipa, and faraway Loja. The files included many supporting testimonies from Peru's bishops, eminent theologians, educators, and local elites. To these the scribe added papal bulls, powers of attorney, and a University of Lima ordinance dating from mid-1576 to late 1584. In January 1584, the notary's large signature sealed all of these volitions into one unified meta-volition.[1] *Pedro Rengifo received this document and would take it to Spain, thereby becoming the personification of the legal effort, a single man who could act and speak "with the power of attorney and voice of all the sons of Spaniards and Indians they call mestizos," who constituted a "family of ... native mestizos ... of ten thousand men."*[2]

Drawn in the messy but uniform hand of the ecclesiastical notary, and sewn together into a cohesive whole, the file exuded neatness and agreement. Pedro's subsequent declarations at the royal court reinforced this impression of a concord of volitions. However, beneath this veneer the dossier's contents reveal a complex scaffolding of rather reluctant actors. All signees had ceded power of attorney to two otherwise elusive individuals named Hernán González and Juan Ruiz, who collected and assumed the "voice" of every one of the "sons of the Spaniards and Indian natives of this kingdom" of Peru.[3] *These*

[1] Van Deusen, *Global Indios*, 127. [2] AGI, Lima 126, 115r. [3] AGI, Lima 126, 1r.

two agents had complained before an important gathering of Peruvian bishops that they had been labeled mestizos, *that part-Indigenous nuns had been denied the equal status of their Spanish counterparts, and that part-Indigenous men were unjustly denied the priesthood. This category of* mestizo *was evidently not one any of the participants eagerly embraced. Indeed, the Arequipa group's collective power of attorney used another category to describe themselves –* "montañeses" *or mountain-men.*[4] *Most of the participants in this effort, including González and Ruiz, evinced deep discomfort about their status as* mestizos, *but pragmatically embraced the term in order to transform it from within.*

Highly coherent, multigenerational social groups of part-Spanish, part-Indigenous vassals never formed in the Spanish Indies, much less under the category of mestizo. *Pedro could nonetheless conjure before the king and the council the fiction of precisely such a "family" of* mestizos *spanning all of Peru. This was no family, of course, but rather a special sort of claim which Pedro could stake by reaching to several years of bureaucratic ceremonies and acts of legal magic summoned by countless actors. Witnesses' oaths before God, several local notaries' certifications, and participants' signatures recorded veridically that each participant had justly acted in his own volition, and had then ceded to legal agents his will, in a sort of magical transfer of living thought and emotion onto cloth-and-ink rectangles. As many individuals' wills became one corporate volition through powers of attorney, and an ecclesiastical notary created one paper dossier out of many, individuals transformed into a unified corporate existence. By the time Pedro met King Philip, 149 signatories fictionally became ten thousand, a handful of towns became the Viceroyalty of Peru, strangers and acquaintances became family, and* montañeses *and sons of Spaniards and Indians became* mestizos. *Through these legal fictions, the* mestizos *became quite real – and, using Pedro as an agent and instrument, collectively communicated their volition by paper across the world with the king and the council as one.*[5]

[4] This was also the preferred category of part-Indigenous vassals in Santa Cruz de la Sierra and Asunción; see AGI, Patronato 29, R. 19, 1565, 1r. Their Spanish parents often used the term "*hijo natural*" or "out-of-wedlock," not *mestizo*. See Mangan, *Transatlantic Obligations*, 45. For their mothers, see Mangan, "Indigenous Women."

[5] For the non-existence of highly concrete, durable *mestizo* communities, see Rappaport, *Disappearing*, and Stolcke, "Los mestizos." For one of many similar examples involving Indigenous vassals becoming *indios*, see Baber, "Categories."

Every day, vassals from throughout the empire participated in crafting *gobierno* petitions which they sent to the king and the council in hopes of winning a royal decree. Petitions constituted portable, storable, sturdy, long-lasting paper ceremonies which could travel across time and space and enable vassals and their volitions to "appear" before kings.[6] This chapter asks a straightforward question: How did petitioners create these *gobierno* proposals? This is an issue which the contemporary historiography has largely overlooked. This owes partly to the literature's widespread conflation of *gracia*, *justicia*, and *gobierno* paperwork into an undifferentiated whole, as well as to scholars' enthusiasm for petitions' contents rather than their manufacture.[7] Historical linguists and specialists in diplomatics (the study of document types) have devoted attention to petitions' formal aspects and language, often at the expense of the social circumstances and praxes surrounding textual production.[8] This omission also likely owes more generally to a widespread understanding of decrees as top-down documents of sui generis royal creation, to the once-popular Lettered City model which understood imperial literacy as an instrument of educated Spanish rule over the illiterate rural masses, and to the sixteenth-century legal fiction of petitioning as an untainted vassal–lord dialogue.[9]

Perhaps the subtlest impediment to understanding the collective work of petition-making is the pervasive search for the "voice" of an "author." Many scholars have argued that these documents *can* contain "the voice of the real petitioner."[10] Others have debated this, noting that sixteenth-century documents required complex intermediation by many actors, posing "problems of identifying the native voice."[11] Analyses of petitions have also often

[6] Corteguera, "Encuentros," 26.

[7] For two of many that commit this error when analyzing "letters' (*cartas*), see Mignolo, "Cartas," 57–109, and Luque Talaván, *Universo de opiniones*, 253–254.

[8] For the four most thorough diplomatic studies of petitions' structures, see Real Díaz, *Estudio diplomático*, 271–274; Heredia Herrera, "La carta," 65–95; Huamanchumo de la Cuba, "Tradiciones discursivas"; Lorenzo Cadarso, "La correspondencia," 1–29; Benítes, "Las cartas," 17–37. For linguistic analysis, see, among others, Andreas Wesch, "El documento indiano." For a fascinating analysis of Maya and Spanish variations in petitioning documents, see Chuchiak, "'Ah Dzib Cahob,'" 159–184; See also Raimúndez Ares, "Cartas."

[9] Ángel Rama, *La Ciudad Letrada*.

[10] Van Voss, "Introduction," 9. For concerns with voice in the writings of non-European subjects of empires, see Ashcroft, Griffiths, and Tiffin, *Empire Writes*, 172–176; Van Deusen, *Global Indios*, 29.

[11] Rappaport and Cummins, *Beyond*, 116, 118, 143, 257. See also, for example, Würgler, "Voices," 11–35; for another example of the concept of voice, see Arndt Brendecke, "Informing the Council," 240.

centered upon finding an "author," although many now conclude that these texts do not conform to today's notion of "individual authorship."[12] Rather, researchers are increasingly focusing on the roles played by intermediaries in imperial paperwork, and have found document creation to be a "highly collaborative process."[13]

This chapter proposes that when subjects crafted *gobierno* petitions (with or without intermediaries), their goal was not primarily to produce authentic voice and authorship as we often understand it but, first and foremost, to affix *voluntad* to their documents.[14] Petitioners' authorship and voice, while important concepts, were often secondary concerns, which contemporaries did not expect to be pure. However, *voluntad* sprung from the domain of the soul, was deeply and exclusively personal, and needed to be untainted and genuine. Without sincere volition, petitions were void; the king (so the legal fiction went) would not consent to a decree if it lacked this attribute.

When we shift attention from these ideas of voice and authorship to *voluntad*, intermediaries' contributions in cocreating petitions appear in a different light. Middlemen now appear not as outsiders who muddled a petitioner's authentic inner voice, but as instruments assisting, capturing, concerting, and amplifying the transmission of the individual will onto a lifeless sheet of paper, which the king and his ministers could then read. Three main elements sustained this ubiquitous legal fiction of petitions-as-ceremonies. The first was a network of symbolic gestures which petitioners (and sometimes their assistants) scored onto each petition with ink. Crosses, salutations, statements of *voluntad* of various sorts, explanations of the case at hand, and then another array of salutations and signatures created an ersatz ritual of direct vassal–lord dialogue. Second was the (non-compulsory) labor and mediation of procurators, translators, notaries, and others who multiplied legal fictions further still, incorporating oaths before God, testimonies, and more signatures.

Of course, the more intermediaries intervened to preserve or amplify a vassal's *voluntad*, the greater the possibility that the chain of transmission could break or become tainted by others' interests. Subjects often loathed such go-betweens, suspecting them of malice and even sabotage. Vassals and officials thus erected a third fictional barricade to protect against

[12] Dueñas, *Indians and Mestizos*, 13.

[13] Premo, *Enlightenment*, 34, 52, 163, 172; Burns, "Notaries," 357; Rappaport and Cummins, *Beyond*, 20; Cunill, "Mosaico," 7; Cunill, "Protectoría," 478; Honores, "Colonial," 2; Yannakakis, "Indigenous People," 931.

[14] Burns, "Dentro de la ciudad letrada," 45.

middlemen's wrongdoings. Intermediaries' less-than-perfect chain of transmission required additional procedural ablutions, including public punishment, so that the fiction of a vassal's traveling *voluntad* could survive intact on its way to the king's desk.[15] Anyone who attempted to use coercion to contaminate legal rituals, misrepresent a vassal's volition, or appropriate a subject's volition risked more than merely being discovered and having the petition invalidated. Just beyond the frontiers of these legal fictions loomed a threat of violence. This all-too-real danger helped ensure the integrity of legal make-believe.

The result was that, despite the colossal challenges which petitioners faced in producing or cocreating these texts, many socially and spatially marginal subjects could produce writings imbued with their volition which would allow them to "undertake paper conversations" with the lord.[16] This was possible thanks to the collective labor of many actors, the web of trust-building ritual and symbolism, and the threat of force against those who counterfeited or adulterated *voluntad.* The serious make-believe of the petition-writing process helped sustain the fiction of vassal–ruler dialogue, upholding the language of a physically proximate ruled–ruler bond in an empire upon which the sun never set.

INTIMATE DIALOGUE ACROSS AN EMPIRE OF DISTANCE

In 1572, the Indigenous commoners (*macehuales*) of Santiago de Guatemala declared to the monarch that they "kneel before you, and we kiss your hands and feet, oh great lord Your Majesty."[17] In 1601, a large group of Inca petitioners of Cuzco proclaimed in Quechua, "*Chunca chunca muchai coscaiqui, capac apo, sulcachariqui yanaiqui chaquiqui, maquiqui muchai, cuiqui, ynga cona*" – that is, "We kiss you most fervently, o powerful lord. Your lowly children, the Incas, kiss your feet and hands."[18] Countless petitioners similarly referenced, in imitation of the in-person vassal–lord greeting, a bodily contact with the king.[19] These references to physical touching were a mere outward metaphor,

[15] For a similar view of Maya petitioning in the Yucatan before Spanish officials as ceremonial of dialogue inflected with prayer, see Hanks, *Converting*, 170, 315–323. See also Rivero Rodríguez, "De todo," 269.

[16] Corteguera, "Encuentros imaginados," 140.

[17] Lutz and Dakin, *Nuestro Pesar*, 5, see also 74; Olko, "Alphabetic Writing," 186.

[18] Glave, "La gran vejación," 37.

[19] Cepeda Adán, *En torno*, 73; Puente Luna, *Andean Cosmopolitans*, 135; Cañeque, "Emotions of Power," 97–99.

a ceremonial beginning of an even more profound fiction: that of direct, unmediated dialogue between the hearts and innermost thoughts of ruler and ruled.[20] For all the importance of this closeness of body, it was also essential that there be a closeness of soul – not at all unlike a subject's intimate pleas to God.[21]

Contemporaries understood such materially close, emotionally intimate ruled–ruler relations to provide important foundations of the acquittal of the royal conscience and the collective creation of a more perfect Christian society. Was the written word the best medium for this sort of encounter? Some thinkers in the sixteenth century boldly claimed that the most ideal substitute for dialogue was actually written correspondence.[22] No doubt, paper was a remarkable vehicle. Letter-writing could not have thrived without a cheap, reliable material medium. Parchment required the skin of animals treated by leather-workers, and was unaffordable for most subjects. Rag-cloth paper, on the other hand, was flexible, durable, and quite water resistant. By the thirteenth and fourteenth centuries, Iberian royal administrations, the church, and society in general had embraced paper as their preferred documentary base, and factories rushed to meet demand; Catalan and Italian production kept paper prices "reasonable."[23]

Transforming the prayer-like, immediate nature of the in-person petition into a cloth rectangle required a considerable measure of make-believe. For the king to "listen" to faraway vassals, petitioners needed to first fasten their volitions to these paper rectangles. Virtually all subjects insisted, in one form or another, that these letters communicated their purest volition. In an undated petition (post-1584), the *cacique* don Diego de Torres wrote the monarch that he "had served his king and natural lord with so much love and *voluntad* . . . what moves me is the love I have."[24] One Francisco Núñez wrote from Lima in 1574 that the "intent and *voluntad* of Your Majesty is the same . . . as that of his loyal vassals."[25] Petitioners constantly insisted upon the fiction that they could assert their pure volition via paper and ink, enabling them to vanquish distance. Conquistador Andrés de Escobar wrote from Concepción de Chile in 1551 that King Philip II's "love" and its "infinite perfection within the

[20] Puente Luna, *Andean Cosmopolitans*, 135; Corteguera, "Encuentros," 33.
[21] Hanks, *Converting*, 316.
[22] Castillo Gómez, "Hablen cartas"; Texeda, *Cosa Nueva*, iii.
[23] Valls I Subirà, *Historia del papel*, 57, see also 14, 18, 47, 63, 91, 106, 132–133, 140, 193.
[24] Archivo General de Simancas, Consejo de Guerra (GYM), Leg. 0171, 139r–v.
[25] AGI, Lima 123, "Todos los vasallos" Francisco Núñez, June 22, 1574.

Catholic Faith" humbled and blessed "we who live in the ends of the Earth."[26]

And yet some recognized that the transubstantiation of an abstract innermost conviction to a written document was not an entirely straightforward or smooth process. The Indians of Chiapas complained that they could not personally inform the monarch due to their great distance from Madrid. They also bemoaned that "we can also not manifest [our problems] through writing as they are so many and so great that it would be sorely irritating to Your Majesty."[27]

Remoteness was not the only problem. How, exactly, could a vassal embed one's living volition into a lifeless material object of ink and paper? For many, the central limitation was one of rhetoric, which could stir the embers of the king's volition and thereby transmit their desire across enormous expanses, like a sort of Olympic torch. Many stated that they simply lacked the rhetorical skills to invoke in the monarch's soul their own feelings of good will. The soldier Andrés de Escobar wrote from Concepción de Chile in 1551 that "I wish I had the illumination [*lumbre*] and understanding [*entendimiento*] to write [the king's] praises which I have in my *voluntad* and heart."[28] One anonymous petitioner – perhaps Hernán Cortés – wrote a brief letter to the king around 1526 stating that he wished to "manifest" and "signify" countless events in Honduras to the emperor, but "not even I would know how to signify them."[29] The New Granada-based Spanish soldier Juan Ruiz Clavijo stated in 1573, "I wish I had the ability to match the need that currently corresponds to me, to have the power to signify to Your Highness the great persecution that many of your vassals suffer in this realm."[30] From Mexico, Gómez de Cervantes bemoaned in 1588, "Oh, who could or would deserve to put his lips on one of Your Majesty's royal ears to say what my quill refuses."[31] The challenges of expressing *voluntad* and explaining circumstances on the ground troubled the purity of the vassal–lord dialogue. However, as Janet Gurkin Altman has noted, letters can be "both a reflection of the gap and an instrument for gap closing."[32] In the Spanish Empire, they would

[26] AGI, Lima 120, "Príncipe el más alto," January 20, 1551, Andrés de Escobar.

[27] AGI, México 168, N.56, 172r. See also AGI, Lima 134, Indiferente, 1088, L.12, 314r, Indiferente 1088, L.12, and Indiferente, 738, N.40, Quito 9, R.1, N.3, AGI, Lima 134, "Los días pasados."

[28] Andrés de Escobar, AGI, Lima 120, Concepción January 22, 1551.

[29] AHNM, Diversos-Colecciones, 43, N.11, 1r–v.

[30] AGI, Santa Fe, 83, N.9, 170r.

[31] AGI, México 110, "Grande fue la misericordia de Dios," June 6, 1588.

[32] Gurkin Altman, *Epistolarity*, 189.

play precisely such a role of "presence and absence ... mania and cure, bridge and barrier."[33]

THE GOBIERNO PETITION: CREATING PAPER ENCOUNTERS IN AN EMPIRE OF DISTANCE

Scholars are increasingly understanding medieval textual production as part of a wider system of rituals, many involving vassals and lords. Indeed, these documents often stood in "for the physical presence of people as ritual participants."[34] When observing the structure of each *gobierno* petition, there is an unambiguous imitation of an ideal in-person encounter between a vassal and a lord – or perhaps even of a Christian praying to the Lord.

When vassals created petitions, including *gobierno* ones, they did so by textualizing the ceremonial steps of an idealized face-to-face encounter with their monarch.[35] Two concrete examples help illustrate some of the general formats of these documents: a 1524 petition by Hernán Cortés (Figure 1.1) and a 1543 petition by the Bishop of Chiapas, Bartolomé de las Casas (Figure 1.2). These writings, like every petition, began with a simple cross, positioned in the top middle of the first page. This was an invocation of God as judge – and an echo of vassals' face-to-face invocation of the Lord with the sign of the cross when encountering his or her monarch. This simple intersection of two lines of ink reinforced the ubiquitous fiction that all involved in reading and writing each petition were engaging in a matter of Christian conscience – in effect, it took the place of the making of the sign of the cross which vassals made during virtually all legal rituals.[36] The Spanish word for making the gesture of the sign of the cross is *persignarse*; the symbol upon the petition was a signification (Lat. *signus*) that the letter was by a Christian, for a Christian, and written under the all-seeing, all-judging eyes of God.

The second element after the cross was the subject's salutation of the monarch. During the reign of Holy Roman Emperor Charles V, the top of

[33] Gurkin Altman, *Epistolarity*, 43.

[34] Rappaport and Cummins, *Beyond*, 216; Bedos-Rezak, "Medieval Identity," 1489–1533, 1508–1509, 1528; Fraenkel, *La signature*, 96.

[35] Goody, *Logic*, 106–110.

[36] Rappaport and Cummins, *Beyond*, 21; Bedos-Rezak, "Medieval Identity," 1511; Fraenkel, *La signature*, 61; Schmidt-Wiegand, "Rechtshistorische Funktion," 66, 73; Diederich, "Bedeutung," 160–166; Hanks, *Converting*, 316; Koziol, "Early."

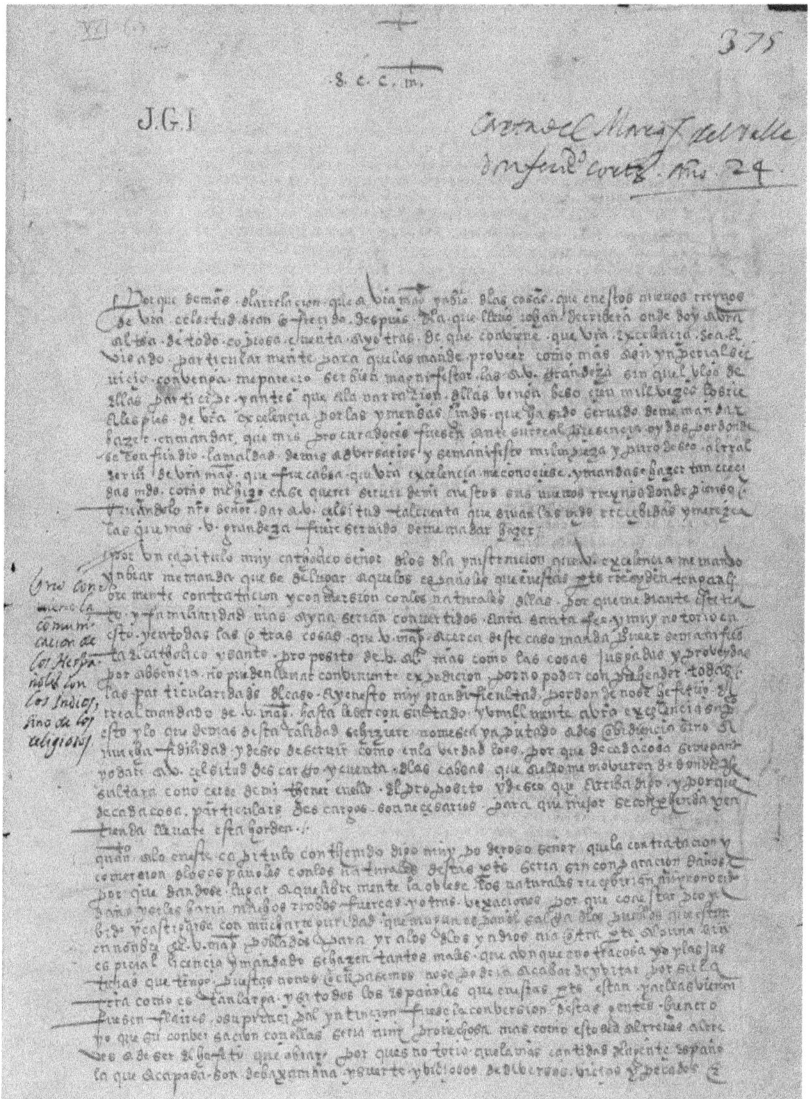

FIGURE 1.1 A 1524 petition by Hernán Cortés, Mexico (NLBLC, JGIC XXI-1 375 r)

each document contained the letters *SCCM*, or "Sacred Catholic Caesarean Majesty."[37] Petitions to King Philip II featured many other types of addresses, generally the simple "Lord" and "Very powerful

[37] Heredia Herrera, "La carta," 131.

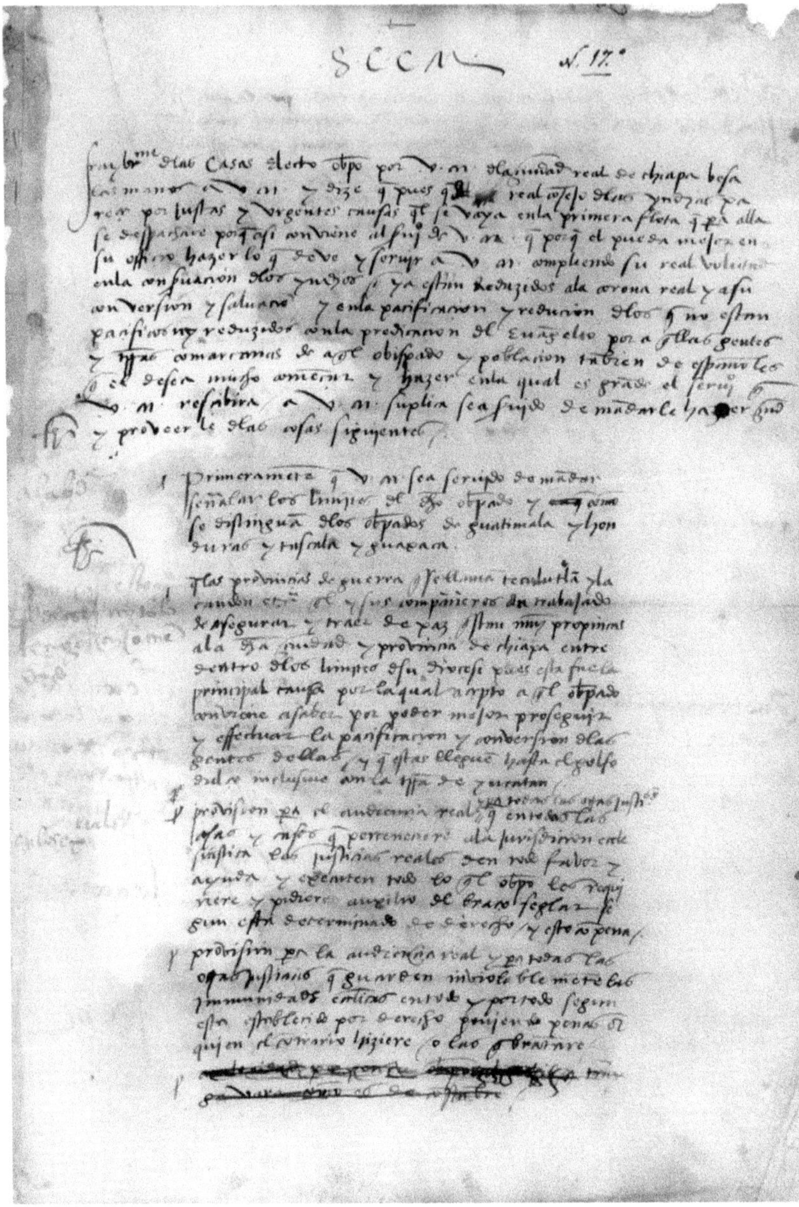

FIGURE 1.2 A ca. 1543 petition by Bartolomé de las Casas, then Bishop of Chiapas (LOC, Kislak MS 191)

Lord."[38] Here, again, the petition imitated speech. Many letters contained salutations and flattering overtures – words which a vassal would likely have uttered when bowing before the monarch.[39]

This tendency came to a head in the 1580s. In 1583 the treaty-writer and occasional royal adviser Fadrique Furió Ceriol noted that vassals used many titles for the king, including *sereníssimo* (Most Serene), *muy alto y poderoso señor* (Very High and Very Powerful Lord), *ilustrissimo* (Most Illustrious), *excelentísimo* (Most Excellent), *muy magnífico* (Most Magnificent), and countless other lesser designations. Ceriol complained that only the Spaniards and Italians were so florid in addressing themselves and others. Officials eventually grew so irritated by these endless sobriquets that the Council of Castile convened in 1584 to discuss solutions. Many deliberations and petitions later, the monarch ratified the 1586 Law of Titles banning *excelencia* (Your Excellency) and *señoría* (Lordship). Petitioners were to use "Señor" and "Catholic Majesty" instead.[40] The result was that by the late 1580s most subjects began to use the simple header, "To the King our Lord."[41]

After the customary cross and salutation, vassals had considerable leeway in formatting their requests. Some petitions adopted brusque tones; others flattered. Some texts spanned more than a hundred pages; others were several sentences long. Some invoked highfalutin humanist and Biblical sources; others went straight to the heart of the issue in layman's terms.

Throughout almost the entire sixteenth century, monarchs did not ratify any other guidelines for how vassals were to write *gobierno* letters.[42] Pragmatic vassals nonetheless clearly sought to provide Crown officials with petitions in a format which would facilitate these officials' decision-making process. This did not only mean that subjects attempted (not always successfully) to write in clear, legible handwriting. They also tended to subdivide petitions into chapters or *capítulos* which would facilitate Council of the Indies scribes' transplantation of their phraseologies into each decree. In many cases they also left blank spaces on either side of the petition, to allow ministers and their subalterns to make the

[38] For "Señor," see AGI, México 364, "*Con la de vra magd*," May 22, 1595 or 1596; for "*My poderoso*," see "Juan de la Peña," AGI, México 98, March 5, 1568.

[39] Lagomarsino, "Furió Ceriol," 89.

[40] Lagomarsino, "Furió Ceriol," 98–104.

[41] Heredia Herrera, "La carta," 133.

[42] For example, in 1585 the city of Mexico sent a 50-page petition with 160 separate proposals; see AGI, Patronato 183, N.1, R.4.

marginal annotations which were so important for the lawmaking assembly line.

It was only on October 15, 1595, that council officials delineated relatively clear guidelines for how viceroys, high judges, and governorships were to send their reports ("*cartas … recaudos, informaciones, y papeles*").[43] They were to send all written material on paper folded vertically down the middle, leaving the left side blank and writing on the other. This would allow ministers to make their annotations in the left-hand margins. Local officials would also write a brief excerpt next to every *capítulo* to facilitate ministers' reading. Moreover, they were to separate all letters into four thematic groups: *hacienda* (finances), *guerra* (war), *justicia* (issues relating to court cases), and *gobierno* (other administration). Save for the 1586 Law of Titles and this 1595 decree, there were no sixteenth-century rules dictating the style or contents of subjects' letters.

Each petition concluded its proposals as it began – with ritual elements echoing face-to-face encounters between vassals and their lord. Vassals often closed their petitions with a final statement of "submission and valediction," featuring the author's name and signature, a date, and a location.[44] Valedictory statements varied substantially. Cortés' letter affirmed that he was a humble vassal of the emperor, and as a farewell kissed his lord's "royal feet and hands." However, this was not obligatory. Las Casas merely signed his name and wished that "God increase" the king's "estates and realms." After the 1586 Law of Titles, vassals were to end their texts with a simple, "God save the Catholic person of Your Majesty."[45]

Letters also tended to include a date, place, and name. The 1595 decree established that all documents officials sent to the council were to have a date. However, some did not, especially those by subjects not in royal employ. The somewhat rare petitions lacking these crucial specifics pose a challenge to historians hoping to understand the chronology of imperial legislative history.

Last came the signature. This ink scribble transformed the petition into a material vessel carrying the ideator's otherwise intangible *voluntad*. By the late medieval period, writers in the Latin West had accepted certain

43 For the council's copy of this decree, see AGI, Indiferente 427, L.30, 451v–452r. For a live decree, see also AHNE, Corte Suprema, Sección General, Gobierno, Cedularios Caja 1, 598r.

44 Huamanchumo, "Tradiciones discursivas," 1942.

45 *King Philip II, Pragmática en que se da la orden de…cortesías de palabra. Granada: Hugo de Mena, 1586.*

symbols as substitutes for an individuals' presence – a "presence not actual but nonetheless real."[46] Signs such as seals and signatures became ubiquitous and took on an agency in their own right.[47] When individuals inscribed these signs they did so with the intent of achieving the "incarnation" of their consent under various types of oaths before God.[48] Signing was simultaneously a simple everyday act, a powerful ritual, and a binding responsibility before God and the law. By putting autographs to paper, supplicants linked their text to the great vassal–lord relationship. In this way, the petition also became a carrier of a piece of the vassal – specifically, the subject's intentionality.[49] In a remarkable feat of legal fiction, they primed a lifeless cloth rectangle for the monarch and his officials to read as if it were an intelligible and authentic reflection of a face-to-face encounter, validated by the vassal's sincere volition.[50]

THE THEMES OF GOBIERNO PETITIONS

Gobierno petitions could cover a wide gamut of proposals for innovation and reform. They could feature many issues – military, financial, religious, moral, medical, agricultural, administrative, demographic – sometimes all at once. This thematic range was extremely common in officials' petitions. Moreover, other gobierno petitions could deal with issues they could also have solved through gracia or justicia channels, as did the 1561 letter of the nobility of Xochimilco, whose signees sought to force conquistadors to recognize their privileges and obligate disobedient Indigenous commoners to respect their authority. In the process, they sought numerous adjustments to the justice system, ecclesiastical procedures, local Indigenous governance, and other subjects – revealing that *gobierno* could not only intrude on *gracia* and *justicia* paperwork channels but also transform how officials structured privilege and litigious justice in general.[51]

Some petitions addressed highly local concerns which scarcely rose to the status of legislation. In 1564, the monarch issued a decree ordering officials to remedy the priest Juan Barva, aggrieved because the bishop of Panama's estate managers had unjustly confiscated a box of clothes and

[46] Bedos-Rezak, "Medieval Identity," 1505.
[47] Bedos-Rezak, "Medieval Identity," 1491.
[48] Bedos-Rezak, "Medieval Identity," 1509, see also 1507; Rück, "Beiträge," 24; Schmidt-Wiegand, "Rechtshistorische Funktion," 77–79.
[49] Bedos-Rezak, *When Ego*, 153–167 and Jeay, *Signature*, 42, 90.
[50] Fraenkel, *La signature*, 10–23. [51] AGI, Patronato 184, R.50.

an image of the Virgin Mary.[52] In 1599, the council responded to the viceroy's May 1, 1598 request about the positioning of the windows in a Mexico City university.[53] In 1579, the Jesuits of Oaxaca won a decree which gave them the king's blessing to create a "humble hut" with some cattle and a piece of land.[54] Many scholars have depicted this type of minutious text as a reflection of Habsburg obsessions with controlling the minor aspects of vassals' lives. In reality, however, this is a sign that vassals determined many of the agendas which came before Crown officials, and that monarchs and ministers alike welcomed these correspondences.

On the opposite side of the spectrum were *gobierno* petitions featuring sweeping proposals. Some suggested new and substantial reforms of imperial institutions. In the Yucatan, Franciscan Juan de la Puerta had two major proposals in his 1547 petition on behalf of the friars of the region: his province should become part of Mexico instead of Guatemala to give its residents direct access to the viceroy's justice, and should receive a bishop.[55] The sovereign issued a decree stating "nos somos informados" (we have been informed) of this or a similar proposal, and shifted the Yucatan to Mexico City's jurisdiction in a decree of April 13, 1548.[56] Council officials later credited the friars for the initiative.[57] Non-Spanish subjects without formal royal positions could also make bold and eclectic recommendations directly to the council. A group of self-described *mulatos* from New Spain prompted two *gobierno* decrees: the first from 1570, which sought to force priests to baptize newly arrived slaves; the second from 1571, which sought to place limits on Indigenous merchants' mobility to facilitate officials' collection of tribute.[58]

Many similar proposals succeeded in creating new institutions as well. The most famous case is the decades-long debate about the novel Indies system of Indigenous tribute, the *encomienda*. In theory and practice, Indians could participate in such processes as well. The Nahua city of Tlaxcala wrote the king to request a *juez de cochinilla*: a new type of judge to oversee the proper production of the red dye-producing insect, cochineal. The monarch approved and dispatched a March 3, 1592 decree crediting them with the initiative.[59]

[52] AGI, Charcas 418, L.1, 76r. [53] AGI, México 1064, L.3, 191r.
[54] AGI, México 1091, L.9, 58v. [55] AHNM, Diversos-Colecciones 23, N.7, 1r-2v.
[56] AGI, México 2999, L.1, 36r–37r. [57] AGI, Indiferente 737, N.68, 68v.
[58] AGI, Mexico 1090, L.6, 170r, 247r.
[59] AGI, México 1092, L.14, 55r–v, March 3, 1592.

Subjects did not always succeed when making these grand proposals. Nonetheless, their efforts show that they often aspired to restructure imperial governance. In 1562, the procurator of Lima requested, among many things, that the council establish a new high court in the Canaries to act as a partial overseer of the Indies, due to the long distances to Madrid.[60] In an undated petition, the Justice of Quito suggested that the Crown establish another high court in the coastal city of Guayaquil, to help pacify the restive region, prevent pirates, encourage faster travel to the city of Popayán, and stimulate the local economy.[61] In 1554, in addition to proposing that the Crown license a formal institutional Inquisition, the friars of New Galicia suggested that the council send a special representative for the joint secular and religious church, the Patriarch of the Indies, to reside with them and defend them.[62] The council did not respond to either of his proposals. One Crown attorney (*fiscal*) of Peru suggested in 1567 that the Crown create a division of the Council of the Indies in Panama, to guard the isthmus from any revolts or attacks and to expedite matters of government, grace, and justice. He also suggested *reducing* the number of high courts.[63] In 1583, Manila's city councilmen requested that the Crown provide the city with a high court to spare them from dealing with their affairs in Mexico.[64] These major efforts were not successful, but show that subjects inside and outside royal employ were perpetually thinking of and suggesting major institutional reforms.

QUANTIFYING GOBIERNO PETITIONS

How many vassals petitioned? There are no easy answers to this question, for petitions often resist quantification. This owes partly to these texts' flexible format and contents. Some featured a single minor proposal. Others featured dozens or even hundreds of major suggestions for reform. This discrepancy alone makes comparisons between one petition and another perilous. The same applies for counting their signatories – most were solitary, but some claimed to represent many thousands. Tallying and tabulating these works in any precise and meaningful way would be nearly impossible without an army of researchers working with dozens of variables. Highly sophisticated methods would also be necessary to splice petitions featuring both *gracia* and *gobierno* requests. And even a busy

[60] AGI, Patronato 188, R.30, "Después," May 5, 1562.
[61] AGI, Patronato 171, N.2, R.3. [62] NYPL, ORMC, Reel 3, "Por la experiencia."
[63] BL, Mss.33983, 6v, 7r-8v. [64] AGI, Patronato 25, R.2, 1583.

team of scholars could not compensate for the large number of petitions which have gone missing.

Some documents bring us closer to understanding the scale of the petition-and-response system. One somewhat manageable source is the council Scrivener Juan de Ledesma's petition registers for 1571–1594. Scholars have scarcely begun to analyze these books, though they offer a panoramic view of the decree-making process. Under each abstract, Ledesma and other officials would scrawl ministers' decisions, often summarized versions of the marginal resolutions they wrote on petitions. These registers' numbers hint at the empire's massive petition-and-response system. A thorough count of each entry would be nearly impossible; they span 14,373 pages of dense excerpts, sometimes in erratic handwriting. One preliminary report on the first volume counts 270 petitions in 48 days, implying (albeit very roughly) that 1572 alone saw approximately 2,050 individual supplications.[65] Assuming that petitioning continued at roughly the same rate until 1594, these volumes catalogue some 46,000 supplications for *gracia* licenses and privileges, as well as *gobierno* reforms. These entries likely represent only the supplications vassals submitted in person or via procurators in Madrid, which would mean these might fall far short of the actual Indies total.[66] If these registers only represent Madrid supplications then the total number of petitions almost surely was in the hundreds of thousands (exactly how many were *gobierno*, however, is impossible to say).

Reckoning who petitioners were is even more complex. Petitions and petition registers certainly reveal non-Spanish vassals' participation in the legislative process. Prominent Indian elites, *caciques*, and Indian towns appear often in the registers. Ledesma also recorded supplications of Indian laborers and women, *mestizos* and *mestizas*, *mulatos* and *mulatas*, free black men and women, and black slaves.[67] Many of these individuals

[65] Manzorro Guerrero, "Prácticas documentales," 133 and boxes AGI, Indiferente, 1084 L.1 to 1091 L.22.

[66] There is a distinct possibility that vassals' letters were vastly more numerous even than these roughly 50,000 in the petition registers. These logs are likely incomplete as they do not match many other correspondences in the AGI's *Gobierno* and *Patronato* sections. Moreover, many entries pair with the series *Indiferente General* 1373–1413. These massive forty-one volumes of petitions of all sorts feature letters which subjects gave to the council by hand in Madrid. In this case, the true number of supplications might be far superior to the number I have estimated. However, many were likely *gracia*.

[67] The following list of references to petitions (not all successful) and their authors is illustrative but very far from exhaustive: Inés Gómez India, AGI, Indiferente 1091, L.22, 134v; Catalina Rodríguez, mestiza of Cuzco, AGI, Indiferente 1084, L.2, 67r;

were not wealthy, such as one prolific group of "penniless Indian laborers" (*indios maceguales*), a number of "poor damsels" of Mexico, and a group of "impoverished prisoners" (*pobres desvergonzados*) in Madrid.[68] We also find the Moorish galleon slave Hali Tupuli; one "Gaspar from China"; Antonio Ungaro, a would-be scribe from Hungary; two Macedonian Greek brothers, Publio and Simeon; and a Cypriot bishop from the town of Amathus.[69] Such individuals and groups appear infrequently, and few proposed radical administrative changes. Nonetheless, their appearance in the registers testifies to the social breadth of the petition-and-response system.

Ledesma's registers and other documents suggest women also petitioned quite often. They tended to do so to defend their rights to their deceased husbands' pensions and property, to force their husbands to live with them, and to allege poverty, among other topics related to family life and patrimony (mainly issues of *gracia* and *justicia*).[70] While not legally prohibited from petitioning for sweeping legislative reforms, women did not request measures affecting Indies society very often. The reasons for this remain a puzzle for scholars to study. Perhaps sixteenth-century Indies society had gendered views that very strongly discouraged women from becoming outspokenly involved in Indies legislation. For instance, in a private 1562 correspondence sent from Mexico, doña Mariana de Morguiz told her father that she had not written often because "women are not as equipped to write … as men."[71] This does not mean that women's interests do not appear in legislation; they may have preferred to seek out a male petitioner, perhaps a friend or family member, to represent them.[72]

Proposing legislation thus remained largely the domain of wealthier, more educated Spanish men. Viceroys, governors, presidents, high judges,

Juan de Zafra, *mulato* of Puebla de los Ángeles, AGI, Indiferente 1085, L.4, 109r; Mari Fernández, viuda *mulata* (*mulata* widow) of New Granada, AGI, Indiferente 1086, L.6, 316r; Juan de Pineda, de color *mulato* (*mulato*-colored) of Lima, AGI, Indiferente 1088, L.11, 84r; Benito, *criollo esclavo* (local-born slave) of San Juan, AGI, Indiferente 1087, L.9, 19v; Casilda de Rojas, *negra atezada libre cristiana* (free Christian woman of black skin), AGI, Indiferente 1084, L.1, 6v.

[68] AGI, Indiferente 1089, L.14, 192v; AGI, Indiferente 1088, L.11, 5v; AGI, Indiferente 1091, L.29, 89v.

[69] AGI, Indiferente 1087, L.9, 81r; AGI, Indiferente 1089, L.15, 148v; AGI, Indiferente 1085, L.5; AGI, Indiferente 1090, L.17, 268r; AGI, Indiferente 1091, L.22, 245r.

[70] Mangan, *Transatlantic Obligations*, 86–96.

[71] AGI, Indiferente 2050, N.8, n.p.

[72] This was the case for Lima's *mestiza* nuns, whose blood purity self-described *mestizo* petitioners defended in 1582–1588. See "Los hijos de españoles," no date, AGI, Lima 316.

attorneys, city aldermen, archbishops, bishops, friars, conquistadores, and merchants wrote long letters and wrote often – sometimes multiple times a day.[73] This constant stream of proposals meant that ministers heeded the cries of wealthy Spanish men more often than those of marginal vassals. However, the record suggests that the council did not let these powerful individuals and groups seize the reins of petition-and-response process. Nor did these elites prevent Indians, *mestizos*, *mulatos*, Afro-descendants, women, or other less prominent groups from proposing legislation. The petition registers, along with surviving documents, and the royal decrees their letters produced, offer incontrovertible evidence that between 1524 and 1598 the monarchy was a very responsive institution with a broad base of Indies participants.

INTERMEDIARIES AND PETITION-WRITING

A sixteenth-century Nahuatl text records how, in 1564, a friar spoke with a group of Nahua artisans from Mexico City about strategies to persuade Spanish officials to reduce their tribute burden. Friar Miguel de Navarro counseled: "Do not write anything in your petition chapter [*capítulo*] except about your tribute. Attempt to reduce this [tribute] to 4 *tomínes*, my children ... converse, unite, write a petition, send it to us."[74] Friar Navarro reminded them that if local officials refused, "Do they decide, after all? The one who knows is the Emperor our Lord."[75] The friars would speed the petition to the royal court, complete with the artisans' petition and the impressive painting which they themselves created as proof of their request. Many thousands of vassals would have experienced similar conversations when crafting petitions, coordinating with others in the process.

Unlike their often-complex contents, *gobierno* petitions' formats posed only a minor challenge. They were almost always far simpler than the testimony-heavy *gracia* (often dozens or hundreds of pages long) and the lumbering, back-and-forth litigation of *justicia* (hundreds, even thousands, long). The latter two genres were particularly cumbersome due to their more complex evidentiary burdens, and always involved intermediaries. Moreover, subjects could submit *gobierno* petitions directly to the Crown without local authorities' intervention or approval.

[73] For example, Viceroy Martín Enríquez wrote four consecutive letters on October 10, 1573; see AGI, México 19, N.s112–15; October 31, 1576, AGI, México 19, N.s176–78.

[74] *Anales de Juan Bautista*, ed. Luis Reyes García. Mexico: CIESAS, 2001, 233.

[75] *Anales*, 233.

Though *gobierno* petitions theoretically did not require intermediaries, in practice many vassals did indeed require additional assistance. The greatest problems facing Indies subjects were literacy and language. Most Christian men were highly or somewhat literate in the sixteenth century; scholars have estimated that in Spain an impressive 72.3 percent could sign their names.[76] However, these abilities existed on a spectrum. Somewhere between 10 to 15 percent of the Castilian population was highly proficient.[77] Around 8 percent of Christian women could write. Outside of the Christian community, the ability to write in Spanish was far more limited.[78] In the New World, Indigenous and Afro-descendant subjects did sometimes achieve varying degrees of alphabetic Spanish literacy. In the case of Indians, many acquired the basics, with some learning eloquent Latin.[79]

The translator was often an essential intermediary. After all, Spanish was a minority language in the Indies and in many cases would remain so until the beginning of the national era.[80] Ministers could commission translations of Italian and Portuguese texts with few problems; highly educated Indigenous subjects could also be sure that council officials could understand letters they sent in Latin.[81] Vassals might also submit documentation in other languages, such as Náhuatl, Mayan, or Chinese – always with an accompanying translation.[82]

[76] Houston, *Literacy*. [77] Kagan, *Students*, 200.

[78] Viñao Frago, "Alfabetización," 45–48.

[79] For excellent analyses of Indian petitioning in the High Court of Mexico City, see Owensby, "Pacto," and *Empire of Law*. For several articles on Indigenous petitioning, see Belmessous, ed., *Native Claims*; Chuchiak, "'Ah Dzib Cahob"; McDonough, "Indigenous Rememberings"; Baber, "Categories." For *mestizo* petitioners see Dueñas, *Indians and Mestizos*; Ares Queija, "Inca Garcilaso"; For Afro-descendant men and women's engagement with writing in Lima, see Jouve, *Esclavos*; McKinley, *Fractional Freedoms*. In many areas friars, clerics, and wealthy allies taught Indians grammar and writing; see Gómez Canedo, *Educación*; Menegus and Aguirre, *Los indios*. For women, see Premo, "Before."

[80] Lope Blanch, "Lenta propagación."

[81] For Portuguese, see AGI, Indiferente 425, L.24, 377r, February 5 1568. For the two-ducat costs of a translation from Portuguese into Spanish for ministers in 1563, see AGI, Indiferente 425, L.24, 133r; For two petitions in Latin written by various Indian men and women of Mexico City, see AGI, México 168, N.108, "Cum sit peculiare," March 17 1566, and AGI, México 168, N.119, "Natura ipsa," February 12 1556. Mariner Juan Bautista Gesio submitted his request in Italian; see AGI, Patronato 48, R.3, "Molti anni," (no date). An anonymous, undated letter is located at AGI, Patronato 37, R.3, "Il gran regno." For a petition translated from Italian to Spanish, see Patronato 231, N.1, R.14, "Copia de los apuntamientos" (no date).

[82] For an example of petitioners using Chinese characters, see the 1598 petition of the "Chinese infidels" (*chinos infieles*) in AGI, Mapas y Planos, Escritura-Cifra, 28. For Náhuatl, see, for example, AGI, México 168, N.53, "Entendido tenemos," December 19, 1554; AGI, Guadalajara 51, L.1, N.33, October 1557; AGI, México 369, no date (ca.1599–1602),

Many different types of officials might help vassals with writing and translating their proposals. As Charles Cutter notes, "nearly every official in the colonial administrative network had the duty of watching out for Indian interests."[83] Bishops, who from the years 1527 to 1550 were the primary officials entrusted with helping Indigenous vassals reach justice, often assisted illiterate vassals both publicly and behind the scenes.[84] By the mid-sixteenth century, and increasingly by its final third, royal protectors of Indians working under viceregal supervision largely took over this task.[85] In local courts and around the Council of the Indies, subjects could avail themselves of the pro bono services of the royal procurators for the poor.[86] In general, then, these services were free for viceregal society's neediest.

Beneath bishops and other high-ranking officials was a middling stratum of intermediaries. For better or for worse, the empire housed a thriving – and often manipulative – "lettered marketplace." In the center of every Spanish city was a hectic open bazaar of writing, perpetually open for business, populated by legal specialists eager to ply their wares. Lawyers (*abogados*) might occasionally counsel petitioners with learned legal strategies drawing from Roman law and other sources. However, they generally did not dedicate themselves to the nitty-gritty bureaucratic details of *gobierno* petition-writing, and generally served as assistants for the more complex *justicia* cases.[87] More often, a would-be petitioner would seek out low-ranking *solicitadores*, or legal assistants, and procurators (*procuradores*), who had their offices in the buildings near or on the plaza.[88]

Legal intermediaries of all sorts proliferated far beyond the already substantial high-and-middling world of royal officialdom. Friars and priests often filled this role in an informal capacity (see Figure 1.3).[89] Indigenous elites, and sometimes commoners, might be sufficiently literate and skilled

"Matu.o Dios," and "Do maviz"; AGI, México 357, "Obispo de Antequera," April 1, 1595. For Mayan, AGI, México 104, "Yoklal," January 8 1580, trans. Juan Ruiz. For Latin, See also Laird, "Nahuas"; *Nahua Humanism.*

[83] Cutter, *Protector*, 7.

[84] Cunill, "Protectoría," 478; Bayle, *Protector*, 12–99; Cutter, *Protector*, 1–19.

[85] Cunill, "Protectoría," 479–481.

[86] Mirow, *Latin American*, 20; Cutter, *Protector*; Schäfer, *Consejo*, 73; Milton, *Many Meanings*, 282–283, footnotes 13 and 14; Sarabia Viejo, *Don Luís*, 25; Cunill, "Justicia," 18–28. Caciques might pay in full; in some cases Indigenous communities petitioning together paid half. See AGI, Mexico 2999, L.3, 77r.

[87] Honores, "Sociedad legalista," 290.

[88] Mirow, *Latin American*, 41; Honores, "Sociedad legalista," xi, 60–61, 221–230, 257, 289–290, 432. For lawyers, see Pérez-Perdomo, *Latin American*, chapter 1.

[89] For a history of the go-betweens, including translators, in central Mexico, see Yannakakis, *Native Intermediaries* and "Making Law"; See also Cunill, "Protectoría," 478–484.

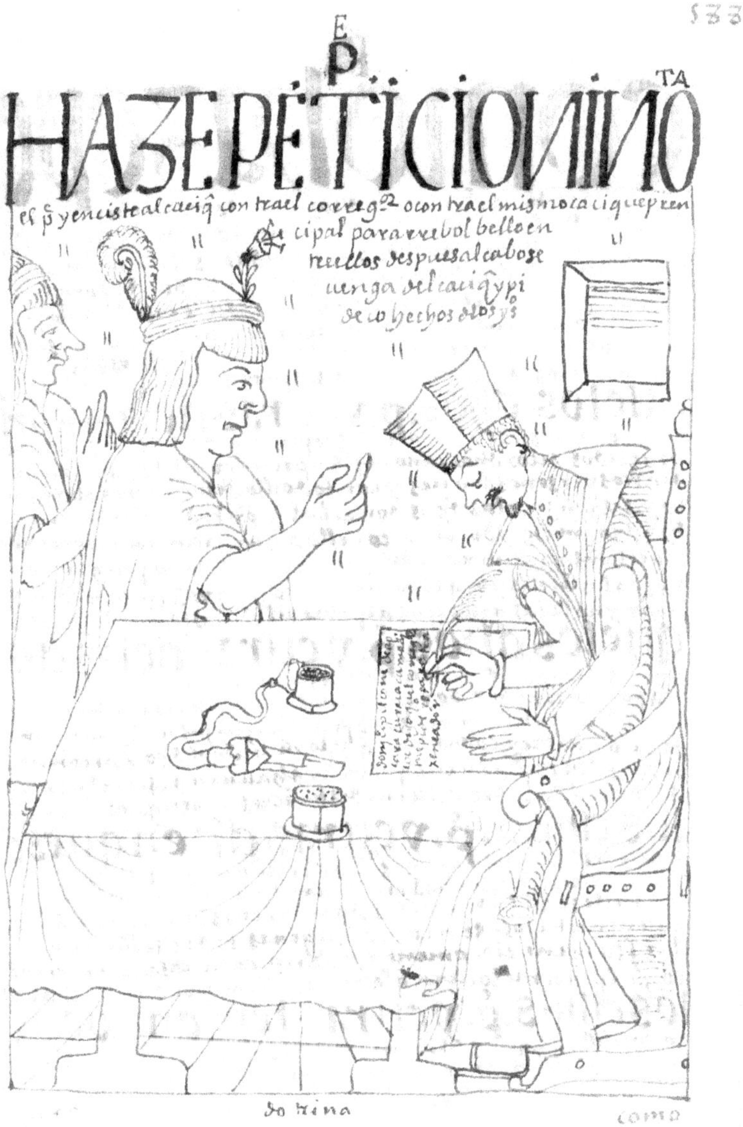

FIGURE 1.3 A priest in Peru helps Indian leader don Juan Pilcone draft a petition against a corrupt field justice (*corregidor*). Subjects who could not write in Spanish could turn to pro bono intermediaries, or seek out other friends and allies, for help in crafting *gobierno* petitions (Guaman Poma, Nueva Corónica, KB Codex GkS 2232, 588/602).

to help their peers and subjects – a small number were perfectly literate not only in Spanish but in Latin.[90] Translators might also provide informal free help to Indigenous vassals hoping to petition.[91] Word of mouth likely helped the confused navigate this system both in the Indies and in Spain.[92]

These rich formal and informal strata pooled contributions from a substantial amount of non-Spanish individuals, generally men. While women did sometimes act as interpreters in the crucial early conquest phase, by the 1530s translators in Mexico tended to be male: a mix of conquistadors married to Indigenous women, those who arrived young to the Indies, those born of Spanish parents in the Indies, those with an Indigenous parent, or those with two Indigenous parents.[93] In some regions, Afro-descendant translators occasionally appeared to help Indigenous subjects reach justice.[94] Notaries were generally Spanish, but might be born in the Indies, and a small number were Indigenous, especially in Mexico, but also occasionally in Cuzco and other areas of Peru.[95] Lastly, anyone of any social background could act as a legal agent – although women very rarely did so.[96] These go-betweens were thus mostly male, but were not always Castilians – meaning that these individuals' labor, and much of the petition-and-response system itself, were not entirely Spanish.

TRANSMITTING VOLUNTAD: THE FICTION OF THE PODER

Most vassals could not travel to court and press their cases before the king and Council. However, they could transfer their *voluntad* to legal agents and have them act and speak in their stead. Appointing a legal representative meant passing one's volition to another individual, who would act as an instrument in ruled–ruler dialogue. This legal fiction was made possible by a specific written ritual: the creation of a *carta de poder* (certificate of power of attorney) before a notary.[97] These notarized documents often cemented vassals' *voluntad* to a dossier, frequently with formulaic contractual clauses

[90] These often received the less-than-flattering moniker of *ladinos*; see Adorno, *Polemics*, 24–25; Aguilar Moreno, "Indio ladino"; Charles, "'More ladino." See also Puente Luna, *Andean Cosmopolitans*, 12–14, 67–68; McDonough, "Indigenous Rememberings," 75.

[91] Cunill, "Mosaico," 37; Puente Luna, "Many Tongues," 153; Yannakakis, "Indigenous People," 935.

[92] Van Deusen, "Oralidad." [93] Cunill, "Mosaico," 34.

[94] Machuca, *Intérpretes*, 41–42.

[95] Burns, "Notaries," 363–365; Navarro Gala, *Libro de protocolo*.

[96] Risly Clemence, *Harkness*, vol. 1, 275. For Indigenous and part-Spanish legal agents, see Puente Luna, *Andean Cosmopolitans*, 45–47, 78–81.

[97] Mazín Gómez, "La corte," 120; Post, "Roman Law."

such as "I … grant/say/do/give/declare."[98] Those present might seal this transaction of wills with oaths before notaries. In this way, the petitioner's volition and voice passed to the procurator for the duration of the contract – this intermediary received the supplicant's agency. This act of legal magic enabled individuals to conduct complex business in court as if they were themselves face-to-face with their lords. This recreated, in a way, an ersatz version of the vassal–lord relationship's sustained in-person dialogues.

Another transformation which could take place in a *poder* was the fusion of individual *voluntad* into the volition of a corporation. Cities, ecclesiastical bodies, local religious orders, and others often fused their many volitions into a single body by giving a professional procurator or any other legal agent their *voluntad* through a contract.[99] In 1551, Jilotepeque governor don Juan de la Cruz and his fellow Indigenous elites Juan Ramírez, Francisco de Guzmán, and Miguel García appeared before the high court notary, a translator, and a witness to produce a *poder* which they sent to an agent in the royal court. This enabled the agent to speak "on our behalf and those of the other Indian elites and commoners of the said town."[100] In even more astonishing acts of paperwork alchemy, small groups could claim, through their use the *poder*, to manifest and represent whole categories of humanity with no formal institutional or social cohesion. For instance, Pedro Rengifo could claim, with only 149 signatures from a handful of towns, to "speak in the name of" the "entire family" of "ten thousand mestizos" before the king and the council – despite the lack of a unified *mestizo* community stretching throughout Peru.[101] Similarly, in 1568 the self-described *mulato* tailor Juan Bautista claimed to speak for the *mulatos* of Mexico City, whom he counted at "more than six thousand."[102] These *poderes* not only created the illusion of a chorus of volitions, then – they were also central in the bottom-up transformation of inchoate categories of human difference into large fictive communities.

98 Argouse, "Otorgo," 220; Luján Muñoz, *Los escribanos*, 94; Mijares Ramírez, *Escribanos*, 75–77, 101; Burns, "Dentro," 49.

99 Seoane, *Buenos Aires*; Gaudin, "Acercamiento"; Bahena Pérez, "Negociar"; Cunill, "De Yucatán"; Mazín, *Gestores*; Rubial García, "Religiosos viajeros."

100 AGI, Mexico 96, "En al gran çiudad," 1551, no folios.

101 AGI, Lima 126, 115r–v; For more on this case, see Ruan, "Andean Activism"; Duve, "Concilio." For this social absence, see Graubart, *Hybrid Thinking*, 222 and Rappaport, *Disappearing*, 61.

102 AGI, México 98, "Joan de la Peña" and accompanying documents, 1568.

A battery of legal fictions was also necessary for vassals and the king to assuage their consciences regarding the translation of *voluntad* into Spanish. Before taking office, all official intermediaries had to swear before God that they would act with honor and rectitude. While these declarations sometimes varied in structure, in general the inductee needed to declare his (or, rarely, her) intention to "use the said office" of translator "well, faithfully, without fraud or deceit."[103] Translators might swear, for example, to "employ well and faithfully all secret in said occupation, and to interpret the whole truth … without diminishing anything."[104] In order to certify that these texts preserved vassals' volitions intact, the individual who provided the translation might also add a clause upon a petition which served as an oath of fidelity. For instance, in 1580 Juan de la Vega stated that he had provided certain Mayan petitioners with an "interpretation of the said letter (*carta*) … extracted faithfully and truly, sentence by sentence, from the language of the Yucatan into Castilian."[105] These assertions were not always duplicitous. Indeed, scholars have also shown that, in some cases, translations maintained a considerable amount of the original language's subtleties, and by and large adhered to the sentiment of the petitioners as expressed in the original Indigenous texts.[106]

The notary was one of the surest guarantors of legal agents', interpreters', and witnesses' fidelity and legality.[107] This official was "the versatile workhorse of Spanish government."[108] Vassals and officials alike generally embraced the myth of notarial proof as a privileged form of evidence.[109] Like translators, they were to be upright Christian bureaucrats, and were to keep careful archives of their proceedings in case their clients needed evidence further down the road.[110] Indeed, notarial oaths and signatures were more than just bureaucratic procedures. They summoned God himself to witness the proceedings, ensuring that everyone involved would work in good faith to affix the subject's volition to paper. One subject swore before a notary to translate before "God and the Cross," promising to act without "any fraud … God help him if he [is

[103] Hillerkuss, *Documentalia*, 81–82; Rojas Rabiela, Rea López, and Medina Lima, *Vidas*, 82, 92, 152, 174, 182, etc.
[104] Cunill, "Mosaico," 37; Puente Luna, "Many Tongues," 146; Machuca, *Intérpretes*, 32–37.
[105] AGI, México 104, N.2 [106] Raimúndez Ares, "Cartas," 228.
[107] Burns, *Into the Archive*, 4; Guajardo-Fajardo Carmona, *Escribanos*, 87–93, 248–255.
[108] Lockhart, *Spanish Peru*, 77. [109] Burns, "Notaries," 351; *Into the Archive*, 3.
[110] Burns, "Notaries," 372.

honest], and if not, may He sue him."[111] These officials were also to provide pro bono services to the needy.[112]

Vassals might also need help signing their names, demanding a new battery of rituals. For example, in 1566 the notary of the Peruvian town of Xauxa confirmed the legitimacy of the signatures of certain Huringuanca municipal officials, which they inscribed upon a petition to the king. The notary stated upon the petition that "they wrote this letter and signed their names on their own volition" (*de su voluntad*).[113] In order to dispel further doubts, the same group of Indigenous councilmen also summoned certain friars to testify and sign themselves.[114] This episode centered mainly around the validity of one of the most essential parts of a petition: the signature. Even the idea that the indexical subjectivity of a signature, which allegedly marked a document's link to its ideator, was something of a fiction. Since most Indigenous subjects could not sign, an intermediary – often a translator or an official entrusted with helping Indians – would have to do this for them.[115] Many other illiterate subjects often resorted to similar actions by having witnesses sign on their behalf before notaries.[116] Whether penned by the petitioner or not, in the Spanish Indies these ink scribbles could thus incarnate an individual's intrinsically subjective *voluntad* upon paper.

Petitioners hoping to convey to the monarch that their letters contained their pure *voluntad* thus could scaffold legal fictions upon one another. The more written proofs, the firmer the king would find the volition. A 1567 collective Maya petition reflects this layering of fictions and intermediaries' labors in transmitting volition:

Hetun cathan lae	Here we speak:
Coltic udzaab ufirmasob	We want the signatures to be placed of our helpers,
Cah antulob	We want the signatures to be placed

[111] Machuca, *Intérpretes*, 35; Cunill, "Mosaico," 15.

[112] See, for instance, AGI, México 1090, L.6, 349v, 21 October 1571, 374v, 26 December 1571; AGI, México 1090, L.7, 18 May 1572. Notarial costs varied; see Guahardo-Fajardo Carmona, *Escribanos*, 496. For estimates, see 240–241; see also Luján Muñoz, *Los escribanos*, 129.

[113] AGI, Audiencia de Lima 121, 60r.

[114] AGI, Audiencia de Lima 121, 48r.

[115] Raimúndez Ares, "Cartas," 228. In this case, it was the General Interpreter of the Indians of the Yucatan who undertook this. See also Machuca, *Intérpretes*, 36; Noack, "Los caciques"; For Peruvian Indigenous understandings of the signature, see Rappaport and Cummins, *Beyond*, 202–209.

[116] Burns, *Into the Archive*, 126; AGI, Mexico 96, "En la gran çiudad," 1551, no folios; Mijares Ramírez, *Escribanos*, 85.

laobi defensorob	the [legal] defenders,
cau tzac auoheltic	so that you might know
hach talil ti col	that this truly comes from our heart.[117]

Signatures, translation under oath, notarization, and supporting testimony created the impression that *voluntad* had indeed transferred from the Indigenous officials to paper. Many documents were thus, as Joanne Rappaport and Tom Cummins argued, "collaborative ventures," the outcomes of a rather elaborate "process marked by extraliterate ceremony as well as by graphic notation."[118]

HUMAN FAILINGS AND THE INIQUITIES OF PROCURATORSHIPS

Intermediaries were to be, as one decree put it, "instruments through which justice is to be spoken."[119] Curiously, notarial documents, which served as important auxiliary supports for some petitions, were also called "instruments" and were also to be receptacles containing and transporting subjects' volitions.[120] Yet intermediaries were embedded in complex social circumstances in which they did not always fulfill their duties – sometimes out of ineptitude, other times because the workload was too great.

Professional procurators at the court provide a case in point. They were to keep track of various petitioners' letters, consult lawyers if necessary, schedule hearings with the council, and patiently wait in the halls and courtyards outside the ministers' offices to lobby on their clients' behalf.[121] However, this responsibility entailed substantial labor, and exposed vassal–lord dialogue quite literally to the elements. For example, in 1570 the Church procurator Sancho Sánchez de Muñón complained that he endured the freezing winter cold outside the council's doors during a long and fruitless winter of lobbying.[122]

This fiction of volitionless instrumentality often ran up against substantial obstacles as all-too-human middlemen failed in their tasks to provide justice for all. Pressed for time, financially stressed, or perhaps simply eager to escape the cold, certain agents came to favor some over

[117] Hanks, *Converting*, 325.
[118] Rappaport and Cummins, *Beyond*, 118 and 21. See also Goody, *Logic*, 42–43.
[119] AGI, México 1064, L.2, 118r–118v [120] Burns, *Into the Archive*, 3.
[121] Honores, "Una sociedad legalista," 245–247; Mazín, *Gestores*, 46, 91.
[122] Mazín, *Gestores*, 47, 57, 124; Honores, "Una sociedad legalista," 230, 251.

others. Indeed, some petitioners found that without deep social ties to protectors, cases might receive less attention and might flounder.[123]

For example, two 1580 Quito letters provide detailed descriptions of how this iniquity might arise. The High Court of Quito's *relator* (court reporter) Alonso Martín de Amores wrote two long and thorough letters to his brother, Alonso de Herrera del Puerto, the Council of the Indies' official procurator. Martín listed the numerous vassals clamoring for his help in pressing the council for justice, as well as the quantity they were to pay him. These letters reveal a number of aspects of how legal agents might work through patrimonial networks. Court procurators seem to have used Indies family members to procure clients and funds. These connections likely facilitated vassals' access to royal justice. Legal agents also favored the wealthy. A nobleman was about to arrive at Quito, noted Martín, and, if they could help him become president, "if our luck were to have this succeed, I understand that I would be very rich, and your Lordship very remedied and gratified."[124] Amores also accepted payments on credit from wealthier clients, and surely was more cautious with those of more limited means. Procurators, far from passive instruments, were embedded in networks of interests – and their own ambitions could either move a petition forward or impede its success.

Some documents reveal that vassals' reliance on procurators could end in bitter disappointment. According to one Alonso del Rincón, Herrera had botched a vassals' *justicia* court case out of pure negligence. Thirteen years later, in 1580, Amores wrote him from Quito regarding a similar complaint. He tactfully warned his relative in Madrid that "certain fools [*maxaderos*] ... have wanted to say that Your Grace is lazy, and that Santander and Uribe and Juan de la Peña are diligent." Amores knew Herrera's illness may have been to blame, but warned that they both had money and honor to lose if these errors and deficiencies continued. Herrera had indeed come down with a high fever in 1577, and died on December 14 of that year.[125] His widow appointed Herrera's pending paperwork to a new procurator, her brother Pedro Hernández de Narváez, who would ultimately carry Herrera's cases to the court. All of this brought about a major delay in his clients' cases.

[123] Cunill, "Protectoría," 483; Puente Luna, *Andean Cosmopolitans*, 77.

[124] Otte, *Cartas*, N.392, 346. The previous president had died not long before. The original document is located in AGI, Indiferente 2092, N.74.

[125] AGI, Contratación 220B, N.1, R.24, no title.

Herrera was not the only procurator who caused friction in vassal–ruler dialogue. One Gonzalo Alonso Peñafiel complained on November 12, 1586 that he had given certain papers to a clergyman who was also his procurator, but that his agent had failed to submit certain important papers to the council.[126] In 1588, the Indian don Antonio Silquigua of Quito complained that his procurator Gerónomio Gómez lost his paperwork, including the decree his agent had won; the council's marginal statement suggests they instructed the Crown attorney to find it in their archive and issue a duplicate for him.[127] In an April 7, 1589 letter, a group of angry friars in Lima blasted their Madrid procurator Friar Bartolomé de Bermúdez, stating that "we fathers of this province are all shocked in not having received letters from you." They complained that they had paid him handsomely – fifty ducats – for him to support the interests of the monastery of Our Lady of Copacabana. Now he had gone silent, though they continued to send him "many letters."[128]

TWISTING VOLUNTAD

The labor of other intermediaries raised similar questions about whether they were capable and honest instruments of vassals' volition.[129] Translation was one central problem: could the transmission of *voluntad* from individuals to legal agents survive the transfer of one language to another? Interpreters were often present whenever non-Spanish speakers needed to notarize their *poderes*.[130] They also often acted as Indigenous vassals' legal agents.[131] However, the very act of translating concepts in petitions, as well as those within *poderes*, led non-Spanish speakers into a series of hazardous circumstances. Since the early conquest, Indies subjects feared translators' ability to distort words and disrupt imperial dialogues.[132] Indeed, translators might sometimes distort a petition's statements or even outright reverse its meaning.[133]

Officials occasionally discovered concrete instances in which an interpreter might seek to twist a vassal's *voluntad* through malicious translation. For example, certain Indigenous elites in Cuzco accused the city's

[126] AGI, Indiferente 1401, "Gonzalo Alonso."
[127] AGI, Indiferente 1404, "Don Antonio," August 22, 1588.
[128] AGI, Indiferente 1403, "Gra. et pax." [129] Burns, *Into the Archive*, 353–354.
[130] Puente Luna, "Many Tongues," 153–155.
[131] Puente Luna, "Many Tongues," 153–155 and Yannakakis, "Indigenous People," 935.
[132] Lentz, "Intérpretes generales," 141.
[133] Puente Luna, "Many Tongues," 143–170, here 143.

translator, the part-Indian Antón Ruiz, of having been a "very biased translator" and having forced a large number of these lords to sign a petition addressed to the king against their will.[134] The high court exiled Ruiz and warned him not to return lest he be given 200 lashes. However, Ruiz protested that he was a "God-fearing man and a man of conscience" simply trying to inform the king and, after a spirited defense, persuaded the judges to overturn his sentence.[135]

Solicitors, lawyers, procurators, notaries, and translators may have enabled Indies justice to function smoothly, but many vassals viewed them with bitter contempt. Some subjects were incensed by procurators' tendency to make legal molehills into profitable and drawn-out mountains. Others warned that they hurt Indians by luring them into petty or never-ending legal conflicts.[136] These experts also had the final say about the content of their clients' supplications. This meant that they could maliciously insert contents into customers' writings to their personal benefit. On one occasion, the City Council of Lima accused a procurator of secretly altering a petition and adding falsehoods in order to benefit his cronies.[137] This sort of extreme event seems to have been rare, but subjects nonetheless had little love for these legal intermediaries. Even the Council of the Indies noted in its 1542–1543 New Laws the "malice of some lawyers and procurators."[138] As Kathryn Burns has argued, notaries too appear periodically as ruffians who attempted to corrupt subjects' statements of volition – and they certainly did occasionally engage in outright deceit to swindle customers.[139]

Subjects often loathed legal specialists in general. Juan Griego complained in 1567 that Peru had been better off before the conquest, for the Inca ruled without "lawyers and procurators and scribes" who "have destroyed the realm" by bankrupting their clients.[140] Friar Pedro Juárez de Escobar went so far as to recommend that Mexico City have "one

[134] AGI, Justicia 434, N.2, R.1, 2r, 5r–6v.

[135] AGI, Justicia 434, N.2, R.1, 44r–48r; Glave Testino, "*Simachi*," 134. For similar accusations against Santa Fe's Muisca translator, see Augusto Gamboa, "El primer," 97–120.

[136] Honores, "Imágenes sociales"; Burns, "Notaries," 353; see also the Viceroy of Mexico's comments on this system and his transcriptions of several of his edicts in his 1592 letter, AGI, México 22, N.72, "Despues," March 1592.

AGI, Lima 121, "Vra voluntad," December 1567, and AGI, Lima 122, "En estos rreynos," January 1 1568. See also BNF, Espagnol 325, "Si era bien," by Fray Juan de Mansilla and the Council of the Indies, 258r, undated, and BNF, Espagnol 325, "Memoria," 267r, undated and Friars Pedro de la Peña, Francisco de Torres, and Alonso de la Vera.

[137] AGI, Lima 108, "Muy poderoso," April 4 1580.

[138] BNE, Mss.3035, 11v.

[139] Burns, "Dentro," esp. 46; *Into the Archive*.

[140] AGI, Lima 121, "Vra voluntad," December 16 1567.

doctor of law [*letrado*] only and one procurator and one translator, all very examined Christians," for "with such a sum and confusion of lawyers, procurators, and translators" the Indians were losing their goods and land. Meanwhile, he alleged that these intermediaries "construct[ed] their illustrious houses and raise up very splendid buildings."[141]

Intermediaries were not the only sowers of mischief, however. Vassals themselves might provide fraudulent documents, signatures, or testimonies under oath when presenting petitions and their auxiliary documents. Officials might punish subjects of voluntary perjury with lifetime bans from office, confiscation of goods, public humiliation, the shaving of the head, exile, forced labor, physical punishments such as the pulling of teeth or nailing of the tongue, or even death.[142] Forgers of ordinary judicial documents, the falsification of signatures, counterfeiting of *poderes*, and so forth might be subject to exile, confiscation of goods, physical punishments, or the death penalty, depending on the determination of the judges.[143] Legal fictions were not truths in the strictest sense, but were nonetheless tied to very tangible worlds of justice enforcement and violence.

That being said, intermediaries tended to avoid outright wrongdoing. Some sources suggest that many of these agents, likely fearful of earning a bad reputation, sought to stick quite closely to subjects' requests.[144] Likewise, notaries did not always faithfully translate an individual's testimonies, and they frequently abbreviated or embellished oral statements, but generally they shied away from distorting subjects' *voluntad*.[145]

CONCLUSIONS

Gobierno petitions were remarkable technologies. Through them, the act of speaking with the lord was spatially collapsed from palace halls into wafer-thin texts. The process was thus rendered nearly weightless, especially in the case of *gobierno* administration, which did not generally require heaps of supporting evidence. This saved vassals from traveling

[141] AGI, Patronato Real 171, N.2, R.1, "A la sacra catholica."
[142] Mayer Lux and Vera Vega, "Historia," 359–361; Iglesias Rábade, "Falso testimonio," 99.
[143] Iglesias Rábade, "Estudio comparado," 319–323
[144] AGI, Quito 18, N.52, "Memorial," November 11, 1580. This section features several other nonnumerated documents that also show procurators submitting petitioners' contracts to the council directly as if they were petitions; see also AGI, Santo Domingo 73; AGI, Santo Domingo 201.
[145] Burns, *Into the Archive*, 34.

to court, and freed monarchs from time-consuming face-to-face dialogue. The vassal–lord relationship had been made portable – featherweight, affordable, highly mobile, stackable, and storable. An empire of dialogue could now extend as far as vassals could sail, without subjects risking the absolute rupture of their (fictional) presence from the court.

Despite petitions' convenience, simplicity, and affordability, creating them was often a deceptively complex process. Few subjects could simply produce these documents, and even elites often needed the help of middlemen in more complex efforts. Transmitting *voluntad* from vassal to ruler via intermediaries could usually only endure if multiple parties expended substantial physical, ritual, and conceptual labor. This ritual buttressing required the participation of a wide range of actors, including many non-Spaniards. They, not just the supplicant vassals and lawgiving lords (as the contemporary ideal had it), were protagonists of this dialogue.

This talk of fiction, however, should not obscure the very real consequences of this system. Petitions, through a series of rather flimsy legal rituals, enabled what no in-person vassal–lord relationship could ever have achieved. These texts and the many labors of will-validation which went into their production enabled vassals, officials, and monarchs to partake in hundreds of daily vassal–lord rituals. Constant maintenance, and even violence, was needed to uphold this great fiction.

The overall effect of these petitions and their supporting rituals was a general (if never ironclad) basis of trust in the validity and integrity of the empire's communications system. Thanks to this legal alchemy, through which volition became affixed to paper, petitions began to change the nature of empire – and the world as well. A system of exclusively face-to-face encounters would have far more heavily skewed dialogue toward magnates physically near in the ruler's circle. Thanks to a robust if imperfect infrastructure for petition-making, most subjects – even those who were illiterate or did not speak Spanish – attained the possibility of influencing royal pronouncements in decisive ways. Most would have had only modest difficulties producing these texts – but also were not oblivious to the enormous logistical challenges that lay ahead, for these texts would now have to travel enormous distances to the court. It is to this highly convoluted process that we now turn.

2

The Cocreation of the Imperial Logistics Network

Sometime in 1584, the legal agents Ruiz and González handed Pedro Rengifo the great 224-page petition of the sons and daughters of Indians and Spaniards. He was to personally carry the case to the council and perhaps even the king. The legal fiction of the family of 10,000 mestizos *prostrating themselves before the monarch might satisfy the consciences of all involved, but this was to be no simple dialogue. For before Pedro awaited an odyssey – thousands of leagues of water, wind, jungle, mountains, and a maze of human contingencies. No petitions – be they in-person or compressed into paper ceremonial – could succeed without first facing the grim reality of imperial distances.*

Hoping to catch the seasonal armada as it arrived in Cartagena and Nombre de Dios, Pedro likely arrived to Panama in late May 1584.[1] *He was fortunate, for the armada had been delayed when two boats sank, and when Cartagena's cash-strapped residents could not afford the fleet's merchandise due to piracy-related delays in Peruvian silver.*[2] *Popayán gold miners also delayed departure by five days when they failed to procure enough mules.*[3] *The summer was now approaching – and, with it, hurricane season. Local officials began to panic that the armada would*

[1] AGI, Contratación 1080, N.3; AGI, Panama 13, R.23, N.159.

[2] AGI, Patronato 258, N.1, G.2, R.3; AGI, Patronato 258, N.1, G.2, R.5; AGI, Panama 13, R.23, N.161 chapter 1; AGI, Panama 13, R.23, N.159.

[3] AGI, Panama 33, N.130.

have to winter in the Indies, lest wind and rain tear apart its crew and cargo.[4]

The armada nonetheless sailed forward, remaining in Havana only for a brief time. By late August, it was well across the ocean. Near the Azores, Pedro would have spotted certain French pirate-merchants from Dieppe, Normandy, whom Spanish warships quickly arrested after a brief volley of artillery.[5] *Now less than a month from Seville, the armada dodged Moroccan- and Ottoman-allied ships not far from Lagos, Portugal.*[6] *Under heavy escort, the armada's passengers arrived at Seville sometime before September 1584. Yet Pedro only appeared before the council in Madrid on February 11, 1585, likely having fallen ill in Andalucía.*[7] *He did not fail to emphasize that ministers owed him "consideration" due to his "long voyage, expenses, dangers, and work."*[8]

Vassals often mentioned the great difficulties of transporting letters to the court. In 1596, the Indigenous Andean elite don Juan Astubarcaya told council ministers he lost "the papers he brought, which were thrown into the sea by a certain storm."[9] One Spanish vassal from San Cristóbal, a small town outside of Santa Fe de Bogotá, lamented to his sister in Spain that he had entrusted letters for her to a priest, but these never arrived, saying, "I do not know to what I can attribute this, unless it was death on the sea, and [his] not having arrived to that land."[10] In 1554, a Franciscan complained from Chiapas that he could not send Bishop Las Casas (then in Spain) a letter "that cannot suffer delays" because he "had no-one to take it." He fretted because "the rains" would soon begin; "I think I must be the messenger."[11] As don Juan Astubarcaya, Pedro Rengifo, Las Casas, and many thousands of others well knew, logistics were not a detail but a central problem for the transmission of petitions to Iberia.

Petitions represented human encounters between subjects and lords, but in almost all cases vassals were not physically present in the Spanish imperial court. Some vassals were fortunate enough to live in the relatively nearby Caribbean, but as the empire expanded up great rivers, into

[4] AGI, Panama 13, R.23, N.159; AGI, Panama 33, N.130.

[5] AGI, Patronato 258, N.1, G.2, R.42, 2v–7r.

[6] AGI, Indiferente 740, N.274.

[7] AGI, Indiferente 740, N.287; AGI, Lima 126, 1r.

[8] All of this is located in AGI, Patronato 127, N.1, R.11, which has no foliation.

[9] AGI, Indiferente 1414, "Don Juan," February 15, 1596.

[10] Otte, *Cartas*, N.362, 317.

[11] AGI, Patronato 252, R.15.

measureless deserts, and into rugged highlands, so did its challenges. Every year, subjects' proposals and volitions traveled upon tens of thousands of cloth-rag parchments, each undergoing a perilous journey to the capital. Some had to travel within Iberia, others through Europe, but most had to traverse vast oceans or even some of the world's densest forests and highest mountain ranges – and brave human sabotage as well. Before them was a world of human and natural peril – and in order for ruled–ruler dialogue to take place, many of these papers had to first survive an odyssey of global proportions. The great fiction of untrammeled dialogue underpinning Habsburg rule over the Indies had met its greatest enemy in the tyranny of distance.

An empire is not a discrete, bounded entity which exists a priori. It is, rather, the repeated consummation of patterned interpersonal networks. How to keep together these empire-networks and protect against collapse? The perpetual maintenance, expansions, and transformations of these vast, ultra-complex linkages do not mechanistically occur. Here, the *work* in *network* becomes crucial.[12] Imperial law was likewise also a network, linked inextricably to many others. This book's understanding of law as a labor process attempts to reframe the question: Who (and what) undertakes the labor of legislation? This answer cannot remain within the domain of the legal alone. The labor of imperial decree-creation encompassed many domains – including, among others, the all-important field of logistics. Even Latour's ethnography of the Conseil d'État did not extend his insights into networks deep enough to link the worlds of ministers' work to what we traditionally have considered to be "non-legal." As a result, he inadvertently reinforced the exact type of arbitrary distinctions which his theories have aimed to erode, such as the dichotomies of idea and matter, between product and process, between lawmakers and the rest of society.

Latour's study of the conseil also neglected to critically explore who (and what) counts as a worker within this process. Yes, French ministers undertook what we commonly understand as the essential legal work of the conseil – but where would these practices be without litigants, legal agents, postal workers, the automobile industry who moved documents, the electricians, inventors, technicians, and countless others? By refraining to cross beyond the French administration's own conceptual border of legal/non-legal labor, his study has in some ways created a newly opaque and mythological account, at the expense of a more accurate sociological

[12] Latour, "Network Theory," 796–810, 797.

one which reaches for the full potential of his iconoclastic network theories.

Neither the processes of empire-making nor of decree-making can exist without logistical networks, which (despite scholars' frequent reinforcement of the illusions of law's immateriality) are always tied to work and matter.[13] In the Spanish Empire, *voluntad* had traveled from vassals' souls and minds onto paper. But how did the paper itself travel to the monarch? Callon and Latour have called for exploring how "our wills flow" through "canals and networks" – for documents containing the legal fiction of *voluntad* to reach the monarch's desk, this was no leisurely drift from periphery to center.[14] This chapter studies the role of logistician-laborers who contributed to the greater process of lawmaking. Rather than sacralizing the law as an autonomous sphere of labor, and meeting lawmakers on their own mythological grounds, I argue that the logistical labor of countless actants was fundamental to determining the transmission of volition, and ultimately of shaping Spanish imperial *gobierno* decree-production.

The Indies' case provides a quintessential example of the importance of labor networks' operation in conjunction with legislative procedure. After all, the Spanish New World faced some of world history's greatest logistical challenges. All early modern polities struggled with communications, and the Latin West's overseas dominions were no exception.[15] But this empire was unique in combining globe-spanning dominions with "an unprecedented combination of land and sea transport."[16] Simply put, no other early modern empire combined such a global reach, populous inland dominions, and a dedicated commitment to ruler–ruled communications.[17] It was not just the empire's size also but its logistics networks which counted among its defining characteristics.[18]

Scholarship on early modern European empires is in the midst of a "spatial turn" that complements and expands upon earlier research on navigation, communications, and conquests.[19] Despite the increase of scholarship explicitly about space, historians have mostly neglected to see the movement of legal documents as a central element of Spanish Indies

[13] McLuhan, *Understanding Media*, 89. [14] Callon and Latour, "Unscrewing," 289.

[15] Steele, *English Atlantic*; Banks, *Chasing Empire*, esp. 71; Naylor Pearson, *Coastal Western India*, 43; Rahn Phillips, "The growth"; Oliveira e Costa, "A correspondência"; Rodrigues and Lobato, "Circulaçao."

[16] Braudel, *Mediterranean*, 371–374. [17] Ross, "Legal Communications."

[18] Anderson, *Estado absolutista*, 70; Garrett, "'En lo remoto," 19.

[19] Roberts, *Transporting Visions*, 3; Dym, "Taking a Walk."

society, and as an issue that realigned many parts of its society to ensure the endurance of ruler–ruled connections. Historian Sylvia Sellers-García's important recent study on Guatemalan high court bureaucratic logistics in the eighteenth century is one of a limited number of works that meditate in depth upon these issues. Echoing communications theorist Marshall McLuhan, Sellers-García notes that distance was a factor not only in delaying justice, but even in shaping the nature of Indies letters and its society's "particular contents, forms, and practices" of knowledge transmission and accumulation.[20] David Garret has also studied how slow imperial logistics affected vassals' search for redress in late 1600s Cuzco, concluding that distance did indeed have a transformative effect on the timing of justice and on society more generally.[21] Throughout this era, remoteness and the logistical adaptations vassals developed in order to overcome it were not merely nuisances. They altered how subjects wrote, what they wrote, how they lived, and how empires legislated. Nonetheless, as Nelson Fernando González Martínez notes, "analyses regarding the mechanisms which enabled the circulation of millions of letters during the colonial period are scarce."[22] Most have focused exclusively on official postmen, not on the more organic, ad-hoc, bottom-up arrangements which moved most imperial letters. Nor have scholars yet attempted a panoramic overview of Indies *gobierno* paperwork's labor and timing.

The problem facing petitioners was not simply distance expressed in the number of leagues separating subjects from the court – the problem was one of time and labor.[23] Networks of letter-carriers had to confront powerful weather forces, the challenges of mustering human and animal work, economic considerations, the hostile interventions of saboteurs within Indies society, and bandits and resistance fighters at its margins. Overcoming these challenges involved the combined labor of Spanish, Indian, and Afro-descended trail-sweepers, Indigenous leaders, foot couriers, horseback postmen, conquistadors, bargemen, sailors, ship captains, dockworkers, merchants, local officials, viceroys, council ministers, and the king – among many others. And each of these individuals' contributions could decisively shape the legislative process, determining not just whether a petition arrived quickly or belatedly to the court, but whether it arrived at all. The legislating process thus always bore the fingerprints of the countless historical actors involved in communications logistics,

[20] McLuhan, *Understanding Media*, 19. [21] Garrett, "En lo remoto," 17–43.
[22] González Martínez, "Correos y comunicación," 40; see also "Communication."
[23] McAlister, *Spain and Portugal*, 206.

a reality which traditional accounts of legislation have obscured by refusing to consider the wider networks integral to the lawmaking process.

This multicausal, multiactor overview also acknowledges the iniquities of the petition-and-response system. True, the vast majority of subjects could expect that their pleas would reach the court. On the other hand, commercially and demographically peripheral areas never achieved the coverage which core Indies routes enjoyed, meaning that an artisan in distant but silver-rich Charcas might enjoy better communications than a bishop in poor and economically isolated Caracas. Where the empire did not possess a monopoly on violence, such as in sovereign Indigenous territory or the open seas, this coverage was also weak or even impossible.

The following pages, then, seek to outline how each petition's success was contingent upon complex human and nonhuman actors and labor demands. It overviews how imperial networks overcame different geographies and ecosystems, developed certain strong but incomprehensive mercantile corridors, certified a limited official postal system, and struggled against sabotage from inside and out. Lastly, it considers the financial costs which may have been involved in sending petitions to the court. These obstacles ultimately tested the Habsburg-era fiction of a vassal–lord dialogue untrammeled by intermediary forces – and yet through the logistical system's titanic collective efforts, communications survived mostly intact – albeit in a badly hindered and extremely slow state.

ACROSS THE WATERS OF THE MERCANTILE ATLANTIC

During the Spanish Empire's troubled infancy in the 1490s and 1500s, this logistical odyssey was initially one of water and wind. During the first three decades of the conquests, most Indies vassals who petitioned the king and council lived either near or directly on the Atlantic. Travel began by setting out across an open and relatively safe Atlantic. There, the powerful winds of the Atlantic Gyre often helped ships speed to court. One record-breaking trip from Santo Domingo took twenty-five days, but most took roughly fifty-five.[24] Havana was about twenty-seven days to the Azores, and another three weeks or so to Spain.[25]

Between the Indies mainland and the south of the Caribbean islands loomed a somewhat more treacherous weather pattern. Where the

[24] AGI, Patronato 260, N.2, R.43, undated.

[25] BNE, Mss.2825 2r-3r and Ordoñez de Zevallos, *Historia*, 418v.

Atlantic Gyre and the South Equatorial Current collided, there arose the Caribbean Current system, which often featured numerous minor gyres, weak winds, and hurricanes.[26] Still, travel in the Caribbean could be measured in days – from Havana to the Yucatan in one, Cartagena to Honduras in as little as seven. In inclement weather, some itineraries took three times as long.[27] Altogether, however, the Caribbean was not terribly far from Iberia.

Nature may have often conspired in Caribbean residents' favor, but due to social iniquities many ordinary and poorer vassals hoping to write the sovereign were disadvantaged. In the late 1490s and early 1500s there was still no royal courier system. Traveling personally back to Spain could also be quite expensive and complex. After all, no petition could cross this ocean without the help of many hands. Ships, undoubtedly the era's greatest and most complex machines, needed specialist workers. Dozens of deck hands toiled to operate their sails, ropes, hundreds of pulleys, artillery, pumps, and other components.[28] Men and even young children on deck variously kept watch, undertook repairs, led prayers, and, if attacked, prepared to fight.[29] At the helm of this elaborate division of labor were pilots, various officials, and captains.[30] Passengers and crew also relied on other forms of labor, especially Old World agricultural work, for sustenance, including dairy products, grains, oils, salt, and goods like firewood, cargo which was harvested and loaded onto boats largely "by the force of human muscles."[31]

The expenses of undertaking and affording travel to Spain therefore threw the imperial communications network primarily into the hands of those who could profit from long-distance trade. Vassals' access to Crown justice often required social connections with merchants and others headed either to the House of Trade in Seville, or to the court.[32] This meant that subjects' ability to communicate with the court went hand-in-hand with a number of exploitative mercantile ventures which made the Atlantic crossing profitable for businessmen – including enslavement of

[26] Centurioni and Niiler, *On the Surface*, 1–4; See also Chaunu and Chaunu, *Seville*, image "Vents et courants," n/p; Schwartz, *Sea*, 13; Gutiérrez Álvarez, *Las comunicaciones*, 20.

[27] For Yucatan-Havana, García Bernal, *Campeche*, 45 and "Afianzamiento." For Cartagena-Havana, AGI, Patronato 258, N.7, G.2, R.1. For Honduras-Havana, AGI, Guatemala 39, R.12, N.66. For slower Honduras travel, Mss.291, 26r. It is possible that the author was referring to the slower fleet ships, however.

[28] Pérez-Mallaína, *Spain's Men*, 63–66.

[29] Pérez-Mallaína, *Spain's Men*, 70–82.

[30] Pérez-Mallaína, *Spain's Men*, 83–90.

[31] Pérez-Mallaína, *Spain's Men*, 68.

[32] See, for example, AGI, Patronato 251, R.6.

Indians, pearl-diving, and other commodities trade. The initial successes of these ventures in the Caribbean increased vassal–ruler dialogue; whereas only twelve ships sailed yearly for Spain in 1506, by the 1530s this number never dropped below thirty-two, thanks to the Indies' improving economy.[33] Inversely, throughout the entire sixteenth century, commercial marginality remained a curse for many subjects – even in coastal areas. The Yucatan's geographically enviable location contrasted with its poverty, as one ship visited roughly every seventeen months.[34] Caracas, a poor coastal town positioned on very favorable trade winds, suffered similar problems.[35]

These itineraries of water and commerce gradually expanded. The agents of the mercantile and military Atlantic increasingly explored lowland riverine systems such as those in Panama and Tierra Firme beginning in the first decade of the 1500s. These fluvial environments demanded a distinctive labor system dependent on small boats and rafts, often operated by both free and enslaved Indigenous and Black deckhands. Initially, these complex arrangements were not available, creating logistical havoc. In Tierra Firme, the first major region of inland conquest, the first Spanish invaders were at the mercy of the very rare travelers leaving for the court. Historian Bethany Aram has studied the private correspondences and Indies–Spain delivery logistics of these conquistadors, and paints a dire picture of imperial communications. Outbound letters to Iberian family and friends from the 1510s and 1520s might take between 4.5 to 19 months, with an average of 12.3 months.[36]

Even after Spanish society became more firmly rooted in the continental New World, riverine communications remained a problem. Traveling from the Andes to Cartagena or the small port of Santa Marta involved hot, slow, rainy, insect-infested journeys down the treacherous Magdalena river, on Indigenous rafts or *bogas*.[37] All of this navigation could take travelers a month during the dry season.[38] Some stretches were much more grueling than others; in the 1580s, salaried Indian raftsmen could row as far as two weeks at a time, worrying reformers.[39]

Panama offered a similar maze of dangerous malarial rivers, but provided conquistadors and merchants with one of their earliest tastes of

[33] Chaunu and Chaunu, *Séville*, 331. [34] García Bernal, "Afianzamiento," 201.
[35] AGI, Santo Domingo 193, R.8, N.16, "Como no biene" 1r, December 24, 1578.
[36] Aram, "Distance," 235.
[37] Gómez, *L'envers*, 147–159, 204. See also AGNC, Sección Colonia, Fondo Visitas SC 62, Subfondo Visitas-Bolívar SC 62, Leg. Cartagena, 10, D.3, Alonso de Arteaga, 1551.
[38] Gómez, *L'envers*, 204; AGI, Santa Fe 18, N.4. [39] HSA, 9/V/2, point 11.

another logistical challenge: inland mountains. To cross from the City of Panama on the Pacific to the Caribbean without encountering rapids, voyagers had to traverse a challenging strip of land which witnesses noted claimed the lives of many free and enslaved black and Indigenous cargo-bearers.[40] In the 1530s, Indigenous guides helped Spanish officials discover new routes, and after substantial clearing of rainforest and dock construction, overland transport by human and animal labor took only eight hours to reach the Chagres.[41] The immense hauls of mineral wealth and other goods (including petitions) which began to arrive in the city from Peru that decade would swell the number of mules to around 600, and the Chagres soon teemed with medium-sized boats which took some two weeks to reach the Atlantic.[42]

HIGHLAND POLITIES, MOUNTAIN COMMUNITIES, AND THE ANDEAN PACIFIC

The imperial logistics system expanded dramatically in scale and complexity when conquistadors and their Indigenous allies expanded into the populous, mineral-rich Indigenous regions of Anáhuac and the Andes. In the 1520s the Habsburgs incorporated millions of Indigenous vassals to their purview, most in Mexico and Peru. Numerous Spanish settlements arose and prospered, and often co-opted Mexica and Inca delivery systems. By the 1530s, the Indies had three major communications routes: the Caribbean to Seville, the Manila–Mexico–Veracruz artery, and the Potosí–Lima–Panama chain, with communications clusters focused in Veracruz, Cartagena, and Seville. This new trinity greatly diminished the Caribbean port of Santo Domingo's grip on maritime traffic.[43]

Indigenous polities' extensive communications networks formed the basis of the Spanish Indies' inland dominions. When Cortés subdued the Mexica and the Habsburgs incorporated Tenochtitlán in the 1520s, the Spanish inherited this polity's vast centralized logistical arrangements.[44] Before the Mexicas' surrender to the Spanish, Tenochca potentates had entrusted the oral delivery of messages to

[40] AGI, Patronato 193, R.18, N.12 and AGI, Patronato 193, R.18, N.24.

[41] AGI, Patronato 193, R.18, N.25 and AGI, Patronato 193, R.18, N.27. For indications of improved transport, Chaunu and Chaunu, *Seville*, VI-1, 166.

[42] See, for instance, AGI, Panama 236, L.9, 415r and Castillero Calvo, "Los transportes," 147.

[43] Chaunu and Chaunu, *Seville* VI-1, "Trafic Español," n/p.

[44] Gargurevich Regal, *La comunicación imposible*, 48.

runners, or *yciuhca titlantli*, and also employed learned couriers, called *paynani*, to relay news throughout their domains.[45] Fray Bernardo de Sahagún observed four types of Nahua trails: the wide and organized *ochpantli* ("swept trails"), the narrower *ohpitzactli*, the shortcuts between major arteries or *ixtlapalohtli*, and, lastly, the rugged, dangerous, secret *ichtaca ohtli*. Merchants (*pochteca*) often used these routes. These Nahua and other Indigenous routes of pre-contact Mesoamerica featured dense intercity networks in the central plateau, various routes to highland Maya towns, and connections to both coasts. Longer preconquest routes had coupled the center to what is today the Sierra Nevada, and as far south as the Darien gap or perhaps even beyond.[46] At the heart of this Mexica complex was Tenochtitlán-Mexico City, an island city within a valley located atop a temperate plateau that rose dramatically out of the tropics. Despite its height, the city was not far from the Atlantic coast.

After the conquest, vassals living in this bustling viceregal capital would have few difficulties contacting the court. Bridges and 1,000-plus Indian canoes linked the lake city to its surrounding valley roads. Letters could then travel to the Atlantic port of Veracruz on the back of one of some 3,000 mules, steered in large part by Afro-descendant drivers.[47] Much of the trail and road maintenance had been undertaken by Indigenous laborers since the 1530s, after the high court and viceroys assigned hundreds of Indians for its improvement.[48]

Central Mexican logistics were not so fraught, but did face one major obstacle. To reach Havana and the open Atlantic from Veracruz, ships had to traverse the Gulf of Mexico, which was distinct from the rest of the Caribbean and Atlantic and possessed its own difficult weather patterns. Sailors had to be wary of Gulf currents as well as hurricanes, which limited travel from the summer months to about November.[49] Historian Ricardo Cerezo Martínez estimates the journey from Veracruz to Havana to have taken an average of 10 days, whereas Huguette Chaunu and Pierre Chaunu have shown ships traveling as fast as 3 days and as slow as a staggering 198 – the latter surely due to captains' struggles to dodge either hurricanes or pirates, or both.[50]

[45] Alcázar, *Historia del correo*, 24–25; Corona Núñez, *Estudios*, 36–37.

[46] Escalante Gonzalbo, "Los caminos," 37.

[47] Slicher van Bath, *Hispanoamérica*, 147.

[48] Del Valle Pavón, "La economía," 41–45.

[49] Gutiérrez Álvarez, *Comunicaciones*, 20; Otte, *Cartas*, N.487, 434.

[50] Cerezo Martínez, *Armadas*, 91.

The empire's second major inland route, that of the Andes, was also shaped profoundly by a major Indigenous polity. The Inca dominion of Tahuantinsuyo left Spanish invaders a vast road network stretching some 40,000 kilometers.[51] During Inca rule the *chasqui* couriers relayed news over short distances between road stations or *tambos*, enabling very quick communication across extensive and rugged terrain. Spanish officials called them *chasqueros* and relied on them throughout the sixteenth century and beyond. However, war and demographic decline did substantial damage to this network. By the 1540s, vassals were using a mixed system of *chasqueros* and informal Spanish couriers.[52] While merchants could take about three weeks to travel from the former Inca court of Cuzco to the new Spanish capital of Lima, a team of *chasqueros* could likely achieve this much faster.[53]

Spanish-led conquistadors, having captured the two great capitals of the Mexica and Inca, needed to master two further geographies: the rugged mountain hinterlands beyond the core Indigenous population clusters, and the Pacific Ocean. Isolated highland towns often struggled to remain open to communications. Guatemala resident Pedro Elsar told his wife María de Alcocer that the route connecting Honduras' port of Puerto Caballos took travelers fifteen days to the Guatemalan capital by land. She could also take another route, the three-month option via Veracruz, then Puebla, then a long mountain trek.[54] Further into Honduras, matters were even worse; according to a 1547 report, the city of Gracias a Dios was virtually cut off by its "fierce, bent … rugged … and fearsome" geography.[55] Like Guatemala, Santa Fe de Bogotá was relatively close to the Caribbean, but travelers nonetheless faced a grueling trek. Its residents would head down in a heavily armed convoy to the Andean mountain towns of Tunja and Velez, then to the Magdalena river valley, and finally to the coast.[56] Popayán lay some three to four treacherous months of travel from Panama via Quito, and a shorter but still grueling trek to Santa Fe.[57] In between Popayán and

[51] Hyslop, *Inka Road*, 223–225. Some of these roads may predate Inca rule; see 270–274; Gargurevich Regal, *Comunicación imposible*, 48; Glavee Testino, *Trajinantes*.

[52] Vaca de Castro, "Ordenanzas," 427–492. For a reference to the informality of the mailing system, see AGI, Patronato 190, R.43, 14v.

[53] Gutiérrez Álvarez, *Las comunicaciones*, 178; Cobb, "Supply."

[54] Bosch García, "Hombres," 33–34; Otte, *Cartas*, N.251, 270.

[55] AGI, Guatemala 44B, N.43.

[56] AGI, Patronato 195, R.17.

[57] AGI, Patronato 27, R.13. The merchant who authored this text did not specify times from Popayán to Santa Fe.

Santa Fe de Bogotá lay the challenging Antioquia region, whose trails were to be maintained by local encomenderos using "all the Indians necessary," via paid labor.[58] Quito's residents faced either a massive journey past Popayán to Santa Fe de Bogotá and Magdalena, a counterproductive southbound expedition to Lima, or a quick but dangerous voyage to the Pacific.[59] By the 1570s, one could travel from Quito to the city of Riobamba by wagon, then down the Andes by foot to the Pacific port of Guayaquil; in the early 1600s this took five to seven days.[60] Tucumán's governor summarized its transit by couriers in a 1586 letter: thirty days from Lima to the regional capital of La Plata (today Sucre), twenty-five from La Plata to Tucumán, and another twenty from Tucumán to the newly founded port of Buenos Aires.[61] It was only by the 1590s that Tucumán and La Plata had relatively robust communications, and no regular interference from sovereign Indigenous groups.[62]

Indigenous leaders and communities always played important roles in the imperial communications system, but in the mid-to-late sixteenth century their contributions become much clearer with Spaniards' increasing engagement with the highlands.[63] Commoners in highland Guatemala complained repeatedly that their trail-sweeping went unpaid.[64] According to one 1570s report on the Quito area, the mountain delivery system was undertaken by Indian men on horseback, assisted by page-boys and by Indian women's cooking and washing, for a pittance. They received a pitiful pay of two blankets, two shirts, and two pesos a year, plus tips.[65] In 1567, the Bishop of Quito even complained that Spaniards were not paying these Indian couriers at all.[66] Spaniards hoping to traverse the harrowing Quito–Guayaquil route sometimes resorted to forcing Indigenous communities to clear trails without pay, obliging officials to intervene and levy taxes on merchants to pay Indian salaries.[67] These compensation issues persisted; for instance, in 1581 the High Court of Quito ordered a local field justice (*corregidor*) to pay an Indian courier whom he had obligated to deliver certain letters to the dock of Guayaquil

[58] AGNC, Colonia–Caciques & Indios 63, D. 26, 1598. [59] Zúñiga, "Camino."

[60] Suárez Fernández, *Historia general*, 328. This is also the estimate provided by historian Uría Maqua, *Alonso*, 130.

[61] AGI, Charcas 26, R.5, N.11, 142r. [62] AGI, Charcas 16, R.27, n. 143, 3r.

[63] Glave Testino, *Trajinantes*. [64] Lutz and Dakin, *Nuestro Pesar*, 33, 73.

[65] Jiménez de la Espada, *Relaciones geográficas*, V.III, 95.

[66] AGI, Patronato 189, R.34, 1567. [67] AGI, Patronato 28, R.13, 5r.

during a storm.[68] Three years later, local *cacique* don Pedro de Henao won a decree which compelled local authorities to pay him the substantial sum of ninety ducats, which he said they owed him for his trail work around Ipiales, between Popayán and Quito.[69] In 1598 a group of Indians from the town of Buituma, led by the Captains Andrés Chalu and Gonzalo Matalamí, counterpetitioned their *corregidor*, complaining that it was not their duty to care for the province's many trails of the province. They received a pitiful wage, and were exposed to enemy Indians. Chalu and Matalamí made clear that a local *encomendero*, Hernando de Hierro, was responsible for finding a suitable solution to these trails' poor state, not them.[70] Indigenous laborers and elites were far from passive in their contributions to the imperial logistics system, both providing and contesting work obligations.

The Spanish-led conquests of the New World's mountainous interior, which mainly occurred between the 1520s and the 1540s, entered a new phase when miners struck silver. The northern and northwestern provinces of New Spain had remained difficult for imperial logistics into the 1540s, but by the 1550s the silver boom towns of Zacatecas and Guadalajara ensured not only robust economies built on slave and wage labor, but regular travel to Mexico City, which was roughly two weeks' journey away.[71] In the 1550s, communications with Lima and the court improved dramatically as Potosí became a global center of silver production. Subjects could now count on massive mule trains and many *chasqueros* traveling up and down between Lima and the Andes, especially Potosí and other major mining towns. Historian Secundino José Gutiérrez Álvarez has found that merchants could move goods from Potosí to Cuzco in roughly thirty-three days, and another twenty-two down the Andes to Lima. However, he states that *chasqueros* could move about twice as fast; they could probably relay the mail from Potosí to Lima in about a month.[72] And along the routes which silver flowed, so did petitions.

Overcoming the Peruvian Pacific proved a mostly uncomplicated affair in comparison with the Indies' logistically daunting and labor-intensive mountainous interiors. A scaled-back version of the Atlantic experience, its boatmen generally faced easier weather and shorter journeys. While there is no sixteenth-century information on the Guayaquil–Panama

[68] AHNE, Presidencia, Fondos Caja 1, Especiales, Sentencias Caja 607, Exp.1, N.78, 1581.

[69] AGI, Quito 211, L.2, 134r, September 5 1584.

[70] AGNC, Colonia–Caciques & Indios 63, D. 26, 1598.

[71] Bakewell, *Silver Mining*, 6–24.

[72] Gutiérrez Álvarez, *Las comunicaciones*, 178

route, it probably took around a week. Travel by boat from Lima's port of Callao to Panama averaged three weeks.[73] By contrast, Chile faced major logistical trials. Its overland route to the Pacific Ocean was not the problem; the capital, Santiago, was only two days on horseback, and ten days by mule, from the port of Valparaíso.[74] The challenge was the region's oceanic wind: the court geographer Velasco stated in his *Demarcación* that ships leaving Valparaíso took six months just to arrive at Lima, perhaps due to inclement seasonal weather patterns.[75]

Subjects and officials gradually began to work around the natural obstacles which they could not change. Through a gradual process of trial and error, local observers in the Caribbean began to predict hurricane season and sailed accordingly.[76] Perhaps thanks to Indigenous allies' explanations, mariners noted the Indies' tropical weather patterns. Travelers soon learned that the Magdalena river was too turbulent for rafts and small ships in the rainy season.[77] They could only leave the eastern Andes town of Zamora for Quito in the dry season.[78] In Panama, parts of the Chagres were unnavigable without rains.[79] Those hoping to cross over from Panama's Pacific to the Caribbean during the dry season had to traverse the province's central mountains to Nombre de Dios – an infamously difficult trek of some four days.[80] Sometimes all seasons conspired against any easy solution. The Pilcomayo River near Asunción was too unpredictable and dangerous for travel – too shallow in the summer, and full of rapids and waterfalls in the winter.[81]

Disease was another inescapable reality. Many travelers perished en route. Panama's Caribbean port towns of Nombre de Dios and Portobelo earned reputations as particularly hazardous. This danger might provide Peruvian letter-writers with an opportunity to excuse using routes prohibited by royal decrees. The High Court of Charcas wrote in 1583 that it had considered sending an urgent letter through the River Plate because "persons of understanding (*ciencia*) and practice" had said it was "more direct, safer, and more

[73] Velasco, "Demarcación," BNE, Mss.2825, 5v, and Schäfer, "Der Verkehr Spaniens," 442.
[74] Encina, *Resumen*, 85. [75] Velasco, "Demarcación," BNE, Mss.2825, 5v.
[76] Schwartz, *Sea*, 13, 35–42. [77] Gómez, *L'envers*, 204; AGI, Santa Fe 18, N.4.
[78] Pimentel Carbo, *Caminos*, 30–31. [79] Uría Maqua, *Alonso*, 78.
[80] Ordoñez de Zevallos, *Clérigo agradecido*, 391r. [81] AGI, Charcas 16, R.6, N.31.

comfortable" than Panama.[82] The labor of imperial logistics included a seamless blend of brain- and musclework, especially when confronting natural perils.

THE CHIEF POSTAL SYSTEM IN THE INDIES

Whenever possible, ordinary vassals and officials alike sought royal intervention to help their letters reach the king and his ministers. By 1513, one local captain noted "thefts and damages" which had been inflicted upon petitions headed to the court, and ordered "the letters of individuals [*particulares*] will be placed in the box of gold" which delivered Crown's tributes.[83] Only a year later, a Chief Postal System for transporting Indies letters began to emerge to combat similar cases of theft and negligence. In 1514, don Lorenzo Galíndez de Carvajal, then a minister in the Council of Castile, noted these problems, asking the king for the privilege of overseeing the entire mailing system.[84] Galíndez received the lifetime and hereditary office of the *correazgo mayor* or Chief Postmastership. He was henceforth to personally appoint and oversee a network of Indies and Spanish mailmen, and ensure the proper delivery of personal letters and royal correspondence alike.

This royal postal system apparently did a poor job of keeping pace with the conquests, and only in exceptional cases would have it been available to petitioners before the 1580s.[85] Spanish merchants' and officials' rapid expansion into Peru and Mexico outpaced the post by decades. When Chief Postman Galíndez's successor Diego de Vargas Carvajal traveled to Peru as a Council of the Indies commissioner during the 1558 *encomienda* crisis, he was surprised to learn that the exasperated viceroy had appointed another *correo mayor*, Marcos Correoso. He was to dispatch horseback couriers every two months between Lima and the major cities of La Plata, La Paz, Chuquito, Cuzco, and Huamanga.[86] In the ensuing 1560s litigation between Correoso and Galíndez' heir, the viceregal appointee observed that he oversaw a very expensive and labor-intensive operation which barely broke even; he would complain many times that "he would give his profession to the Devil."[87] The Galíndez family won in

[82] AGI, Charcas 16, R.22, N.101, 1r–v. [83] AGI, Patronato, 26, R.5, 19r.
[84] Vallejo García-Hevia, "El Correo," 1786.
[85] Sellers, *Distance and Documents*, 81; González Martínez, "Correos y comunicación."
[86] Correoso based his claims on 1557 and 1560 viceregal grants; AGI, Justicia 434, N.2, R.4, 125r–v. See also AGI, Lima 118, "Abra nuebe," Bernaldino de Romani, 1557.
[87] AGI, Justicia 434, N.2, R.4 128r and 135v.

1568, but in 1570 sold the Peruvian branch of the postal service to another buyer, who continued the previous owners' trademark mismanagement.[88]

Until the tenure of Viceroy Martín Enríquez (1580–1583), Peru's petitioners had mainly relied on irregular, slow, and unprofessional messengers. He instituted a new, regular *chasqui* system whose couriers left Lima and Potosí at the beginning of every month, passing through La Plata, La Paz, Cuzco, and Huamanga, before finally arriving to Lima. He financed this system through additional Indigenous labor, this time an *encomienda* near Huanuco.[89] This seems to have functioned to an extent, but exacted a heavy toll on the *chasqueros*. In 1593 the king ratified a decree addressed to the viceroy in response to an anonymous petition stating that some 500–600 Indians were delivering "public and private" letters – that is, royal and personal documents.[90] He was concerned, stated the decree, that this work was too grueling. To make matters worse, certain "Spaniards who have no order in their lives, and mestizos, mulatos, and free blacks" harassed them as they undertook their duties.[91] The resulting 1599 ordinances sought to guarantee certain labor protections to these Indigenous couriers.[92]

The Chief Postmen likely failed to oversee even Mexico's less complex itineraries. In the late 1570s, the Mexican viceroy sought to entrust the mailing system to one of his household dependents, who would oversee four to six regular deliverymen.[93] Not all were happy with this monopoly – in 1582, the Mexico City councilmen complained to the king that they preferred to rely on the many travelers and merchants streaming to the coast.[94] The result, it seems, was that viceroys regularly sold the office of chief postman instead.[95] By the final two decades of the century, these officials offered express couriers on horseback who could now reach Veracruz in four days instead of nine.[96]

Another rather mysterious avenue was an official postal collection service which Indies inhabitants called the *pliego del rey* – roughly, "the parcel of the King."[97] These envelopes accumulated in important centers

[88] AGI, Justicia 434, N.2, R.4.
[89] AGI, Patronato 190, R.43, 14v.
[90] AHNM, Códices L.691, 79r.
[91] AHNM, Códices L.691, 79r.
[92] AHNM, Códices L.691, 79r.
[93] AGI, México 20, N.8; AGI, Indiferente 739, N.179.
[94] AGI, México 1091, L.9, 96v-97r; AGI, México 20, N.8.
[95] González Martínez, "Correos y comunicación," 44–45.
[96] See the Mexico-to-Veracruz *vaya* from AGI, Contratación 4325, McAlister, *Spain and Portugal*, 207.
[97] See, for instance, a 1562 Lima reference in AGI, Justicia 434, N.2, R.4, 132r. Another vassal referred to this itinerary as the *via de la corte* or the route of the court; see Otte, *Cartas*, N.124, 128.

of Spanish governance and periodically went to the fleets for delivery, and often collected petitions to the council, other royal paperwork, contracts for procurators, and private letters. The collection and distribution of the *pliego* is not clear; historian Margarita Gómez Gómez briefly suggests that high court secretaries managed them.[98]

SABOTAGE FROM WITHIN

The collective work of ensuring imperial communications logistics was not always just a matter of mustering the social connections, physical labor, and know-how to conquer oceans, rivers, forests, and mountains. Everyday vigilance, along with policing and justice, were also necessary. Many petitions contained sensitive information implicating officials and elites in serious wrongdoing. Those hoping to intercept incriminating letters might seek to destroy or alter them.

Sometimes, vassals suggested the direct perpetrators were hard laborers. For instance, when rumors of a "case of treason" in which Havana sailors dumped letters overboard reached Santa Fe de Bogotá in the late 1570s, one judge noted that "nobody will dare write with freedom" if this practice continued unpunished.[99] Vassals often hinted at the hand of shadowy figures. Licenciado Juan Bautista de Monzón, Lima's Crown attorney, protested in 1563 that unknown forces in Panama were not handing his and others' petitions to the captains of ships bound for Spain.[100] Another subject complained in 1566 that "this land is so spied upon," for hostile parties were forcibly taking the "travelers' letters and the dispatches they bring," patting persons' bodies down and ripping apart cushions to find secret writings.[101]

It was not these laborers but local officials whom petitioners most often accused of masterminding this sabotage. In 1571, the Franciscan Juan de Bélmez alleged that certain friars were colluding with the president of New Granada to destroy outgoing letters. Bélmez insisted that the president had the "custom" of "taking and tearing the dispatches that he finds do not go in his favor, even though they are headed to the royal hands of

[98] Gómez Gómez, *Sello*, 160. She notes she was not sure about the meaning of this *pliego*, however.

[99] AGI, Santa Fe 16, R.23, N.92. See also AGI, Santa Fe 37, R.5, N.29.

[100] AGI, Lima 92, "Por el mes," January 2, 1563.

[101] AGI, Lima 92, "E rrecibido," January 28, 1566.

the King our Lord."[102] In 1578, the *cacique* don Diego de Torres alleged that the king remained ignorant of a slew of injustices authorities were committing against Indians and royal interests in New Granada, because a local justice official blocked Spain-bound petitions with a counterfeit document of permission.[103] Even viceroys might be suspects. In 1557, a royal treasurer from Lima, Bernaldino de Romani, delivered his petition with the help of a sailor. He stated that, "here it is taken as a fact that the viceroy ordered all the letters [vassals] wrote to be seized."[104]

Crown officials took these transgressions seriously. Both Roman and Iberian legal tradition defined tampering with sealed letters as crimes against justice and good government. Citing a number of these ancient and medieval juridical commentaries, Jerónimo Castillo de Bobadilla's 1597 *Política para corregidores* stated that "those who open the letters of the King" and of "individuals ...[,] in addition to sinning," committed the crimes of falsity and treason against the Crown.[105] By 1509, the king had ratified his first decree banning authorities from preventing vassals from petitioning, in response to complaints in Hispaniola.[106] The law appeared again in 1521 and 1530.[107] In response to Bishop Juan de Zumárraga's complaints about the viceroy's obstructions, the king ratified another decree of July 31, 1529 for the entire Indies. During the violence of Peru in the 1530s, the king signed yet another decree in 1538, specifically castigating Governor Pizarro for having jailed his sworn enemy don Diego de Almagro and having confiscated his petitions; the monarch also demanded Pizarro reopen all sea communications with Peru, which he had apparently blocked.[108] The residents of Buenos Aires sent a procurator to the king in 1546 alleging that certain individuals were not honoring these edicts, and confirmed their obedience to the law in 1593.[109] In 1575, the council once again sent a decree to the Indies' high courts, reminding all subjects not to interfere with "anysoever letters and dispatches that may be sent to us ... by anysoever cities, villas, and places and individual persons [*personas particulares*] of any estate," so that the council ministers "can receive them and be informed."[110]

[102] AGI, Santa Fe 233, N.27, 654r. A cathedral chaplain also mentioned unknown individuals interfering with outgoing petitions in Quito; see AGI, Quito 82, N.5, January 8, 1577.
[103] AGI, Santa Fe 85, "La principal causa," March 1, 1578, 618v.
[104] AGI, Lima 118, October 15, 1557, "Abra nueve meses."
[105] *Política*, 486.
[106] Brendecke, *Empirical Empire*, 261, and AGI, Indiferente 418, L.2, 43r–v.
[107] AGI, Patronato 275, R.12.
[108] AHNE, Corte Suprema, Sección General, Gobierno, Cedularios Caja 1, 592v–593r.
[109] AGNA, Período Colonial 24–6–25, 12v.
[110] AGI, Indiferente 427, L.30, 270r–270v.

Local authorities occasionally also moved against perpetrators. When the council's own Licenciado Sandoval undertook a *visita* of Veracruz in 1550, he issued an ordinance in response to certain complaints which cited a previous 1544 royal decree punishing any shipmasters or other perpetrators with the confiscation of half their goods and ten years' exile from New Spain.[111] Viceroy Luis de Velasco's April 5, 1599 *Capitulaciones* for the correo mayor similarly warned that anyone caught by officials opening letters, no matter how highborn or lowly, faced a 200-peso fine and lifelong exile from Peru.[112]

At least occasionally, officials did prosecute offenders. In 1591, the High Court of Quito sentenced two Indians, Alonso Sicho and his accomplice Lorenzo Indio, for stealing five letters from Alonso Ordaz and "others from this city." The former received a public humiliation, 200 lashes, and banishment for life; the latter seems to have escaped scot-free.[113]

Round-the-clock vigilance was difficult in an empire stretched so thin. Nonetheless, by the early 1550s some officials were monitoring the strategic communications corridors of Mexico and Peru. In 1550, *visitador* and council minister Licenciado don Tello de Sandoval established ordinances which stated that Veracruz's *alcaldes mayores* were to safeguard petitions, and then deliver them to ship captains for their voyage to Spain.[114] In 1551 the council reissued these Veracruz ordinances for Cartagena, where all Peruvian dispatches arrived by way of Panama or Nombre de Dios.[115] These collective attempts to prevent the Indies powerful and ordinary vassals from usurping the petitioning system surely did not succeed in every case. Nonetheless, a combination of effort and the threat of violence against perpetrators together buttressed the fiction of vassal–ruler dialogue.

SOVEREIGN INDIGENOUS RESISTANCE TO IMPERIAL LOGISTICAL ROUTES

Protecting correspondences from internal saboteurs was daunting work, yet this paled in comparison to the challenges posed by the empire's enemies. In a very tangible sense, the efforts of sovereign Indigenous

[111] AGI, México 1089, L.4, 196r–198r. [112] AHNM, Consejos 21343, Exp.5, 17v.

[113] AHNE, Presidencia, Especiales, Sentencias Caja 607, Exp. 2, 1591. The *fallo* or sentence indicates that the high court did indeed carry out this penalty but Lorenzo's fate was unclear.

[114] AGI, Mexico 1089, L.4, 196r–198r. [115] AGI, Santa Fe 987, L.3, 47r.

peoples, Afro-descendant maroon communities, and Old World rivals influenced and deformed the empire's justice system. Sovereign Indigenous peoples were major protagonists in the disruption of invaders' lines of communication. In northern and northwestern New Spain, alliances of Indigenous communities which imperial authors called "Chichimecs" would actively resist Spanish presence in the area until around 1590, forcing miners to travel in armed convoys and thus almost certainly slowing transit.[116] Caracas Governor Pimentel's proposal to establish a land route to Santa Fe de Bogotá or Cartagena collapsed under hostile Indians' threats.[117] Similarly, Mapuche military supremacy in Chile perpetually jeopardized isolated Spanish bastions, compounding the province's major logistical problems.[118]

Perhaps nowhere did independent Indigenous forces isolate Spanish settlers quite like the Chiriguanos did to impoverished, distant, and outnumbered Asunción and Santa Cruz. Residents from these towns could scarcely reach the viceroy in Lima, or even the high court in Charcas, let alone the royal court. Sometime around 1566, a Charcas judge wrote the king that Asunción was desperately isolated, "because there has been no gold nor silver nor other things [to sell], and communication has ceased." When the City's representatives attempted to reach Charcas with fifty heavily armed settlers, a company of Chiriguanos killed three conquistadors, a Mercedarian friar, and the City procurator.[119] In 1588, Charcas High Judge don Juan López de Cepeda described the Eastern Andes and the Santa Cruz lowlands as a "closed box" so isolated and dangerous that only large armed convoys could transport supplies, communications, and settlers.[120]

PIRACY, THE ARMADAS, AND THE INDIES' COMMUNICATION BREAKDOWN

It was the Caribbean and the Atlantic where the empire's enemies most devastated vassal–ruler communication. Ironically, it was the same ease of movement which sped vassals' letters over the oceans which enabled sea bandits to imperil communications. Before the 1530s, these oceans had

[116] For a 1569 petition of the men and women of Zacatecas on this matter, see AGI, Guadalajara 51, L.1, N.139, 436r.

[117] AGI, Santo Domingo 193, R.8, N.16, "Como no biene" 1r, 24 December 1578.

[118] Riquelme, "Comunicando."

[119] AGI, Charcas 16, R.6, N.31. See also AGI, Charcas 16, R.7, N.34.

[120] AGI, Mapas y Planos, Buenos Aires 12.

been "a locked box, with the Spanish Crown holding the key."[121] Only along the Spanish coast was Moroccan and French piracy a major issue. However, this danger quickly spread to the Indies' shores. By the 1540s, mining discoveries meant that one-fifth of Spain's entire revenues would have to sail the Atlantic every year.[122]

Treasure fleets swollen with mineral wealth quickly became an easy target for French vessels, initially off the coasts of the Iberian peninsula.[123] War between France and the Habsburgs broke out in 1551, and extremely violent pirate raids in the Caribbean became commonplace by the 1560s.[124] Spanish vassals lost at least 250 ships to pirates between 1536 and 1585: 162 in the Antilles, 72 on the coasts of the mainland, and 16 off of Central America.[125] Between 1550 and 1650, pirates were to blame for up to 15 percent of total Spanish ships' losses in the busy months of July and September.[126] Many of these losses surely aborted subjects' petitioning efforts. At the sight of pirates, ship captains were to dump all correspondences overboard to avoid the risk of the enemy using any information against the empire.[127]

These pirate attacks could also reach the shore. Around this decade of crisis a new alliance against Spain formed, when in the 1570s *cimarrones*, Afro-descendant communities who escaped Spanish slavery, joined with British pirates. Sir Francis Drake and the *cimarrones* besieged Panama and Nombre de Dios, seizing a major Peruvian silver shipment.[128] One British captain even raided the Pacific. The Spanish only defeated him and recovered his plunder when the British–*cimarrón* alliance frayed.[129]

The damage these naval and coastal conflicts inflicted upon the petition-and-response system would prove enormous. Against the backdrop of increasing piracy, Crown officials moved to create two separate yearly galleon convoys. These would escort treasure ships, merchant vessels, and mail couriers. Fleets had operated periodically since the 1520s, but the council and the House of Trade formalized the armada system in 1561.[130] There were three main convoys: the Isles fleet, the New Spain fleet, and the Tierra Firme fleet.[131] By the second half of the sixteenth

[121] Peterson, *Funnel*, 97. [122] Bakewell, *A History*, 226–227.
[123] Lane, *Pillaging*, 20–24. [124] Lane, *Pillaging*, 29–33.
[125] Cerezo Martínez, *Armadas*, 180.
[126] Chaunu and Chaunu, *L'Amérique*, "Pourcentage des pertes," n/p.
[127] This occurred with Quito correspondences in 1594; see AGI, Quito 8, R.28, N.111.
[128] Gerhard, *Pirates*, 57–100, 132–137, 145–151. [129] Lane, *Pillaging*, 57–60
[130] Lane, *Pillaging*, 13.
[131] García-Baquero González lists a fourth "assorted" South Atlantic and Pacific fleet featuring unorthodox stops such as Buenos Aires, Valparaíso, and Lima. These routes were virtually nonexistent in the 1500s. See *Carrera de Indias*, 181.

century, the vast majority of traffic was divided between the latter two fleets, each of which left annually from Spain.[132]

The Indies Armada consisted of dozens or even hundreds of boats, whose staff was organized into its principal directors (*hombres de mando*), military and middling labor providers (*gente de cabo*), and lower-rank laborers (the rabble or *chusma*) who could provide their work either willingly, as prisoners, or as slaves.[133] In the latter group, many were Spaniards serving time for major crimes. Many others were Muslim prisoners of war from North Africa or the Ottoman Sultanate.[134] Officials' and mariners' efforts to equip the Armadas often took far longer than planned.

Once these convoys disembarked, they generally followed the recurrent, predictable Atlantic Gyre.[135] Both fleets would sail from Spain to the Lesser Antilles, normally making landfall in Dominica or the nearby isles of Guadalupe, La Deseada, and Martinica.[136] The Tierra Firme fleet arrived in the months of April to May.[137] It might stop by the port of Santa Marta, about sixteen days' travel.[138] It usually headed directly from the Antilles for Cartagena, the biggest port of the province of Santa Fe de Bogotá, arriving in about twenty days.[139] This convoy would then proceed on a one-to-three-week voyage to the major Panama port of Nombre de Dios, where goods and letters of the Viceroyalty of Peru awaited.

The Tierra Firme fleet would then return to Cartagena, where its sailors and locals would repair and restock. The longest time it stalled in Cartagena was sixty-two days; others would stay for around two weeks.[140] Sometime in the summer, normally May, June, or July, it would head across the Caribbean and arrive at Havana, a journey of roughly twenty-two days.[141] It normally gathered in the Cuban port in June, July, or August, where it generally lingered some three weeks to resupply and rest.[142] It would arrive at Spain sometime between August and October.

[132] García-Baquero González, *Carrera*, 182–186.

[133] Pazzis Pi Corrales, *La Armada*, 152. [134] Pazzis Pi Corrales, *La Armada*, 152–155.

[135] For a basic overview of these routes, see Schäfer, "Der Verkehr Spaniens," 435–455.

[136] Chaunu and Chaunu, *Seville et l'Amerique*, "Évolution des routes maritimes," n/p

[137] Chaunu and Chaunu, *Seville et l'Atlantique* 6.1, 215.

[138] Chaunu and Chaunu, *Seville et l'Amerique*, "Vitesses Comparees," n/p.

[139] Chaunu and Chaunu, *Seville et l'Amerique*, "Ensemble du movement: Allers," n/p.

[140] Chaunu and Chaunu, *Seville et l'Atlantique* 6.1, 190.

[141] Chaunu and Chaunu, *Seville et L'Amerique*, "Ensemble du movement – rotation des convois," n/p.

[142] This assumes the same restocking time of the New Spain fleet; see Chaunu and Chaunu, *Seville et l'Amerique*, "Rotation des concois, Nouvelle Españe," n/p.

After reaching the Lesser Antilles in July or August, the New Spain fleet would begin its separate route. In the 1560s to mid-1580s it would stop by Santo Domingo, normally in August. By the 1590s, however, the threat of pirates in the area marked the end of the convoy's arrival to the island.[143] Vassals seeking to send a letter to the king could either wait for the fleet's smaller ships to approach or send their own vessels directly to them.

The New Spain fleet would collect goods and correspondence and continue to the Mexican port of Veracruz, aiming to dock by the fall. Ships would normally port in mid-September, where they usually remained until mid-March. It was the captain's duty to collect New Spain's letters during these eight and a half months, and by the 1580s this probably occurred in conjunction with the chief postman's subalterns.[144]

Mexico's convoys would then return to life in the spring. In mid-March the fleet would head to the Gulf of Mexico, often becoming mired for days or weeks in its complex currents. It would dock in Havana in early July, and resupply for some two to three weeks. The empire's Atlantic and Caribbean settlements would relay last-minute requests to Havana in small, swift boats while the fleets waited. One document suggests that the Cuban High Court coordinated and delivered petitions to the fleet captains. On June 30, 1581, a notary certified that the Governor of Cuba, Gabriel de Luján, had entrusted to Gaspar de Torres, Captain of the Fleet of New Spain and master of the mothership Santa María de Begonia, "a bundle of letters, closed and sealed, with an address that says 'to the Catholic Royal Majesty of the king don felipe our lord.'"[145] The fleet would depart in late July to the Azores and then the Spanish coast, averaging some seventy days and generally setting sights on Cadiz in late September.

Armada-related delays in correspondence could be dramatic. The Tierra Firme circuit added two medium-length stops in Cartagena and Havana, generally totaling five weeks' time; the New Spain convoys anchored in Veracruz (averaging 8.5 months) and Havana (averaging three weeks).[146] Petitioners expecting their letter to arrive promptly might find their desired reforms set back half a year, or even more.

[143] Chaunu and Chaunu, *Seville et l'Atlantique*, 6.1, 235.
[144] Chaunu and Chaunu, *Seville at L'Amerique*, "Rotation des convois – Nouvelle Espagne," n/p.
[145] AGI, Patronato 256, N.2, G.1, R.6.
[146] Chaunu and Chaunu, *Seville at L'Amerique*, "Ensemble du mouvement," n/p.

Weather could also force both fleets to stay in Havana the entire winter. For instance, Panama's high court officials lamented that they were "disconsolate" because "the Galleons are wintering in Havana ... many things that required brief processing [*breve expediente*] ... have been sepulchered an entire year."[147]

Overall, the armada system created a far more secure delivery system but almost doubled the amount of time petitions took to reach the court. This arrangement also interrupted the fluidity of outbound information, creating a stop-and-go pattern in which petitions arrived at the court in spurts (March, mid-August, and September–December) followed by long dry spells.[148] A certain "communications weirdness" also took hold. An early petition might arrive at the court the same day a much later one did; in one case, two Chilean petitions sent in April 1571 and February 1573 arrived simultaneously in January 1574. One took 316 days and the other 691 – a difference of 375 days.[149] Other cases were even more irregular. A later petition might reach ministers significantly earlier than a more recent one. On August 15, the council also received a Lima petition from November 17, 1576, and two days later opened one from March 15, 1575: a 405-day discrepancy.[150] Indeed, 5–10 percent of petitions went badly astray before reaching the court.

As dreadful as the 1570s were, the 1590s were even slower. Letters from 1590s Santo Domingo, by then a decrepit port city constantly besieged by pirates, averaged the same time to Madrid as correspondences from the Philippines had in the 1570s, for example. Mexico's communication in the 1590s was slower than Peru's in the 1570s. The culprits were pirates. In 1590, President Antonio González complained pirates had all but severed communications between the cities of Río de la Hacha and Caracas and Santo Domingo. Boats seeking safe passage had to take a six-month route to avoid them.[151] Only Havana and Cartagena (busy and well-armed port centers of imperial communication) and Atlantic-facing Puerto Rico, could relay their letters in less than 200 days.

[147] AGI, Panama 14, R.11, N.61.

[148] The tendency for most petitions leaving Mexico to arrive in August matches neatly with the New Spain fleet's general yearly path. See Chaunu and Chaunu, *l'Amérique*, "Rotation des convois, Nouvelle Espagne," n/p.

[149] AGI, Chile 8, R.5, N.16; Chile 28, N.56; Chile 28, N.49.

[150] AGI, Lima 93, "Por el mes," AGI, Lima 310, "Quando don Fran.co."

[151] AGI, Santa Fe 17, R.7, N.42.

THE NAVÍOS DE AVISO

Indies officials' most urgent correspondences could not wait many months or even years. During the late 1560s and 1570s, Crown paperwork increasingly mentions a solution: the *navíos de aviso*, or courier ships. They were often either the brisk caravels, or, increasingly in the 1580s and 1590s, a smaller class of vessels: barques, *pataches*, or brigantines.[152] Some accompanied the Armadas, and would inform Indies subjects of their impending arrival.[153] This ensured that subjects knew when to prepare their lists of complaints to the monarch. Many of historian Enrique Otto's transcriptions of 650 Indies letters between private vassals reflect that this system enabled vassals not only to anticipate the best time to write and send petitions, but that subjects had a general awareness of these arrivals even in distant areas like Popayán and Buenos Aires.[154]

These small vessels complemented the role that independent merchants had occupied before the fleet system, heading across the Atlantic every so often with letters. Indeed, when they sailed to Iberia their primary function was to provide Crown officials with information about the impending arrival of the treasure-laden fleets.[155] The *navíos* left virtually no paper trail, however, because (at least in theory) they were to carry only correspondence, and would therefore not pay or record import taxes to the House of Trade. From time to time, their pilots would stand trial for illegally transporting goods, a practice many officials abhorred because it incentivized pirates to seek out these undefended vessels.[156]

The *navíos* in the 1570s and 1590s sometimes did preserve the communications speeds of earlier years, or at least prevented some correspondences from traveling as slowly as the fleets. A letter from Quito might reach Spain in a comparatively fast 140 days. In the 1590s, some missives arrived from Cuba to Spain in only 46 days, and from Nombre de Dios in 55. Nonetheless, perhaps due to safety concerns, after 1594 the sovereign decreed that *navíos* were no longer to simply cross the Atlantic but would make an obligatory stop in Havana before heading to Spain.[157]

[152] Chaunu and Chaunu, *l'Amérique*, "Types des navires," n/p.
[153] AGI, Panama 13, R.8, N.11 and Panama 14, R.4, N.24.
[154] Otte, *Cartas*, N.403, 355. For Lima, N.429, 377–378, N.628 561.
[155] See, for example, AGI, Indiferente 738, N.122; N.165; N.177; N.238; Indiferente 739, N.14; N.167; N.181; N.217; N.218; AGI, Indiferente 741, N.248; AGI, Indiferente 742, N.79; N.130.
[156] AGI, Indiferente 1956, N.2, 18v-19r, AGI, México 1092, L.14, 212r-213r, and AGI, Justicia 931, N.1.
[157] AGI, México 1064, L.3, 23r–v.

THE DELIVERY SYSTEM IN EUROPE

Despite staggering delays and sabotage from within and without, most petitions arrived at Spain thanks to various types of hard labor, as well as vigilance and coordination. As fleets and smaller mail ships approached the southern Spanish coasts, petitions faced another challenge: to reach the royal court. A unique 1580 instruction shows how special official agents on *navíos* might ensure documents' arrival in Spain. Don Francisco de Eraso was to leave Havana on the *navío* San Miguel on August 26, 1579, and speed to the House of Trade in Seville. His sailors were to scan the horizon for pirates at every minute of the day, being prepared to flee, or if necessary, to dump the correspondences into the ocean. They would travel with the House's couriers to Seville, give certain documents to them, and proceed immediately with the rest to Madrid and the council.[158] While this case clearly was exceptional, it outlines the trajectory which the Indies' most urgent petitions might take.

Few could afford such agents, and so their letters traveled under the custody of ship captains. Officials might have disembarked documents either in Cadiz, the first Iberian port, or at the estuary docks of Sanlucar; some large ships simply could not navigate the Guadalquivir river's treacherously shallow waters. Captains seem to have delivered a significant segment of Indies letters to the House of Trade in Seville. In 1589, for example, two Tierra Firme fleet captains handed House officials about fifty bundles of documents dealing with *gobierno*, *gracia*, and *justicia* issues. These included bundles or *pliegos* and *embueltos*, and larger parcels or *bultos*, which featured correspondence from Cartagena, Popayán, Guayaquil, and Lima.[159]

By the 1510s, documents located on Spanish soil fell under the jurisdiction of the Spanish branch of the Chief Postmen. This postal system was not without its own labor problems and irregular service, and like other parts of the logistics network this required occasional official efforts to punish wrongdoing. In a 1545, the chief postman sued a lieutenant for negligence and corruption while relaying letters from Seville to the court. The accused had entrusted deliveries to friends to cut costs, embezzled funds from his subalterns, employed peons instead of honorable couriers, opened letters, and abused rented horses, among other crimes and misdemeanors. The lieutenant was fined and barred forever from his position.[160] In 1580, royal

[158] AGI, Indiferente 1391, "Instrucción," August 27, 1589.
[159] "Relación," no pages, AGI, Contratación 4325.
[160] AGI, Justicia 942, 22v–24r, 133r–148v, 183r.

investigators again found that the Chief Postmen had committed numerous abuses. They lacked regular pricing charts, failed to deliver on time, overcharged customers (sometimes double), opened parcels (*mazos grandes* and *empanadas*), and kept inadequate horses. The king ratified a decree fining the owner and his lieutenants, and suspended them for a year.[161]

The European theater of the logistics system was more regular, less vulnerable, and less inequitable than its Indies counterpart. However, the correlation between wealth and communication persisted. As the famous chronicler Gonzalo Fernández de Oviedo complained in 1548, "these Chief Postmen always piggyback with bankers."[162] He mocked the Chief Postmen's' personal aversion to peril, noting that the poor working under them "broke their necks."[163]

Official postmen played essential roles in Europe, especially because until the 1560s the court had no permanent residence. Queen Isabel rarely stayed in one city for more than a few weeks, visiting even remote communities.[164] When the Habsburg Holy Roman Emperor Charles V took the throne, he was "probably the most peripatetic ruler of Europe (if not, indeed, the world)."[165] Spain's postmen could not keep pace. Philip the Handsome had already begun linking Habsburg lands to Spain by 1506, with the help of the Tassis family, who oversaw 106 mailmen. By 1518, his son had consolidated the postal service under this family's management. They would oversee Spain's connections to Italy, France, the Netherlands, and Germany.[166] During the reign of Charles V, the core centers of operation were Brussels and Innsbruck.[167] Brussels was almost three weeks from Granada, about two weeks from Toledo, and a week from Burgos, and could connect Spain to Austria in a week.[168] Charles V's constant movement beyond Brussels and Innsbruck could deal substantial setbacks to the petition-and-response system. Fast letters could leave Barcelona for Genoa in twenty days, while those from Valencia took thirty. From Genoa, letters could reach Milan in six days, Rome in ten, and Venice in roughly two.[169]

By contrast, when King Philip II rose to power, he ended his father's constant nomadism and settled the capital in Madrid in 1561. As prince he

[161] AGI, Indiferente 524, L.1, 227r–230v. [162] Blake, *Libro de la cámara*, 114.
[163] Ibid. 115. [164] Kamen, *Empire*, 8; Vassberg, *Village*, 171.
[165] Vassberg, *Village*, 171; de Cadenas, *Caminos*, 13.
[166] Borreguero Beltrán, "Los problemas," 405.
[167] Borreguero Beltrán, "Los problemas," 409.
[168] Borreguero Beltrán, "Los problemas," 407
[169] Braudel, *The Mediterranean*, 375 and 364.

undertook only one major voyage to his Italian, German, Burgundian, and Dutch possessions between 1549 and 1551, along with a handful of later travels to England, the Netherlands, and Lisbon.[170] Already by 1551 Philip had taken up a prolonged residence in the medium-sized town of Madrid.[171]In 1561, he set about expanding the city and its palace.[172] Philip would also build a second, private base of operations: the Monastery of San Lorenzo, in the village of El Escorial, a half-day's journey from Madrid. This would be his enormous cloister-palace, begun in 1562 and finalized in 1584. However, he would also travel frequently inside Spain, spending prolonged amounts of time in Aragon, Andalusia, and Portugal.[173]

Now that Madrid was the permanent seat of the Council of the Indies, the European segment of the logistical system became substantially simpler. By the 1570s, most mail headed for the council traveled along the Seville–Córdoba–Ciudad Real–Toledo–Madrid corridor, though some deliverymen may have opted to travel through Extremadura by way of Seville–Cáceres–Toledo–Madrid. Voyagers often complained that these routes were dangerous and offered bare-bones accommodation. In some ways, the critical routes of Mexico–Veracruz and Cuzco–Lima may have been safer and had more amenities.[174] Royal express couriers galloping at full speed could connect coastal Cadiz to Sanlucar in a minimum of ten hours, Sanlucar to Seville in four and a half hours, and then reach Madrid in four days. Slow couriers took two weeks. Ordinary vassals' paperwork would have traveled far slower, taking about two weeks to a month to reach the court.[175]

THE FINANCIAL COSTS OF DELIVERY FOR OFFICIALS AND VASSALS

Details about the costs of mailing logistics are very scarce. Historian Werner Stangl located thirty-three references to the delivery costs of private letters from the Indies to Spain in the sixteenth century, revealing that these correspondences might run between one to eight reales, with an average of around three reales. This suggests that correspondence could be quite pricy: a humbler

[170] Parker, *Imprudent King*, 15–18, 36, 39–40, 43.
[171] Parker, *Imprudent King*, 19, 39–43, 49. [172] Kamen, *Philip*, 178–180.
[173] Parker, *Imprudent King*, 100–105.
[174] Madrazo and Fontana, *El sistema*, "Red de caminos," n/p. [175] Casey, *España*, 41.

worker might earn some 3–4 reales a day.[176] However, it is highly likely that the ordinary royal delivery option was free, and travelers to Madrid likely often delivered letters without charging fees for this service.

The costs of compensating postal workers appear most clearly. Express Indigenous *chasquero* runners in Peru seem to have charged two reales per delivery by the 1580s, a price which the viceroy formalized in 1599.[177] Vastly more expensive were the "*servicios extraordinarios*" or emergency couriers, which cost three reales per Spanish league, and were likely by horse.[178] These *servicios* were surely only affordable for high-ranking royal officials, who paid for them with Indigenous tribute revenues from Huánuco. By the 1560s, Spain's official postal couriers charged the council different rates over time, from five ducats per hour to ten per day.[179] That suggests that the cost of a horseback courier to travel from Seville to Madrid alone could reach astronomical sums – assuming 10 hours' riding a day, this might average between 90 to 460 ducats one way.

The *navíos* were even more complex and capital-intensive. In response to French piracy, in the 1520s a group of Seville merchants petitioned for royal officials to levy an insurance fee on all traders' goods leaving for and arriving from the Indies.[180] This system, the *avería*, would permit merchants to finance armed, defensive escort vessels.[181] It fluctuated from 1 percent to as much as eight percent, depending on the year. In the 1520–1540s it tended to range between 1 percent and 6 percent, between the 1540s and 1570s from about 2 percent to 5 percent, and then climbed progressively as piracy worsened. By the 1590s, it ranged between 3 percent and 6 percent. Beginning in the 1560s with the advent of a proper fleet system, the *avería* would also cover some or all of the costs of the *navíos de aviso*.[182] Exactly how expensive these ships were is unclear; one *navío*'s emergency round-trip voyage cost the royal treasury 612,533 *maravedís*, the amount a peasant might earn in 4,500 to 9,000 days of work.[183] However, that the letters of ordinary subjects traveled in these courier ships suggests that vassals themselves did not bear these costs. Surviving private correspondence from Indies

[176] Stangl, *Zwischen Authentizität*, 198–199; Larson, *Cochabamba*, 58.

[177] AGI, Patronato 190, R.43, 14v. For a 1586 reference to the two-real cost, see Otte, *Cartas*, N.484, 432.

[178] AHNM, Códices L.691, 79v.

[179] AGI, Indiferente 1400.

[180] The council did not yet exist; it would emerge clearly as a separate entity in 1524. See Céspedes del Castillo, *Avería*, 27/543 and AGI, Indiferente 420, L.9, 29v-31v.

[181] Céspedes del Castillo, *Avería*, 3–4 or 519–520.

[182] AGI, Santa Fe 1, N.90 and Indiferente 744, N.115C.

[183] AGI, Indiferente 433, L.2, 127v; Motomura, "New Data," 348.

individuals of diverse social backgrounds often reported having used these *navíos* to communicate with family on the peninsula, further suggesting that they were either affordable or free for ordinary subjects.[184]

The petitioning system thus seems to have been largely affordable, perhaps even free for most. High-ranking officials could always expect their letters to travel the fastest, although sometimes these avenues might include nonelite correspondence as well. Nonetheless, the wealthy had one clear advantage over the less fortunate: they could also send agents to court to press their arguments in person. This could be a terribly expensive affair. One 1577 document suggested that an agent's one-way travel from the Indies (it did not specify from where) cost 600 ducats.[185] Many of these costs owed to life on ship, as well as room and board in Seville and the court.[186]

Some petitioners did brave the ocean without recourse to legal agents. Friars, priests, merchants, encomenderos, outgoing officials, and others traveled quite often, sometimes heading back to Spain for good. Some relied on friend and allies already en route to Madrid, as did the *mestizos* of Peru with court-bound Pedro Rengifo. Hundreds of Indigenous vassals also made the voyage themselves, often by joining the retinues of friars and other travelers. In Peru, Viceroy Toledo was considerably irritated by Indigenous travel, partly because of the possibility of human trafficking, but mostly because he and subsequent officials found it difficult to prevent them from heading to court.[187] Many Indigenous vassals' complaints to the council that they were mired in poverty in Madrid may have been exaggerations, but some were so poor that doormen had to arrange for them to receive clothing, food, haircuts, and shoes.[188] Certainly, travel to Madrid was not for the down on their luck.

CONCLUSIONS

The collective labor of many actants made transporting hundreds of thousands of texts affixed with the legal fiction of vassals' volitions possible, sustaining the legal fiction of vassal–lord dialogue. This required

[184] See Otte, *Cartas*, numbers 19, 23, 30, 32, 43, 47–49, 52, 54, 57, 66, 78, 80, 93, 94–98, 101, 106, 115, 124, 125, 142.a, 144, 146, 158, 172, 174, 178, 179, 183, 186, 191, 192–193, 196, 213, 215–216, 221, 226–227, 249, 254, 309, 312, 315, 323, 325, 327, 336–339, 343, 353, 431, 463, 483, 486, 498, 500, 507, 524, 527, 555–556, 598, 600, 602, 639, 640.

[185] AGI, Indiferente 1391, "Instrucción," 27 August 1589.

[186] Pérez-Mallaína, *Spain's Men*, 67–68.

[187] Puente Luna, *Andean Cosmopolitans*, 59–64, 75, 97, 129, 147–148, 241n42, 253n32.

[188] Puente Luna, *Andean Cosmopolitans*, 150 and "A costa."

a great logistical network comprised of multicausal, multiactant components. This was not merely a system upheld by Spanish couriers, or even by European merchants and sailors. Indigenous rangers, canoeists, oarsmen, couriers, trail-sweepers, and others joined Afro-descendant muleteers, raftsmen, and others in providing essential – and often coerced – labor.

The legal fiction of vassal–ruler dialogue was truly at its most strained here. One of the world's greatest logistical undertakings, spanning from northern Mexico to Patagonia and beyond, very often failed. Perhaps as many as 10 percent of letters went badly astray. Other iniquities abounded. Economically isolated regions, even when comparatively close to Iberia, were often bereft of justice due to a shortage of merchant go-betweens. Paranoid officials, sovereign Indigenous and Afro-descendant peoples, and pirates also played their part by nearly crippling logistics in crucial imperial areas. By the 1570s and especially the 1590s, piracy had slowed communication to a crawl, with letters traveling in the lumbering armada convoys at drastically slower speeds than in previous decades. Officials developed extremely expensive courier alternatives for urgent news, but most vassals were restricted to using the very slow ordinary mail.

Contemporaries imagined a vassal–lord dialogue of human volitions, but the logistical system was not cocreated by humans alone. Currents of wind and water, seasonal weather patterns, geography, disease, and substantial animal labor played major roles in determining whether vassals and lords could communicate or not:. Lifeless technologies, from cloth paper to cotton sails, also played a major part. Imperial logistics could only be overcome through many actants, whose contributions exemplified, perhaps more than any other part of the decree-production assembly line, the hard labor of lawmaking and the law's embeddedness in a complex causal ecology. It was thanks to this extraordinary collective labor that the Spanish rulers largely succeeded in maintaining the legal fiction that they ruled over a monarchy of volitions in motion, an empire of dialogue.

3

Distant Kings, Powerful Women, Prudent Ministers

The Gendered Creation of the Council of the Indies

Pedro Rengifo was among a select group of Indies vassals who managed to personally speak with King Philip II. Their meeting must have taken place sometime between 1585 and 1587. The Council of the Indies' secretaries would have arranged for this encounter via the king's secretary, settling on a strict date, down to the minute – probably between 9am to 10am, or 5pm to 6pm.[1] *In preparation, Pedro would have probably invested in a set of Madrid's finest clothes, and nervously practiced his brief speech.*[2]

The king had likely been at the royal palace, an austere building perched upon the western bank of the city. Pedro would have stepped through its great entrance, with doormen directing him to the king's office. There he would wait outside, joined by a cohort of officials, friars, and other petitioners. Or perhaps he would stand in line at the Monastery of the Escorial, the king's monastery retreat about a day on horseback away. Time would have spilled over from an hour to the next, as the monarch's constant business delayed the meeting. At last, the royal secretary would summon Pedro into the room, perhaps the bedchamber itself.[3]

There, the part-Indigenous agent would have been greeted by a white-haired figure clad in simple black attire, of somewhat

[1] Parker, *Imprudent King*, 77, and Kamen, *Philip*, 223.

[2] One Roman veteran named Alexandro Orsino mentioned needing to invest in proper clothing; see AGI, Indiferente 1392, "Alexandro Orsino," February 19, 1581, no folios.

[3] For a map of the Escorial, see the 1587 image by Pedro Perret, in BNE, Invent.28851, which functions in conjunction with Herrera's *Sumario*.

slight stature, with a courteous but exhausted expression, crouched over a desk full of papers. Upon the secretary's signal, Pedro would have delivered his speech, handing in a written copy for official paperwork. The entire time the king would have remained eerily silent. It was likely only after Pedro's monologue was over that the monarch finally spoke, promising cryptically with a soft voice and faint smile that he would consider the case.[4] *Pedro then returned to petitioning the council through early 1588, repeatedly submitting reminders lest his case be forgotten.*[5]

In 1580, one scholar living in Madrid would marvel that the king's proximity and visibility to vassals was a "very praiseworthy custom, which has been gradually forgotten."[6] *Even Pedro, who had been lucky enough to receive an audience, would have experienced the royal appointment and his work with the council as distant, sterile encounters. This distancing of lords from vassals was a half-century in the making, a consequence of a growing empire.*

Vassals often wondered: was there no way to appeal to ministers in a more personal way, perhaps over card games, drinks, gifts? Maybe ministers' wives or daughters might put in a word for him, in appreciation of a generous gesture – would a present, perhaps a pearl necklace or a piece of Indigenous gold, suffice? Anything seemed a small price to pay for a vassal hoping to leave the expensive, overcrowded court. Others had tried the route of gift-giving, and some had even become entangled in ministers' lives – to their benefit. Surely Pedro had heard the rumors. But he likely had also learned that King Philip was investigating several of the council's unscrupulous ministers for precisely this approach, with royal auditors attempting to keep vassals – especially women – distant from ministers. Even in Madrid, the vassal–lord dialogue thus remained almost entirely on paper, under the vigilance of a suspicious and enigmatic monarch. Embittered vassals would leave no stone unturned to accuse ministers who disappointed them before the monarch's inner circle. Pedro would have to follow the melancholy route of paper to see his case to fruition.

[4] See the account of Venetian ambassador Federico Badoaro in Prosper, *Relations*, 41–42 and Kamen, *Philip*, 223.

[5] AGI, Lima 126, 114r. [6] Zurita, *Historia*, Ch.XII, 15v.

Countless volition-bearing papers traveled from around the world, their portable, stackable bodies accumulating in one space.[7] This was the Royal and Supreme Council of the Indies, the premier institution of counsel for the Spanish New World. This chapter explores both the rise of this institution and the Habsburg court administration's gradual embrace of social distance from its own vassals. Most historians of the council have tended to enumerate key dates in its existence or provide collective biographies of ministers' strategies of ascent. Instead, I explore how the monarchy's style of rule emerged and evolved, transforming the council, its practices, and its ethos along with it.

The distancing of kings from ministers was an inevitable by-product of imperial expansion, a phenomenon which greatly increased officials' influence over the actual *gobierno*, *gracia*, and *justicia* decision-making processes. The meteoric rise of ministers' power stimulated considerable anxiety among royal advisers and vassals. At the heart of these concerns was a similar question to the dilemma posed by Indies intermediaries and couriers. Ministers were to be but neutral instruments in the transmission of volition from subjects to rulers. In theory, their roles consisted only in assisting monarchs by supplying them with advice – especially prudence (*prudencia*) and awareness (*noticia*). King Philip II wrote his son on his deathbed that "prudence is the mistress of life, the meter of virtue, and the wall of the princely realm."[8] Sixteenth-century jurists, and many vassals, agreed that prudence and counsel formed a central part of improving the ruler's decision-making, even if the monarch's law-creating *voluntad* was ultimately what gave decrees their binding power.[9] The king warned his son that greedy ministers risked transforming imperial administration into a plaything of "the powerful few."[10] The contamination of the chain of *voluntad* by the mighty would bring "grave damages to the people . . . and not lesser ones to the land."[11] King Philip also admonished his ministers that they were to "disrobe themselves in all matters of passion [*pasión*], bias [*afición*], and personal ends, placing in their view only the pure service of God and the good of my affairs and those of these realms."[12] Ministers' dispassionate prudence was a tool to free the people

[7] A version of this chapter appeared in the *Renaissance Quarterly as* Masters, "Influential Women."

[8] BNE, Mss.10861, 161r.

[9] Suárez, *Tretado*, Ch.3, T.10, 61–65, Ch.4, T.5 75, Ch.8, T.1, 146, Ch.12, T.2, 216, Ch.5, T.12, 102.

[10] BNE, Mss.10861, 161r, see also 161v–164r.

[11] BNE, Mss.10861, 168v.

[12] IVDJ, E.29, C.42, 4, 10r.

from "rapacious officials" and to "protect, reward, and defend the powerless, and the innocent."[13]

Virtually all *gobierno* petitions would pass before royal ministers, but would these flesh-and-blood individuals allow their personal desires to win over the good of the monarchy, the empire, and the least powerful? Would their own private volitions quash those of vassals? Bottom-up efforts against over-powerful enemies of the republic repeatedly reminded Emperor Charles V and King Philip II of the importance of keeping ministers' intents dispassionate and maintaining clear, written expectations of their ethos. The expansion of the empire, monarchs' increasing reliance on paper over oral ceremonial, and the growing power of ministers in decision-making had consequences for the administration which few could have suspected. By the early 1520s, Indies rule was only partially conducted by paper. Moreover, courtier-ministers often emulated the early Habsburgs' patrimonialist style of administration-through-family.[14] This meant that the powerful few did indeed influence Indies decision-making in its early decades, often unbeknownst to rulers.

By the early 1500s, Castile and Aragon became a central component of the Habsburgs' sprawling dominions. This Austrian dynasty was in dire need of novel approaches to rulership: King Charles' often patrimonialist style provoked a civil war in 1520s Castile, after which communities demanded he replace his trusted courtiers with a robust system of councils. The Habsburgs' embrace of these institutions also transformed the Indies into Europe's first overseas collegiate bureaucracy and inaugurated an era in which officialdom was increasingly central to imperial administration.[15] Indies ministers' practices and ethos gradually became more complex, more well-defined, and less patrimonial, a process epitomized by Charles' foundation of the council in 1524, its 1542 New Laws guidelines, and its 1571 ordinances, which established most of its *gobierno* guidelines.

And yet, council ministers' gradual (and never entirely complete) movement toward an ethos of social detachment from vassals, and hostility toward passion (*pasión*), favoritism through social proximity

[13] BNE, Mss.10861, 161r.

[14] Bendix, summarizing Weber, defines patrimonialism as "government . . . [which] . . . treats all political administration as [the ruler's] personal affair," in *Max Weber*, 345. Bureaucracy, in turn, among other things constrains officials within "impersonal criteria" with "business and private affairs . . . strictly separated," *Mex Weber*, 418–419.
See also Magali, *Spanish Bureaucratic-Patrominialism*.

[15] Anderson, *Lineages*, 60. Elliot, *Imperial*, 70. Brendecke and Martín Romera, "Habitus," 23–60.

(*familiaridad*), and partiality (*afición*), was not merely the result of a mechanistic process of state formation. Nor were the Crown's all-male officials the only actors involved in stimulating this restraint of affects or *Affektbeherrschung*.[16] The reforms of 1542 and 1571, as well as ongoing royal audits of the council into the early 1590s, frequently involved gendered concerns about the illicit influence of women over decision-making, and ministers' corresponding need to demonstrate masculine impartiality against earthly charms. Royal attempts to disentangle ministers from developing illicit ties with female subjects and to ensure the council's "pure service" to the Habsburg family had transformational effects on the petition-and-response system. These efforts culminated not only in the 1542 and 1571 ordinances, but in a court culture of increasing enmity toward influential women, a gendered ethos of ministerial masculinity, and the legal fiction of the council's capacity to protect the empire's weakest vassals equally against the temptations of beauty, wealth, and the power of the mighty few.

This chapter thus points to certain concrete reasons why early modern European officialdom and governance in general took on an increasingly gendered and misogynistic ethos. As polities became larger, patrimonial dynasties ceded much of their de facto power to all-male cadres of officials to impartially administer rulers' dominions. As kings became more distant, ministers' roles became increasingly important. To preserve the voluntarist fiction of vassal–lord communication, ministers had to divest themselves of their own patrimonialist inclinations, inventing themselves as masculine enough to resist powerful men and tempting women in the interest of the common good. The council guidelines and ministers' ethos were not simply royal impositions upon officialdom. Women played a leading role, sometimes intentionally and often inadvertently, in prompting the council's move away from pure patrimonialism, which not only transformed Europe's premier conciliar system but also extended this model across the oceans.[17]

SPANISH MONARCHS: FROM PUBLIC LAWGIVERS TO RECLUSIVE BUREAUCRATS

In the early sixteenth century, Spain's culture of rulership was undergoing a crisis of its own success. The Trastámara dynasty had once upheld both the fiction of vassal–lord dialogue and

[16] Duindam, *Myths*, 18.

[17] Kelly-Gadol, "Did Women," 45; Armon, *Masculine Virtue*, 35; Lehfeldt, "Ideal Men"; Rohr and Benz, "Introduction," xx.

monarchs' very real in-person appearances throughout Iberia. Yet by the 1520s the Habsburgs had overseen a dizzying imperial expansion and were transitioning away from the in-person vassal–lord ceremonies which had helped unify the peninsula. The result was that the Habsburg rulers relied more and more on paper ceremonials, a shift of material and medium. This extended monarchs' dominions, but paradoxically diluted their own power, as ministers increasingly became the most powerful agents of decision-making.

The Catholic Kings, facing Iberia's strong localist traditions and seeking to unite Castile and Aragon, had long been "exceedingly itinerant."[18] Queen Isabella in particular was a familiar face throughout Castile. She "visited every corner of the kingdom, covering in some years well over two thousand kilometers of terrain. Few residents of Castile did not see her directly at some time in their lives."[19] She did not engage terribly often with Indies affairs, however, considering the limited scope of conquests at the time. After her 1504 death, Las Casas observed, bishops and friars alike might speak directly with her survivor Ferdinand II of Aragón – some by entering his palace quarters and banging on the door before delivering petitions.[20] The Aragonese ruler acted as regent in the name of his daughter Juana, the rightful claimant of Castilian and New World rule, who many contemporaries regarded as mentally unfit (a controversial diagnosis then as now).[21]

Ferdinand's 1516 death passed the Castilian scepter to Juana's son Prince Charles of Ghent. In contrast with the supremely Iberian Catholic Kings, the new King Charles was a Habsburg deeply entangled with affairs in the rest of Europe. In some ways, Charles' constant movement and inattention to Indies affairs inaugurated a more paper-based regime. Only a select few Indies vassals could afford to follow him throughout Europe, and ministers could not always keep apace, meaning vassal–king communication was thus increasingly limited to letter-writing.[22]

Even those vassals who could personally approach Charles for redress found audience rituals elaborate, aloof, and far too infrequent.[23] Las Casas, who followed the monarch to Aragón in 1519, described one such hearing. Charles sat upon an elevated throne against the back wall

[18] Vassberg, *Village*, 171. [19] Kamen, *Empire*, 8.
[20] BNE, Mss.2814, B.3, Ch.5, 9v–13r; AGS, Patronato, L.69, Doc.34.
[21] Jansen, *Monstrous Regiment*, 75–79.
[22] Espinosa, *Empire*, 265, and Pieper, "Cartas," 434.
[23] BNE, Mss.2814, B.3, Ch.98, 306v.

in the middle of the chamber. Counselors sat at specific places on benches before him. The meeting began in total silence. The king's chancellor instructed Las Casas, "His Majesty commands you speak if you have anything to say about the Indies."[24] The first respondent to rise and speak was the Bishop of Tierra Firme, who denounced abuses against Indians at length. Next it was Las Casas' turn. Imperial Chancellor Mercurino di Gattinara said to him, "Monsieur Bartolomé, His Majesty commands you speak."[25] The reformer removed his hat and launched into a long monologue. Next came a Franciscan friar, who presented his case in support of these pro-Indian testimonies. Las Casas requested to speak again, but Gattinara instructed him to submit a written statement instead.[26]

A 1548 report by a Frenchman named Baylo de Amont described a similar audience, but in greater detail.[27] On weekdays, the emperor ate his breakfast, and then, upon a chair draped in silk, perched upon a raised platform decorated with fine tapestries, held a public hearing. Before him at all times was the chancellor. Around him were other courtiers, seated by rank of blood and seniority. These courtiers would take their seats, and petitioners would approach the hall. The emperor then engaged in "hearing and dispatching all the petitions ... principally of the poor and low people" (this considerably irritated the blue-blooded de Amont).[28] These oral entreaties had a written component; after speaking, subjects would hand their petitions to certain "masters of requests."[29] Not far away was a secretary to register resulting decrees. Another immediately sewed the letters into a bound volume for consultation and archiving.

Once the crowd and the petitioners dispersed, the royal deliberation would begin. Servants erected a tapestry wall around the emperor and his courtiers, which his fifteen personal guards shielded. Petitions entered through one of the two portals, presumably in the hands of an official (likely the secretary). Then, the emperor "decrees according to his taste, and according to the case ... dispatches all of them before leaving that place, and during this time all are quiet and guard their order."[30]

Even more distant was the administrative style of Prince Philip, Charles V's son and a young prodigy of imperial governance. During the early 1540s, the ever-absent emperor increasingly appointed the prince as

[24] BNE, Mss.2814, B.3, Ch.147–150, 479r–492v.
[25] BNE, Mss.2814, B.3, Ch.147–150, 479r–492v.
[26] BNE, Mss.2814, B.3, Ch.147–150, 479r–492v. [27] BNE, Mss.9089, 144r–v.
[28] BNE, Mss.9089, 144r. [29] BNE, Mss.9089, 144r. [30] BNE, Mss.9089, 144r–145r.

regent of the Indies. In 1543, Charles departed Spain for the last time and delegated Philip the authority to govern in his absence and respond to council ministers' written questions.[31] The rise of the paperwork empire also seems to have spelled the further decline of vassals' and even officials' frequent face-to-face communications with their ruler. Very rarely did Philip speak directly with ministers via a *consulta a boca* or oral consultation.[32]

Nonetheless, subjects might sometimes personally approach Philip with petitions. In 1543 Charles commanded him to "continuously hear public mass, and on the Sundays and festivities you deem fitting to go to the churches and monasteries that you please, and eat publicly and assign certain hours every day to listen to those who come to speak, and receive petitions and accounts (*memoriales*)."[33] To these he was to give "general answers" that were pleasing to his vassals and forward their written requests to his secretary Juan de Sámano for processing.[34]

These audiences generally took place between 9 am to 10 am and 5 pm to 6 pm. During these meetings, the presidents of each council might approach him and discuss highly sensitive matters face to face. Philip conducted these meetings out of a sense of obligation and to satisfy his elite subjects and foreign dignitaries, but he repeatedly stated that he wished he could simply conduct all of his affairs through writing.[35] He once said to the poet Alonso de Ercilla "speak to me on paper."[36]

Two Italian observers provide further details regarding these audiences with Philip. In 1557, the Venetian ambassador Giovanni Micheli described the king as a man of "benevolence and amiability" always eager to accept petitions directly, either during his regularly scheduled public hours or even during his moments of family time. Anyone might "freely" submit his or her "petitions and memorials."[37] That same year, Venetian ambassador Federico Badoaro elaborated further. He stated that for Philip's first hour awake, and for an hour before dinner, he listened to "petitions [*suppliche*]" which "he accepts from all, being as he is most intent on gathering the things said unto him." In spite of this eagerness for information, Philip acted less than enthusiastic about dealing with

[31] AGS, Patronato L.26, Doc.75.

[32] Schäfer located only three of these from 1568, 1569, and 1571; he noted that none of them resulted in royal decrees on sweeping administrative issues because the king insisted on conducting these in written form; see *Consejo*,151. See also Gómez Gómez, "Consejo Real."

[33] AGS, Patronato L.26, Doc.67. [34] AGS, Patronato L.26, Doc.67.

[35] Parker, *Imprudent King*, 77–79 and Escudero, *Felipe II*, 18.

[36] Kamen, *Philip of Spain*, 223. [37] Gachard, *Relations*, li.

subjects face to face. Badaoro stated that he "does not normally look at the person with whom he deals, and keeps his eyes looking low to the ground, or, when he raises them, he turns them in this or that way." His answers were as noncommittal as his body language: "He responds with brevity of word, and promptly … without making any decisions" on the spot.[38]

Other contemporaries agreed with these assessments. Philip was famously quiet during these face-to-face meetings, often "disconcerting" subjects with his silence.[39] One Italian petitioner stated that God had made the monarch's heart from "the diamond, the hardest, the roughest, the roughest of all the metals."[40] New World vassals would encounter even more difficulties than Europeans in communicating with the king. The Indies' remoteness forced most subjects to resort to paper communications. Sure enough, the documentary record suggests only a handful of these vassals managed to speak in private to the monarch. Some were elites, such as Hernán Cortés and his son, the Marquis don Martín. Whether these meetings resulted in decrees is unclear.[41] Generally, however, Philip seems to have emulated his father in providing audiences mainly to nonelites, especially friars and Indians. We have one surviving transcript of the petition the part-Spanish, part-Indian *cacique* of Turmeque in Santa Fe de Bogotá handed to the king in 1584, for example.[42] We also know that sometime around 1585–1587, Rengifo presented his case about the eligibility of Peru's "ten thousand mestizos" for the priesthood.[43] Overall, these audiences were terribly scarce during the administrations of both Charles and Philip; one friar complained (on paper) in 1571 that the king had become "totally inaccessible."[44]

THE DILUTION OF ROYAL POWER WITHIN THE RULING FAMILY: REGENCIES AND CONSULTAS

The larger the empire became, the more kings delegated and diluted their role in lawmaking. During Spanish monarchs' absence from the peninsula, especially during the nomadic tenure of Charles V, regents took the

[38] Gachard, *Relations*, 41–42. [39] Kamen, *Philip of Spain*, 222.

[40] AGI, Indiferente 1392, "Alexandro Ordino," February 19, 1581, no folios.

[41] For a letter detailing Hernán's meeting with Charles V in Barcelona in 1529, which does imply that the meeting culminated indirectly in new legislation, see AGI, Patronato 16, N.1, R.7; AGI, Patronato 171, N.1, R.20.

[42] AGI, Patronato 196, R.16. [43] AGI, Lima 126; see the procurator's cover letter.

[44] Feros, *El Duque*, 112–113.

reins of Indies affairs. Little is known about how petitioners approached these placeholders. Charles' de facto rule over Spain had begun through a regent, Cardinal Francisco Jiménez de Cisneros. He oversaw Castilian and Indies government from 1516 until his death in 1517. One contemporary regarded him as an intimidating man of few but prudent words, who "dispatched succinctly all those who approached him," and expected his meetings to be quick and to the point.[45]

Cisneros shared his regency with two different Flemish coregents. One was Ambassador Charles de Poupet, Lord of La Chaulx. The other was Cardinal Adrian of Utrecht, who would also act as coregent of Castile in 1516–1517, and late 1520 to late 1521. Petitioners often addressed their letters to the cardinal, though he did not sign his name frequently on decrees; one historian has suggested that he was a passive ruler who had Charles V's trust but little interest in Indies governance.[46] None of these three have attracted sufficient attention from scholars of Indies law. Notably, it was during Cisneros' tenure that an informal committee within the Council of Castile emerged, which one anonymous official referred to in 1516 as the "*Consejo de Yndias*."[47]

During kings' absences, Habsburg women often took control of Indies legislation. King Charles V married Isabella of Portugal in 1526. The queen soon became a major political force in the European theater of the empire.[48] On multiple occasions her husband departed, and beginning in March 1529 he made her the de facto first-in-command over the Indies.[49] In one 1539 letter, her husband called her his "lieutenant-general and governess of these aforementioned realms" and the supreme authority, next to himself, over the "administration and governance" of the empire.[50] Charles V was clear that he trusted her to make decisions of maximum importance. He affirmed that she was a "person in whom we recognize that exist ... excellent and great virtues" for the "good administration" of the Habsburgs' dominions.[51] Isabella's tenure thus involved decisions on the New World. Some of these probably involved minor

[45] Ruiz-Crespo, *Cisneros*, 212.

[46] See, for example, AGI, Patronato 34, R.12 and R.12, Patronato 172, R.20, Patronato 174, R.25, R.27, and R.28, Patronato 176, R.9 and R.12, and Patronato 295, N.84, and Ruíz-Crespo, *Cisneros*.

[47] AGI, Patronato 170, R.21.

[48] She was regent as early as April 23, 1528; see AGS, Patronato, L.26, Doc.26 and Doc.27.

[49] Jiménez Zamora, "La Emperatríz," 231–237, AGS, Patronato L.26, Doc.14, Doc.15, Doc.32; AGS, Estado, L.21, 231–237.

[50] AGS, Patronato L.26, Doc.50.

[51] AGS, Patronato L.26, Doc 80.

issues, as Charles V also expected her to uphold regents' tradition of receiving subjects' petitions after mass. There is no definitive study of her exact contributions to Indies affairs nor did she leave a long paper trail, but she may have signed into law some seventy-six major *gobierno* decisions during her years as regent.[52]

Another set of regents during the reign of Charles V included his Habsburg relations from Central Europe. This time the President of the Council of the Indies, Luis Hurtado de Mendoza, acted as coregent; decision-making would (at least in theory) include the input of María of Austria and Maximilian II.[53] María was Charles V's eldest daughter and Philip's sister, Queen of Bohemia and Hungary, and Empress of the Holy Roman Empire.[54] She shared her regency with her cousin and husband Maximilian, King of Bohemia. He held this position until 1550; she would serve until 1551.[55]

Though Prince Philip had ruled Castile and the Indies de facto since 1551, political circumstances in Europe later forced him to leave Spain and temporarily disconnect himself from most legislative activities. Beginning in mid-1554, he was headed to England and would soon leave for Brussels. There, the following year his aging father crowned him King Philip II. On July 12, 1554, he appointed his sister Princess Juana of Austria, a mere eighteen years old, as regent. As Philip had done as prince, she was to hold public mass and accept petitions afterwards.[56] Like her brother, she was a vigorous sovereign; one Venetian contemporary said that she was "so energetic in her decisions that she even expressed regret at not being born male."[57] Juana's tenure lasted until 1559; no scholar has yet explored whether her approach to Indies rule differed from that of her fellow rulers.

Regencies reinforced Habsburg kings' reliance on paperwork. It was during these early regencies that the council's practice of elevating written requests for decisions or *consultas* to the ruler seems to have arisen or at least become commonplace. The earliest *consultas* date to the late 1520s, when Charles V was frequently absent from Spain.[58] Only five survive for 1529, seven for 1530, eleven for 1531, four for 1532, twelve for 1534, four for 1535, and two for 1536. They were probably once very

[52] Jiménez Zamora, "La Emperatríz," 243. [53] AGS, Patronato L.26, Doc.108.
[54] AGS, Patronato L.26, Doc.98. [55] Sánchez, *Empress*, 62–70.
[56] AGS, Patronato L.26, Doc.137. For a study of Juana's regency, see Buyreu Juan, "Princesa."
[57] Monter, *Rise*, 104. [58] Herrera Heredia, *Catálogo Tomo 1*.

numerous, but have disappeared due to the time period's poor archival practices. In subsequent years, with the rise of Charles' ambitious and capable young son Philip, the *consultas*, and council paperwork in general, would increase exponentially.

As Philip's duties pushed him further from his subjects, and ministers grew more powerful, he endeavored to remain vigilant toward officials. A handful of documents attest that sometime during his first years of rule, Philip developed a line of direct communication between himself and Indies viceroys that bypassed the councils and routed instead through his royal secretaries.[59] This channel also allowed ordinary subjects' urgent denunciations of official abuse. These secret letters must have involved only a small fraction of overall communication. This itinerary nonetheless ensured that a "vigilant triangle" of suspicious vassals constantly kept ministers' passions from completely usurping the king's prerogatives and reinforced a widespread fiction of ministers' upright behavior strong enough to keep subjects' faith in petitioning.[60]

THE APOGEE OF THE INDIES' PATRIMONIAL STYLE, 1492–1523

The steadily increasing social distance between monarchs and petitioners sometimes put regents in control, but most often considerably expanded the role played by royal advisers. Indeed, Council ministers would occasionally act as regents themselves, becoming de facto rulers of the Indies. The Bishop of Ciudad Rodrigo, Gonzalo Maldonado (ruled 1524–1530) assumed the regency briefly in late 1529.[61] Between 1539 and 1541, Council President and Cardinal of Seville Juan García de Loaysa y Mendoza governed with the assistance of Cardinal of Toledo Juan Pardo de Tavera and thus could "decree all that which the Emperor himself could."[62] Loaysa once again assumed this role in 1543.[63]

The era of the minister was gradually dawning. Kings now had two profoundly different administrative approaches to choose from. One was patrimonial administration: treating officials as extensions of the royal household and granting them the king-like prerogatives of forming and

[59] Schäfer, *Consejo*, 150; Parker, *Imprudent*, 69; AGI, México 19, N.13; AGI, Indiferente 875, "Leyendo," September 7, 1570; AGI, Lima 126, "Memorial."

[60] Brendecke, *Empirical Empire*, 113.

[61] AGS, Patronato L.26 d.33; d.35.

[62] Schäfer, *El Consejo*, 2003, 74, and AGS, Patronato L.26, d.58; d.63.

[63] AGS, Patronato L.26, d.73.

favoring family connections with vassals. This style was a natural fit for an absolutist dynasty which viewed its family affairs as inseparable from its administration of the public good. The other major option was for rulers to view council officials as servants of the public good, working under numerous restrictions and stipulations. In this approach, ministers would not treat governance as an extension of their own family business; they would instead banish their own volitions as thoroughly as possible from the decision-making process.

Whichever choice the monarchs elected would have major consequences for the petition-and-response system. Patrimonialism would create close ties with Indies elites, favor high-ranking women's and men's influence over the administration, and reduce paperwork. A more socially distant approach promised the opposite, to the benefit of increasing accountability and garnering legitimacy among weaker Indies groups, and especially Indigenous interests. A system of decision-making consisting mostly of paper communication would, however, exact a heavy toll as ministers would document their movements through a time-consuming, burdensome administration ill-suited for a monarchy on the move.

Before the early modern era, Iberian rulers employed patrimonial cliques to oversee their dominions. The collapse of Roman authority over Spain did away with most bureaucratic elements of administration. The ruling circle went by numerous names. The sixth-century Visigoths of Toledo employed a small imperial *comitatus* or *Gefolge*, and by the seventh century there was a primordial distinction between the royal household's ministers, the *officium palatinum*, and the outer circle of enforcers in the *aula regia*.[64] The ninth-century Leonese realm similarly envisioned its officials and family as part of a single household *palatium regis* or *familia regis*. By the late twelfth century, the ascendant Astur-Leonese administration had expanded their *curia regis* substantially, but it was during the reign of Alfonso X the Wise (1252–1284) that a stronger ethos of official service to the monarchy emerged.[65]

By the fourteenth and fifteenth centuries, kings' delegation of advisory roles to ministers and their subalterns began to mature due to petitioners' increasing pressure upon monarchs.[66] The ruling family's confidantes could simply not keep pace. The Catholic Kings created new and more

[64] Porras Arboledas, Ramírez Vaquero, and Sabaté i Currul, *Época medieval*, 69–74; Díaz, "Visigothic," 345.

[65] Porras Arboledas, Ramírez Vaquero, and Sabaté i Currul, *Época medieval*, 70–104.

[66] De Dios, "Ordenanzas," 271–272.

specialized councils to respond to this flood of petitions. Their reign saw the rise of the Councils of Brotherhoods (1476–1498), Inquisition (1488), Aragon (1494), Military Orders (1495), House of Trade (1503), and Crusade (1509). Legal dispositions governing these bodies also became far more specific than they had been in previous centuries.[67]

Though Castilian administration became increasingly specialized, it remained quite patrimonial. This was doubly true of the Indies, which in the early 1500s was of little concern to the Catholic Kings. Ferdinand, never enthusiastic about Indies rule, delegated nearly unlimited advisory powers to a tiny cabal of Council of Castile ministers, who would treat New World affairs as family business. The powers of bishop, lawyer, and minister Juan Rodríguez de Fonseca and his secretary Gaspar de Gricio were only limited by their common-sense desire to avoid angering the king.[68] After Gricio died in 1507, Fonseca replaced him with Lope de Conchillos, a pair which would oversee the Indies' lawmaking process into the early 1520s.[69] Fonseca's nearly three-decade rule prompted some contemporaries' disapproval. Some regarded him as harsh and impartial, whereas Bartolomé de las Casas depicted him as a tyrant indifferent to the plight of Indigenous subjects.[70]

Though communication with King Charles was mainly paper-based, before the 1520s subjects could communicate personally with ministers with some ease. The committee for Indies affairs often met in ministers' homes to debate important issues.[71] Las Casas recalled friars cursing at Fonseca, and he himself once personally upbraided the bishop.[72] Subjects from outside the Council of Castile who nonetheless boasted Indies experience might even form part of ministers' committees without royal appointments.[73]

Las Casas recalled navigating the royal decision-making process during this early period of imperial rule. Few seem to have complained about Regent Cisneros. However, this Castilian official's professional and detached style of Indies administration was limited, for Charles also appointed two courtiers, Ambassador Poupet and the Cardinal of Utrecht,

[67] Lorenzo Cadarso, *Documento real*, 36.

[68] Martínez Martín, *Juan*, 33. See also Gricio's petition before the king seeking (successfully) to help the governor of Santo Domingo, Nicolás de Ovando, win certain decrees, in AGI, Indiferente 418, L.1, 53v, September 9, 1501.

[69] Schäfer, *Consejo*, 43–50.

[70] Guevara, *Libro primero*, lxx; BNE,Mss. 2814 B.3, Ch.103, 326v and 328r.

[71] BNE, Mss.2814, B.3, Ch.101, 321v.

[72] BNE, Mss.2814, B.3, Ch.103, 326v.

[73] BNE, Mss.2814, B.3, Ch.6, 12r.

to share power with him. Petitioners also wrote to the cardinal.[74] Las Casas also cultivated personal ties with William de Croÿ, Lord of Chièvres, whom contemporaries sometimes referred to as the monarch's *alter rex*.[75] To isolate Fonseca he also befriended Ambassador Poupet and the Flemish courtier Mosior de la Mure.[76] With friends in high places, Las Casas won victory after legislative victory on behalf of millions of Indians.

In 1517 another courtier, Chancellor Jean le Sauvage, took a leading role in handling New World legislation.[77] The king gave him near-all-powerful faculties to appoint officials.[78] Las Casas would describe le Sauvage as the "head and President of all the Councils."[79] The Dominican celebrated the rise of the chancellors, for they had ousted the deceased King Ferdinand II's favorite ministers, especially Fonseca. Though le Sauvage died in 1518, Las Casas also was on good terms with his successor, the eminent and politically savvy Piedmontese diplomat and statesman Mercurino di Gattinara.[80] The friar initially found Gattinara to be interested in "pure temporal interests," but later described him and his Flemish associates as reliable allies and steadfast enemies of Fonseca.[81]

The friar gradually discerned an action plan for other would-be reformers. This involved using the king's patrimonial networks in, above, and around the Council of Castile. First, reformers would "fraternally" try to persuade this council, which, based on past experiences, they suspected was unlikely to work for their particular mission due to Fonseca's power. If this failed, they would appeal to Chancellor Gattinara. If they still could not achieve their goal, they would seek the intercession of Croÿ. Their penultimate approach was to rather desperately attempt the direct attention of King Charles. If all else failed, they would resort to pressuring their legislators and their ruler through public opinion, "publicly preach[ing] against all of them, giving part of the blame to the King."[82]

Las Casas' dexterous use of personal relationships which he crafted with the king's courtiers landed him an informal position as colegislator in

[74] See, for example, AGI, Patronato 34, R.12 and R.12; AGI, Patronato 172, R.20; AGI, Patronato 174, R.25; R.27; R.28; AGI, Patronato 176, R.9; R.12; AGI, Patronato 295, N.84; Ruíz-Crespo, *Cisneros*; Castro, "Adriano."

[75] BNE, Mss.2814, B.3, Ch.132, 425r; Headley, *The Emperor*, 26.

[76] BNE, Mss.2814, B.3, Ch.102, 322v-323r; Ch.137, 446r.

[77] BNE, Mss.2814, B.3, Ch.98, 306v; For his biography, see Vermier, "Chancellor."

[78] Headley, *The Emperor*, 23; BNE, Mss.2814, Ch.139, 454v.

[79] BNE, Mss. 2814, B.3, Ch.98, 306r.

[80] Headley, *The Emperor*, 20.

[81] BNE, Mss. 2814, B.3, Ch.130, 417v; Ch.133, 426r.

[82] BNE, Mss. 2814, B.3, Ch.133, 428v.

the Council of Castile. He befriended the king's Spanish secretary, Francisco de Cobos, who had been Gattinara's subordinate and who was in charge of bringing finalized petitions to Gattinara and the emperor. The pro-Indian lobbyist became so close to Cobos that, beginning in 1517, the secretary would first give Las Casas any incoming petitions from the Indies and supposedly even had the friar produce summaries of incoming letters in Latin with his opinions for an unspecified period of time. If true, the friar had briefly become more powerful than the "tyrannical" Indies minister Fonseca and his underling Conchillos.[83] An ordinary vassal, a simple priest, was directing an empire's legislative process in the face of powerful ministers through his masterful patrimonial string-pulling – at least for the time being.

COUNCIL DEPATRIMONIALIZATION AND ITS LIMITS, 1524–1531

Las Casas' case demonstrates that, before the 1520s, strong interpersonal connections close to the Habsburg household trounced the small clique of ministers who oversaw Indies lawmaking (officials who were themselves hardly a bureaucratic corps). For the Dominican, this maze of social relations was an opportunity. For many in Castile, however, King Charles' foreign courtiers represented the worst ills of patrimonial administration.

Gradual reforms proved too little, too late for many of Spain's discontented subjects. When Charles, Holy Roman Emperor since 1519, departed Spain in 1520, a major revolt broke out among Castilian cities. Though the king and his Spanish allies defeated the insurgents in 1521 and secured his position as the supreme ruler of Spain, he would heed the writing on the wall: Spaniards demanded that kings pay very close attention to their demands and uproot the undue power of the Flemish ministers.[84] In 1523, Spanish cities demanded Charles V bring his venal, swollen government under control. Among the institutions they singled out for reform was the Council of the Indies, then still a subcommittee of the Council of Castile.[85] Simultaneously, perhaps because of these and other pleas, Chancellor Gattinara began to envision a more formal conciliar system.[86] Charles ratified the establishment of the Council of the Chamber in 1518 (for the distribution of privileges), the Council of State

[83] BNE, Mss. 2814, B.3, Ch.99, 309r-310v; Ch.139, 455r. [84] Espinosa, *Empire*.
[85] AGS, Patronato L.70, Doc.9, 51r-v. [86] AGS, Patronato L.70, Doc.11.1.

in 1523–1524, the Council of War in 1524, the Council of Finance in 1525, Works and Forests in 1545, and the Council of Italy in 1555.[87] Thanks to these changes after 1521, legislative decisions would pass from the hands of the Flemish courtiers to a less patrimonial corps of mostly Spanish officials. Charles also officially ratified the foundation of the Council of the Indies in 1524. While this council's crucial foundational documents are unfortunately missing, seventeenth-century historians placed its formal beginning as August 1.[88] According to eighteenth-century officials' observations, a decree from that year which apparently no longer exists established that the council was no longer a subcommittee but independent and fully equal to the Council of Castile.[89]

The 1524 advent of the Council of the Indies as a separate institution brought about a major change in its staff and praxis. The Council of Castile's President Juan Pardo de Tavera sought to staff the new Council of the Indies with subjects who had been loyal to Charles V during the great *comunero* revolt. Tavera also broke somewhat from the previous years of fluid, personalistic influence by appointing candidates with a proven history of "competence and accountability."[90] Minister Fonseca died in 1524, just after the Council of the Indies appeared; Charles and Tavera replaced him with Dominican friar García de Loaysa, the bishop of Osma. The council also received its own secretary, Juan de Sámano, another sign of the institution's growth and growing reliance on paperwork.[91]

Chancellor Gattinara largely oversaw council affairs and did not merely relay decisions to King Charles. By the late 1520s he had replaced Francisco de los Cobos as the Habsburgs' unchallenged chancellor. The Italian thus briefly became the de facto ruler over the Indies, making all final administrative and grace decisions and overseeing the dispatch of the new council's documents – he signed more than 450 during his tenure.[92] Cobos regained his role directing New World affairs in 1530, but unlike his rival Gattinara did not press any clear vision of empire upon the council other than personal enrichment.[93]

Already by the 1520s the council's practices were fundamentally paper-based, and with ministers perpetually on the move, vassals had few means

[87] Parker, *Imprudent King*, 65. [88] Schäfer, *El Consejo*, 62–63.
[89] AGI, Indiferente 454, L.4, 175v, 29 July 1773. See also Indiferente 545, L.2, 196r.
[90] Espinosa, *Empire*, 99, 133. [91] Schäfer, *El Consejo*, 64.
[92] Schäfer, *El Consejo*, 65–67; Ard Boone, *Mercurino*, 38.
[93] BNE, Mss.2814, B.3, Ch.99, 310v.

to influence the system through illicit means. However, documents reveal that some subjects had successfully bribed ministers with gifts. On April 4, 1531, the king and Secretary Cobos issued a decree strongly prohibiting that "my Council, judges of my High Courts, or other judges ... receive, neither directly nor indirectly, for themselves nor for others," any gifts "of any value ... publicly or secretly." The ruling also banned ministers from buying from or selling to Indies vassals. It strongly castigated them for placing in doubt "the laws of ... my realms." Clearly, something had gone foul and displeased the emperor, probably in a court case; the edict implied that the problem related to "those undertaking their affairs [*negociantes*] and litigants [*pleyteantes*]."[94]

Overall, by the 1520s a faint ethos of social distance was gradually triumphing over the more patrimonialist style of Ferdinand and young Charles, as the council became an independent institutional entity, assembled key staff, and operated under a less interventionist royal secretary. Still, its rules and esprit de corps remained rather vague. In subsequent decades, however, the council would become a model institution for European overseas rule – after a series of strongly gendered crises which in many ways were peculiar to the Indies' unique context, and which were linked to women's power and Indigenous labor.

CHANGES IN THE COUNCIL, 1531–1542: WRONGDOING, WOMEN, AND REFORM

Until 1542, Council ministers operated under threadbare legal guidelines. Only in that year would they adopt somewhat more concrete administrative rules: the New Laws. Scholars have considered these extensive ordinances to be the most important in Indies history, largely because they sought to weaken conquistador power, establish stronger royal oversight, and protect Indians against abuses.[95] Many historians have suggested that the Crown promulgated these ordinances almost entirely due to the powerful rhetoric of Las Casas. Yet two mysteries regarding the New Laws remain: these also reformed not only Indies governance but also the Council; and were tied in unclear ways to an equally enigmatic royal investigation. Two nearly century-old historical mysteries loom

[94] AGS, Cámara de Castila, Diversos 1, 15.

[95] Van Deusen, *Global Indios*, 7 and 222; Raup Wagner and Rand Parish, *Life*, 114; Ybot León, "Juntas," 431; Huerga, *Fray*, 201; Zavala, *Encomienda*, 423; Getino, "Influencia," 265; Lucena, "Crisis," 163.

unanswered: why was there an audit of the Council in the early 1540s which culminated in its reform, and who prompted this strange measure?[96] The 1542 New Laws marked a milestone in the depatrimonialization of the Council and of Indies rule in general. They sternly prohibited ministers from having illicit connections with vassals under pain of exile, proscribed third-party intercessions when issuing judicial rulings and other decrees, and dictated ministers' workdays and voting.[97] Unfortunately, the probe's proceedings are missing.[98]

Most historians have suggested it was Las Casas who inspired the royal investigation.[99] However, two documents hiding in plain sight at the Royal Library of El Escorial offer crucial clues regarding the nature of a separate conflict which gave rise to this inquiry and the council's reform, a struggle which in the 1530s and early 1540s nearly saw the organization transform into a plaything of powerful conquistadors. These texts also reveal the centrality of women as agents of patrimonial administration and, in one notable case, acting as a bulwark against Indies elites' usurpation of the decision-making process. The Escorial documents, and a constellation of texts which they lead to, reveal the origins of the early 1540s reform process. These lay not in the agitation of Las Casas, but in the mêlée of pen and sword between two conquistador dynasties of Peru: the Pizarro and Almagro clans. During their conquests in Peru, Captains Francisco and Hernando Pizarro marginalized their partner don Diego de Almagro from the spoils. After a heated series of jurisdictional struggles which turned violent, the Pizarros executed Almagro in a sham trial in 1538.[100] Almagro's son, the part-Indigenous Diego the Younger, took the Pizarro family to court, beginning a legal struggle of titanic proportions in which these rivals exposed how almost all council ministers had pursued patrimonialist ties to both exorbitantly wealthy conquistador dynasties.

Years of bitter litigation revealed that since 1535 Diego de Almagro the Elder had planned to marry his son in Spain with the help of enormous sums of Indigenous-mined gold.[101] He dispatched agents to the court with hopes of forming ties with council president García de Loaysa and minister Diego Beltrán as well as with the royal secretary Francisco de los Cobos. The terms were strictly patrimonial; the agent was to "show

[96] Schäfer, *Consejo*, 77. [97] BNE, Mss.3035, 4r–15v. [98] Schäfer, *Consejo*, 79.
[99] Toro Garland, "Carta," 63; Brennan, *Las Casas*, 36–37; Pérez Fernández, *Cronología*, 34.
[100] Lockhart, *Men*, 6–15.
[101] Himmerich and Valencia, *Encomenderos*, 1996, 68; Cieza de León, *Obras*, I, 336. See also Risly Clemence, *Harkness*, vol. 2, 24.

them clothing and jewels . . . offering my person's absolute disposition to their servants and dependents."[102] By 1537, the conquistador planned to wed his son Diego the Younger to a certain doña Natalia de Carvajal, daughter of council minister Juan Suárez de Carvajal. President Loaysa himself had arranged the marriage.[103]

These patrimonialist liaisons collapsed with the Pizarros' execution of Almagro the Elder. By 1539, Hernando Pizarro was en route to the court in chains. The council's attorney prepared a slew of charges against him – bolstered largely by the Almagro faction's alarming accusations.[104] By 1540, Pizarro sat in a royal jail in Spain.[105] Lawyers assembled in their paperwork trenches. Volley after volley of allegations revealed that council ministers had developed deep patrimonial ties with both cliques. President Loaysa and Beltrán abandoned Diego the Younger when his bride-to-be suddenly died, throwing their support behind the vastly wealthier and more powerful Hernando Pizarro, whose brother Francisco was also favoring Beltrán's sons in Peru.[106] Beltrán vehemently denied this.[107]

The Almagros also argued that minister Suárez de Carvajal's relatives in Peru received Francisco's favor.[108] They even blamed Hernando and his brother of having bought the council president and the emperor's secretary Cobos.[109] The council recused minister Carvajal. However, Pizarro then faulted minister Gutiérre Velázquez for impartiality, as his wife's distant cousin was involved with certain Almagro supporters. He, too, was recused.[110]

By early 1542, the recusations had paralyzed the Council of the Indies, and various ministers from the Council of Castile took up the case. The two anonymous Escorial documents reveal how this crisis prompted the royal investigation of the Council of the Indies. One, from early 1541, describes how two ministers from the Council of Castile learned that Hernando Pizarro attempted to co-opt one of their colleagues, Sancho Díaz de Leguizamón, by sending two agents to bribe his wife, doña Mencía de Esquivel.[111] The two ministers reported the issue to the emperor. The second document, dating from sometime before

[102] AGI, Escribanía, 1007B, "Orgoños," 372r–373v. [103] AGI, Escribanía 1006B, 247v.
[104] AGI, Patronato 90B, N.2, R.9, July 6, 1539; Medina, ed., *Colección*, 1889: Doc.LIX, 324–325; AGI, Escribanía 1007B, xxxii recto–xxxviii recto.
[105] AGI, Indiferente 737, N.48a. [106] AGI, Escribanía 1007B, cxxi recto.
[107] AGI, Escribanía 1007B, clvvv recto, June 17, 1540.
[108] AGI, Patronato 294, N.4, 16v-19r. [109] AGI, Patronato 294, N.4, 18v-19r, 40v.
[110] AGI, Justicia 1164, N.2, R.3, 62r and 102r. [111] BSLE, &-II-7, 459v.

February 1542, urged the emperor to order an investigation of the Council of the Indies in consideration of the inducements of Hernando Pizarro and others who had discovered "a good manner to negotiate" with their "great treasures."[112] Pizarro was poised to take over the council through his "close and intimate and well-known friendship" with ministers.[113] The title of the dossier including the two Escorial texts features a title from some years later, "causes for which it is necessary that the Council of the Indies be investigated."[114] The wheels of reform were turning, thanks largely to the intervention of doña Mencía, who clearly understood that injustice was afoot and boldly resisted Pizarro's entreaties.

Las Casas arrived at the court at this opportune moment. He appears to have made his first formal denunciation of Council of the Indies wrongdoing in early April 1542, before the Parliament (*Cortes*) of Castile and the emperor.[115] The Dominican accused council ministers of having placed the interests of their families, friends, and dependents before those of the realm and of entwining their blood ties and loyalists into Indies society.[116] Las Casas and a number of his allies gathered in a special committee beginning in May to remedy Indies government: the Junta of Valladolid.[117] Between July 1542 and February 1543, the council ceased to operate, and around this time the royal investigation seems to have been underway.[118] It seems the emperor himself was in charge until June 1542, when he appointed don Juan de Figueroa to the task. While the probe continued, the emperor ratified the New Laws in November 1542.[119]

INFLUENTIAL WOMEN ON CENTER STAGE

By the 1530s, a ubiquitous theme had emerged in accusations of Council wrongdoing: influential women were beginning to help powerful vassals adulterate the petition-and-response system. Though both the Council of the Indies and the enterprise of conquest were heavily male undertakings with ever-present masculine overtones, the networks of family power had also sometimes allowed women to become highly influential. Matrimonial ties, and the connections they brought between Crown officials and vassals, had once been a legitimate vehicle through which women could shape

[112] BSLE, &-II-7, 460r. [113] AGI, Lima 565, L.3, 224r y BSLE, &-II-7, 460v.
[114] BSLE, &-II-7, 461v–462v. Loaysa died in 1546.
[115] Pérez Fernández, *Cronología*, 568 and 570. [116] Las Casas, *Obras*, I, Doc.XI, 121.
[117] Pérez Fernández, *Cronología*, 574. [118] Martínez Millán and Morales, *Corte*, 235.
[119] Schäfer, *Consejo*, 79 footnote 109. AGI, Indiferente 423, L.20, 102r.

decisions regarding the New World. Here the paradox of ministers' rising power becomes apparent. All contemporaries agreed that monarchs' dynastic networks required family ties and powerful women to forge them. But should officials imitate their superiors in this regard? Initially, the answer was yes. In the 1510s, when patrimonialism was the stock-in-trade of the court, the famous court humanist Francisco López de Villalobos wrote to a nobleman praising women's power to unite Spain with Charles' foreign courtiers. True, Castilians and Flemish officials were as different as "horses are to asses," but he maintained that "women can participate in the governance" of the kingdom by forging connections between such dissimilar groups.[120] In the right context, a certain stratum of courtiers – like the European counselors who initially assisted Charles – could weave the Empire together, one marriage at a time. By the 1540s, this was no more.

The results of the council audit showed that this acceptance was fading fast by the mid-1500s. Investigator Figueroa's February 1543 determinations have not survived, but other documents summarize the outcome. President Loaysa was indeed guilty, but the emperor did not punish him. Minister Carvajal lost his position for accepting huge bribes from the Almagro faction.[121] Minister Beltrán paid a colossal fine and was exiled – Figueroa had found he had accepted gifts from Diego de Almagro de Elder, Hernán Cortés, and Pizarro's clique – all through the hands of Beltrán's wife.[122]

The Peruvian fiascos of the 1530s and 1540s threw a harsh spotlight not only on the council but also on the courtly confusion between aristocratic practice and official integrity. Ministers had nearly wedded their families into the murderous Pizarro and Almagro clans. Suddenly, both patrimonialism and women were on Emperor Charles' mind – and in the early 1540s his diagnosis of the problem differed sharply from his youthful acceptance of mixing official business and family interests. In 1543, he warned his son, Prince Philip, that certain high-ranking ministers in the court were engaging in wrongdoing – and they had the young regent in their crosshairs. The emperor alerted him not to allow himself to be overpowered by palace grandees – especially those who worked "through the voices of women."[123] In the emperor's spotlight was none other than his royal secretary, Francisco de los Cobos. He considered Cobos

[120] BL, Mss.Add.8219, 25v–26r. [121] BSLE, V-II-4, N.69, 197r.
[122] AGI, Patronato 185, R. 34 y AGI, Indiferente 737, N.53.
[123] BNE, Mss.10509, 15r–v.

a faithful secretary, but warned Philip that "his wife fatigues him, and is the cause of involving him in *pasiones*" – that is, biased conflicts.[124] This has "not ceased to give him a reputation ... all that is necessary is a few presents, that they [vassals] give his wife."[125]

This was not idle gossip. One high-ranking officials' private letters from late 1542 reveal that Cobos' wife doña María de Mendoza, as well as an array of other officials' spouses, had previously played essential roles in shaping the Council of the Indies' decisions. The governor of Peru, Cristóbal Vaca de Castro, privately admitted women's extensive power in the court in a letter to his wife doña María de Quiñones. The letter ended up in the royal archive in Council Secretary Sámano's hands, after the royal accountant of the Panama port of Nombre de Dios intercepted it – perhaps as part of Investigator Figueroa's ongoing investigation of the council.[126]

The Peruvian governor's approach mirrored the patrimonial playbook of the Almagro and Pizarro factions, but rested even more explicitly upon the importance of court women's influence over Indies decision-making. The governor instructed his spouse to head to court, where she would visit certain council ministers "in style, on your mule, well accompanied with a squire and an old and venerable chaplain, and servant boy and pages."[127] Her task was to sway imperial Secretary Cobos and the Secretary Sámano, the council's interim president Count of Osorno García Fernández Manrique, and President Loaysa.

She was to do so almost entirely by befriending women. The governor's spouse would appeal to Cobos' wife doña María de Mendoza and the Countess of Rivadavia Doña María Sarmiento. She was also to "stay on speaking terms with doña María de Mendoza, and visit her and give her some things, and that way she will do as we wish." The governor also noted that "if you should think proper to give some of the gold alloy items to doña María de Mendoza, do it, for I'll send plenty" from Peru.[128] Of course, these matters required that the governor's wife be flexible and strategic. If Cobos' wife and the Countess were for any reason unavailable, she should seek out any other "wife of a Councilor of the Indies or

[124] BNE, Mss.10509, 16r. [125] BNE, Mss.10509, 16r.

[126] Ministerio de Fomento, *Cartas*, 710; AGI, Lima 565, L.3, 224r; BSLE, &-II-7, 460v. Figueroa would have likely heard the Almagro clan's accusation that Governor Vaca de Castro was a friend of the Pizarros and a dependent of pro-Pizarro President Loaysa. AHNM, Diversos-Colecciones 22, N.43, and in Lockhart and Otte, *Letters*, 181–182.

[127] AHNM, Diversos-Colecciones 22, N.43, and in Lockhart and Otte, *Letters*, 181–182.

[128] AHNM, Diversos-Colecciones 22, N.43.

someone else ... do there as you see fit, since it is good to please people."[129]

This episode was one of several involving Secretary Cobos' wife doña María de Mendoza. She may have even attempted to leverage her influence not just over her husband but the Council of the Indies' ministers as well. Chronicler Bernal Díaz del Castillo suggested that in 1528 Hernán Cortés had tried but failed to woo her sister, doña Francisca, in order to recover his governorship of Mexico. Bernal Díaz also provided a colorful account of how Cobos' wife enlisted the conquistador-surgeon-healer Alonso Muñoz (himself badly afflicted by thyromegaly) to cure her infertility in the late 1530s. In exchange, she promised him 2,000 ducats and a grant of Indian labor using her favor with the council. Muñoz failed to cure doña María, but nonetheless received his tribute grant.[130]

Powerful women – especially the wives of ministers and secretaries – thus played roles within the highest echelons of royal decision-making from the 1520s to early 1540s. Their influence was encouraged by the blurry lines dividing the Habsburg culture of household administration and officialdom. Three major forces seem to have prevented the council from becoming entirely infested with family interests, however. The first was the Habsburgs' own dislike for officials' subterfuge against their own patrimonial sphere. The second was the perpetually agonistic nature of petitioning and litigation, which offered vassals prime vehicles for denouncing rivals' wrongdoing. A third force owed to the court's constant movement, which limited freewheeling patrimonialism.

COUNTERING ILLICIT VOLITIONS IN THE COUNCIL

When King Philip II decided to permanently move the court to the unremarkable town of Madrid and break with his father's itineracy in 1561, a major sociolegal transformation took place.[131] Once more, concerns about patrimonialism leapt to the fore, with even greater strength. Women again took center stage. The outcome would be an even more fundamental reform of Council praxes in 1571, and the rise of far more explicitly hostile commentaries about female involvement in imperial decision-making.

[129] AHNM, Diversos-Colecciones 22, N.43, and in Lockhart and Otte, *Letters*, 181–182.
[130] Díaz del Castillo, *Historia*, 758.
[131] Cadenas, *Caminos*; Parker, *Imprudent King*, 15–18, 36–43, 62–105.

Madrid was ecstasy and agony: a spectacular court milieu and an overcrowded town of distressed justice-and-privilege-seekers. Many were desperate to escape its expensive, often unsanitary living conditions. One official complained that because litigation dragged on interminably, Madrid was full of "sad men, disconsolate and desperate."[132] One subject complained in 1567 that because of paperwork delays, "those who seek resolutions procure not very licit methods, be it with grandees, or lawyers, or procurators, or guests of those [ministers] of the abovementioned Council, or with others."[133] True, the council now boasted the organizational advantages of fixed lodgings, offices, and archives – but upon the palace's stone walls, the mildew of wrongdoing began to gather.

At the heart of Madrid's vibrant and melancholy scene was the royal palace's courtyard, comprised primarily of men (and some women) from all over the world, conducting every sort of personal, communal, and imperial affair.[134] The powerful and the meek of the Indies rubbed elbows there, gathering around the doors of the various councils. There was also a retinue of professional procurators conducting business there and perhaps seeking new clients.

Subjects just outside the council doors were always vigilant, eager to eavesdrop on ministers' latest decisions. Many traded information with one another on their experiences and on the best way to reach a favorable determination. In the late 1560s, Indies justice-seekers had their eyes on one man: Secretary Ochoa de Luyando, the gatekeeper of the institution. Luyando (and perhaps his doormen) would have informed subjects on their cases' progress.

Vassals in the courtyard soon began to hear whispers of corrupt ministers.[135] One jurist noted Secretary Luyando's conspicuous accumulation of wealth and wondered how exactly an official with a modest income could have built up such an illustrious patrimony.[136] Licenciado Salazar heard that a procurator for the City of Guatemala had heard in the courtyard from Pedro de Avendaño that there were "many rumors said against those of the aforementioned Council of the Indies."[137] When the Guatemalan pressed Avendaño, he suggested cryptically "he had negotiated with those of the Council as he had pleased," specifically

[132] Escudero, *Felipe II*, 19. [133] BNE, Mss.9855, 156v; BL, Mss.Add.33983, 84v.
[134] Lorenzo Cadarso, *Documento real*, 65. [135] BL, Mss.Add.33983, 306r.
[136] BL, Mss.Add.33983, 193v. [137] BL, Mss.Add.33983, 37r.

with ministers Licenciado Alonso Múñoz and Licenciado Juan Vázquez.[138]

In 1567, the king appointed Council of the Inquisition's minister Juan de Ovando to audit the Council of the Indies, under circumstances which are far from clear.[139] His sprawling investigation unraveled these intrigues like a ball of yarn. By 1571, he would be the Council of the Indies' president and would help draft the 1571 ordinances which would govern this institution until the early 1600s. In the process of Ovando's career-defining audit, witnesses revealed how the excesses of officials' patrimonialism could pervert royal justice. The probe often disclosed how certain council subalterns developed troublesome conflicts of interest through patrimonial ties to ministers. The Council of the Indies' own procurators' livelihoods depended on pushing their cases before ministers, giving them strong incentives to develop ties. Witness Licenciado Ramírez noted the rumor that procurator Sebastián de Santander was minister Santillán's dependent – a clear conflict of interest.[140] Witness Licenciado Barrionuevo claimed the City of Panama's procurator spoke of having made himself "of the house of [minister] doctor Vázquez" with these payments.[141] Others whispered that minister Licenciado Encinas was considering one of procurator Juan de la Peña's servants for a plum position in the Indies.[142] Clearly, the division between council officials and procurators was fragile in the 1560s, with some legal agents behaving not as public defenders but as ministers' household dependents.

Juan López de Velasco, a longtime council scribe, singled out officials' page-boys and servants for eroding ministers' impartiality and secrecy. Visitors who managed to secure brief face-to-face audiences with ministers to inquire into their cases' progress often brought their assistants. Velasco was strongly suspicious of these dependents and recommended

[138] BL, Mss.Add.33983, 37v–38r.

[139] Poole, *Juan de Ovando*, 95–97, 2004. It is quite conspicuous that in the late 1560s the same pattern of ministers accusing powerful conquistadors of treason swirled around Hernán Cortés' son, don Martín, and that just as in the Pizarro-Almagro trial, the litigants recused multiple council ministers. Don Martín complained in two undated petitions that President Tello de Sandoval was related to his enemies through marriage (he was the uncle of the wife of a Mexico judge); see HSA 9/IV/5. Don Martín's wife, the Marchioness, also complained of this in an undated letter; see HSA 9/IV/7. However, this issue requires further investigation, and I have found no "smoking gun" akin to the Escorial documents linking the Cortés trial to the 1567 audit.

[140] BL, Mss.Add.33983, 84r.

[141] BL, Mss.Add.33983, 190v.

[142] BL, Mss.Add.33983, 305r.

Ovando ban the entry of all nonessential staff to prevent "the friendships and negotiations of the doormen, page-boys, [and] servants of lords."[143]

Ovando mainly uncovered wrongdoing among ministers themselves. The investigation often led not to the council, but to ministers' private abodes. The president of the council was to live within the palace, placing him under considerable royal scrutiny. Other ministers, however, conducted of all sorts of business at their Madrid homes long after work hours.

The returns for crossing the threshold into ministers' homes could be great. The interim president, minister Licenciado Vázquez, hosted important figures from the Indies – some of them, perhaps, were distant relatives, others strangers with something to offer. High Judge of Guadalajara Licenciado Francisco de Mendola suggested that he heard that Licenciado Vázquez "allowed ... pretenders and justice-seekers" into his house, mainly "from Peru and New Spain."[144] Witness Pedro Gómez del Valle heard there were "persons linked to the house of the said doctor Vázquez" who were necessary for those "seeking to dispatch their business with the Council."[145] Indeed, Gómez said that "many times he had heard the house of said Doctor Vázquez be called the Golden Door, for behind it much gold is beaten from the dealings of many Indies subjects [*indianos*]."[146] Witness don Diego de Carvajal singled out minister Licenciado Barrionuevo's household wrongdoings as particularly egregious. In the court there was "no other refrain between all of the litigants" that "he who does not pay the aforementioned Barrionuevo do not succeed in this Council."[147] Carvajal suggested that ministers Vázquez, Barrionuevo, and Muñoz kept a list detailing their bribes.[148]

Council ministers clearly were in the public spotlight while they conducted affairs in Madrid, whether in the palace or at home. Many thus sought the privacy of the countryside, especially secluded gardens. These spaces could be the sites of more illicit behavior. Licenciado Salazar alleged that it was "very murmured among justice-seekers" that ministers Licenciado Vázquez, Villafañe, Salas, and Aguilera would abscond to a certain "garden in Burgos" on weekends; Licenciado Ramírez testified the same.[149]

143 BL, Mss.Add.33983, 294v.
144 AGI, Guadalajara 5, R.13, N.23, 8r.
145 BL, Mss.Add.33983, 309r.
146 BL, Mss.Add.33983, 309r.
147 BL, Mss.Add.33983, 269r.
148 BL, Mss.Add.33983, 269v.
149 BL, Mss.Add.33983, 103v.

WOMEN AS POWER-BROKERS IN MADRID AND THE 1571 ORDINANCES

Justice-seeking vassals aggressively sought to exploit patrimonial ties of friendship and dependency with ministers. The wives and other relatives of officials now gained considerable status within Madrid's milieu. Their growing influence would generate a scandal that would play a substantial role in the Council's most fundamental reforms.

Vassals who wisely studied up on the names of ministers' female family members would have started with remembering doña María de Luna, wife of council president Vásquez himself. According to one witness, vassals could influence Vásquez through doña María de Luna's dependent (*criada*) María de Lizcano, a "very public and very notorious ... route" to a positive outcome. Subjects could also directly approach doña María de Luna, who often picnicked in the royal gardens. She and licenciate Juan Briviesca de Muñatones' daughter were frequently visible from the city's windows, publicly seeking "great friendship" with Indies vassals.[150] Those who preferred their shoes clean could also meet doña María by the cathedral door after evening Mass.

There were other routes of access to these influential brokers. Licenciate Barrionuevo's wife could apparently facilitate connections to doña María de Lizcano. One witness heard rumors that subjects could give Lorenzo Vaca's sister money to "negotiate well."[151] One could also seek doña María de Luna out through her brother. According to Lima High Court attorney Licenciate Cristóbal Ramírez de Cartagena, the wife of Minister Alonso Muñoz, doña Catalina de Otálora, provided intercession for subjects seeking to "soften the condition" of her insufferable husband. Word in Seville and Madrid was that she could also sway other ministers too. Doña Catalina apparently traveled to Burgos and conducted unspecified Indies-related "business" there, perhaps in one of the gardens that certain ministers fancied for gambling with Indies vassals.[152]

Investigator Ovando's witnesses painted a picture of an institution gripped by an integrity crisis that enabled well-connected women to rule the Indies. Nonetheless, having concluded his investigation, Ovando did not fire ministers or subject them to major penalties. He appears to have fined several officials, but seemingly lacked hard evidence to substantiate

[150] BL, Mss.Add.33983, 278r–279r. [151] BL, Mss.Add.33983, 190r.
[152] These were Ministers Vázquez and Aguilera.

most allegations. Moreover, since many ministers were on the verge of retirement, he refrained from prosecuting them, instead turning his attention to reforming the council's next generation of officials.[153]

When Ovando assumed the presidency on August 28, 1571, he introduced additional rules to prevent influential women and others from adulterating the ruled–ruler bond. He and his new ministers drafted the *Ordenanzas reales del Consejo de las Indias*, which the king ratified on September 24, 1571.[154] These again barred gift-giving and ministers' favoritism toward their families, friends, associates, and dependents, including women. The 1571 ordinances would not be dead letters during President Ovando's lifetime, and no documents suggest that women influenced ministers until the mid-1580s despite constant royal vigilance.

SURVEILLING THE COUNCIL, 1574–1589

Madrid's structural challenges remained despite these major reforms. The capital only became more crowded with justice-seekers desperate for favorable outcomes. Crown officials soon began to fear that many temporary and permanent residents had begun shedding their Christian values as they left their hometowns for the court. In response, the king, his firebrand confessor Friar Diego de Chávez, his secretaries, and his closest advisers repeatedly gathered into a special committee to combat moral decline: the Junta de Reformación or Junta of Reformation.[155]

Junta members viewed their moral mission as central to the empire's affairs.[156] The committee first convened on October 11, 1574, dispatching investigators, especially priests and field justices (*corregidores*), to uncover wrongdoings throughout Madrid. They reported that the city was indeed infested with sin. One testimony suggested that the "liberties of women" in the palace had become a problem.[157] Indeed, the junta's late 1570s and 1580s findings frequently alleged women's political corruption of the republic through their illicit dealings with ministers.[158] By the late

[153] BL, Mss.Add.33983, 103v. For fines, Macías Rosendo, *Correspondencia*, 56; Schäfer, *Consejo* 333–339.

[154] Schäfer, *Consejo*, 136, says the ordinances' original copies have disappeared. For a 1585 printed version, see BNE, Mss.3035, 19r–37v.

[155] Ezquerra Revilla, "Reforma," 1998; "Junta," 268; BL, Mss.Add.28340, 270r, August 28, 1577.

[156] BL, Mss.Add.28340, 270r, August 28, 1577. [157] HSA, 5/III/2.

[158] For a 1577 report regarding a Granada high judge, see BL, Mss.Add.28340, 224r–233r.

1580s, the junta's scrutiny aimed squarely at women's patrimonial ties to ministers.[159]

During the mid-1580s' context of increasing scrutiny of court women, high-ranking royal officials found further wrongdoing within the council. An undated, anonymous petition from sometime around or before 1584 warned the king that in the court certain "friends of gifts ... [had] the proverb that it is not serving your Majesty that is important, but the Council of the Indies." He further alerted that the council was gripped by "the merchants of favor" and had therefore ceased to listen to the less fortunate; after all, ministers "are called *oidores* [listeners] so that the great and small, the rich and poor, the healthy and the sick" could all receive justice.[160] Perhaps this report alarmed the junta. In 1585 council president Hernando de Vega cryptically told the king that he must uphold "the Ordinances that Your Majesty has made for this Council after the audit of President Juan de Ovando," and which demanded ministers "be clean" ("fuesen limpios"), especially when making ecclesiastical appointments.[161] It was perhaps in this context that the council first printed the 1571 ordinances in 1585.

In 1586 the king appointed Francisco de Villafañe, a trustworthy minister of the Council of Castile and the Chamber, to investigate Indies ministers' wrongdoing.[162] Villafañe's inquiry proceeded from mid-1586 to early 1587.[163] His work responded partly to a major political crisis in the relatively backwater Indies province of New Granada. In 1578 the Council of the Indies had ordered that Licenciate Fernando de Monzón investigate the New Granada High Court. Monzón stirred major controversy by alleging more than 1,000 different abuses by the judges and president. A former Council of the Indies attorney, Pedro Zorrilla, worsened matters by imprisoning Monzón. Alarmed, council officials sent another investigator, who ordered all involved back to Madrid to stand trial.[164]

[159] HSA, 7/II/25; see also HSA, 7/II/26; HSA, 7/II/28R; HSA, 7/II/30.

[160] HSA, 9/I/13, no date. This document must be from spring 1584 or earlier, for it mentions Minister Henao, who died in March that year; see Schäfer, *Consejo*, 1, 338.

[161] IVDJ, CA, E.23, C.36–373. [162] BL, Mss.Add.28346, 337r–338v.

[163] Villafañe was bedridden with gout by early 1586, which may explain why his investigation only began later in 1586; see IVDJ, CA, E.23, C.36–319.

[164] Gálvez Piñal, 13n26; Mayorga García, 168–185. Zorrilla accused Monzón of, among other things, inciting rebellion, marrying his daughter to a local, and illegally importing merchandise.

The New Granada judges, desperate and wealthy, developed a reputation in Madrid as particularly unscrupulous in their dealings with the council. By early 1586, Secretary Vázquez and President Vega y Fonseca already regarded them as *indiano* troublemakers; Vázquez fretted that they were "most dangerous" and believed they wished to corrupt ministers.[165] Dire petitions to the king reinforced this fear. A member of the anti-Zorrilla party, Pedro Muñoz de Salazar, wrote a blistering tell-all. Minister Saabedra's ties to Zorrilla ran not only through his brother's wife's father but also through his own wife, who was Zorrilla's first cousin.[166] Salazar testified that the whole court, and its lettered men [*letrados*] are amazed and shocked, and those who see it can hardly believe ... the great favor which Licenciate Zorrilla has."[167]

Zorrilla's ally and codefendant Francisco de Velázquez, the secretary of the New Granada High Court, also appeared to be befriending women in several testimonies. Monzón's secretary Luis de Mármol reported that he once headed to the Crown attorney's house to insist on the crimes of Velázquez and Zorrilla, but that the attorney's mother-in-law, doña María de Montoya, closed the case. The two defendants openly boasted of having befriended her. Monzón also suggested Velázquez had befriended and bribed doña Catalina de Montalvo de la Cárcel Bernardo y de Anaya, the wife of Minister Gedeón de Hinojosa. He had heard her tell Velázquez, "Gentleman ... have no shame, for I will promise to send you gratified to your home."

The former president of New Granada, don Lope de Armendariz, may have also had similar connections. Mármol suggested that Council of the Indies President Vega was a dependent of don Lope's wife, doña Juana de Saavedra. As a result, "Vega has shown himself very partial in defending those under investigation."[168] The council's exact rulings did not survive, but ministers did appear to favor the high judges over Monzón, fining the magistrates minor fees and the investigator the large sum of 4,000 ducats.[169] Other high-ranking Indies officials' long trials in Madrid also stirred fears of women's ability to illicitly sway ministers. Licenciate

[165] IVDJ, CA, E.23, C.36–294, C.36–296, C.36–297.

[166] IDVJ, CA, E.23, C.36–313. I have not found evidence of Saabedra's time in the council; it is possible he served in another council or junta.

[167] BFZ, CA, E.170–1, 48r

[168] BFZ, CA, E.170–1, 6r–7r, 15r–v, 21r, 34r, 48r. It is unclear which attorney they attempted to speak with because the council had several who died within months of each other in the 1580s; see Schäfer, *Consejo*, 350.

[169] Mayorga García, *Real audiencia*, 190–191.

Rodrigo Ribero, who had arrived in Santo Domingo in 1580 as an investigator, was back in Madrid by 1586, defending his excessively harsh actions. Two witnesses claimed Ribero was an "intimate friend" of minister Doctor Lope de Vayllo. Another recalled hearing Ribero boast he had bribed Doctor Lope's wife, doña Juana.[170]

While many subjects seeking women's intercession were litigants seeking to resolve litigation and investigations, privilege-seekers of various sorts also posed problems. One crucial intercessor seemed to have been Minister Hinojosa's wife, doña Catalina de Montalbo. One Juana Rodríguez was also crucial for obtaining privileges and licenses, especially with Minister Espadero.[171]

One witness implicated President Vega himself. Don Francisco de Valverde suggested that the blue-blooded doña Ángela de Tassis, daughter of Spain's chief postman, often traded vassals' bribes for interceding on her behalf before ministers in cases regarding important Indies ecclesiastical positions. Valverde suggested President Vega also committed many other offenses. A friar had told him Vega not only knew this, but also accepted bribes from "some little woman" nicknamed "Gradina the Weaver" (*la Texedora Gradina*) for an Indies office. Investigator Villafañe stated in his findings that, as the President of the Council of Finance, Vega had earned a reputation for receiving petitions from "loose and unmarried women in the royal courtyard," and at the helm of the Council of the Indies he even accepted their money. Villafañe summarized one witness's allegation about the president as "he is so given to women that he has lost his authority and credit."[172]

Villafañe's investigation was a partial failure. He produced 228 pages of witness testimonies, but Secretary Vázquez deemed his charges inconclusive.[173] The sovereign and his closest confidantes nonetheless took several measures. Vega asserted that former minister (and current president of the House of Trade) Hinojosa was "very thorough in cases in

[170] AGI, Indiferente 739, N.245. For the council's 1583 suspicion of his abuses, see AGI, Indiferente 1956, L.3, 200v–201v. See also BFZ, CA, E.170–1, 2r and 53v–54r. Lugo provided a general overview of Ribera's investigation; see *Edad media*, 47, 54–55, 79, 98, 214, 224–229.

[171] BFZ, CA, E.170–1, 5v, 11r, 12r, 13v, 33r. As Sebastián de Covarrubias defined the term, "we call *amo* to the lord whom we serve, because he feeds us . . . and *ama* to the lady, and so the terms *amo* and *moço* [youth] are correlative": Covarrubias Orozco, *Tesoro*, 62. It is also possible this was a euphemism for "lover."

[172] Salazar Mir, *Expedientes*, 79; For Gradina, BFZ, CA, E.170–1, 59r; for Vega, BFZ, CA, E.170–49.

[173] IVDJ, CA, E.25, C.40–263.

which his wife is not biased [*aficionada*] or captivated [*prendada*] – of this I have heard somewhat bad talk."[174] The king promoted him to the Council of Castile in 1594, separating him from Indies affairs.[175] The monarch also chastised Minister Espadero, who responded with a groveling letter defending his actions. He claimed to have worked "free and clean," treating vassals with "equality." Though the council was constantly assailed by vassals' gifts, he had shown "resistance."[176]

Throughout 1586 and 1587, the Junta of Reformation worked alongside Investigator Villafañe to uncover further illicit dealings. On May 24, 1586, President Vega reported that another minister was allowing earthly enjoyments to interfere with his work.[177] This was Minister Antonio González, who was to experience considerable Crown scrutiny until his demotion in 1589. He had a checkered past. While Guatemala's president, an investigator banned him from Indies officeholding and fined him more than 2,500 ducats. President Vega lamented that though González was a "talented jurist" he nonetheless had many flaws.[178] González spent time in "monasteries of nuns and especially in the Franciscan [convent of] the Conception." Minister González apologized to Confessor Chávez, promising to no longer attend comedies or cavort with court women.[179]

After Investigator Villafañe's inconclusive findings, the king's inner clique selected a more assertive figure, the Archbishop of Mexico, Pedro Moya de Contreras, to conduct yet another examination of the council. The archbishop had resided in Spain since 1587, after undertaking a major investigation of the viceroy of Mexico.[180] By 1588, he was secretly investigating the council. That year, President Vega hinted to Secretary Vázquez that yet another scandal was brewing. He and Investigator Contreras were probing what Vega called "the greatest disturbance, the greatest outrage, the greatest injustice, anyone has ever heard of in a court case."[181] The scene was a major trial over the Duchy of Veragua, a patrimonial holding of the Columbus dynasty in Panama. When the Duchy's last heir died in 1578, a fierce legal struggle began.[182] The case went to the council and became one of its most expensive and convoluted trials ever. When one litigant, the admiral of Aragón, died, his sister, the

174 BL, Mss.Add.28349, 141v. 175 Schäfer 1:338; IVDJ, CA, E.23, C.36–396.

176 IDVJ, CA, Envío 25, Caja 40–266. 177 HSA, 7/II/22RB.

178 IVDJ, CA, E.23, C.36–447. 179 HSA, 7/II/29 180 Poole, *Pedro*, 125–134.

181 BL, Mss.Add.28349, 142r.

182 Veragua was part of what is today Western Panama. For the context of this conflict, see Martínez Cutillas, *Veragua*, 442, 474–96, 511–15; BNE, *Por Doña Iuana Colon*, Porcones 833(19).

third Marchioness of Guadalest, doña María Ruiz de Liori Colón y Cardona, picked up his case in 1583. In 1584, and again in 1586, the council ruled in the marchioness's favor, but her opponents appealed and the trial dragged on.[183]

What happened next triggered a remarkably bold act of infiltration by an elite woman into the council's decision-making process. Witnesses alleged the marchioness groomed at least two of the council's *relatores* (court reporters) to sway the case in her favor, along with two ministers. One witness claimed she paid a middleman the enormous sum of 16,000 ducats to sway Relator Villarroel.[184] Indeed, Villaroel had formerly been the marchioness's lawyer – a clear violation of council ordinances.[185] Another *relator*, Doctor Salvador Núñez Morquecho, was also swept up in the investigation. One litigant, don Baltasar Colón, discovered that Núñez was deliberately misrepresenting the arguments of the marchioness's opponents before the council in order to disqualify their strongest arguments. Colón noted Núñez's summaries were different "in more than twenty ways . . . all against this witness and the other claimants and in favor of the Marchioness."[186] There can be little doubt that she and her lawyers were aware of the illegality of these actions.

Minister González and Minister Espadero also played a central part in boosting the marchioness's chances. González had apparently forced a dying minister to sign a favorable sentence for an unspecified litigant in the case in 1587.[187] On July 12, 1589, Vega warned the king of González's terrible reputation. He was still involved in "perditions of all sorts," and "it would please me in every extreme to see him out of the Council." Ultimately, the marchioness failed to secure the Duchy of Veragua, having spent many years in court and a massive fortune for naught.[188]

183 RBPR, XIV/2995, "Memorial del pleyto," 1497–1584; RBPR, XVI/3015, "Memorial del pleyto," 1506–1607, 93r–v/56r–v.

184 I have not been able to find information about Juan or his wife. Moreover, Villarroel's first name has proven elusive. Schäfer suggests he departed to the Council of Castile in 1585, but was still overseeing the Veragua case; see Schäfer, *Consejo*, 358.

185 HSA, B2883, 15r–17r.

186 HSA, B2883, 42r–48r. In 1590 don Baltasar printed a tract, the *Demanda y oposición*, which insisted "Relator Villarroel, and Relator Núñez. . . fooled the said council, giving a false account of the proceedings, and producing false summaries"; BNE, *Demanda y oposición*, 30r.

187 BL, Mss.Add.28349, 142r–v. The dying minister was one Valcázar.

188 BL, Mss.Add.28349, 107r, 142r–v, 147v. The Marchionesse died childless in 1591. The lawsuit raged on until the Count of Gelves triumphed, at least temporarily, in 1605: see RBPR, XVI/3015, "Memorial del pleyto," 1506–1607.

Investigator Moya's findings are unclear.[189] His charges and penalties against the *relatores* are missing. Núñez did not lose his job, and in the 1590s he was the *relator* for the Junta of Puerto Rico, an important royal military committee.[190] Minister Espadero died in early 1589. The king demoted the disgraced González to the presidency of New Granada.[191]

INDIES WEALTH, INDIGENOUS GOLD, AND GENDERED ANXIETIES IN THE COURT

From the 1540s to the 1580s, one of the Crown officials' overarching fears was the flourishing culture of gift-giving for favorable outcomes. These concerns extended far beyond the Council of the Indies. A 1582 report to the Junta of Reformation by Doctor Villagómez mayor of the court of Navarre, offered an extended diagnosis of this evil. Vassals spent "billions of ducats ... sending to the court many and very curious presents to persons who were close to the royal [court] of Your Majesty and their women." Madrid was nothing but "tyranny and robbery and infernal negotiations." Indeed, this was the "principle cause of all the bad government of Spain, and in all the states of Your Majesty." Villagómez pleaded that the king investigate "how many mules loaded with presents and gifts enter every day in the court, and where they come from, and who sends them to whom."[192]

Important women were again key in these networks. Villagómez suggested that the trail would lead to "the houses of the most principal dependents and ministers of Your Majesty and secretaries ... look at their jewels and gold and silver and tapestries ... that they have, they, and their women." The mayor suggested a radical solution: banning all gift exchange in the capital. Officials should lose their jobs should they accept even the smallest present. Ministers' "wives and children and family members and dependents" were to follow the same rules, only deviating with special written permission from the king.[193]

Villagómez's preoccupations repeatedly underscored the gendered relationship between women and gift-giving. Indeed, many throughout Europe considered gift-giving and gift-receiving to have female or effeminate connotations.[194] Some even suggested that men could become

[189] Poole, *Pedro*, 262. [190] AGI, Indiferente 426, L.28, 103r.
[191] Schäfer, *Consejo*, 338. [192] BL, Mss.Add.28343, 241r–243r.
[193] BL, Mss.Add.28343, 241r–243r. [194] Zemon Davis, *Gift*, 210–211.

effeminized and sexually debased if they opened the doors to bribes. For instance, witness Licenciate Ramírez informed Investigator Ovando in 1567 that one Peruvian vassal boasted how his gifts turned the Council of the Indies' ministers into putative prostitutes and homosexuals, saying "all that was left for him was to sleep with the [ministers] … he swore to God that if he wished, he could marry anyone in the Council."[195] For Villagómez, patrimonialist wrongdoing revealed the character of a man to be vain and weak and therefore effeminate and ignoble.

This disorder afflicted the entire court, not just the Council of the Indies, Villagómez warned. He and other moralists described court women as very inclined toward wealth and material luxury – and the court had plenty of treasure to go around.[196] The Indies had peculiar characteristics, however, which made these illicit exchanges especially problematic. The three sixteenth-century investigations into council ministers' conduct revealed royal administrators' constant preoccupation with bribery, especially involving Indies wealth. This bribery took on an additional patrimonial touch, for when officials accepted gift from others they became their dependents. Would the royal administration allow vassals to overpower ministers? Would New World commodities allow elites to destroy the Indians and the royal conscience, or could its ministers steel themselves against temptation and adhere to their official responsibilities?

Scholars have noted that the Indies' abundant and often-peculiar commodities played a part in creating widespread anxieties about increasing moral laxity in the late sixteenth century.[197] Vassals may have preferred to bribe women in officials' circles, exchanging influence disguised as innocent gifts. They could mask these transactions as innocent acts of kindness and magnanimity and conceal the size of their bribes by gifting items of exceptional novelty and exquisite craft.

Gift-giving practices, including opulent works by Indigenous craftsmen, had deep roots during the heavily patrimonial early phase of Indies rule. Cortés' 1528 attempts to woo Secretary Cobos' sister-in-law doña Francisca included Indian-made offerings for the entire household, including "many treasures of gold … to all those ladies … crests of green feathers full of silverwork and gold and pearls."[198] In the 1540s,

[195] BL, Mss.Add.33983, 69v. [196] Vives, "Estructura administrativa," 160.

[197] Warsh, *American Baroque*, 11, 173; Vilches, *New World*, 17, 261, 292; Martínez Vega and Pérez Baltasar, *Madrid*, 142; Bridikhina, *Theatrum*, 283.

[198] Díaz del Castillo, *Historia*, 725.

Minister Beltrán lost his position partly because of emeralds that one vassal gave his wife's cousin. Emperor Charles suspected his own secretary's wife, doña María de Mendoza, of accepting gifts, which the governor of Peru confirmed when he instructed his wife to pass her certain Peruvian "gold alloy items."[199] The governor listed valuables worth more than 5,800 pesos, many likely destined for council ministers and other officials: gold ingots, a saltshaker, fine gold and turquoise necklaces, small emeralds, and gold and silver chalices, including one "of fine gold, made by Indians."[200]

In the late 1560s, witnesses told Investigator Ovando that Minister Muñoz's wife, doña Catalina de Otálora, treasured such fine gold products, likely from the Indies and made by Indigenous craftsmen. Ramírez had heard from one Alonso Castellón that her support had cost him a golden parrot, a barrel of anchovies in escabeche, and "certain moneys." Lima's chief postman, don Diego de Carvajal, also alleged that the same Castellón slipped doña Catalina a "golden parrot."[201] A witness mentioned a rumor that doña Catalina accepted payments in gold and fine handkerchiefs.[202]

Investigator Villafañe discovered a similar pattern in the mid-1580s. Peru's former viceroy, don Francisco de Toledo, under investigation at the court, allegedly had an agent attempt to pass a gold chain to his niece, Marchioness of Villena doña Juana Lucas de Toledo.[203] She was to use this to persuade Assistant Secretary Pedro de Ledesma for a favorable outcome.[204] Licenciate Ribero allegedly tried the same tactic. Witness Francisco Marmolejo stated that Ribero told him he secured his position as investigator thanks to Minister Vayllo's wife and planned to repay her with a superb silver reliquary made in Santo Domingo. Marmolejo could not confirm whether she received this gift. However, he had seen Minister

[199] AHNM, Diversos-Colecciones 22, N.43. and Lockhart and Otte, 175.

[200] Ministerio de Fomento, *Cartas*, 502–503.

[201] BL, Mss.Add.33983, 103v, 268r.

[202] Ramírez overheard in the palace courtyard that doña Catalina helped House of Trade scribe Christoval de Santistevan, who sought a positive ruling against a rival British plaintiff; Santistevan had promised her "as many reales as he could muster." Ramírez also heard that one don Eugenio de Palta had boasted about "the friendship that he had with the abovementioned doña Catalina," noting that she met often with him and Pedro de Casadevante, of Honduras, who sought a royal office in Veracruz. Casadevante was hoping to win doña Catalina over with embroidered handkerchiefs: see BL, Mss. Add.33983, 103v–104r.

[203] Ávila, *Collected Letters*, 1:509n14.

[204] IVDJ, CA, E.23, C.36–498, 113v. Ledesma became a salaried official in 1596: see Schäfer, *Consejo*, 353.

Vayllo's daughter wearing an opulent strand of pearls, which he claimed he saw in Ribero's possession.[205]

Guatemala high judge García de Valverde, in Madrid defending himself after his turbulent tenure, was also reportedly part of the capital's gift exchange. Witness don Diego de Guzmán claimed Valverde commissioned a magnificent silver platter and saltshakers for Minister Espadero. Guzmán was unsure whether Valverde passed this gift on, but noted that when Espadero traveled to Cáceres, Valverde's wife suspiciously left Seville to meet him there. Another witness reported that Juana Rodríguez, connected to Espadero, helped a captain receive the position of *corregidor* (field justice) in Peru in exchange for a large golden saltshaker. Yet another suggested that Minister Hinojosa's wife repeatedly sought out gold, gems, and emeralds from High Judge Zorrilla and Francisco de Velázquez, unbeknownst to Minister Hinojosa. Muñoz also complained of this case, calling the gifts "the greatest bribes in the world."[206]

A conspicuous number of the gifts which witnesses alleged passed from Indies vassals' hands to ministers and their female family members were of Indigenous make. Only on rare occasions did these offerings appear to be simply minerals and gemstones in species.[207] More often, these were Indigenous craftworks whose value seems to have derived from their exquisite beauty.

Here, the fingerprint of Indigenous artisan labor was crucial. Sixteenth-century Europeans greatly esteemed the aesthetic quality of Indies goldwork. Artisans' production varied from region to region, but usually required the proficiency and substantial effort of complex expert supply chains and workshops. Workers had to painstakingly extract mineral pellets from rivers and mountains. Other laborers smoothed stones into anvil-like surfaces. Metalworkers manufactured brass and copper hammers for flattening gold and silver (and other alloyed mixes), often achieving a near-perfect smoothness. Artisans created molds, covered these with beeswax and resin, and added a second mold segment to encase the wax. They then melted the wax, leaving a gap into which they would pour

[205] BFZ, CA, E.170–1, 3r–v.

[206] BFZ, CA, E.170–1, 39^{v}, 49^{r}–50^{r}, 62^{v}–65^{r}. Muñoz also suggested Velázquez had the council's favor because his sister was married to don Francisco Beltrán de Caizedo, a relative of Minister Gasca de Salazar; BFZ, CA, E.170–1, 45r.

[207] For one example of apparently unrefined gold "alloy' shipped to Spain, AHNM, Diversos-Colecciones 22, N.43. and Lockhart and Otte, 175.

molten alloys.[208] The golden bird figures, chalices, and other items, which were likely prized by Indigenous people as lordly ornaments, took on a new power when they circulated Madrid.

It was not primarily these objects' weight nor their karats which made them powerful. It was this refined handiwork which endeared them to gift-givers as ideal gendered objects for the women at court. For instance, Cortés' gifts of Mesoamerican featherwork headdresses decorated with gold and silver for the ladies of the court is a case in point. It did come with a twist, for in Mexica society such *tlahuiztli* crests were martial adornments for elite male warriors, or ritual insignia for priests, not curiosities for courtly women's enjoyment.[209] As with Madrid's Indigenous metallic products, it was extremely skilled artisans' work which transformed bird feathers into spectacular objects. The *amanteca* – male and female feather-workers – operated large workshops with hierarchical and gendered divisions of labor and occupied tribute-exempt status in Tenochtitlán.[210] Feathers adorned with valuable decorations had little value by themselves, but *amanteca* craftsmanship bestowed them with great aesthetic and social power in the courtly context.

RESISTING PASSION WITH "MASCULINE BREASTS": MINISTERS' GENDERED ETHOS

Among Madrid's officialdom, overcoming dazzling beauty presented only one part of a greater challenge of resisting social temptations in general. Officials were to have no room for greed (accepting gifts, gambling), lust (caving to women's beauty), anger (undue bias), and sloth (entertainment and laziness). Gambling, a problem in the Council during Doctor Beltrán's tenure which officials probably curbed after his 1542 dismissal, once again appeared in Ovando's late-1560s investigation as a major source of injustice.[211] Witnesses testified having seen Minister Santander angrily respond to subjects who sought to "interrupt" his enjoyments.[212] As we have seen, others claimed Licenciado Vázquez often allowed gambling to derail his duties.[213] The 1580s probes which Villafañe and Moya de Contreras undertook also found evidence of this illicit behavior. For

[208] Bray, "Gold-working."
[209] Olko, *Insignia*, Appendix: Table A.8, 109–132, 406–426.
[210] Castelló Yturbide, *Art*, 56–57
[211] Lorenzo Pinar, *Fiesta*, 157, footnote 3, and BL, Mss.Add.33983, 27r.
[212] BL, Mss.Add.33983, 50r.
[213] BL, Mss.Add.33983, 34v and 193r.

instance, in the late 1580s minister González spent "a great part of his day in gambling with priests and with women, and, they tell me, with Indies vassals [*indianos*] as well." These practices reinforced patrimonial administration by bringing nonofficials into a familial space of social and financial obligations. Gambling also encouraged bribery, for ministers who owed subjects money, like Licenciado Vázquez in the 1560s, might seek gifts to continue betting or favor petitioners to repay debts owed.[214]

Emotional mastery entailed more than rejecting "womanly" behaviors or refusing to gamble. Officials had to master their overly aggressive impulses more generally. Even when on their best behavior, they could violate Spanish norms of politesse important to the petition-and-response system when vassals approached them during and after their official hours. Officials were public figures and could expect to confront throngs of obsequious and even desperate vassals. Ovando's investigation frequently recorded complaints that ministers could become very rude, even abusive, toward these subjects. An acquaintance of Captain Gómez de Acosta stated that Minister Muñoz was so discourteous that he would not speak again with him for "one thousand ducats' pension."[215] Muñoz did indeed have quite the reputation for being short-tempered both inside and outside of his home; one witness stated that "everyone complains about his condition."[216] Another vassal told Ovando that Minister Francisco Ramírez de Alarcón said Vázquez was "an angry man, and a bigmouth [*hablador*]."[217]

Secretary Ochoa de Luyando was also prone to fits of rage. According to Licenciado Ramírez, the council procurator Juan de la Peña had approached the secretary to dispute a judicial ruling, informing him he would soon petition again. Luyando begged to differ, calling Peña a "knave." He swore to God he would punch Peña repeatedly in the face. The procurator supposedly responded, with great patience, "sir, here I have no need to respond," at which point Luyando physically forced him out of the council hallway into the courtyard.[218] Ramírez concluded dryly: Luyando was "somewhat harsh by condition."[219] The anonymous early 1584 report accused Ministers Henao, Gasca, and Espadero of having "ox tongues, uttering such cutting words" that vassals refused to petition them.[220] Curiously, during the 1580s investigations' witnesses did not emphasize ministers' difficulties controlling their anger, suggesting

[214] López de Gómara, 193v; BL, Mss.Add.33983, 104r. [215] BL, Mss.Add.33983, 177r.
[216] BL, Mss.Add.33983, 98r. [217] AGI, Guadalajara 5, R.13, N.23, 12r.
[218] BL, Mss.Add.33983, 109r. [219] BL, Mss.Add.33983, 109r. [220] HSA, 9/I/13.

that perhaps Ovando's postinvestigation reforms had indeed created a more measured office culture in the council.

Before the 1570s and 1580s, very few statements theorizing ministers' ethos seem to have reached the king's desk. Increasingly, officials in Madrid began circulating memorials detailing the values that the perfect official would possess to better navigate the opposite poles of palace patrimonialism and distance from vassals. These virtues included loyalty, organization, promptness, learnedness, experience, knowledgeability, secrecy, Christian rectitude, prudence, respectability, incorruptibility, impartiality, mastery over emotions, and approachability for justice-seekers.[221] Masculine steadfastness against the mighty was also important. An anonymous letter to Secretary Vázquez emphasized that the perfect president would be a "man who deals with the powerful with a masculine breast [*pecho varonil*] so that he can resist" the powerful.[222] Whereas many Spanish commentators urged noblemen to be knightly by pursuing martial valor, building a household of dependents, and rejecting the inertia of court life, officials were to become masculine by remaining inert, aloof, and detached from vassals. Only this way could they become morally strong and impartial – not unlike friars and churchmen.[223] These traits together undergirded a ministerial ethos of "public utility" where "public peace and royal authority" could reign.[224]

Royal officials' efforts to reduce passion and emphasize masculine impartiality, coming very often at the behest of vassals, posed a challenge to officials steeped in courtly patrimonialism. One anonymous letter, likely by a royal secretary, complained that he could no longer "go, deal, converse, gamble, stroll" without appearing suspect.[225] In 1584, Royal Secretary Jerónimo Gasol complained to his colleague Secretary Vázquez that, "Being a public minister [*ministro público*] I cannot close

[221] These values are also detailed by Antonio de Padilla y Meneses, President of the Council of Orders from 1572 to 1579 and later the President of the Council of the Indies from 1579 to 1580: BL, Mss.Add.28366, 117r–119v. For reflections on secrecy, see BL, Mss. Add.28381, 47r–57r, 70r–71r. On gravity and respectability, see reports discussing ministers' clothing from 1581 in BL, Mss.Add.28357, 392r–405v.

[222] BL, AM-28360, 202r–202v.

[223] Lehfeldt, "Ideal Men"; Armon, *Masculine Virtue*, 36.

[224] BL Mss.Add.28366, 117v, 118r.

[225] BL, Mss.Add.28362, 30r–31v (15 January 1584). He was likely a high-ranking official, indicated by his use of a rubric to sign his name; however, I have not been able to determine whose rubric this is.

the door to anyone, and being a man and not a stone I must have friends and entertainments, and I must rest and desire honor and reward."[226]

Officials seem to have embraced this ethos of masculine distance to a considerable extent. According to Janine Fayard, Spain's seventeenth- and eighteenth-century ministers were perhaps the most chaste of the monarchy's nonreligious officials. Though some likely continued to illicitly allow female influence, their dedication to controlling their sexual impulses, evidenced by their few legitimate and illegitimate children, and their tendency to marry late in life, suggest ministers took previous decades of admonitions to heart.[227]

Indeed, Ovando's research also turned up relatively or entirely positive accounts of ministers' behavior. Some favorable evaluations suggest longstanding good practices in the council. Don Diego de Santillán critiqued specific ministers, but noted that he "had not known or heard anything whatsoever that he holds as true" about the rest.[228] Others found ministers to be adequate or even excellent. Secretary Juan López de Velasco stated that he considered them "good Christians, well-intentioned in the service of God and of His Majesty and of good judgment and comprehension."[229] Licenciado Ramírez stated that President Tello de Sandoval had always struck him as "desirous of concerting the benefit of the service of God Our Lord and His Majesty."[230] Juan Augustín Osorio of Santo Domingo said he considered all ministers "to be good Christian men and zealous of the honor of God Our Lord and his Royal Majesty."[231] Bartolomé Vásquez of Panama found President Vásquez to be very courteous, and most other officials to be prompt and available.[232] He had a good experience with the secretary: "for me, he has always processed my papers well."[233] He even affirmed that the famously ornery Licenciado Muñoz was kind and available. Licenciado Muñatones similarly testified that for the most part he did not know "anything contrary to that [the ministers] conduct their offices as they should."[234] He praised minister Antonio de Aguilera as "a friend of justice and purity," minister Licenciado Fernando de Salas as upright, the lawyer Licenciado Hernando Pereira de Castro as "modest," and relator Licenciado

[226] BL, Mss.Add.28362, 38r–39v. For a copy see BL, Mss.Add.28345, 54r–v.
[227] Fayard, *Miembros*, 268–89.
[228] BL, Mss.Add.33983, 192r.
[229] BL, Mss.Add.33983, 294v.
[230] BL, Mss.Add.33983, 85r.
[231] BL, Mss.Add.33983, 293r.
[232] BL, Mss.Add.33983, 178r.
[233] BL, Mss.Add.33983, 178v.
[234] BL, Mss.Add.33983, 10r.

Santander as particularly careful and effective.[235] Almost all in the Guadalajara dossier agreed. High Judge Francisco Ramírez de Alarcón thought well of most, calling them "very saintly" and stressing their "great care in proveying and administering all the affairs touching upon the Indies."[236] Six other witnesses stated that they had not heard anything but good reports about council officials.[237]

WOMEN AND THE GENDERED PETITION-AND-RESPONSE SYSTEM

The 1570s and 1580s Junta of the Reformation made tangible strides in restricting women's influence over high officials. The committee not only investigated, scolded, fined, and sometimes demoted ministers, as demonstrated earlier; its officials also chastised and even exiled certain women. In September 1586, the Count of Barajas informed the king of his progress in "impeding that women go to negotiate with ministers."[238] He and Confessor Chávez had found five court women engaging in major wrongdoings and exiled one, but provided few specifics.[239] He warned cryptically that one doña Blanca had a powerful husband, and that "it would [do] much damage to the Republic" if she remained in Madrid, for "it could be possible that she would have all the governance and affairs at her command." He also expelled one doña Leonor. He did not reveal the nature of their wrongdoing or if this related to Indies affairs specifically. King Philip was pleased. He wrote, "This is good," before reflecting upon the importance that officials "be elderly and have a reputation of much honesty, for having to deal with so many women."

The count then directly raised an important issue that arose from this enforcement. What did the junta's measures mean for women seeking legitimate access to royal justice? Surely, to exclude them would be a new injustice. Confessor Chávez's report informed the count that certain exiled women had complained that ministers "did not hear them well" and that these women defended their illicit efforts as symptoms of

[235] BL, Mss.Add.33983, 107v–108r, 109v. For Pereira's appointment see AGI, Indiferente 741, N.262.

[236] BL, Mss.Add.33983, 12r–v.

[237] AGI, Guadalajara 5, R.13, N.23, 29v–58r.

[238] HSA, 7/II/30.

[239] These were doña Juana de Zarate, doña Juana de Arteaga, and two whom he identified only by their first names, Ysabel and Sylvia. The latter was probably Leonor de Sylva, whom he mentioned on the following page.

a system biased against them. These women had taken illegal actions out of desperation. The king, who rarely commented on issues at length, provided an unusually elaborate solution. Ministers were to discourage women with families from petitioning, while providing special attention to those without. He suspected that many women used their feminine powers of persuasion on ministers to further the interests of their male family and friends. As for "the widows and others who have no one to speak for them, it would not be fair" for royal justice to deny them. Women with families would approach ministers only through their male kin via formal written supplications. Widows and orphans would petition without hindrance. No concrete legislation came of the king's proposed solution, but his sentiment nonetheless suggests the extent of royal hostility to court women's influence.

Women did maintain several licit channels through which they could impact the council's operations and decision-making. The first pathway was through patrimonial ties to the ruling house. Queens and regents would continue to have great say in royal governance in subsequent centuries.[240] This applied, naturally, only to a select few. The second was through petitions and lawsuits. Aristocratic women very often requested privileges from the sovereign and litigated as representatives of their dynasties' estates; they remained "some of the most influential women in Europe."[241] Irene Olivares has estimated that some 6 percent of petitions during the reigns of Philip II to Philip IV were submitted by women.[242] She did not determine how many sought to change administrative policy, though my own research suggests this was exceedingly rare.[243] Most nonaristocratic and lower-aristocratic women requested pensions, largely based on their male family members' deeds. Others, especially Indian, part-Indian, and Spanish women, often pursued court case resolutions.[244] While litigation only produced one-off sentences that did not form precedent, petitions of privilege and administrative reform could shape policy for centuries, meaning women sometimes prompted important imperial decisions through licit means. By the 1580s and 1590s, their opportunities to shape royal decisions were nonetheless narrower than before, for well-connected women had largely lost much of their ability to illicitly sway ministers' major determinations.

[240] Mitchell, *Queen*. [241] Coolidge, *Guardianship*, 8, 119–39.
[242] Olivares, "Politics," 76. [243] Masters, "Invisible Architects," 378, 392–393.
[244] For instance, Van Deusen, *Global Indios*.

CONCLUSIONS

The Habsburgs, Europe's greatest kinship network and a sprawling dynastic imperial family, paradoxically did not assent to the patrimonialism of officials' decision-making process. Busy monarchs empowered ministers to act as instruments of rule, only to discover through vassals' complaints and lawsuits that these officials were adulterating the ruled–ruler dialogue. Whistleblowers repeatedly warned that, unbeknownst to the kings, their ministers were usurping the patrimonial prerogatives of the Habsburgs – and powerful women were central actors in this wrongdoing.

The early years of Indies legislation were dominated by a clique of virtually all-powerful courtiers and ministers. However, King Charles V's 1520s post-revolt reforms gradually distanced vassals from the empire's legislators. By the 1550s, the council petition-and-response system ran through quite clear administrative channels, having at least theoretically removed most direct, interpersonal connections between subjects and the ministers. This Crown–vassal divide was detrimental to rich and powerful subjects who wished to influence legislation by befriending the monarchs, their courtiers, and ministers. For ordinary and marginal vassals who would have to conduct business through writing, this social and physical remoteness played a leveling role against Indies elites and seeded the petition-and-response system with a degree of equity. Ministers who sought to breach this distance and receive conquistadors' gifts met with the king's investigations in 1541–1542 and 1567–1571; the New Laws and the 1571 ordinances, as well as an increasingly explicit emerging ethos of ministerial masculinity, served to safeguard the volitions of vassals and rulers alike.

The major shift in the decision-making process was not created only by kings and their counselors. This chapter has also shown that the cocreators of the *gobierno* petition-and-response system and the council itself involved a multiplicity of actants. Women – elite brides-to-be, cousins, sisters, and wives – played an outsized part. So did nuns, commoners, and widows. Most appeared in audits when they sought to bribe ministers, but some – like the notable doña Mencía – played the role of whistleblower at a crucial moment in Indies history and ultimately set into motion the sweeping reforms of the New Laws. Male courtiers, treatise-writers, and ministers also played key roles either as model officials or all-too-human seekers of pleasure and power. The dazzling beauty of Indies pearls, silver, and gold – especially fine crafts made by Indigenous artisans – also incited passions and lubricated illicit dealings.

These actors subtly but fundamentally, wittingly and unwittingly, shaped Europe's first institution of overseas administration. The end result was not only a less-elite dominated petition-and-response system, but a quite robust legal fiction of good government. With ministers distanced from vassals, they could at last act as mere instruments for helping their own socially withdrawn king reach his decisions. The collective, multiactant defeat of ministers' volitions impacted subjects' understandings of their ruler – as a single man with the ability to rule the world through dialogue with his subjects and with the help of the good, pure advice of his sage advisers. Philip had become the *Rey Prudente*: the Prudent King.

4

Lawmaking in a Portable Council

Gobierno *Decision-Making Technologies Before 1561*

Had Pedro Rengifo reached the court in the 1530s instead of the 1580s, he would have faced substantial challenges in pressing the case of the 10,000 mestizos *of Peru. Before the 1560s, the council was perpetually on the move, following itinerant monarchs through Spain and Europe. Pedro could have scarcely afforded to travel for years on end. The monarchs' travels were so difficult to keep pace with that they paradoxically reduced nonelite vassals' ability to co-opt the petitioning process. Pedro would have likely resorted instead to sending a barrage of letters from Peru or would have contracted a court procurator instead. Moreover, ministers would have also dealt with his case differently. Whereas in the 1580s council subalterns compared his dossier to their archive of decrees and other documents, this institution hardly had the ability to effectively utilize its papers before the 1560s. Nonetheless, before the 1560s its ministers were developing a series of decision-making technologies which might have steered Pedro's case in one direction or the other, not relying so much on archival sources as in the 1580s, but on ministers' rather nebulous guiding principles.*

Once ministers had collected petitions, it was time for them to scrutinize them and consider which ones they would recommend that the monarch ratify. Now royal officials confronted a major informational challenge. How to sort the just petitions from the unjust, the false from the true, the prudent from the imprudent? By the end of Emperor Charles V's reign, the Council of the Indies was likely sixteenth-century's Europe's greatest single collector of world knowledge. Later observers would note in awe that "the globe of affairs and documents which this council oversees, and the materials it deals with and grasps, is so great, and so universal."[1] In spite of the council's transcendental importance within the history of knowledge and governance, scholars of knowledge and governance have overwhelmingly ignored this institution as well as how its officials made use of information.

In a radically different approach, a smaller specialist historiography on Indies society and administration has generally depicted imperial knowledge as an extension of top-down power and control – as if the Crown's uses of information were self-evident and effortless. In the process, the specialist historiography has argued that *colonial knowledge equals colonial power*. Recently, Arndt Brendecke has sharply undermined this formula, especially the simplistic postcolonial mantra linking "the production of knowledge about the colony with the generation of colonial power."[2] He has established that the relationship between information and overseas mastery was never simple or linear. Indeed, the council's 1570s quest for total knowledge (*noticia entera*) was thwarted by the "communicative penetrability of the court" – that is, by ministers' embeddedness in their social milieus and by the heavily biased bottom-up initiatives from distant peripheries which vassals constantly pressed upon the council.[3] Interests and knowledge were inextricable and mutually reinforcing. He concludes that while the council achieved its primary goal of fostering loyalty-building communication with royal vassals and amassed a mountain of information in the process, this pile of documents "rendered a dubious service" to the Crown's capacity to achieve New World domination through knowledge.[4] Paradoxically, the world's premier repository of Indies knowledge could not make effective use of its colossal holdings.

Throughout this book, I have argued that the empire was held together by the legal fiction of vassal–lord dialogue, in which the monarch and his officials played a more passive role than most historians have assumed. In this formulation, during the early postconquest decades it was not knowledge but conversation which created the social consent necessary to legitimate Habsburg rule. The almost total lack of actual face-to-face subject–ruler interactions and interpersonal relations between vassals and ministers paradoxically increased the Crown's capacity to

[1] BNE, Mss.7677. [2] Brendecke, *Empirical Empire*, 9, 14.
[3] Brendecke, *Empirical Empire*, 275, see also 6–7.
[4] Brendecke, *Empirical Empire*, 281; see also 286.

communicate with Indies subjects. Vassal–lord dialogue by paper ceremonial was faster for ministers to process and better included those from the geographical and social periphery.

However, communication was a double-edged sword for the king and his ministers. This presented a great imperial paradox: paper enabled dialogue, which created both legitimacy (and power) while also creating a counterproductive information overload. On the one hand, ministers were generally in a terrible position to make informed decisions. On the other hand, they often could not even keep track of the kings' past determinations.

A heap of decrees soon towered over the empire. While a ruler's precedent was not strictly binding since his new volition superseded any past decisions, vassals could become quite distressed if the monarch reneged on his promises or challenged his own decisions. Contemporaries noted this often-incoherent proliferation of royal decisions. One priest wrote in 1614 that the result of ministers' "infinitely" busy processing of *gobierno* petitions had produced deep "contradiction" within its many decrees.[5] The historian of the council, don Antonio de León Pinelo, stated in 1658 that his and other officials' efforts to tame 650 decree registers into a 9-volume book was slowed down badly by this problem. For more than two decades, he, the famous jurist Juan de Solórzano y Pereira, and others had wrestled to harmonize 600 highly incongruous fundamental decrees at odds with other edicts – somewhere under 10 percent of the total of fundamental edicts they had selected for inclusion in the *Recopilación*.[6] The liberal reformer José Servando Teresa de Mier declared in the early nineteenth century that this legislative phase had produced a "jungle ... of many decrees absurd, extremely jarring, contradictory."[7]

This and the following chapter ask three questions. First, how did ministers make *gobierno* decisions? Second, how did technologies assist these ministers' resolutions and change vassals' ability to propose reforms and new policies? And third, how did the evolution of ministers' social contexts and decision-making criteria incorporate new actants in the lawmaking process? These two chapters are divided to reflect a major cleavage between decision-making before and after 1561. This chapter explores the decision-making process within its portable context – a circumstance in

[5] BNE, MS.2825 2r–3r and Ordoñez de Zevallos, *Historia*, 429v–430r.
[6] AGI, Indiferente 1651, "Informe del Licenciado," October 15, 1658.
[7] Servando Teresa de Mier, *Escritos*, 282.

which ministers traded communication for coherence. From town to town, Spanish imperial councils wove their way through Europe within Charles V's massive mule-and-ox-driven wagon train. A document issued circa 1535 hinted at the scale of this operation: the president of the council alone required twelve wagons and twelve beasts of burden to move his official archives and possessions; each of his ministers received four.[8] An undated document (circa the 1550s or 1560s) referring to travel within Spain stated that "in years in which the court moves, six wagons are needed to move the lawsuits and books and other writings relating to His Majesty."[9] In contrast, between 1561 and 1598 – the year of King Philip II's death – the court received permanent offices in Madrid, which enabled a series of transformations in ministers' praxes in which new archival and social technologies enabled a greater consistency of decision-making, costing vassals a degree of influence over decrees.

These two chapters thus study ministers' and subalterns' everyday practices, their decision-making technologies, and their social milieus. In the process, they trace a slow but unmistakable shift from the monarchs' dialogue-heavy approach to a more moderate balance between communication and decision-making consistency. This interpretation provides a different group of causal explanations than the most careful and sophisticated theory on kings' and ministers' shifting approaches to lawmaking. Victor Tao Anzoátegui famously posited a legal dichotomy of case-based versus systematic legislation; sixteenth-century decrees responded to highly concrete cases, often presented to officials via petitions. Only by the eighteenth century, Tao Anzoátegui argues, did case-based legislation fade and did system triumph, with Crown officials making decisions according to a consistent, inflexible legal framework.[10] Anzoátegui further argues that the shift from case-based to system-based decision-making was largely an outcome of Enlightenment thinking.[11] Here, I offer another interpretation: at least from the perspective of Crown officials, who were not proper casuists, the division was not casuistry versus system, but passive dialogue versus increasing royal assertiveness and consistency. Moreover, the currents which influenced this growing systematicity were not Enlightenment ones, but rather were sixteenth-century officials' pragmatic responses to the frustrating experiences borne from the petition-and-response system itself.

[8] BNE, Mss.904, "Papeles referentes," 262r. [9] AGI, Patronato 171, N.1, R.4.
[10] Tao Anzoátegui, *Casuismo*, 336–339 [11] Tao Anzoátegui, *Poder*, 120.

BETWEEN ACTIVE AND PASSIVE REASONING: SATISFICING, LEGAL FACTS, AND DESCRIPTIVE FACTS

To explain inconsistent *gobierno* decrees we must not treat them as the rulings of a self-avowedly casuistic magistracy. Rather, these edicts were the products of a small collective of patrimonial-bureaucratic rulers and officials who not only sought constant dialogue but were working under badly subpar informational and social circumstances. Latour argued that French counselors within the Conseil d'État created law through a "collective process of review – with its revision, discussion, conclusion and deliberation" which provided a means "of kneading and of cracking a file."[12] He likened these discussions – deeply steeped in French legislative tomes, to "burners of great industrial furnaces" which could blast a dossier through "violent and continuous agitation" into a legal determination.[13] It was not the mythical omniscience of lawmakers but this deeply human, agonistic, and labor-intensive process, built from debates and a "palace of laws and mountain of paper," which transformed the conseil's dossiers into its laws.[14] However, the Council of the Indies had very different decision-making technologies and visions of rule. On the one hand, the king's volition was unbound by precedent. On the other, there was scarcely any normative or factual context to guide the reasoning of council ministers to begin with. Ministers and monarchs alike groped their way through the dark as they attempted to find a balance between passive and active postures.

Throughout the entire sixteenth century (and well beyond) ministers and monarchs settled for a decision-making method useful in information-poor situations which social scientists today call "satisficing."[15] Each petition, be it about a miniscule case or a major reform, posed major moral and evidentiary problems. Ministers, lacking time and contextual cues, did not tend to view their roles in terms of mustering optimal evidence to judge past events. Nor did they often attempt a deep understanding of the consequences of a given policy.[16] Instead, their core decision-making technologies served to maintain dialogue with vassals and to exonerate the king's conscience.

Following these technologies closely, this chapter argues that between 1492 and 1561 the council developed nine such conscience-satisficing tools: paperwork technologies, guiding values, textual hermeneutics,

[12] Latour, *Making of Law*, 92. [13] Latour, *Making of Law*, 92.
[14] Latour, *Making of Law*, 69. [15] Simon, *Administrative Behavior*, 57.
[16] Simon, *Administrative Behavior*, 57.

debate, consultation with the monarch, corpuses of legal fact, special committees or *juntas*, expertise, and delegation of decisions. By the 1560s, ministers did establish an edifice – or, better said, a shaky moral shelter – which consisted of a rather haphazard body of legal and descriptive facts. These, in turn, operated on different epistemological planes. First came legal facts, which emerged from two sources. The first was pre-existing collections of law, and the second was the constantly evolving assemblage of decrees which monarchs had imbued with their law-forming volition.[17] Legal facts were generally "ought-to" statements such as "I, the King, hold that mestizos should be allowed into the priesthood." Descriptive facts, on the other hand, contained information which ministers regarded as truth statements independently of whether they contained the king's volition.[18] These read like "Cuba is an island" or "the Treasury will be depleted if this year's Armada is delayed."[19] Both types of facts' intrinsic differences were crucial for shaping ministers' decision-making "assembly line."[20] By the 1550s, ministers were growing more aware of the need to clearly establish fundamental descriptive facts about the Indies in order to uphold the royal promise of justice – and in the process to shed some of their passive attitudes for more active stances.

MONARCHS' AND MINISTERS' GUIDING VALUES

The first technology which ministers used, surely both consciously and not, was their repertoire of guiding values. The historiography on Crown administration of the Indies has confused its royal decrees with the monarchy's own concrete worldviews. However, Horst Pietschmann has correctly noted that scholars "have studied very little the form of systematic politics the Crown adopted regarding the Indies," meaning that scholars do not understand "the guiding ideas that steered the politics of each moment" of Crown rule.[21]

[17] Not all legal facts in the empire contained the king's *voluntad* – see municipal acts, for example. However, for the purposes of this chapter, I will not call them "legal facts of royal volition."

[18] Here, I am using a very loose adaptation of the definition of the "descriptive fact" provided by Greenberg, "How Facts."

[19] The council distinguished legal from descriptive facts quite sharply, but did not classify them in these terms. Rather, ministers explicitly identified royal decisions on the one hand and implicitly grouped all other truth-statements in a separate domain with no explicit name.

[20] Simon, Administrative Behavior, 23. [21] Pietschmann, "Corrupción," 48.

Royal decrees generally did not neatly reflect the king's or ministers' guiding values, as these often jarringly contradictory policies reveal. Indeed, they seem to have lacked the sorts of strong state programs so common to administrations in the nineteenth and twentieth centuries. However, the Trastámara and Habsburg dynasties did have certain parameters which ministers deployed as decision-making technologies.[22] These values loosely guided the outcome of petitions, through generally speaking vassals' requests were neither controversial enough to elicit outright rejection nor so straightforwardly conformant with imperial interests as to earn ministers' enthusiastic embrace.

Before the 1520s and 1530s, royal officials had developed three principles. The first was spreading and defending Christianity. In Queen Isabella's secret 1504 testament, she instructed future monarch Juana and her regent husband Ferdinand II to uphold this mission in the New World: "our primary intention" had been "to procure and induce and attract its peoples and convert them to our holy Catholic faith, and to send to the said islands and mainland prelates and friars, clerics, and other educated people, to indoctrinate them and teach them good customs … without any grievances against their persons."[23] All subsequent rulers and ministers explicitly and tacitly embraced this mission. A powerful second guiding idea was that of profit. The new Council of the Indies, eager to help King Charles "resist the Turk," fight Protestant heathens and fund European wars, sought financial solutions – including taxing Indigenous vassals.[24]

The third principle was defending vassals and the royal jurisdiction within a framework of legality. Immediately upon hearing of Columbus' voyages, the Catholic Kings had pressured Pope Alexander VI for the 1493 papal bull *Inter Caetera*, which granted the Crown the privilege of Christianizing virtually the entire New World, and at least in theory legitimized their claims to the Indies against Christian powers – including the papacy.[25] That same year, the monarchs were negotiating with Portugal over the extent of its Asian dominions, which it naturally wished to be as broad as possible in order to profit from the Spice Islands.[26] By the 1530s and 1540s, monarchs and ministers also developed what might be

[22] Tao Azoátegui, *Casuismo*, 326–327.

[23] For two versions of this segment of her testament, see AGI, Patronato 1, N.5, and Patronato 170, R.20, 1r.

[24] AGI, Indiferente 737, N.2, December 4, 1529, see also AGI, Patronato 170, R.40.

[25] AGI, Patronato 1, N.1.

[26] AGI, Patronato 170, R.2, R.3, R.4, R.5, R.6, R.7, R.8, R.10, etc.

considered a fourth guiding value: that of simultaneously undermining conquistador jurisdiction and protecting Indigenous vassals. These views were ultimately refractions or expressions of a common royal goal: to defend the good of all.

Ministers nonetheless did not attempt to rigorously impress their four guiding principles upon every concrete and general reform which petitioners suggested. They faced, fundamentally, a labor problem: establishing petitions' merits required much more information about cause and effect than they could ever muster. Should the king approve the disbursal of funds from Peru's viceregal treasury to build a bridge over the Apurímac River?[27] Order officials to cut off the tongue of a lying royal interpreter in Mexico City?[28] Expand one *cacique*'s jurisdiction over the Indigenous towns of Tenango and Zuchalco?[29] Abolish Seville's trade monopoly?[30] Obligate all Indian vassals to speak Nahuatl?[31] Ban *mestizos* from the priesthood? Prevent conquistadors from passing their tribute allocations to their daughters? The imperial administration was often woefully ill-equipped to impose active Indies projects when faced with these questions.

TEXTUAL HERMENEUTICS

To make matters much worse, most petitions simultaneously made dubious claims and provided highly biased facts.[32] Ministers always suspected that these letters represented not the common good but a vassal's one-sided description of a problem. Sure enough, most *gobierno* supplications did not include supporting documentary evidence of any kind. And because vassals knew that the ministers and the king were pressed for time, they often subdivided their letters into brief paragraphs or *capítulos*, greatly reducing these letter-writers' ability to explain themselves in depth on a given topic. In this way, many (though not all) petitioners embraced a "thrifty economy of narration" – a terse writing style which favored speed and conveniently met the template of royal decrees – but that was also very poor in factual content.[33]

These problems forced ministers to use rudimentary textual hermeneutics for detecting bias and other potential problems within petitions. Before the reforms of the 1560s and 1570s, however, ministers had almost

[27] AGI, Lima 92, "Aunque," June 5, 1566. [28] AGI, Patronato 184, R.7, 5v
[29] AGI, Indiferente 1089, L.4, 9v–11r. [30] AGI, Patronato 172, R.9.
[31] AGI, México 1090, L.6, 135v–136r. [32] Brendecke, *Empirical Empire*, 136.
[33] Becker and Clark, "Introduction," 7.

no ability to reach to readily available descriptive facts in order to cross-reference vassals' statements. Petitioners, keenly aware of the council's lack of supporting descriptive evidence, sometimes provided these officials with another technology, which we might call "consensus certification." Whereas simple petitions featured extremely brief expositions of a problem from one point of view, vassals could also attach supporting evidence which certified that other groups, or even the entire community, agreed that a measure was just and correct. Many such petitions featured witness statements by community leaders, and some even included notarized copies of royal decrees, viceregal edicts, or other official orders, which served to reduce subalterns' archival labor and thus speed their requests to a conclusion. Pedro Rengifo's *mestizo* dossier, buttressed by notarized documents and signed by university professors, Jesuits, bishops, Spanish elites, and others, is a clear example of a petition seeking to demonstrate consensus certification.

Multiperspectival reading provided ministers another technology for textual hermeneutics. Most incoming petitions were monoperspectival; each buttressed a single fundamental point of view. Rengifo's case, for example, was avowedly pro-*mestizo*. Another very rare circumstance was that the council might receive a single group of petitions whose contents featured conflicting claims, enabling ministers to cross-reference them and to discern the best possible solution. For instance, the High Court of Mexico forwarded a local dispute between one don Francisco Ahuí on the one side and, on the other, numerous Tarascan laborers, his Pátzcuaro rival don Antonio Huitzimengari, and the Bishop of Michoacán. The dossier featured not only Ahuí's paperwork before the high court and his favorable witnesses but also the Bishop of Michoacán's defense and the third-party recommendations of the Archbishop of Mexico. This case almost resembled a *justicia* process, with its back-and-forth agonistic structure featuring competing perspectives, but functioned as a *gobierno* case once it reached the council because its cocreators sought a royal decree, not a judicial sentence. This case featured multiperspectival elements which would have provided a powerful cross-referencing tool for ministers to sift out involved parties' bias from issues of the common good and royal interest.[34] This type of case was rare and, in any case, such a petition was merely curated to provide the illusion of multiperspectivity.

[34] AGI, México 96, "En la gran ciudad," 1551.

COUNCIL DELIBERATION AND CONSULTAS

After ministers read each text, a new phase in the *gobierno* assessment process began: discussion. This was one of the council's most central but also weakest decision-making technologies. After ministers read the petitions' *capítulo* proposals, they would engage in debate and then cast votes. In one of King Philip II's 1590s informal instructions for ministers in general, which he modeled on decades of earlier practice, certain details emerge about how deliberations and ministers' voting process were to proceed. The president or the most senior minister would briefly explain his stance regarding a specific measure, followed by the next most experienced one. If all ministers rejected a measure, it failed. If all agreed on a case, then it would move to the king's desk for his approval. Differences of opinion also appear only rarely in internal council correspondence, but not upon petitions themselves. This was no coincidence. Philip provided his rationalization for such a terse style of administration. He discouraged extended oratory and disputes: "long discussions are to be excused, so as to not waste time on them ... proceed to the substance, and work in as few words as possible to avoid delays."[35]

Dialogue alone could generally not guide ministers to a firm decision. This was mainly because of their limited time, but also because, especially before the 1560s, it was so difficult for these officials to reference any corpus of sources and help them restrict the parameters of any arguments. Ministers' dispassionate discussion was nonetheless an important component of the decision-making process, for its appeal to their collective prudence certified these officials' efforts to satisfice the royal conscience.[36]

Crown officials and monarchs only regarded discussion as authoritative if it generated consensus. For this reason, when officials could not unanimously agree on an issue, they were to improve the satisficing process further by elevating their doubts about a petition's proposals to the monarch through a written document or *consulta* featuring ministers' doubts.[37] This process of *consulta* further safeguarded the royal conscience and provided additional legitimacy to a decree and thus constituted another satisficing technology. King Philip II wrote his son on his deathbed that deliberation led to "prudence" and gave rulers' decrees "more foundation."[38] Of course, the monarch was generally even less informed than ministers about a given issue, meaning that *consultas* often

[35] IVDJ, E29,C42,4, 9v. [36] IVDJ, E29,C42,4, 9r–10r.
[37] Real Díaz, *Estudio diplomático*, 92. [38] BNE, Mss.10861, 163v and 162v.

tended to produce erratic decisions even as they bestowed royal legislation with greater legitimacy.

PAPERWORK TECHNOLOGIES: MARGINAL COMMENTS AND SUMMARIES

Abundant but opaque evidence attests to ministers' *gobierno* praxes. The most abundant sources of information on ministers' internal decisions before the 1560s are the comments ministers and other officials wrote in the margins of petitions and *consultas*.[39] This marginalia often survives because it assisted officials' *gobierno* tasks, enabling them to keep track of recent decisions and to instruct each other or subalterns as to the next paperwork step. As Carolina Cunill notes, these acted as "traces of the activities carried out by a wide array of the Consejo's officials," but also often appeared as anonymous scribblings with uncertain impacts.[40] Nonetheless, they clearly "proved useful in the process of decision-making," namely by allowing officials to record their votes, express doubts, prompt subaltern officials into action, or classify a document within a certain genre or case.[41]

Some petitions were extremely short, to the point where ministers could hardly discern potential biases and problems from close readings. Others, such as those with consensus certifications and compound multi-perspectival dossiers, were often too long for ministers to exhaustively consult – sometimes by hundreds of folios. For these longer cases, ministers often entrusted court reporters, or *relatores*, to write summaries or *relaciones* of long petitions' contents.[42] This was most common in *justicia* and *gracia* cases, which tended to be long due to witness statements and other supporting documents, but also occurred in the longest *gobierno* petitions. Sometimes *relatores* or other officials scribbled their annotations next to petitions themselves, while *relaciones* were generally orderly summaries on separate sheets of paper.

If the ministers approved of a petition, they would scrawl something to the effect of "*fiat*," "it is good" (*está bien*), "as is" (*así*), and so forth (see Figure 4.1a).[43] This signaled that the council would draft a decree from the petition.

[39] Cunill, "Margins." [40] Cunill, "Margins," 384. [41] Cunill, "Margins," 385–386.
[42] For more information on the term *relación*, see Escudero, *Felipe II*, 26–28.
[43] Escudero, *Felipe II*, 33.

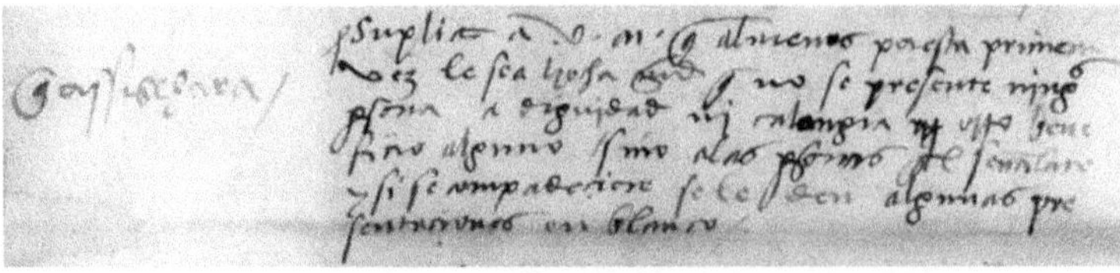

FIGURE 4.1A An example of a petition capítulo (right) and the council's decision (left). This is a 1543 petition by the Bishop of Chiapas, Bartolomé de las Casas, in which he requests that the emperor not grant additional employments to his cathedral canons unless he expressly requested them. The council's ruling reads "q assi se hará" – "it shall be done this way." This positive ruling indicates that the council resolved to create a decree from his proposal.

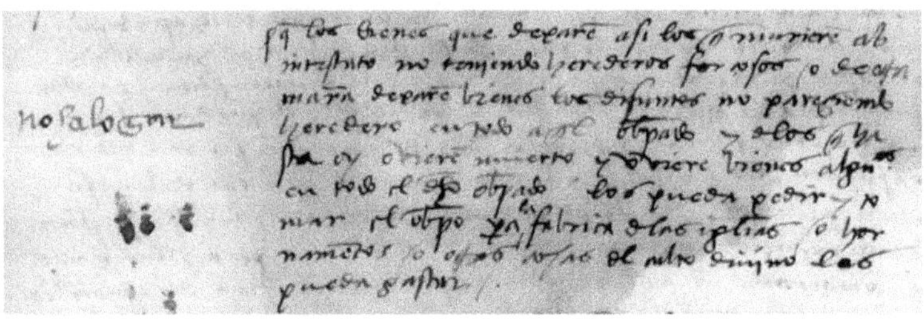

FIGURE 4.1B The council's rejection of one of Las Casas' proposals. This capítulo would have allowed the bishopric to inherit anyone's land if the deceased failed to leave a proper will. A minister wrote, "no ha lugar" (roughly," it has no grounds").

Ministers might also reject a vassal's suggestion with a phrase such as "*no ha lugar*" – roughly, "it has no place" (see Figure 4.1b). In other cases, surviving petitions contain no ruling at all (what happened in these cases is unclear). Unfortunately, these brief marginalia appear somewhat inconsistent.[44] When they do, they do not always reveal which minister made a given decision, or why.[45] As these cases show, these brief statements provide clues as to which specific parts of a petition became decrees.

Ministers, in addition to writing marginal comments on petitions, were often forced to resort to other types of paper technologies in order to assist

[44] This often occurred if a minister ruled on a copy of a petition that has since gone missing, or if a subaltern drew up a *memorial* which no longer exists in the AGI.

[45] Ministers occasionally identified themselves through a small rubric. For a guide to match rubrics to their respective ministers see Schäfer, *Rúbricas.*

the decision-making process.[46] For instance, secretaries and ministers (or at least their assistants) tended to write brief comments on the front or back pages of petitions to describe the basics of each case – normally the name of the petitioner, the year, the region, and perhaps the theme. These descriptive annotations would have helped streamline everyday decision-making as well as sorting papers into *gobierno*, *gracia*, and *justicia* bureaucratic channels.[47]

This marginalia poses major drawbacks for researchers. First, some are nearly impossible to read. Others provide the *decisions* but not the *opinions* of ministers. To make matters worse, these annotations are generally anonymous; there is often no way for researchers to tell which individual minister wrote them into the margins, unless he left his rubric next to the determination.[48]

REPOSITORIES OF LEGAL FACTS: DECREES AND DERECHO

The satisficing technologies of reading, deliberation, and annotation were extremely weak tools for ministers hoping to come to a just decision. Fundamentally, vassals themselves provided the descriptive facts of each proposal. In general, before 1561 facticity in ordinary royal decision-making therefore played a reduced role, largely because officials generally had no facts of their own from which to draw.

A fourth technology – ministers' collection of legal facts – was the most important *gobierno* decision-making technology both before and after the 1560s. The first archival repository to emerge in Indies decision-making was the royal archive of manuscript tomes of royal decrees. When ministers could locate earlier policies which reflected the monarch's volition, they saved time and effort in deciding and phrasing a new edict (see Figure 4.1c). Noting past decisions also had the benefit of producing a less-heterogenous corpus of policy, with fewer duplicates and contradictions. For instance, on November 14, 1514, ministers of the Indies subcommittee received a petition from the government of Santo Domingo, in which officials urged ministers to hurry in resolving certain affairs for new discoveries in Castile of Gold (Castilla de Oro, later Peru), to which a marginal comment reads "it has already been provided."[49]

This repository of legal facts was a very powerful satisficing technology and even early on promised to help ministers create more coherent

[46] Klein, *Experiments*. [47] Cunill, "Margins," 389. [48] Cunill, "Margins," 384.
[49] AGI, Patronato 172, R.5, 130r.

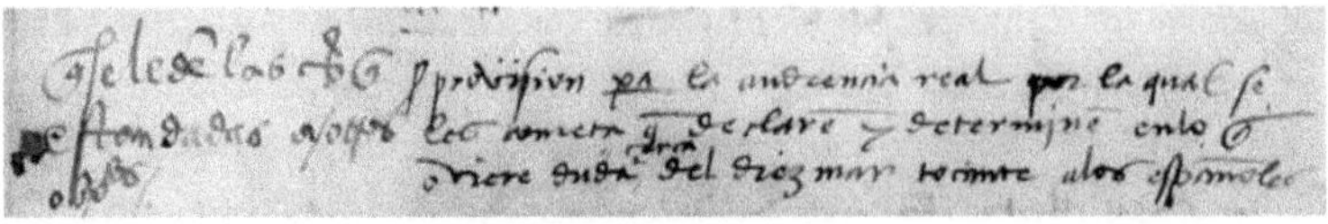

FIGURE 4.1C An example of Las Casas' 1542 petition (right), in which he requests that the emperor prompt the high court to decide how much Spaniards should tithe. The council's ruling (left) reads, "that he be given the decrees that have been given to other bishops." Bartolomé de las Casas, LOC-HKC, 191.

policies. However, it posed a number of problems. First, these sources were merely legal facts, not descriptive ones. Ministers could not always be sure that reissuing a decree was appropriate for a new context; in fact, the earlier decree might have been based on faulty information as well.

The growing size of the decree registers also diminished ministers' ability to use this resource. Officials initially had no finding aids, no subdivisions by region or theme, mixed *gobierno* and *gracia* indiscriminately, and combined both *oficio* and *partes* edicts. The only rational element they contained was their simple chronological organization; an official could locate individual decrees within each tome only by the date which the king signed them. In other words, the process through which subalterns located edicts could be labor-intensive and time-consuming.

This landslide of decrees and tomes began as a small stack of papers. In the earliest years following the conquests, the Council of Castile, and by 1524 the Council of the Indies, had few decree collections to consult. The first manuscript volume, which concerned the earliest discoveries, spanned between April 17, 1492 and December 23, 1505 and was a mere 360 pages long.[50] Another series, likely the second, spanned February 20, 1503 to August 10, 1513, and was 700 pages long.[51] The third spanned from June 14, 1509 to May 30, 1511 and had 358 pages.[52] By about 1511 ministers could still easily manage these tomes while answering petitions. However, the number of decree registers soon began to steeply rise. Officials had organized these books by chronology, but having noted the difficulty of managing specific topics by time alone, introduced new decrees which they separated by institutional and geographical themes.

Perhaps the first such division was the 1507 emergence of a new decree collection of 292 pages related to the Seville House of Trade, spanning

[50] AGI, Indiferente 418, L.1. [51] AGI, Indiferente 418, L.3.
[52] AGI, Indiferente 418, L.2.

from September 20, 1507 to November 20, 1509.[53] The Tierra Firme books added another 742 folios of decrees between 1513 and 1524.[54] Then there were the great bulk of decrees which did not fit institutionally and geographically into House of Trade or regional affairs, which ministers would later call "General Indifferent." Between mid-1512 and late 1518, General Indifferent added 1,662 more pages of *gracia* and *gobierno* policies.[55]

This chronological-geographical arrangement was no panacea. By the early 1520s, officials were already staring down a minimum of 3,414 pages of handwritten decrees that scribes had distributed throughout 9 massive series of books. Their thematic areas, especially "General Indifferent," were extremely broad, and the internal contents of each volume remained chronological, without onomastic or thematic indices. To make matters worse, scribes entered both *gracia* and *gobierno* decrees together, meaning that a subaltern searching for a decree on taxation had to leaf through dozens of pages of travel licenses and nobiliary privileges. In this situation, it was only an official's recollection of a specific decree's location which could enable ministers to quickly compare earlier decisions and better resolve petitioners' requests.

Of course, this multiplication of tomes was only the beginning of a worsening problem. The Spaniards' subjugation of Mexico and Peru caused a major diversification of decree areas, further legislative subsections, and exponential numbers of edicts. In 8 decades, the council's registers went from around 9 volumes to at least 300.[56] By the 1530s, this landslide of legal facts, which officials had clearly not prepared for, was obstructing the *gobierno* process. If a policy was hidden deep within thousands of chronological handwritten pages, ministers could not always find it. The problem became so serious that ministers often had to resort to asking Indies vassals to comb their own archives and report back about what the king had previously decided. For instance, in 1533 council officials issued a decree – quite possibly of its own sui generis confection – in which ministers requested Mexico's high court send whatever decrees they had because they could not find them in Spain.[57] Two decades later, ministers also requested that Peruvian authorities send copies of their edicts.[58]

[53] AGI, Indiferente 1961, L.1.
[54] AGI, Panama 233, L.1.
[55] AGI, Indiferente 419, L.4, L.5, L.6, and L.7.
[56] AGI, Contaduría 7B (no numeration).
[57] Manzano Manzano, *Recopilaciones*, vol. I, 8–9.
[58] AGI, Indiferente 532, L.1, 126r.

Ministers generally had no reliable legal sources which they could turn to beside decrees. Though Castile had many of its own legal codes, there is almost no proof that ministers reached decisions by referencing these compilations. While many ministers had profound juridical training and had studied Roman, Papal, medieval Castilian, and modern law, they almost never left behind evidence that they submitted these texts to this juridical rigor. The argument that these officials were "content to rely upon legal precedent and narrow precepts of law ... [and] tended to be overly cautious, punctilious, and unimaginative in the administration of the Indies" could not be further from the truth.[59] Indeed, one only finds reference to Castilian *derecho* in a handful of cases among many tens of thousands. For instance, in response to a Peruvian viceroy's report about a forged decree, ministers wrote that he should prosecute the counterfeiter "in conformity with law [*derecho*]."[60] They did not even bother to cite *which* piece of *derecho* they meant. Nor did they explicitly invoke the concepts of natural or divine law in ordinary *gobierno* undertakings, although petitioners could and did often invoke these principles. The simple reality was that these officials had too much work to laboriously comb through tomes upon tomes of Castilian jurisprudence. This casuistry-like reasoning through barrages of sources was the task of jurists engaging in litigation or reflecting on recurring moral problems, but not for the busy ministers at the helm of the sixteenth-century *gobierno* petition-and-response system.

JUNTAS

The *gobierno* process thus had three main approaches to decrees: a yes, a no, or a consultation with the king. Ministers could also avail themselves of legal facts (with considerable difficulty). Another major avenue, which was not common but was quite important, came in the form of special committees or *juntas*. Crises in the Indies could jolt ministers to ask rulers to ratify such committees, which unlike ordinary *gobierno* deliberation entailed phases of deep contemplation involving vassals from outside the council. They were not permanent but did gradually transform the monarchy's guiding values, its use of legal facts, and its accumulation of descriptive facts. A petitioner, or more likely a series of them, could prompt a committee by warning the ruler of grave consequences if an issue was not resolved.[61] For instance, regent King Ferdinand summoned

[59] Dworkoski, "The Council," no page. [60] AGI, Lima 31, "De lo que tengo," 1586.
[61] Ybot León, "Juntas," 403.

one major theological junta after Dominican Friar Antonio de Montesinos pounded on his door in 1512 warning of the great crimes Spaniards committed against Indians.[62] If the monarch felt it necessary, he might declare a temporary junta to study the issue for weeks, months, or even years.

Many of these committees focused on moral issues and therefore relied heavily on legal facts. Their participants often used a more complex and rigorous technology than was customary in ordinary *gobierno* decision-making: theological-juridical debate. In an April 16, 1495 decree, as the admiral was returning to Spain with 500 Indian slaves, the monarchs stated that he could keep them according to an earlier decree, but was to abstain from this practice in the future until a gathering of theologians could lay the issue of the legality of slavery to rest.[63]

These juntas soon became quite common and increasingly shaped *gobierno* policies.[64] Theological-legalistic debate-by-committee brought in a range of textual resources which ministers rarely, if ever, employed – indeed, they were markedly more casuistic in their rigorous reasoning style and careful proceedings. Whereas day-to-day council business made almost no reference to Castilian *derecho* or scholastic law, these theologians brought Aristotle, the Old and New Testaments, the writings of Pope Silvester, and French vassalage theory to the table.[65] The Council of Castile issued the 1512 ordinances of Burgos as a result. These ordinances reiterated under full penalty of law the monarchy's goal of Christianization and care for Indians, decried the Indians' mortality rates, and forbade conquerors from receiving tribute from more than 300 able-bodied Indians at a time.[66] Throughout the decade, thanks in part to the agitation of Las Casas, "there gathered in Burgos more than twenty times many Dominican theological masters, and many bishops and some members of the Council" to find solutions.[67]

Participants in these juntas soon noted the weaknesses of theological-legalistic debate. These deliberations tended to go in circles, demanding that all involved commit to exhaustive – and exhausting – textual production and debate. Already by the 1510s an anonymous insider complained that they "never provide[d] a resolution" to concrete issues.[68]

[62] Ybot León, "Juntas," 403–404. [63] AGI, Patronato 9, N.1, 85v.
[64] Ybot León, "Juntas," 424. [65] BNE, Mss.2814, B.3, 20v.
[66] AGI, Indiferente 421, L.13, 44v–47r.
[67] AGI, Patronato 170, R.21, 1516. As I have noted, the author of this text may be Cardinal Cisneros.
[68] AGI, Patronato 170, R.21, 1516.

The process of legal satisficing by theological committee also could veer into radical territory and tarnish the empire's image. At the suggestion of the Bishop of Mexico and his agent, the council summoned the eminent theologian Francisco de Vitoria to a junta to discuss certain problems relating to the "education and conversion of the natives," which, because they were "theological matters, it has seemed that it is convenient that they be seen and examined by theological persons."[69] Vitoria and his colleagues apparently put into question "the right that we have to the Indies, islands and mainland."[70] The emperor declared his findings "scandalous" and ordered Vitoria to never again broach the subject.[71] And yet a similar debate reared its head again in the 1550s, during the 1550–1551 Juntas of Valladolid, regarding the status of Indigenous peoples. Theologian-jurist Juan Ginés de Sepúlveda and the Salamanca-trained Las Casas faced off through a back-and-forth of major writings, but produced no concrete legislative outcomes.[72]

Juntas' frequent reliance on legal facts – specifically juridical texts and debates – helped shape the administration's guiding values, transforming everyday decision-making. However, theological-juridical juntas rarely solved issues once and for all. Both scholastic and humanist texts, theoretical readings of the Bible, and other approaches were simply too open-ended; they satisficed the royal conscience, but left the Indies in turmoil. By the 1530s and especially the 1550s, this arena of decision-making began to lose its centrality.

Committees which drew heavily from descriptive facts, on the other hand, offered concrete benefits which all involved quickly noted. For example, as early as 1495 and well into the 1520s, monarchs were assigning juntas to negotiate with Portugal over the extent of its Asian dominions, which they naturally wished to be as broad as possible in order to profit from the Spice Islands.[73] These cosmographic committees sought to understand where the delimitation between Portugal and Spain rested in the Pacific.[74] Ursula Lamb has noted that these meetings managed to recruit cosmographers who displayed disinterestedness and skepticism,

[69] AGI, Indiferente 423, L.18, 207v–208r. For the Bishop's early efforts, see AGI, Indiferente 423, L.18, 207v., AGI, Indiferente 423, L.18, 76v.

[70] AGI, Indiferente 423, L19, 67v/296v–69v/297v.

[71] AGI, Indiferente 423, L19, 67v/296v–69v/297v. Lupher, *Romans*, 60–68; Vitoria, *Relecciones*, 13, 45.

[72] Pagden, *The Fall*, 109–122.

[73] AGI, Patronato 170, R.2, R.3, R.4, R.5, R.6, R.7, R.8, R.10, etc.

[74] Lamb, "Spanish Cosmographic," 51–64.

even if Castilian ministers often twisted these reports – with the help of lawyers – to defend royal jurisdiction against the Portuguese.[75] Promisingly, from such encounters arose a by-product which could also act as a technology: the repository of descriptive facts.

THE RETREAT OF THE THEOLOGICAL JUNTAS

By the late 1520s the empire was sleepwalking into a crisis which neither pious theology nor torrents of communication alone could solve. Monarchs and ministers had found themselves battling conquistador power, a struggle which pitted the virtually unarmed council against very mighty local warlords. Legal facts alone would not do; administrators needed certain factual assessments of its position in order to tactically outmaneuver the conquistadors. In 1529, behind closed doors, ministers from the Councils of Castile, Finance, and the Indies fretted that any effort to defend the Indians – whom "God made . . . free" – would soon encounter conquistador resistance. Officials wished to protect Indians but noted that if they attempted to dismantle the *encomiendas* "in one fell swoop," then "they bring about other upheavals." The king did not have any means to truly stop them, at least not yet, for "your Majesty has no other force there but the Spaniards." In the event of an uprising, moreover, the first principle of the empire would be doomed, and the Indians would revert to their "rites and bestialities."[76] The ministers and secretary Juan de Sámano advocated a strangulation of the conquistadors both by gradually restricting their privileges and by overseeing a slow buildup of loyal Spanish officials in major Indies cities and ports.[77] In 1533, the Council of Castile urged upholding the freedom and Christianization of Indians, the defense of the New World, and the dangers posed by the conquistadors.[78] These internal debates reveal that committees had grasped certain factual elements about Indies society, geography, and arms which they could muster to defeat their vastly more powerful rivals.

Juntas never fully abandoned theological debate in decision-making, but pragmatism based on descriptive facts did slowly win adherents. The

[75] Lamb, "Spanish Cosmographic," 54–56. [76] AGI, Patronato 170, R.41.

[77] AGI, Indiferente 737, N.4. This was likely the same junta that appeared in historian Juan Bautista Muñoz's papers; see RAH, CJBM, A-105, 179r.

[78] AGI, Patronato 170, R.41, November 18, 1533. It bears the signatures of the Council of Castile's Juan Tavera, Lic. Santiago, Doctor Guevara, Licenciado Acuña, Doctor Vázquez, Doctor Erzilla, Doctor Corral, Licenciado Girón, and Doctor Montoya. For an eighteenth-century copy see BNE, Mss.904, 256v–261v.

1542 New Laws stated in the preamble that its junta had gathered "persons of every estate, prelates and noblemen and friars and some of our Council to discuss and deal" with Indies issues, and that, after furious and drawn-out debates, they had agreed on these measures to be the most just.[79] Pragmatic debate by a committee of vassals and ministers had created one of Indies history's fundamental legal facts – and given the Council of the Indies the New Laws, a major textual resource in its decision-making process alongside royal decrees and other ordinances.

Behind the scenes of the 1542 junta, however, descriptive facts were taking on an increasing importance. Surviving internal documents from the junta show ministers concerned not only with theological problems but also with concrete social issues. Moreover, President García de Loaysa pointed to the dramatic population collapse of the Indians of the Caribbean and the conquistadors' depiction of Indians as "beasts" as signs that their power must be curbed.[80] Others, such as Minister Carvajal and Secretary Cobos, suggested gradual reform in the light of Indies realities.[81] Participants' overwhelming consensus was that ministers could only safeguard the royal conscience if legal facts matched descriptive ones.

Soon enough, petitions against the New Laws flooded the council; by 1545, word spread to the council that these policies had caused an uproar in the Indies, especially in Peru.[82] There, Gonzalo Pizarro and viceroy Blasco Núñez Vela faced off about implementation; soon, hundreds of Spaniards were waging combat to the death throughout the Andes. What had gone wrong? In a new, pragmatically minded 1545 junta, the senior New World official Juan de Salmerón suggested that the council had created laws that were theologically "just" and "saintly" but yet "not decent" for they ignored the Indies' complex realities.[83] Though the members of the 1542 junta had been mainly pragmatic and not theological in their approach, the civil wars marginalized moral debate further than ever and placed the importance of factually informed pragmatism front and center.

EXPERIENCE

One consequence of the 1540s debates about conquistador power was ministers' increasing emphasis on experience as a technology. Broadly speaking, these officials could rely on two subtypes of experience. The

[79] AGI, Patronato 170, R.47, 2r–v [80] LOC-HKR, 129.
[81] LOC-HKR, 129; LOC, HKR, 138. [82] Lockhart, *Spanish Peru*, 5.
[83] LOC-HKR,132.

first was their own experience within the council. This had played a difficult-to-discern role upon decision-making since 1493. However, in the 1540s, the already powerful tendency of junta participants to invoke their experience with Indies matters during deliberations became more pronounced. Debating the causes of the 1540s revolts, Council President Loaysa reversed his previous pro-Indian stance, citing "so many years of experience" to argue to bolster conquistador power and Crown power simultaneously.[84] Minister Garci Fernández Manrique, who had long been the de facto senior member of the council, stated, "it seems to me through experience … Your Majesty should have the Ordinances revoked."[85] The powerful Cardinal of Toledo, Juan Pardo de Tavera, long the emperor's right hand man in the Council of Castile, suggested that the emperor delay the matter and send more friars to dilute the conquistadors' power, which "experience" had shown was so lethal for the Indians.[86]

The second type of experience involved not bureaucratic tenure but eyewitness familiarity with the Indies. Licenciado Salmerón had been an *alcalde mayor* in Santa Fe de Bogotá in the late 1520s and early 1530s before the council named him a High Judge of Mexico in mid-1530. He would serve as a council minister from 1543 to 1548.[87] Francisco Tello de Sandoval, who served as a council minister from 1547 to 1557, had previously seen New Spain with his own eyes; the emperor placed an extraordinary trust in his loyalty that few others enjoyed.[88] Sebastián Ramírez de Fuenleal had not only been Bishop of Santo Domingo, but had acted as President of the High Court of Mexico, returning permanently to Spain in 1537. Three years later he became associated with the council and formally worked as minister from 1544 to 1547.[89] Some ministers embarked to, and then returned from, the Indies. Jerónimo de Valderrama, minister from 1560 to 1567, spent 1563–1565 in Mexico as an auditor.[90]

One interim president, and one president, also had eyewitness experience in the Indies before the 1570s reforms. The former bishop of Santo Domingo and president of Mexico, Sebastián Ramírez de Fuenleal, briefly acted as a substitute president from mid-1543 to 1544.[91] The Inquisitor-priest

[84] LOC-HKR, 127. [85] LOC-HKR, 135. [86] LOC-HKR, 132.

[87] AGI, Patronato 276, N.4, R.105. For his appointment as Crown official in 1525, see AGI, Indiferente 420, L.10, 118v–119r; Schäfer, *Consejo*, 337.

[88] Rubio Mañé, *Virreinato II*, 88; Schäfer, *Consejo*, 337. [89] Schäfer, *Consejo*, 337.

[90] Rubio Mañé, *Virreinato II*, 88. [91] Schäfer, *Consejo*, 337.

Francisco Tello de Sandoval traveled for several years throughout Mexico, starting in 1544 as *visitador*; he returned in 1547 and served as minister until 1557.[92] In 1565 he became the president and ruled until 1567.

Neither Emperor Charles nor King Philip would treasure this experience, however. In the aftermaths of the 1541–1542, late 1560s, and 1580s controversies about ministers' connections with vassals, they saw all too well that conquistadors and other subjects could easily co-opt justice if given the option. Here, again, the subtle but powerful consequences of well-connected women's efforts to variously denounce and facilitate wrongdoing echoed in the decision-making process

DELEGATION

Yet another very common technology was decision-by-delegation. When faced with a sensitive issue, the king and his officials often simply decided to ratify an edict which entrusted a solution or further investigation to a local official or other vassal. According to an anonymous Peruvian official writing the council around the 1620s or 1630s, nine out of ten royal decrees which ministers issued to the Lima High Court did not contain policies, merely requests for additional information.[93] This seems to confirm Brendecke's suggestion that the administration's strategy in the petition-and-response process was to foster communication and ruler–ruled bonds, and that the council did not accumulate useful knowledge.[94] However, it is also true that the council produced tens of thousands of firm policies as well; not all was a mere transoceanic back-and-forth in which monarchs delegated their decisions to officials.

Another type of delegation, which was extremely rare and yielded few results, was direct negotiation between the royal administration and Indies estates in the style of Castilian parliaments. The most important of these *comisiones* or negotiations responded to the most acute crisis facing the Indies: the issue of whether the sovereigns should allow conquistadors and their descendants to exchange a huge sum of money for permanent feudal jurisdiction over Indigenous towns. Opponents of these reforms, including Las Casas, suggested the need for this jurisdiction to return forever to Indigenous lords.[95] The urgency was exceptionally great

[92] Schäfer, *Consejo*, 337. [93] BL, Add.Ms.13992, "Consideraciones," 25r–33v, here 30r.
[94] Brendecke, *Empirical Empire*, 6.
[95] Lorenzo Sanz, *Los indios*, 3; Goldwert, "Lucha," "Lucha … (continuación)"; Pereña, "Pretensión."

in Peru, where a series of major revolts had broken out in the early 1550s.[96] By 1558, the administration had decided to dispatch four trusted royal officials from outside the Council of the Indies, the commissaries of perpetuity, to negotiate with Peru's municipal conquistador lobbies. The king and his ministers desired "that parliaments [*cortes*] be gathered, and that the votes of the city procurators vote concurrently with those of the council, and with the volition of His Majesty."[97] This gathering took years to set into motion – its members did not even leave Spain until 1560.[98] By spring 1562, the commissaries made their recommendations to the king. Having considering the declarations of Indigenous groups, friars, conquistadors, and others, they proposed the monarch divide Indian tribute into three equal parts: one permanent hereditary grant to conquistador families, one-third to be granted on a case-by-case basis for one generation, and the last to be incorporated into royal control. However, by then the commissioners had become enmeshed in acrimonious factional struggles with Peruvian officials, including the viceroy. These officials accused the commissaries of various financial violations; the king ordered a 1563 audit of the viceroy's administration, which not only found that several commissaries had sent undeclared valuables back to Spain but also that they had suspicious ties to the corrupt viceroy.[99]

These in-person negotiations failed miserably to resolve the perpetuity crisis. The parliamentary dialogues had promised to offer kings and ministers deeply extensive multiperspectivity, a rich basis of both legal and descriptive facts, and satisficing dialogue. Yet, this negotiation collapsed into the very bias and factionalism which plagued ordinary petitions.[100] The administration had spent massive amounts of money trying to develop a more active posture regarding its greatest legislative quandary – the problem of Indigenous tribute – and had little to show for it.[101]

CONCLUSIONS

The king, the council, and the empire's many subjects invested enormous conceptual, ceremonial, logistical, and labor resources into creating an enduring channel of vassal–lord communication. Ministers were

[96] Lorandi, *Ni Ley*, 65–68. [97] RBPR, Papeles tocantes a Indias II-175, N.63, 295r.
[98] Lorenzo Sanz, *Los indios*, 6. [99] Lorenzo Sanz, *Los indios*, 6–13.
[100] For an example of this multi-perspectivity, see AGI, Indiferente 1624, "Mandado," 42r-65r, no date.
[101] Lorenzo Sanz, *Los indios* 12, n67.

to assist the monarchs in satisficing the royal conscience – a process which involved not just heeding petitions but also judging these documents' merits with prudence and acumen. While royal officials largely succeeded in establishing this communication with vassals, they struggled far more to provide the king with well-informed counsel. After all, petitions were always biased, and ministers generally had almost no means of fact-checking.

In response, officials developed rudimentary methods of decision-making. The mobile court, weaving its way through Europe, was a demonstration of the supremacy of dialogue. However, the nomadic administration badly limited officials' abilities to effectively develop firm criteria for decision-making. This enabled Indies petitioners to prompt decrees which were extremely numerous, but that were also highly contradictory and difficult for council officials to manage. In fits and starts, the itinerant ministers and monarchs developed threadbare technologies to reject petitions and approve others. They abided by a loose framework of guiding values: defending Christianity, ensuring profit, providing justice, and weakening over-powerful elites' grasps over Indies life. Their principles, deliberations, textual hermeneutics, and rudimentary paper technologies facilitated dialogue and internal paperwork as well. For the most pressing issues, monarchs gathered time-consuming, rather casuistic committees – the special juntas – and initially devoted many resources to satisficing the royal conscience through theological debates.

However, the crisis of the late 1520s to the 1540s revealed the grave weaknesses of imperial policy and the inadequacy of its committees. These issues threw ministers toward new solutions. They developed other decision-making technologies – including the establishment of a rather crude legal archive, and especially the more effective but work-intensive committees for gathering descriptive facts. Eyewitness knowledge of the Indies and ministers' long tenures might add nuance as well, but royal officials' efforts to separate ministers from vassals generally failed to offer ministers major advantages in decision-making. The king and his ministers often ceded much decision-making power to local Indies officials – a strategy which diluted monarchical power somewhat and also failed to bring reliable knowledge on New World issues.

By the 1550s, the council remained largely passive, an institution with limited abilities to fact-check, strategize about imperial policy, and assert a strong, top-down program which conformed to Indies realities. In this context, petitioners enjoyed substantial power to set the imperial agenda through proposals small and large. King Philip's establishment of Madrid as the permanent royal court in 1561, however, began to transform ministers' decision-making processes, shifting the administration's strategy of ruling primarily through communication to one more aggressively incorporating descriptive and legal facts. In the process, a moderately more assertive monarchy would emerge. To wrestle a measure of order from this confusion and respond to the empire's worsening crises, ministers and many others would soon have to undertake a bold new project in Madrid: the creation of Europe's first and largest coherent central system of overseas rule by paperwork.

5

"Bring the Papers"

Royal Decision-Making and the Power of Archives in Madrid, 1561–1598

By late 1587, the increasingly desperate Pedro Rengifo was eager to conclude his business and leave Madrid. The would-be priests of Peru had orchestrated a mighty case in their favor, a chorus of volitions including bishops, powerful Jesuits, and others. How could ministers not appreciate the weight of his case?

The part-Indigenous agent continued to insist – and eventually his diligence paid off. He must have renewed his efforts in the quiet winter months, for some time in early 1588, Minister Fernando Medina de Zarauz wrote a marginal note on his cover letter: "bring the papers that pertain to each one of the chapters contained in this petition."[1] *A January 26 annotation reads "seen by their eminences . . . on 1588," referring to ministers Zarauz, Diego Gasca de Salazar, Alonso Martínez Espadero, Antonio Gonzalez, Luis de Mercado, and Pedro Gutiérrez Flores.*[2] *In the same hand, a minister wrote "bring the decree from the year 1578 and all the others relating to this topic."*[3] *A subaltern named Pedro de Sierralta located the near-total 1578 ban on* mestizos *in the council's decree registers, and appended a copy to the dossier.*[4] *It is also likely that the court reporter or* relator *Salvador Núñez Morquecho helped identify other important documents within Pedro's file, perhaps with the assistance of Scrivener Juan de Ledesma, as both of their names appear on the case's cover letter.*

[1] AGI, Lima 126, 116v; Schäfer, "Rúbricas," 14. [2] AGI, Lima 126, 116v.
[3] AGI, Lima 126, 1v. [4] AGI, Lima 126, 113r–v.

Perhaps it was Núñez, or one of the ministers, who highlighted certain passages in the dossier as worthy of note. The first was the positive testimony of the eminent Jesuit José de Acosta, writing "este" – *"this one" – on the file.*[5] *He also underscored the favorable testimonies of Lorenzo Zamudio and Diego de Agüero that part-Indigenous priests spoke Indigenous languages better than Spaniards.*[6] *Two further comments highlighted the Peruvian bishops' endorsement of petitioners' rich promise as priests.*[7]

At last, on January 26, 1588, the council made its decision. In nearly incomprehensible scribbling on Pedro's petition, the scrivener wrote that "the prohibition of the decree of the year 1578 notwithstanding, issue another [decree] that the bishop and bishops of Peru . . . [ordain them], finding them well-taught and capable of being ordained." These annotations are the only clues which ministers left regarding their decisions on the case – but they nonetheless capture how by the 1580s the nature of royal decision-making had changed from the council's nomadic days. Both vassals and officials were engaging in increasingly complex paperwork, seeking mastery over many written sources, and relying on the labor of council subalterns: who navigated these expanding archives.

The core question of this chapter is straightforward: how did the royal administration's decision-making process transform with King Philip II's establishment of Madrid as the seat of the empire in 1561? Already by the 1520s, vassal–lord communication generated an enormous corpus of petitions and responses. This trove of correspondences and answers came to constitute the papers of the council – *los papeles* – and the monarchy's core collection of Indies knowledge.

This accumulation of paper leads to a paradox about imperial decision-making. On the one hand, sixteenth-century Iberia, especially Spain, was at the Latin West's avant-garde of state archival practices.[8] Moreover, Spanish archival practices became increasingly sophisticated as its empire spread. As we have seen, many poststructuralist and postcolonial scholars have assumed that colonial knowledge equals colonial power.[9] Likewise, just as archives beget power, so too must *colonial* archives beget *colonial* power.[10]

[5] AGI, Lima 126, 43r. [6] AGI, Lima 126, 44v, 47r. [7] AGI, Lima 126, 108r, 109v.

[8] Delsalle, *History*, 108; see also 1–29, and 80, 108. [9] Friedrich, *Birth*, 10, 140.

[10] For a few noteworthy works among many, see Schwartz and Cook, "Archives," esp. 2–14; Schwartz, "Having"; Ketelaar, "Archival Temples"; McEwan, "Building"; Rao,

Taken at face value, such an analysis gives early modern administrations altogether too much credit. The model *colonial archives = colonial power* transforms a gout-ridden king, his handful of overworked flesh-and-blood ministers, and their subalterns into planetary masterminds. It also takes for granted that each piece of new Indies information provided this ruling cabal with a tool highly useful to the central decision-making apparatus. This understanding assigns to rulers a capacity to dominate which is mythical beyond even the Habsburgs' Herculean dreams. True, in 1575 Secretary Vázquez called President Juan de Ovando a "great Hercules."[11] Vázquez did so mainly to remind him that God gave His chosen ones back-breaking work. Hercules wrestled with his Twelve Labors; royal officials were to grapple with operating the "great machine of the Indies" – a task that was by no means straightforward to anyone involved.[12] Secretary Vázquez's statement reveals simultaneous confidence in the empire's might and an air of dread about the challenges at hand. Even more pointed was the king's private comment to his secretary that "I really don't know what" these petitioners "think of me, other than I must be made of iron or stone . . . I'm so tired they will soon find out that I'm human like everyone else."[13]

Some scholars have recently begun to rethink the knowledge-equals-power formula and, in the process, are rethinking the power of archives. Ann Stoler has at once declared the archive to be the "supreme technology" of late-colonial statecraft and critiqued the "reductive equation of knowledge to power."[14] Indeed, she questioned the "conceit that more knowledge secures a more durable empire."[15] Markus Friedrich similarly noted that "archives were not *per se* places of knowledge in the service of power," and that "scholars have hardly investigated whether and how archives . . . functioned in everyday politics."[16] Brendecke, working specifically on the council's papers, has also forcefully questioned the "simplistic" claim of *knowledge = power*.[17]

Indeed, where Brendecke posited that the Crown failed to make archives useful, I argue that ministers, subalterns, and others did

"Affect," 559; Trundle and Kaplonski, "Tracing," 408–409; Caswell, "Hannah"; Lowry and MacNeil, "Archival thinking," 3; González Echevarría, *Myth*, 176; Derrida, *Archive Fever*, 4.

[11] AGI, Patronato 171, N.1, R.22. [12] AGI, Patronato 171, N.1, R.22.

[13] Parker, *Imprudent King*, 61.

[14] Stoler, "Colonial Archives," 87 and 100, see also 91–92 and 98; Head, "Mirroring," 319.

[15] Stoler, *Archival Grain*, 8. [16] Friedrich, *Birth*, 140.

[17] Brendecke, *Empirical Empire*, 6. See also Friedrich, "New Perspectives," 471.

manage to wrest substantial utility from them. True, President Ovando's famous project to create a reference book for descriptive facts had an unclear outcome, and his plan to hire more experienced ministers was largely a failure. Yet this chapter argues that power and the accumulation of documents into archives indeed do not have an entirely straightforward relationship to one another. The dominant Crown paradigm even after the reforms beginning in the 1560s was that papers – petitions and decrees – enabled vassal–lord communication, and that this dialogue was paramount. Document buildup was an undesirable outcome of the true origin of power – namely, interaction, which produced consent and legitimacy. However, as I will also show, beginning in the early 1560s royal officials did indeed begin to master some elements of this heap of papers, creating indices of legal facts, and transforming resolved petitions from communicative residue into descriptive facts. Among these technologies was an archive with limited but powerful faculties, and which offered officials tools for more consistent and rational decision-making.

Ministers and King Philip II became gradually more assertive in their *consulta* determinations, and decree registers greatly improved. Entirely new technologies also emerged during this period. Legal facts became more accessible thanks to thematic decree reference books. A true revolution in descriptive facts also transpired. Office subalterns assembled what they called "the papers" – key collections of petitions on critical issues allowing for more information and multiperspectivity. Ministers increasingly interviewed and cross-referenced unexpecting Madrid vassals for essential knowledge, allowing the administration to collect less-biased reports. A passive administration gained some active faculties. By the 1580s, these reforms gathered even more steam. Ministers appointed a Franciscan expert to act as a de facto censor and fact-checker for petitions relating to the Order. Even more essential was the king's creation of fact-gathering committees for economic and military issues. Thanks to these committees' employment of expertise and fact-gathering, ministers managed to grasp the panorama of Indies' issues quite holistically, especially in the emerging bureaucratic subfields of finance (*hacienda*) and war (*guerra*). Officials working with *hacienda* and *guerra* helped the empire survive against fiscal woes and pirate attacks. These achievements only concerned a fraction of ministers' business – the monarchs and their counselors remained largely passive and dependent on communication from the peripheries. Thus, while these reforms often had incomplete and even inadequate results, ministers did increasingly assemble decision-making technologies which more successfully integrated legal facts and descriptive facts into the overall process of satisficing the royal conscience.

Imperial decision-making became more consistent, and in some cases, such as in Franciscan affairs, substantially more informed. However, three factors undermined ministers' influence. First, the council was always an institution better suited for dialogue than fact-checking. Ministers ceded to special semipermanent committees many issues best solved through hands-on experience and descriptive fact-gathering. Second, the council's increasingly complex archives of legal and descriptive facts displaced much of the basis of decision-making to these material objects and their true masters: subaltern officials and handymen as well as secretaries and their wives. Indeed, just as monarchs delegated powers to ministers and thereby diluted their own might, ministers entrusted many of their faculties to subalterns who lorded over Crown archives. Third, the role of the council secretary also expanded dramatically beginning in the 1580s – this official became not only the *mayordomo* of a wealth of papers but also the social intermediary between the king, the juntas, and the council. The post-1560s reforms thus not only changed decision-making; they unchained a shifting burden of labor and power which diminished ministers' direct involvement and favored the technicians of the empire's paper machinery.

ORDERING THE COUNCIL'S LEGAL FACTS

The story of these reforms in royal decision-making began in 1561, when King Philip II declared Madrid the imperial capital. Ministers now had a permanent office in Madrid and, by the 1560s and 1570s, were making strides in rationalizing their extremely haphazard practices. In 1571, President Ovando concluded after his audit that the council had been insufficiently informed in three ways. First, ministers did not know their own laws – they thus could not deploy legal facts. Second, the council had no collections of descriptive facts which could bring new ministers up to speed when their predecessors passed away.[18] Third, ministers had insufficient eyewitness experience in the Indies. Ovando blamed the first two issues on Secretary Antonio de Eraso's poor handling of papers – after all, he informed the king, the "scribal office … is the foundation of the Council."[19]

[18] Jiménez de la Espada, *Código*, 12, 21. [19] Jiménez de la Espada, *Código*, 20.

An anonymous, undated report regarding Ovando's progress (perhaps by the royal secretary) from around 1571 revealed how this investigator planned to reorder the council's paperwork.[20] This document has Ovando observing in third person that the "papers that there are in the office of the Council" had suffered "great neglect."[21] His 1571 ordinances stated that these texts constituted "the instrument and medium, without which the matters of [the Indies] cannot be well-understood or dealt with."[22] Ovando sought to remedy this, stipulating "so that the important papers not be lost, and in the Council [ministers] can always see what they contain," ministers were to keep careful track of their "important papers," making copies of anything they sent to the Archive of Simancas.[23]

In 1571, the council had two main groups of documents to organize. On the one hand were its few statements of descriptive fact. On the other was a massive repository of texts which, through the king's volition, had become law and legal fact. As president, Ovando doubled down on the limited reforms of his predecessors to compile royal decrees and enable ministers to make their decision-making process faster and more consistent. His tenure thus saw the introduction of yet another decision-making technology: decree reference books.

A first major step which Ovando's staff made toward organizing *gobierno* decision-making was the circa 1569 text known to historians as the *Copulata*. According to its organizer, council subaltern Juan López de Velasco, the project to create a "compilation of laws of the Indies" (*recopilación de las leyes de Yndias*) began around late 1563/early 1564, during the brief presidency of Juan Sarmiento.[24] Work continued under President Tello de Sandoval and "was finished with the investigation undertaken by Sir Juan de Ovando," at which point Velasco "ordered and wrote all the general results."[25]

Velasco's handwritten guide to the council's archives not only provided brief one-sentence excerpts describing between 17,000 and 18,000 *gobierno* decrees.[26] It also added substantial thematic books, with sections, subsections, and then dozens of excerpts pointing directly to the council's handwritten decree registers, down to year and page. Velasco arranged excerpts' metadata in a hierarchical thematic tree, which

[20] I have been unable to consult the original. A partial transcript is found in Jiménez, *Código*.

[21] Jiménez, *Código*, 9.

[22] In 1522, for instance, we know that deceased Secretary Conchillos had amassed certain "books and papers and letters," AGI, Patronato 275, R.4.

[23] *Ordenanzas*, VIIIr. [24] BL, Add.Ms.28345, 67r. [25] BL, Add.Ms.28345, 67r.

[26] De La Peña Cámara, "Manuscrito," 51.

ultimately led to a concrete book and a folio located in the council's archive. For instance,

BOOK: "Fourth Book: of the Spaniards,"
- SECTION: "Title III: Of Municipalities, Councils, and the Governance and Offices and Ordinances Thereof."
  - SUB-SECTION: "Elections of offices by royal officials"
    - EXCERPT: "65: The High Court of Santiago [Guatemala] must not intervene in the provision of municipal offices in the said city, and rather, should allow it to operate freely.
      - ARCHIVAL LOCATION: Year 65, in April, book Guatemala E, folio 219."[27]

The *Copulata* seems to have been the first relatively comprehensive thematic guide for ministers to retrieve legal precedent. Previously, a subaltern might know that Book Guatemala E concerned Guatemala, and upon consulting it realize it corresponded to the 1560s. However, this assistant would then have to comb through Guatemala E's 915 pages of dense and sometimes messy handwritten text, reading each page's incomplete marginal description of every decree, which required a significant amount of time and labor.[28] Velasco's resource saved both officials and petitioners time and labor.

Using this source as a guide, ministers could also consult previous contrasting decisions. For example, according to Excerpt 65, in 1565 Guatemala the high judges could not name municipal officials. However, in Excerpt 68, in 1541 the high judges of Santo Domingo could appoint these authorities – albeit only to rural areas.[29] When we consider the *Copulata* not merely as a reference material but as an actant, we find that on the one hand it offered officials the capability to make faster, more consistent decisions, but also may have reduced vassals' likelihood of phrasing decrees on their own terms. In a way, then, this sort of rich thematic resource helped partially automate subaltern assistants' praxes, moving some of their actions from freer if more chaotic adaptations to concrete issues and toward more constant and repetitive patterns. The tyranny of disorganization receded somewhat, losing ground against the tyranny of regularity.

[27] De Altolaguirre y Duvale, ed. *Gobernación*, 123.
[28] AGI, Guatemala 394, L.4, 219, 218r (modern foliation).
[29] De Altolaguirre y Duvale, ed. *Gobernación*, 123.

Ovando likely considered the *Copulata* a first step toward establishing *gobierno* coherence. Indeed, it was only a messy manuscript draft. As president, by 1571 he had tightened and improved this thematic approach to *gobierno* decrees, which were to form seven major books: (I) the Church and spiritual governance, (II) temporal governance, (III) matters of *justicia*, (IV) the Republic of Spaniards, (V) that of the Indians, (VI) royal finance, and (VII) navigation and trade. He envisioned the principles of this compilation to become "perpetual law" for the entire Indies.[30] The president also stated that the number of thematic entries distributed throughout all seven books totaled more than 2,000, and if each of these contained a handful (or even dozens) of royal decrees, we can surmise that these books contained many thousands of bedrock principles.[31]

The president managed to oversee the completion of at least one of these seven books: the manuscript *Libro primero de la governación espiritual de las Indias* or the *First Book of the Spiritual Governance of the Indies*. It featured 22 titles comprising 400 individual *gobierno* legal principles. This *First Book*'s entries did not provide references to decrees in the council archive as the *Copulata* did; rather, they acted as a single legal tome divided into sections and subsections, with a minimum of internal contradictions. Historian José de la Peña discovered an index, cover, and draft page of Book III, the *Republic of Indians*, and two sheets of an early draft of an index of Book IV, the *Republic of the Spaniards*.[32]

When Ovando died in 1575, no ministers or subalterns had officially assumed the task of compiling existing or new Indies royal decrees into an easy-to-use format.[33] Only in 1582 did one of the council's interim presidents formally appoint one Diego de Encinas, a scribal subaltern since 1556, to attempt this once more. However, Encinas had likely begun to undertake this project earlier than 1582; in a 1596 privilege petition he stated that his work began seventeen years before – that is, in 1575, the year of Ovando's death.[34] After nearly two decades' work, Encinas completed this compendium in 1596. He had taken this long to finalize his project because it featured "all that has been provided for the Indies and Seville" – over a century of *gobierno* decrees.[35] It spanned 4 volumes and 1,741 dense pages of tiny print, each page sometimes containing several decrees. It featured the unwieldy title of *Provisions,*

[30] Jiménez de la Espada, *Código*, 9. For the manuscript, see BNE, Mss.2935.
[31] Jiménez de la Espada, *Código*, 13. [32] Manzano Manzano, *Historia*, 141–145
[33] Manzano Manzano, *Historia*, vol.I, 303. [34] AGI, Indiferente 745, N.102f.
[35] AGI, Indiferente 745, N.102b2.

Decrees, Chapters of Ordinances, Instructions, and Letters Issued and Dispatched in Different Times by Their Highnesses. Scholars simply refer to this as the *Cedulario de Encinas* or the Register of Encinas. Its first pressing was of 500 books; it would thus go on to achieve a relatively high readership.[36]

This work was a milestone in Indies legislation. For the first time, the entire New World had a single decree compilation, in easy-to-read print, and featuring thematic and alphabetical indices. However, its contents are deceptive – this was no exhaustive work. Encinas had envisioned this as a collection of "all the *oficio* decrees" and had omitted many thousands of important *de partes* laws in the process.[37] On face value this was sensible – his book's purchasers were Crown officials in the Indies whose duties corresponded to implementing *de oficio* legislation. However, this criterion eliminated vast swaths of edicts from this book – all those which the council had delivered *de partes* to vassals not in Crown employ. This included, for instance, the 1588 decree establishing equality between Spaniards and *mestizos*, which ministers had given directly to Pedro Rengifo. The decisive Indies compilation of *oficio* and *partes* policies would have to wait until 1681 to see print.

Rather curiously, in everyday work ministers and their assistants virtually never referenced the *Copulata*, Ovando's books, or Encinas' *Cedulario*. Historian Juan Manzano Manzano has shown that at one point, in a 1575 royal letter to the Viceroy of Peru, ministers had responded to one of his doubts with a *verbatim* extract of Ovando's *First Book*'s chapter 60, title IX about Indian tribute.[38] Nonetheless, it is certain that as time passed, and especially after the late 1560s, ministers began to rely on legal facts much more often. When the Peruvian President Licenciado Castro complained in 1567 about Peruvian bishops' ordination of Indies-born Spaniards, the council's 1568 or 1569 response was, first, "bring the decrees that have been provided regarding this," followed by "what is convenient for this has already been provided."[39] When ministers read Augustinian Friar Rodrigo de Loaysa's 1578 request that local miners not exploit Indians like slaves through a new form of labor distribution in Potosí, they responded "this has been provided, and send a duplicate."[40] Petitioners who benefited through the council's more expedient issuance of a previous decree might also lose their power to

[36] AGI, Indiferente 745, N.102a. [37] AGI, Indiferente 745, N.102d.
[38] Manzano Manzano, *Historia*, vol.I, 209. [39] AGI, Lima 92, R.19, N.146, no folio.
[40] AGI, Indiferente 1388, "El presentado," 1578.

create new legal categories or to insert phraseology into decrees when this occurred – a sign that archival technologies could, in some cases, estrange subjects from certain elements of the decree-making process.

These retrieval technologies were not a panacea, however. Even Ovando's reforms officials could sometimes not locate specific decrees. For instance, they encountered this problem when the officials of Popayán made certain proposals on February 8, 1575.[41] These Popayán officials' fifth request was that council ministers send them a copy of a pre-existing decree stating that alcaldes not act as judges, a policy which the king had issued for Cartagena. To this a minister's hand reads, "bring this decree." Another marginal comment beneath this command reads "the decree cannot be found." Yet another states, "The decree is not there in the books, [order] that ... they [the officials of Popayán] send a notarized transcript of it."[42] This sort of problem could have been tied to council practices or perhaps owed to an error by Popayán's officials – it is difficult to say which.

Another important subset of legal sources which Ovando ordered organized were past *consultas*. On February 23, 1575, the sovereign also paid one Pedro Sánchez de la Torre for having drawn up an "inventory and tables of seven *consulta* books in this Council with his Majesty."[43] By 1597, the council possessed about forty-five large bundles of these documents dating from 1575 forward.[44] That ministers would have considered these documents to be useful legal sources makes good sense – they often included marginal comments which suggested the king's law-creating volition. Unfortunately, there is no evidence regarding how often ministers used this repository.

DESCRIPTIVE FACTS AND REFERENCE WORKS

President Ovando's second suggestion, after ministers' more consistent grasp and usage of legal facts, was for their decision-making to rely more heavily on descriptive facts. Until the 1570s, council officials had concerned themselves more with creating legal facts through vassal–ruler communication than with collecting factual statements regarding concrete social realities, except for in specific fact-gathering juntas. This meant that the council generally did not seek out descriptive facts per se. This dismayed Ovando, who developed a more ambitious plan to improve

[41] AGI, Quito 19, N.84, no folio. [42] AGI, Quito 19, N.84, no folio.
[43] AGI, Indiferente 426, L.25, 315v. [44] AGI, Contaduria 7A, L.2 and L.3

the council's hermeneutical tools. His 1571 ordinances stressed that ministers should only make legislative decisions "being first very informed and certified" of an issue before ruling.[45] Without any knowledge of the Indies, "no thing can be understood, nor dealt with as it should, whose subject is not first known by the people related to it" – this included matters of the "land and of the sea, natural and perpetual and temporal, ecclesiastical and secular, past and present."[46]The segment further ordered that the chamber scribes personally care for these documents, as secretaries had in the past, handing them on to their successors with a complete inventory of their contents. The following ordinance stated that these officials were to devise (unspecified) indexes for these documents, filing them into a system of documentary bundles (*legajos*).[47] The chamber scribe was to arrange for the delivery of all documents ministers deemed no longer important to the Royal Archive of Simancas near Valladolid.[48]

Scholars have dedicated ample attention to council officials' attempts to collect massive amounts of demographic and cartographic information about the Indies through its famous questionnaires in the late 1560s, 1570s, and 1580s, which were to help Juan de Velasco write his history and description of the Indies. During and after Ovando's reform, Velasco began requesting massive amounts of information from Indies vassals in a series of extensive questionnaires. He mailed these in early 1569 to the Archbishop of Mexico, as well as to clergymen from sixty-six parishes, and various friars.[49] The president received the responses in 1571 and the next year sent out a follow-up, now stating explicitly that his goal was to help Velasco create a major reference work, the *Geografía y descripción universal de las Indias*.[50]

Ovando suggested he expected that these reports and the *Geografía* would help remedy ministers' ignorance and implied that these sources would be particularly helpful for *gobierno* decisions.[51] However, the Quito High Court judges noted astutely in one 1574 letter that these descriptions were not going to help the administration in Madrid complete any of its primordial tasks of *justicia*, *gracia*, or *gobierno* – especially not the latter. These reports would produce knowledge simply too abstract to serve any concrete everyday purpose in the council.[52] Indeed,

[45] *Ordenanzas*, IIIIr. [46] *Ordenanzas*, IIr. [47] *Ordenanzas*, XVIr.
[48] *Ordenanzas*, XVIv. [49] AGI, México 336A, R.2
[50] Brendecke, *Empirical Empire*, 168. [51] Jiménez de la Espada, *Código*, 21.
[52] AGI, Quito 8, R.8, N.22, 6v, and Brendecke, *Empirical Empire*, 214.

while vassals did send descriptions and maps to the king and the council, these documents' impact on *gobierno* legislation remains mysterious. As Brendecke has noted, "the mere fact that, for example, Philip II could draw on … the *relaciones geográficas* says nothing about whether this actually happened and, if it did, to what end."[53] When Velasco completed his *Geografía* in 1574, he used only the early questionnaire answers. But what was the exact role of Velasco's *Geografía* in helping the council understand, and legislate for, the Indies? There are no clear answers. Quite likely in response to Velasco's own recommendation, in 1582 Philip ordered that ministers store the text in a locked chest in the council's offices (perhaps because it contained sensitive military and economic information and concerned conquistador misdeeds which might offend their descendants).[54] Brendecke has suggested that this meant that the work was "no longer ready at hand" for ministers, though there is always the possibility that ministers consulted its pages.[55] By King Philip II's death in 1598 the larger *relaciones geográficas* project had stalled and the reports were already out of date; moreover, official historians had not produced works that were useful to council ministers' production of legislation.

Ministers did have other factual resources at their disposal. Sometime between 1571 and his death in 1598, López de Velasco also produced a brief manuscript guide to Indies geography, the *Demarcación y división de las Indias*. This divided the New World into its provinces and towns, adding brief descriptions of their populations, administrative institutions, geographical features, economic activities, and histories.[56] It also featured rudimentary jurisdictional maps and a place name index. This may have been very useful for ministers but, once again, we have little information about whether they ever put this resource to use.

TRANSFORMING PETITIONS INTO FACTS

These officials certainly did begin to collect petitions which they deemed noteworthy, and which they would eventually amass into a sort of ad-hoc factual archive. By the late 1560s, on the eve of Ovando's reforms, this

[53] Brendecke, *Empirical Empire*, 235–236. However, Helen Nader's excellent *Liberty* does note that similar *relaciones* for Spain were useful for officials' *gracia* sale of municipal liberty; 115.

[54] Brendecke, *Empirical Empire*, 242–245.

[55] Brendecke, *Empirical Empire*, 255; AGI, Indiferente 740, N.91.

[56] BNE, Mss.2825.

new collection was emerging in a haphazard manner. One 1567 inventory of the recently deceased Crown attorney Jerónimo de Ulloa suggests he had personally safeguarded certain documents, including *gobierno*-related reports. He had several boxes of correspondences with the Viceroy of Peru and the Bishop of Cuba. He also had "ordinary petitions (*peticiones*) and reports (*memoriales*) from previous people." There was even another category of "loose papers of diverse things that because of their variety were not recorded in this inventory."[57] Yet another group of papers of an indeterminate nature remained in the hands of royal secretary Mateo Vázquez, which ministers successfully obtained for their own use in 1569.[58]

On the eve of his reforms, Ovando was already moving to unite these papers and make this important patrimony useful to ministers. He also set out to reunite other scattered papers of royal interest. A royal decree of April 24, 1570 instructed Council Secretary Francisco de Eraso to collect and inventory the "court case papers (*procesos*), letters, paintings, and other writings" that were in Valladolid in the hands of the deceased Secretary Juan de Sámano's two sons.[59] On June 28, 1570, the ruler issued another decree, paying Juan de Ledesma to organize these documents.[60] On November 3, 1571, the king ordered the rector and regents of Valladolid's College of Saint Gregory to send to Madrid the papers of Las Casas, which featured "some books and treatises that he composed and did about the matters of the Indies" as well as "many loose papers of notices and reports [*avissos e rrelaçiones*] he had gathered that had been sent to him from the Indies."[61]

Council officials' creation and management of collections of descriptive facts could help them achieve specialized expertise in a given subject matter. Minister Gedeón de Hinojosa, who had previously served as President of the House of Trade, had experience regarding Indies commerce, and after his death the council inherited his personal archive. This included substantial collections regarding armada routes, and information about Peru and Brazil, but primarily encompassed matters regarding politics and travel in the Portuguese Indies and its adjacent polities from Persia to China.[62] Ministers had clearly become increasingly keen on archiving not only royal decrees but also certain petitions and important

[57] AGI, Indiferente 1383A, "Memorial," 1567. [58] AGI, Indiferente 744, N.16.
[59] AGI, Indiferente 426, L.25, 67r–68v. [60] AGI, Indiferente 426, L.25, 69r.
[61] AGI, Indiferente 426, L.25, 134r–v.
[62] AGI, Indiferente 856, "Relacion," no date (1594?).

figures' personal collections. In this way, petitions – even highly subjective ones – transformed biased information into descriptive facts.

Just as ministers' growing collections of legal facts changed how they read petitions, so too did the new and growing archives of descriptive facts influence the decision-making process. One command that ministers began to write frequently in their marginal responses to petitions was "bring the papers" or something to that effect. This was an order to a scribe or another official to rummage through the council files for information. I have not been able to find references to this practice in petition marginalia before the late 1560s. However, by then they were becoming quite common. Examples abound: on January 4, 1567, President Castro wrote from Peru that he had received letters from Chilean governor Rodrigo de Quiroga requesting military aid for certain frontier towns. Ministers seem to have received copies as well, for a minister's handwriting reads "look here [*ojo*], bring the letters of Quiroga."[63] When the priest Gonzalo de Torres petitioned in March 23, 1583 from Popayán about the state of friar–priest relations, a minister wrote "gather this with the other papers that there might be."[64]

In other cases, ministers' reliance on earlier petitions for their decision-making process was even more obvious. In response to the Ecclesiastical Council of Oaxaca's April 18, 1589 complaint that the bishop had ordained a certain priest with one-quarter Morisco blood, unspecified council officials wrote on October 24, 1596 (!), "place this letter with all the ancient papers … to determine what is convenient."[65] On March 20, 1592, the Archbishop of Mexico complained from Lima that the new viceroy Conde de Villar altered a practice of his predecessor, by issuing *mandamientos* in response to the petitions of his close associates, which spawned many court cases. The petition marginalia reads "bring everything that has been provided about what there is in this chapter and the letters that the [previous] don Viceroy Luis de Velasco has written about this."[66] On November 20, 1593, the Viceroy of Peru wrote about several dozen issues, the fourth of which warned the council about general discontent about a new sales tax, the *alcabala*.[67] A minister wrote in the margin, "bring everything that the Viceroy has written about this and what has been responded to it."[68] These and many other petitions indicate that council officials prized the papers of the viceroys as repositories of

[63] AGI, Lima 92, R.19, N.138. [64] AGI, Indiferente 858, "Copia y relaçion," 1583.
[65] AGI, México 358, "Dos años," 1589. [66] AGI, Lima 274, "La visita," no folios.
[67] Herzog, *Upholding Justice*, 261. [68] AGI, Lima 274, "Todas las ocasiones," no folios.

descriptive facts, and that these documents had given them a new and powerful hermeneutical tool which served to test petitioners' claims.

OUTSOURCING EXPERTISE: SECRET INTERVIEWS AND INFORMED OUTSIDERS

Ovando's third proposal, after the employment of more legal and descriptive facts, was that the council be staffed with the New World's most distinguished and experienced judges.[69] In reality, however, his proposals were largely frustrated, likely due to the reticence of Philip II and his advisers regarding the employment of officials with social connections to Indies-linked women and men. The only minister to serve in the council during Ovando's tenure was Gómez de Santillán, who had been High Judge of Mexico from 1543 to 1551; much later, from 1572 to 1586, he was minister in the council.[70] Antonio González had been a notoriously corrupt but intelligent judge in Guatemala (1570–1573), and had worked in Charcas (1578–1580), before becoming a council minister in 1584. He served until he was sent into a soft exile as president of Santa Fe in 1587 (in large part because of his scandalous dalliances with court women, as we have seen).[71] Pedro Moya de Contreras, who spent twenty years variously as the inquisitor, *visitador*, viceroy, and Archbishop of Mexico, served a year as president until his 1592 death.[72] These traveling officials' first-hand experiences may have influenced the *gobierno* decision-making process, but remained in the minority, just as they had been before 1561.

One major alternative to having a council staffed by ministers with eyewitness experience was for officials to transform unsuspecting vassals into informants in Madrid. This enabled the administration to obtain multiperspectival evidence with fewer risks of vassals' biased testimonies. For example, in 1573, council minister Benito López de Gamboa launched an investigation into Florida governance – specifically, its military fortifications and food supply. Gamboa received richly informative testimonies from five Florida soldiers and did so without having to suffer the months or years-long delays of writing informants in the Indies. Because his approach "surprised" the witnesses as they conducted other business, it gave them little opportunity to coordinate a biased approach.[73] This practice of "surprising" vassals proved useful to officials during a royal

[69] Jiménez de la Espada, *Código*, 15. [70] Schäfer, *Consejo*, 338.
[71] AGI, Santa Fe 56, N.18, and Santa Fe 17, R.6, N.37. [72] Valderrama, *Cartas*.
[73] AGI, Patronato 179, N.5, R.5

inquiry into the failure of a major expedition to erect a fortress and town in the Strait of Magellan in the mid-1580s. In 1585, an anonymous council official delegated a key witness to spy on certain informants in the court, specifically to secretly collect unbiased information about armada commander Diego Flores de Valdés' role in the debacle.[74] That being said, such cases were extremely few in number, perhaps reflecting the council's deep suspicion of vassals, the need to keep Crown affairs secret in a city populated by many foreign subjects and ambassadors, or simply due to the excessive amount of labor and time which undertaking these interviews demanded.

Madrid was a magnet for expertise, but ministers could not forever be tracking down subjects to check the facts of each incoming petition. However, other powerful models of information-checking were at their fingertips. Sometime in the 1570s, the council added another important technology: the outsourced expert advice of the Franciscan General Commissary of the Indies. The role played by this powerful representative of the Order in council decision-making represented both a sharp deviation from previous practices, and a glimpse into what might have become a far more interventionist, active royal strategy of imperial rule.

Beginning around 1571–1572, perhaps in response to suggestions by Peru's Viceroy Toledo, a high-ranking Franciscan in Madrid was to play a major role in the decision-making process. He was not only to provide ministers with descriptive facts to evaluate truth statements of incoming petitions concerning Franciscan issues but also to filter scandalous and impertinent content before these texts ever reached the council. This model of decision-making was deeply alien to ministers' normal practice of insisting on untrammeled ruler–ruled communication from as many petitioners as possible. It effectively outsourced fact-finding to the senior member of a corporation outside the council and also promised to curb petitioners' ability to shape decrees in the process.[75]

The commissary's role was explicitly that of a censor and fact-checker. As one anonymous 1599 petition noted, this official could act as a "perpetual sentinel" against the "sinister reports of biased friars."[76] He could also crack down on friars' constant travel to the court, especially on the "lies [and] false accounts" handed in by "young friars born there

[74] AGI, Patronato 33, N.3, R.55 (Ns.1–11). [75] Borges, "En torno," 156.

[76] AGI, Indiferente 878, "Algunas," 1599; AGI, Indiferente 3058, "Miguel de Carmona," November 28, 1581; Indiferente 3058, "Esta carta," November 8, 1578.

[in the Indies] who normally answer to [its] climate and nurture."[77] This figure thus quashed an unknown number of petitions alleging wrongdoing in the Indies and acted as a powerful censor against Franciscan dissenters.

This adviser would also screen friars' incoming proposals for moral content. In 1597, ministers forwarded a petition by Friar Pedro de Pila from Mexico containing numerous proposals for reforms, writing in the margin "inform the Commissary General of the Indies" and "remit . . . the processes and informations to the Commissary General who resides in this court with his signed recommendation so that he offer his sentence."[78] The Franciscan Commissary replied to a proposal about funding a college, stating that it was "not for the multiplication of friars or convents but for the exercise of learning and to substantiate ministers in the Gospel," which would serve to "banish ignorance" from the province.[79] In a similar case that same year, the leader of a local Franciscan from Santa Marta wrote of the mission's terrible results, blaming the governor and requesting Indigenous labor to rebuild convent buildings. The Commissary General wrote on the petition that this proposal "contained improprieties" and could lead to "abuses upon the Indians." To the petition's implicit request for force, he wrote that this was not "how it was done by Christ."[80]

This official was not merely a moral censor. He was also to collect all Indies-relevant descriptive facts from agents within the Order. He would keep rigorous lists of monasteries and of all their members, their names, personal capabilities and weaknesses, and other characteristics.[81] For example, in 1580 the Commissary provided the king with a list (probably prepared by the representatives of the Orders) of New Spain's 60 Franciscan monasteries and 467 friars.[82]

Indeed, when comparing the powerful reforms which Las Casas and others managed to bring to the king's consideration to the council's climate regarding Franciscans, it is clear that the monarchy was experimenting with a radically less-open system of communication. The intervention of the commissary was so important in Franciscan affairs that in 1591 Gaspar de Ribera complained that, in consideration his having prepared relevant "papers and commentaries," he should receive the

[77] AGI, Indiferente 3058, "Negocio," no date.
[78] AGI, Indiferente 1415, "Frai Pedro," November 10, 1597.
[79] AGI, Indiferente 1415, "Frai Pedro," November 10, 1597.
[80] AGI, Indiferente 2987, "Nro. Señor," October 3, 1597.
[81] Borges Morán, *Envío*, 107–108. [82] AGI, Patronato 171, N.1, R.32.

formal title of "commissary General of the Indies with the vote, seat, and salary of a minister."[83] Ministers informed the king that the President of the Council did not deem this necessary, however. The king requested further input, but I have been unable to find a follow-up; clearly, the project did not advance.

Council members were perhaps not keen on making the Franciscan Commissary a minister, but royal officials were interested in applying this model to the Dominicans, Augustinians, and other Orders. By the late 1570s Dominicans were in discussions about how to achieve this.[84] An anonymous letter – almost certainly by the Viceroy of Peru in the early 1570s – suggested that all of the Orders were in need of "commissaries and general vicars" to oversee and discipline friars. He complained of the "freedom [the friars] have to speak of the government of these realms."[85] However, these talks fell apart due to jurisdictional squabbling within the Orders and with the Pope.[86] Had the Orders embraced this project, perhaps the Habsburgs would have considered abandoning one of their core tenets – that of an untrammeled exchange of vassal–lord *voluntad*. The dynasty wisely refrained from expanding this project further.

THE JUNTA OF FINANCE

Council officials' practice of enlisting a Franciscan supervisor to vet the Order's petitions using his separate institutional archives and experience may have failed to produce an overarching framework for censoring the other monastic orders. However, it revealed that if ministers outsourced or subcontracted fact-finding to other bodies, they could make quite factually informed (if still imperfect) decisions. To an even greater extent, the special juntas of the 1570s to 1580s would demonstrate that the administration was not entirely helpless when it came to transcending its suboptimal decision-making and could take more active stances through expert committees.

In response to a rising tide of imperial crises, the king inaugurated two primary juntas as regular gatherings between the ministers of various imperial councils.[87] The Junta of Finance was the first to emerge, featuring

83 BFZ, CA. E.134–33, July 15, 1591.

84 See AGI, Indiferente 3058, "Oy se han recibido," July 2, 1576; "El buen govierno," July [1577]; "Fray Miguel," November 28, 1581.

85 BFZ CA. E.169–4.

86 AGI, Indiferente 3058, "Noticioso el Consejo," after 1613.

87 Heredia Herrera, *Catálogo Tomo I*, 12.

two ministers from the Council of the Indies, two from the Council of Castile, and two from the Council of Finance. According to historian A. W. Lovett, King Philip II had responded to the monarchy's constant bankruptcies by creating a special committee to oversee the royal budget in 1573. This variously took the names of the Junta of Presidents, the Junta of Greater Accounting, or the Junta of Finance.[88] At the helm were the Presidents of the Royal Council and the Council of the Indies' President Ovando. However, Lovett notes that while Ovando was a very capable statesman, his understanding of finance was weak at best. He did grasp that Crown finances suffered from having three fiscal agencies: the Accountancy of the Economy (*Contaduría de Hacienda*) which farmed taxes, the Accountancy of Expenses (*Contaduría de Cuentas*) which analyzed officials' financial reports, and the Council of Finance, which was to produce legislation that would enrich the empire.[89] The expectations of both King Philip and Ovando were that this committee would rise above the tangled spheres of authority of the empire's councils, direct the reform of its financial institutions, achieve a clear-eyed vision of its treasury, and, ultimately, rationalize imperial assets.[90]

This special junta was not entirely successful. Ovando proposed reorganizing this committee under a single powerful president, and staffing it with ministers specifically devoted to increasing the treasury. One problem was that Ovando never succeeded in prompting a reform of these institutions.[91] Moreover, many of this junta's eligible staff were excellent jurists but feeble economists and financiers. The only member who profoundly understood money was the great merchant Melchor de Herrera, whom the king distrusted due to his suspicious dealings in the Castilian markets. In Lovett's evaluation, this dysfunction "partially explains the bleak financial history of the reign."[92]

Historian Carlos Javier de Carlos Morales suggests that this committee did manage at least to understand the enormity of the empire's debt through the use of double-entry statistics and shows that by the late 1570s the administration had indeed attempted numerous steps to increase earnings by procuring new lenders and increasing domestic revenues.[93] Mauricio Drelichman and Hans-Joachim Voth have argued that though monarchs possessed an array of sophisticated financial tools

[88] Lovett, "Juan de Ovando," 8; de Carlos Morales, "Política," 152, footnote 353.
[89] Lovett, "Juan de Ovando," 8–9. [90] De Carlos Morales, "Política," 157.
[91] Lovett, "Juan de Ovando," 11–17. [92] Lovett, "Juan de Ovando," 21.
[93] De Carlos Morales, "Política," 159–164.

to raise funds, acquire loans, and repay with interest, its bureaucrats "did not keep centralized financial records."[94] However, Esteban Hernández Esteve demonstrated that by the mid-1550s the Habsburgs had indeed attempted to create Europe's first unified, rationalized, highly exhaustive, indexed accounting books for the Council of Finance – the *Libros de Caxa* – and largely succeeded after reform efforts in the early 1580s culminated in 1593–1621 with the double-entry accounting books. While these books – which may have numbered 500 or 600 – no longer survive, abundant evidence suggests their use at the time.[95]

The various committees which coordinated finances beginning in the 1570s thus likely did achieve some of their goals of statistically and synoptically viewing imperial revenues and debts. They also improved their decision-making with improved bookkeeping. Already in 1573, members of this junta were assembling lists of priorities to tackle broad, interconnected financial problems throughout the entire empire, ranging from war and medieval feudal agreements to specific *gracia* appointments, to the every practice of decision-making to the "forming and reforming and ordering of laws and instructions." The list's individual entries totaled 147. Many of these, moreover, concerned improving official and archival practices: training better ministers, improving financial bookkeeping, elaborating lists of noblemen to contribute to war costs, cataloguing towns and offices to be put up for sale, and creating an "inventory of and inquiry into all [royal] possessions which profit and don't profit" among other lists.[96]

Another example of the powerful advantages of these financial committees over regular council praxes appears in a report by Secretary Pedro de Ledesma, probably from the early 1600s. Ledesma had drafted this report to complain (likely to King Philip III) that his colleague Secretary Juan de Ibarra had ceased to bring necessary documents to the Junta of Finance. To press his case, Ledesma praised the accomplishments of this body for the year 1596, noting that "in the brief time which the Junta lasted, more matters, and more important ones, were resolved than in all the past 27 years of juntas combined."[97] He appended a list of seventy different thematic fields which the committee had explored, which included undertaking major reforms of regulating the Armadas and

[94] Drelichman and Voth, *Lending*.

[95] Hernández Esteve, "Pedro Luis," here 222–224, 230–233, 237–243; Soll, *Reckoning*, 109–115.

[96] HSA, 3/II/45.

[97] RBPR, Papeles tocantes a Indias II-175, N.55, 251r.

overseas trade, financing fortresses and artillery, coordinating improved taxation and tithing efforts, producing Spanish and Indigenous mining ordinances, fighting frauds of mines and mints, fostering agriculture, protecting Indians from abuses, and managing the ever-troublesome debate about *encomiendas*.

Though it was in Ledesma's interest to emphasize this junta's achievements, the list's topics also leave no doubt: its members could compare and survey important issues throughout the entire Indies and consider them in a more systematic and less ad-hoc style than in the communication-centered council. Each one of the junta's topics could draw from the council's archives of petitions, creating a rich multiperspectival and quite synoptic portrayal of an issue over time. For instance, the junta surveyed which mines from northern Mexico to Chile had succeeded, declined, stagnated, failed, or had never been exploited and made recommendations to increase their output. Similarly, they could make more interventionist diagnoses about farming. For instance, in 1585 and 1586, when committee members were considering scientific and agricultural remedies for impoverished and depopulated Santo Domingo and the island requested more slaves, ministers suggested another sui generis remedy by encouraging locals to embrace the ginger industry.[98] The passive stance likely still prevailed – after all, the junta's information was also suboptimal and largely composed of biased, bottom-up reports – but its panoramic understanding of the Indies enabled the administration to become far more active and even to make new proposals.

The Junta of Finance may have achieved a vastly superior archive of descriptive facts to that of the Council of the Indies and channeled greater focus and expertise into Indies reforms. However, it would be premature to assume that this committee always succeeded in transforming this knowledge into Indies mastery. For instance, its members struggled to resolve the ongoing conflict over the *encomienda* despite amassing countless papers to help it make decisions. At least one of the junta's huge collections of documents from the 1540s onwards had more than 2,000 pages in total.[99] Some of these were council documents which the junta reshuffled for its own purposes.[100] The *encomienda* sessions drew partly from a list of 1550s and 1560s documents from various Peruvian and Mexican sources as well as various originals and

[98] AGI, Indiferente 1866, September 29, 1585 and July 20, 1586.
[99] These papers are found in AGI, Indiferente, 1624.
[100] AGI, Indiferente 1624, R.3, N.18.

duplicates.[101] One marginal comment confirms its ministers' consultation of Peruvian jurist Licenciado Juan de Matienzo's petitions and a certain "book he wrote about the governance of Peru."[102] This was surely his extensive manuscript treatise *Gobierno del Perú* (ca. 1567), in which he used juridical sources, ethnohistory, and eyewitness statements to strongly argue in favor of the *encomiendas* in chapters 28 to 32.[103]

Multiperspectivity was a major benefit of such a collection. The junta could consider the *encomienda* reforms not only from its critics but also its advocates from numerous regions. For instance, its members possessed the findings of Peruvian commissaries' late 1550s and early 1560s negotiations, which spanned several hundred pages.[104] The junta also possessed an index, and likely many documents, on the matter of property and lordship inheritance rights of the Inca.[105] These papers, and their many perspectives, could not resolve the *encomienda* crisis, however. Indeed, with the possibility of conquistador uprisings so dire even in the 1580s and 1590s, ministers and monarchs sensibly opted – legal and descriptive facts be damned – to avoid any conflictive reforms.

At least as useful as this multiperspectivity was the junta's invitation of vassals living in Madrid to provide expert advice on Indies finances – like several former viceroys of Mexico and Peru, and the procurator of the city of Potosí. Ledesma noted that the junta had "issued a great quantity of decrees" and ordinances as a result.[106] Why exactly Secretary Ibarra opposed the continuation of the junta is a mystery, but his power to freeze its operations certainly points to these officials' rising clout in decision-making; indeed, he may have been angling to be treated as a minister, which he later became.[107]

THE JUNTA OF PUERTO RICO

Even more prolific, and perhaps more successful, was the Junta de Puerto Rico. This was another periodic gathering of various ministers from the conciliar system, which helped the king resolve pressing military issues,

[101] AGI, Indiferente 1624, "Perpetuidad Nueva España," 212r.

[102] AGI, Indiferente 1624, "Relación," 66r.

[103] NYPL, ORMC, *Gobierno del Peru* (ca. 1567), Mss.2570.

[104] AGI, Indiferente 1624, "Todo lo pedido." See also RBPR, Papeles tocantes a Indias II-175, N.63.

[105] AGI, Patronato 192, N.2, R.14. Though not part of AGI, Indiferente 1624, this document has unmistakable correspondences, both stylistically and content-wise, to the inventories of the latter.

[106] RBPR, Papeles tocantes a Indias II-175, N.55, 249v.

[107] De Carlos Morales, "Política," 213.

mainly regarding piracy in the Caribbean. When the House of Trade wrote with alarm to the Council of the Indies that they had received many reports from the Governor of Puerto Rico warning of pirate activities in 1583, the king himself took the initiative of formalizing this committee.[108] This gathering was to feature the senior Indies minister Gasca de Salazar, a Council of War minister, and each of these institutions' secretaries.[109] These officials coordinated the Indies' defensive efforts, especially in Puerto Rico and the wider Caribbean, seeking to safeguard the region with massive fortresses and well-coordinated naval forces. They also considered reforms about the fleet systems, the relocation of the strategic but malarial Panama port of Nombre de Dios, the work of Italian military engineer Giovanni Battista Antonelli, and other urgent issues.

The Council of the Indies' secretaries and scribes archived the Junta de Puerto Rico's petitions, internal paperwork, and decrees separately from ordinary business, and collected pressing petitions for ministers, just as they did for the Junta of Finance. This enabled subalterns to provide ministers and monarchs with a rich base of descriptive facts and a keener sense of military developments on the ground.[110] For instance, one 1585 *consulta* shows that this junta was deeply researching the fortification of the Strait of Magellan after the pirate Sir Francis Drake had passed through it and sacked various Pacific ports.[111] This is probably why, in 1583, council ministers demanded the armada secretary hand over papers relating to the Straight and the Pacific.[112] The junta also turned much of its attention to military defenses in Florida, the Antilles, and Buenos Aires.[113] By 1597, it had scores of boxes of documentation at its disposal about many military and defense topics and at least two specifically dedicated to its own paperwork.[114]

The Junta of Puerto Rico's participants quite successfully analyzed financial data, allocating resources for a new system of Indies defenses capable of repelling major pirate predations. For instance, it appointed

[108] Schäfer, *Consejo*, vol.1, 172, and footnote 267. In what appears to be Schäfer's typographical error, he lists the letters as 1563, but cites a document from 1583.

[109] Schäfer *Consejo*, vol.1, 172.

[110] See, for example, its separate decree registers in Indiferente 541, L.1, Puerto Rico, as well as *consultas* in Indiferente 1866, 1867 and 1883.

[111] AGI, Patronato 33, N.3, R.52. [112] AGI, Patronato 33, N.3, R.36.

[113] AGI, Indiferente 1866, December 24 1585, July 4, 1590, and Charcas 1, N.93, January 27, 1593.

[114] AGI, Contaduría, 7A.

and corresponded with the exceptionally capable Italian engineer Bautista Antonelli, whom the junta dispatched to the Caribbean to construct a line of defense against future arracks. There, he designed fortifications and oversaw their construction from the Cartagena-Panama area, coastal Mexico, and the Islands. Over several years' travels, the Italian had accumulated hands-on experience with the Indies, which meant that junta members did not question his understanding of Indies geography and society.[115] Moreover, junta officials trusted he was not part of any local factions or secret interests. Indies vassals repeatedly petitioned in order to thwart Bautista, accusing him constantly of taking bribes, favoring certain projects over others to benefit his interests, and even revealing the Indies' secrets to his French assistant.[116] However, ministers were confident that Bautista was simply upsetting these subjects' local social and business interests – for instance, by redirecting roads, appropriating local labor, and neglecting to fortify some areas in favor of others.

Bautista's success proved itself on the battlefield. A decade earlier, pirate expeditions led by Drake had torched their way around the Indies with little resistance. Now, the system Bautista had overseen made such plundering much more difficult. In Panama, Spanish forces repelled Drake at the strategic mountain pass of Capirilla.[117] The engineer's Caribbean fort system was instrumental in defeating Drake once again when he attacked Puerto Rico and its fort of El Morro in November 1595. The timely arrival of the Spanish Armada ultimately saved the day after a small contingent of Spanish soldiers kept the invaders at bay. Drake's forces once again met defeat off the coast of Cuba, and when he returned to the bay of Portobelo, Panama, he died of dysentery. A large British force would sack Puerto Rico by land invasion in 1598, but only after a time-consuming battle against the island's badly outnumbered defenses. Disease struck, and the pirates returned to England.[118] The Crown had, at least in this particularly important sphere of military affairs, largely managed to muster descriptive facts and overcome local interests to protect strategic imperial locations such as Panama and the Caribbean.

The rise of the special juntas whose members had direct experience, possessed a body of trustworthy factual sources, and were ready to make decisive legislation from above seems to point to a vigorous administration capable of top-down action. Had the Crown at last achieved mastery

[115] AGI, México 257, "Con un navío," February 10, 1590.
[116] For one such accusation, see AGI, México 257, ""Relación," October 12, 1590.
[117] Broussard, "Antonelli." 519. [118] Andrews, *Last Voyage*, 152, 244.

over the decision-making process? The reality was more complex. True, the king and his officials had become more conversant in many elements of imperial rule thanks to these committees. However, these meetings also had a mixed record. The Junta of Finance did not produce any great financial genius to banish financial woes from Spain or even resolve the *encomienda* debate. The Junta of Puerto Rico temporarily stalled and even repelled major European attacks in the Caribbean. Moreover, if committee members sometimes settled upon wiser decisions, their deliberations also caused major delays. Nor was either junta capable of wrestling with all the claims of the ever-increasing number of incoming petitions. Now military and financial matters had a special channel, yes, but the New World had so many complex and multifaceted problems that a hundred committees would not have sufficed. This ensured that, despite major royal advances toward a more active and informed decision-making process, bottom-up petitions continued to prompt council ministers to respond. For instance, the junta of Puerto Rico seems to have produced a mere 238 royal decrees between 1586 and 1596, and the Junta of Finance produced 560 decrees between 1584 and 1604.[119] By contrast, just the Lima decree books for 1551–1555 alone contained 2,140 entries; Lima's registers between 1584 and 1604 contained tens of thousands.[120] Ordinary decree registers were, of course, mostly *gracia*, and junta registers mostly *gobierno*, but there is no doubt that these committees produced a limited number of *gobierno* edicts in comparison with those decided upon by council officials.

THE COUNCIL AND ITS FACTUAL ARCHIVE, 1597

In mid-1598, on the eve of King Philip II's death, the council's legislative praxis was in an ambivalent state. On the one hand, ministers maintained their stance that vassals should dominate the process by petitioning them for new decrees. On the other hand, these officials sought to use various different archives: a massive collection of legal facts and reference works, a group of elite subjects' reports arranged into descriptive facts, and the king's *consultas* to provide a modicum of order.

What might the council's overall archival resources have looked like? Unfortunately, surviving documents rarely reveal the exact sources ministers might have drawn from. One extensive 1597 testimony lists

119 AGI, Indiferente 541, L.1, Puerto Rico; AGI, Indiferente 606, L.1; L.2; L.3.

120 AGI, Lima 567, L.7.

substantial specifics about how its ministers amassed and used Indies knowledge and reveals that the council had a vast trove of sources on hand.[121] These records span two massive books: the first was more than 2,400 pages, and the second was nearly as long.

These lists offer a snapshot of the 1590s council's epistemic setting. They depicted some of its archives as an indiscriminate mass – half-organized piles of government papers of all sorts. Heaping *legajos* of 1570s to 1590s petitions appear left and right in the notary's writing, often without any discernable order – seventeen here, thirty-one there, and another eleven there. The years jumped haphazardly back and forth. This suggests that the council could not have been using them systematically; they had been in the care of a secretary's wife in a Madrid house, and some were surely awaiting delivery to Simancas.

Others were clearly still in use by the council. A large part of these registers also concerned *gobierno* papers and legislation. Many bundles appeared with labels suggesting ministers used them with some regularity. For example, the notary listed institutional groupings like the "writings of the Junta de Hacienda" and the "Junta de Puerto Rico" papers. Other sections were military in nature, with designations such as "artillery and war," "Fortress of Havana," and "Production of Biscay Galleons." Others were more obviously economic, with titles such as "copper mines," "*almoxarifazgo*," and "pearls." Many seem to have dealt with regional issues, such as "the Molucca Islands," "Brazil and the Port of Buenos Aires," and "descriptions of the lands and provinces of the Indies" (these may have been the legendary *relaciones geográficas*). A smaller group dealt with moral and religious issues, such as the "Royal Patronage" papers, the "the liberty of the Indians" and the Indies' "spiritual government," and "University and Cathedral of Lima," or the "papers on the Inquisition of New Spain and Peru."

Some sources were clearly more important than others. The archival list shows that council officials possessed some 300 registers of royal decrees, which their subalterns consulted often. There were also *consultas* for the years 1575–1597, organized into dozens of rather haphazard

[121] For Ledesma, see Manzorro Guerrero, "Prácticas documentales," 130. For Sopando, see AGI, Indiferente 744, N.71. Council officials had a notary produce this inventory while in the process of merging the position of Scrivener of Justice with the Chamber of Grace and Governance (the 1594 and 1596 deaths of Juan de Ledesma and Francisco Sopando de Valmesada, respectively, had vacated this position). Sopando's widow doña Mariana de Ribera had inherited his *justicia* paperwork. She also received many of the council's *gobierno* and *gracia* papers.

yearly groups. Some concerned crucial thematic issues such as the "*Consultas* about matters of the Strait of Magellan"; others focused on friars' procurators, bishoprics, and *visitas*; and another on Inquisition finances. Others were simply random groupings of *consultas* "of different types."[122]

Another section, "Libros," featured hide-bound tomes of royal paperwork. Considering their special binding, these were probably the most important for ministers after the decree registers and *consultas*. Indeed, these may be the "papers" which officials referred to when they ordered subalterns to consult council repositories. These tomes included documents on tax policies of New Spain, New Biscay, Guatemala, Nicaragua, Yucatan, Peru, Cartagena, Tierra Firme, and Pasto. There were other individual volumes for the tithing systems of Cuzco and Guamanga, and another on the "spiritual governance" of Quito. Others dealt with peripheral but militarily important areas of the Indies, one "Discovery and Pacification of the Darién," a "Settlement of la Trinidad," and a 1536 "Study of the Magellan Straight." A separate book consisted entirely of decrees and letters relating to *encomienda* laws.[123]

In some ways, the two 1597 inventories reveal a wealth of information about the sources the council might refer to when determining *gobierno* paperwork. Ministers mention in their marginal comments that they used certain "papers" located within the council; these were likely the inventory's many large boxes of petitions, *consultas*, and books. However, these registers do not always reveal much about the institution's specific archival arrangements. For one, the notary's brief excerpts merely sketch the contents of this archive, but do not explain how and when each text proved useful for ministers. Moreover, they provide a static image of the mid-1590s state of affairs, but give no indication of how ministers proceeded in previous decades. It is likely that officials kept a dynamic and chaotic archive, shifting with the growing and waning concerns of an empire that was always lurching from crisis to crisis. To achieve a fuller understanding of how the legislative process worked, we would have to have far more information about the papers at the ministers' disposal at any given moment.

[122] AGI, Contaduría 7A, L.2. [123] AGI, Indiferente, 1624.

GLIMPSES OF A MORE ASSERTIVE CROWN

Though it is not always easy to piece together ministers' decision-making, the overall picture strongly suggests that these officials became more active in crucial areas. However, the overall decision-making environment, both in the committees and in the council, was now richer in both social and legal facts. What did these more assertive capabilities look like in everyday decision-making? Certain marginal comments on petitions illustrate the concrete roles' improved factual collections might offer officials and monarchs. The Viceroy of Mexico had reported on May 1, 1572 that the mercury mines needed more slaves; he suggested enticing Indian wage laborers to work, but noted Crown legislation prohibiting this. He said that he would let "His Majesty order what was best." At this point a marginal comment from a council member provided an unusually extensive written reflection on a certain petition, ordering,

> if by his words the mercury mines need more labor, gathering persons of good heart [*bondad*], knowledge [*ciencia*] and conscience [*conciencia*] and seeing the order that exists for Peru, the best order they agree upon should be sent so that the Indians, of their own volition, and paying them a daily wage, work in the mines, giving orders that it not harm them, and taking very great care to inform about if they are mistreated so that they not be [mistreated], and proceed in the matter with much temperance and moderation, and seeing how it proceeds, providing reports of its success.[124]

Even King Philip II himself might sometimes evince a more active stance. During the 1580s, imperial troubles began to accumulate and petitions to the councils surged. Ministers pushed for increasing contact with the king as difficult matters multiplied. Philip answered at least 1,373 *consultas* by 1585, but between that year and his death on September 13, 1598, he answered another 2,281.[125] This increase is partly misleading, as before the 1560s royal archival practices were weaker, meaning more *consultas* survived in the final years of the sixteenth century. Nonetheless, the abundance of these documents beginning in the mid-1580s is no mirage, thanks mainly to rising numbers of petitions, but also to the ever-expanding circles of ministers attending ever more subcommittees.

King Philip preferred to reach his decisions with ample written evidence, explicitly stating the need to "know more particularly" the "reasons, pros and cons" of the *consultas* reaching his desk.[126] *Consultas*, and council

[124] AGI, México 19, N.74, 21r. [125] Heredia Herrera, *Catálogo*, Tomos I-II.
[126] AGI, Indiferente 741, N.109.

paperwork overall, would increase in volume exponentially beginning in the 1560s, as would *gobierno* paperwork in general. Whereas between 1550 and 1555, surviving Council of the Indies *consultas* number 139, between 1556 and the time of Philip's death in 1598, a staggering 3,220 of these documents survive.[127] While these *consultas* were indeed an ordinary part of council praxis, however, it would be a mistake to think that these documents featured most ordinary *gobierno* issues. Rather, only for the most difficult or extraordinary cases would a *gobierno* proposal reach the king's desk; most concerned issues of *gracia*.

The *consulta* paper trail would capture more of King Philip's reflections and reveal a ruler making good use of the Council of the Indies' improving archive. In one 1581 case, for instance, ministers recorded how they summoned a number of documents to help him make nine different determinations. They produced several documents in response to an unspecified vassal's requests (whose name they carefully scratched out on the back of the document). The *consulta* documentation features various lines clearly reflecting the secretaries' retrieval of these papers for the king's final decision (Table 5.1).

By the 1580s, the king was increasingly beginning to insert his opinions on *consultas*. Clearly, he was most informed and involved when facing military issues. For instance, when petitions by Havana's military officials arrived at the council in late 1590, begging the king to send reinforcements to Cuba, he responded that "sending an armada to Havana brings with it great difficulties, and the place was never so secure as it is now." He concluded he would make his decision regarding how many smaller ships to send by reading "the reports [*relaciones*] of its generals that are in the Council or in the hands of [Secretary] Ibarra."[128] The King had checked the Indies reports in the Junta's archive (surely with a subaltern's help) and found them to be exaggerated – a clear sign of his increasing factual mastery or at least his greater confidence regarding New World matters.[129]

The king once again showed that he had at least a basic comprehension of these military and geographical issues when the council brought a *consulta* before him in 1596, also about Cuban military affairs. He suggested spontaneously in a marginal comment that the armada should

[127] Heredia Herrera, *Catálogo*, Tomos I-II. [128] AGI, Indiferente 741, N.248.

[129] For a similar case regarding reforms in the trajectory of the Tierra Firme Fleet, based on petitions from the municipality of Panama, see the king's comments in AGI, Panama 1, N.67.

TABLE 5.1 *Royal decisions and the new council archive*

Ministers' summaries (fragments)	*[King's instructions for council subaltern]*
1. Your Majesty be served to favor the passing of friars to the Indies	1. No need to respond
2. In the [petition's] second chapter … the Viceroy investigated the whole land and set its taxes … in writing … but has not sent them	2. For issue 2, bring the papers that the Viceroy don Francisco [de Toledo] sent
3. In the third … the Indians not be aggrieved … provided by decrees that the tributes be paid in goods … Viceroy has ordered them to pay in silver	3. Bring everything the Viceroy has produced
4. In the fourth … the decrees have been issued for the remedy for this … they will be issued again	4. That the report [*memorial*] of the Viceroy be seen, bring the decrees that have been issued
5. In the fifth … that Your Majesty be served with issuing a decree … viceroys and High Judges inform … [about wicked officials] … Indians should not be aggrieved	5. Bring it to read it with the report [*memorial*] of the Viceroy
6. [Decrees] have been issued a decree [about the sixth chapter] 7. The same for the seventh	6. and 7., That the decree be brought that was ordained with the clause that an investigation be undertaken against the *corregidores* and ministers that have exceeded this
8. For the eighth and [9.] ninth … that the High Courts fix this with much care	8. and 9., [Produce and dispatch] decrees conforming to the *consulta*, ordering that they punish the guilty
(in AGI, Indiferente 739, N.353, Aug. 12, 1581)	

ship cannons to the island using them as ballast or, better yet, should create a single artillery foundry on the island. All Indies-bound ships were to take ore as ballast to the port and begin production.[130] In this instance, the king had modified the original proposal, drawing from his accumulated knowledge of military and naval technology and Indies geography.

[130] AGI, Indiferente 744, N.55, September 8, 1596.

Philip also developed certain firm convictions about economic and social issues based on descriptive facts. For instance, on April 24, 1596 he responded to an undated report on the difficult economic state of Santo Domingo by ordering the gradual buildup of a fortress there. He revealed his opinion about the island merchants' suggestion regarding freer trade: "what matters most is that [officials] be careful to prohibit foreigners and primarily the British from trading in any fashion in the Indies."[131] Military concerns trumped mercantile ones, he had decided. While such comments reflecting his grasp of knowledge unchained from petitions' specific claims were rare, they did become somewhat more common as the 1580s and 1590s progressed.

Philip also might make somewhat more assertive moral and administrative decisions remote from military issues. On May 8, 1581, the king read a petition and proposed his own sui generis solution – an action which in previous decades would have been an extreme rarity. He wrote the council, "I am reading what you responded to the chapters of complaints of the New Realm of Granada." He continued, "it would be a sufficient provision that in the central and marginal areas of all the Indies it be proclaimed that if any Indians or any others feel overworked [*cargados*] ... by the *encomenderos* or anyone else, they should seek help at the High Courts or the other centers of justice to be relieved of these grievances."[132]

The overall advances which the administration derived from repositories of descriptive and legal facts had at least one major downside. The burgeoning *consultas* and special junta consultations caused a substantial slowdown in the decision-making process. When the king read an August 1, 1596 *consulta* about ordering new fleet departure dates and other matters, his secretary wrote, "the President take this to the Junta ... and inform me in what is decided in it." Three weeks later, on August 22, 1596, a marginal comment in the hand of the king's secretary Ibarra states that "having undertaken the diligence that His Majesty here ordered," the president recommended fixing a specific date for the departure of the fleets or the captains would face "harsh penalties." This answer did not solve the problem – or even fix a date – but it had set the legislative process back by twenty-one days.[133] In a similar case, the king responded to a *consulta*

[131] AGI, Indiferente 744, N.182. Soon thereafter, on March 22, 1597, he once again responded to a report – this time from the House of Trade dated May 18, 1597 – that among "sailors it is not convenient that foreigners go."

[132] AGI, Indiferente 739, N.325.

[133] AGI, Indiferente 744, N.38.

about the competing jurisdictions of the House of Trade and the Council of Finance on August 1, 1596 and received his answer on October 24, 1596 – a setback of eighty-six days. Doubt, along with the king's illnesses, was creating slowdowns by forcing these time-consuming backs and forths, and these delays were making it hard for the king to administer his empire in a timely manner.

ARCHIVAL MANAGEMENT, SECRETARIES' POWER, AND CONFLICT IN THE COUNCIL

Documentary archives of legal and descriptive facts had bestowed limited but important advantages upon monarchs' decision-making by the late sixteenth century. As one anonymous report stated in the early 1600s, archives were "the light with which these realms, so extended and far from their head, [are] the papers which have formed and are gathered since their discovery."[134] These "supplement the lack of experience and intelligence of ministers and secretaries who are new."[135] The proposal suggested unifying the many different factual repositories into one so that ministers would not always be "panhandling for news" (*mendigando la noticia*). King Philip II, however, argued sometime in the 1590s for these collections' continued separation, fearing that a single council archive would be more difficult for officials to use.[136]

Certainly, since the 1560s and especially the 1590s these repositories of legal and descriptive facts became prominent actants within the decision-making process in their own right, alongside nontextual technologies like experience and debate. Indeed, even as documents stored within archival systems enabled royal administrators to achieve greater consistency and multiperspectivity, officials also sometimes delegated certain faculties of reasoning and phraseological formulation to these papers. In a way, archival repositories helped ministers stick to a streamlined, efficient script; in other ways, these papers sometimes wrested these officials' active engagement away from a given case, making paper the real protagonist.

Ministers' embrace of archival technologies had another paradoxical effect. Archives (and complex paperwork in general) also exerted their own transformations, as ministers' desire for a more automated assembly line made its subalterns more powerful. By the 1580s, for example, the

[134] RBPR, Papeles tocantes a Indias II-175, N.47.
[135] RBPR, Papeles tocantes a Indias II-175, N.47.
[136] RBPR, Papeles tocantes a Indias II-175, N.47.

importance of the council's social secretaries increased greatly. These officials oversaw all incoming petitions, acted as intermediaries between the council, the juntas, and the king, and acted as custodians of the increasingly useful royal archives. Soon enough, council secretaries began to exert their growing authority upon ministers. Already by the mid-1580s, associates of Mateo Vázquez were pushing for him to have voting faculties in all imperial councils.[137]

Secretaries' ascendance, bolstered largely due to their mastery of royal archives, became particularly clear during an acrimonious debate in the late 1590s. It began when Secretary Juan de Ibarra pushed for a reform of the council's praxes, which produced a reorganization of its scribal offices of *gobierno* and *justicia*.[138] As the new council secretary, Ibarra received direct oversight of and responsibility over the scribal chamber of *Gobierno*; his counterpart, Pedro de Ledesma, received oversight of the scribal chamber of *Justicia*. Ibarra thus oversaw the council's *gobierno* repositories. Moreover, the king gave him the faculty to vote on council affairs as a minister except in cases of *justicia* (which he could not participate in because he lacked juridical training). The council's president and ministers were also terribly irritated by Ibarra's assertion of his right to vote as well, ordering he stay home, often with "heavy words."[139] An anonymous protest from certain council officials stated that though the position of secretary had the "most strenuous workload that there is in this court," Ibarra preferred to play the role of minister.[140] He not only was slow at processing paperwork and deprived the "Council of its authority" but also had since 1597 the duty of opening all incoming documents before bringing them to the president. This enabled him to "stop and conceal those [documents] that he could wish, and to his ends."[141]

Another anonymous report from around 1601 complained that Ibarra's monopolization of incoming correspondence meant that "there is no understanding or ability through which [ministers] can govern the Indies."[142] Ibarra retorted that his management of papers owed not to any sinister plot but to the extreme workload of organizing documents into their respective channels and jotting down the basic details of each case; he

[137] HSA, 7/II/19, March 7, 1586.

[138] AGI, Indiferente 516, L1, 5v–6v. For a post-facto assertion by an insider that Ibarra prompted the reforms, IVDJ, E88,C124,280, n/d.

[139] IVDJ, E88, C124,279, n/d. [140] IVDJ, E88, C124,280, n/d.

[141] IVDJ, E88, C124,280, n/d. [142] IVDJ, E88, C124,282, n/d, no folios.

had to undertake this at home, after council hours, or imperial decision-making would become "impossible."[143]

Ibarra seems to have universally irritated his peers, with considerable consequences for Indies governance. His pretensions created a major rivalry between himself and council secretary Pedro de Ledesma over the Junta of Finance. In this committee, Ibarra formally was a minister, and Ledesma a secretary, but Ibarra insisted on handling all papers and not dealing with Ledesma at all.[144] This all occurred precisely during the last years of King Philip II's life and the regencies preceding King Philip III's rise to power, resulting in the temporary paralysis of one of the empire's most important decision-making organs.[145]

SECRETARIES' WIVES AS ARCHIVAL CUSTODIANS

In the eyes of sixteenth-century contemporaries, secretaries were the foremost managers of Crown repositories. By the late 1500s, they had become much more powerful than mere paper-pushers. In his 1598 *Espejo de Príncipes*, Martín de Carvallo Villasboas stated that each council secretary's mastery of royal paperwork made him the "treasurer of the machine of [the King's] thoughts."[146] Carvallo urged that "the Secretary who is employed in this great machine ... must betroth himself with his bureau, and with its procedures."[147]

This metaphor of matrimony was rich with irony, for indeed the women whom royal secretaries married often played a crucial role in the maintenance of this imperial "machine." Because these secretaries oversaw archives as their patrimonial possessions, these repositories were often located in their homes as part of these officials' patrimonies. As archives sat within this domestic sphere, secretaries' wives very often played a particularly important and sensitive role in taking care of royal documents: the decree books, petitions, court cases, communications with the king, and other repositories of social and legal facts.

In 1508, the Catholic Kings ordered Gaspar de Gricio's unnamed widow to hand over the papers "touching upon the Indies" to Secretary Conchilllos. When Conchillos passed, the king ordered his widow, doña María Niño de Ribera, to create an inventory of his Indies papers in 1522 and to hand all of these documents to Charles V's royal secretary

[143] IVDJ, E88, C124,284, n/d, no folios.
[144] RBPR, Papeles tocantes a Indias II-175, N.55, 251r. [145] IVDJ, E88, C124,284, n/d.
[146] Carvalho Vilas Boas, *Espejo*, 35. [147] Carvalho Vilas Boas, *Espejo*, 38.

Francisco de los Cobos. In 1597, doña Mariana de Ribera, the widow of former official Francisco de Balmaseda, led the effort to inventory the council's paperwork which she had been caring for in her home, and which she handed to incoming secretaries Juan de Ibarra and Pedro de Ledesma. Diego de Encinas and his associate Juan de Miranda noted that since 1563 (and perhaps before) a vast amount of the council's papers had been in storage in Minister Balmaseda's and his wife's two houses. Between these homes, the council stored more than 200 *legajos* and many other boxes, leaving doña Mariana "very aggrieved for these papers take up the greater part of her own homes."[148]

Women thus retained a very important patrimonial role as family custodians over the empire's documents. They did so apparently without direct remuneration or formal recognition from the king or the council and were thus almost entirely excluded from any part in the fiction of vassal–lord dialogue. Nonetheless, by providing these domestic archives with critical work and upkeep, they supplied enough labor to have truly played a "thoroughgoingly constitutive" role as secretarial coworkers.[149] It is in large part thanks to these women that petitions and decree registers – indeed, the entire imperial archives – have survived.[150]

OTHER COUNCIL SUBALTERNS

Secretaries also relied on a network of dependents who operated formally and informally under their employ. Of particular importance to archival operations were the near-invisible but indispensable council subalterns. Scriveners, who were directly under secretaries, played an essential role in archival management. Secretary Ibarra fought hard to keep and expand his privileges, which often came at the expense of Scrivener Pedro de Ledesma's duties – they wrangled over Ledesma's papers, and even over his small cubicle.[151] Unsurprisingly, by the early 1600s, Ledesma was also angling to become a council secretary, reflecting the rather thin line separating scriveners and secretaries.[152]

Scriveners had their own subalterns, who also provided fundamental labor to the decision-making process. Domingo de la Quintana stated in 1592 that he would soon travel to Peru with a new governor, but had

[148] AGI, Indiferente 1415, "Francisco de Bergas," January 24, 1597.
[149] Ludwig, "Verwaltung," 196. [150] McGaw, "Feminine Technologies," 23.
[151] BFZ, E.134–131.
[152] IVDJ, E88, C124,285, n/d. See also Gómez Gómez, "Secretarios."

previously enjoyed working for a year and a half for the *gobierno* scrivener, helping "with much care and diligence, giving good dispatch to all business and papers."[153] In 1597, Pedro Galíndez de Coca worked under Minister Balmaseda and requested payment for "having spent three months in concerting how to order and make the bundles [*legajos*] of all the papers, processes, reports, investigations ... sentences, [and] *consultas*."[154] Galíndez' coworker Alonso de Aybar called foul the next year; it was he who had spent nine grueling months making an inventory of deceased Scrivener Juan de Ledesma's papers, "which has been much work .... separating and dividing different materials one from the other, because they are so many ... working night and day."[155]

No single individual better embodied the growing influence of the subaltern official upon the decision-making process than Diego de Encinas. He had been a subaltern since 1556, working on litigation paperwork under the scrivener of *justicia*.[156] He had worked under secretaries Sámano and Eraso and specialized on the trials against the Pizarro clan, Governor Vaca de Castro, and the ringleaders of Mexico's Cortés-Ávila revolt. Under Ovando and Crown attorney Liébana he began to pore over "all the books and registers" of the council, in order to create a book divided into *gobierno* and *justicia* and by thematic subsections "so that those of the Council could have news of them" – clearly, the primordial version of his 1596 *Cedulario*.[157] Encinas stressed that "because the work was so great ... nobody had wanted to accept" this task, he had "toiled day and night" for twelve years to arrange the compilation's four books.[158] His gradual rise from lowly subaltern to the architect of the first great printed book of Indies decrees epitomizes the essential structural contributions of these nearly invisible workers on decision-making and on Indies society in general.

Even certain doormen might play a direct role in organizing papers. Juan de Morales requested his pay for cataloguing the contents of the papers of secretaries Juan de Ibarra and Pedro de Ledesma.[159] He

153 AGI, Indiferente 1409, "Domingo de la Quintana," June 19, 1592.
154 AGI, Indiferente 1415, "Pedro Galíndez," October 24, 1597.
155 AGI, Indiferente 1416, "Alonso de Aybar," n/d, 1598.
156 AGI, Contaduría 215, no page, no title; AGI, Indiferente 1379, "Diego de Encinas," no date; AGI, Indiferente 1400, "Diego de Encinas," July 30, 1586; AGI, Indiferente 1409, "Diego de Encinas," July 6, 1592.
157 AGI, Indiferente 1419, May 28, 1598, "Diego de Encinas."
158 AGI, Indiferente 1419, May 28, 1598, "Diego de Encinas."
159 AGI, Indiferente 1415, "Juan de Morales."

emphasized how hard the task had been – he worked for five months, even during festivities, spending 30,000 maravedís to produce a 3,000-page inventory. The council awarded him 100 ducats.[160] Doormen and their handymen also participated in producing certain archival collections through less bookish forms of labor. The material conditions which ensured the integrity of legal and descriptive facts were no minor subset of council decision-making. Archives required forms of material support: desks and shelves for organization, leather bindings and string for protection from the elements, and so forth. Handymen built and maintained the council's archival repositories. Doorman Pedro Romero reported in 1583 that he (or perhaps his underlings) had repaired a large secretary's desk made of walnut, added iron fittings, and painted it with the Habsburg coat of arms.[161] He also spent four months with a team of carpenters and other laborers building shelves, fixing locks, binding books, and even repairing the council's map.[162] Three years later, he invoiced the council for similar work.[163]

Handymen also produced Crown papers' physical repositories, often through book-binding or the creation of documentary bundles or *legajos*. Around 1592, a receipt described how Scrivener Juan de Ledesma had entrusted several assistants to cut paper and bind books together, including "the books of the ordinances of the Indies," and "two books of New Spain, and other of New Galicia," among others. These works appear to have been mainly decree registers, but one, "the discovery of New Spain," may have either been a printed book, a long report, or a collection of petitions.[164] The value of this labor came to 1,360 maravedís. One subsequent document from 1608 suggests that the secretaries entrusted these labor assignments to doormen.[165] These contributions enabled the decree registers to withstand the elements in the sixteenth century and even survive until the present.

There were thus multiple types of labor which rendered Crown archives available to the decision-making process. Secretaries and their wives oversaw the custody of these repositories, subaltern officials developed the tools necessary for archival retrieval, and handymen overseen by council doormen ensured the integrity of the archives by constructing and

[160] AGI, Indiferente 1415, "Juan de Morales"; AGI, Indiferente 1416, "Juan de Morales portero"; AGI, Indiferente 1417, "Juan de Morales portero," September 15, 1598.
[161] AGI, Indiferente 1395, "Pedro Romero," November 11, 1583.
[162] AGI, Indiferente 1395, "Pedro Romero," n/d.
[163] AGI, Indiferente 1401, "Quenta," August 22, 1586.
[164] AGI, Indiferente 1408, "Lo que," n/d. [165] AGI, Indiferente 1378, "Febrero 1608."

maintaining the physical repositories of documents. Collectively, this work enabled ministers to take significant if limited strides toward rationalizing elements of the royal decision-making process and had critical impacts on spheres of acute imperial concern, such as protecting the Caribbean from pirates, as well as on everyday decision-making.

CONCLUSIONS

The formula *knowledge = power* and its surrogate clause *archives = power* are too simplistic to explain imperial administration or power in general. These equations mystify, rather than elucidate, the true textual and social resources which enabled polities to operate and expand. They also obscure the actors involved in rendering certain repositories from useless deposits into corpuses useful to rulers, and the social transformations the rise of these individuals brings about. We must provide concrete examples of how officials and subalterns might prime certain groups of documents for use and explain why these works seemed decisive to lawmaking entities in a specific time and place. Only then can we grasp what Brendecke called "the intricate connection between knowledge and the exercise of colonial rule."[166]

The royal administration's great dilemmas were communication versus imposition and passivity versus activity. Ministers' increasing embrace of archival repositories to fact-check and probe vassals' petitions threatened to disrupt petitioners' ability to shape law – the very formula of the empire's success. After all, a complete shift from a passive, listening monarchy to an active, discerning one would also suppose the monarchy's severing of its bonds with many vassals – which would in turn jeopardize the royal conscience and perhaps the empire. Ministers' improving grasp over its Indies legal and descriptive facts made the council somewhat less responsive to subjects' proposals and gave ministers some limited powers to quash whistleblowers, who had played such a large role in reform in earlier decades. Vassals had certainly lost some of their power to set the imperial agenda, especially by the 1580s and 1590s, due to the council's improving archives.

Ministers and monarchs wisely avoided overextending these new technologies. Archives (and outsourced ones such as those belonging to the

[166] Brendecke, *Empirical Empire*, 9. For two additional important works which take this more nuanced approach to council cosmographical-cartographic knowledge, see Portuondo, *Secret Science*; Padron, *Spacious Word.*

Franciscan Commissary) might assist their decisions. However, they could never replace legitimacy and the Crown's thirst for news and dialogue. Even if officials had harbored such a desire, they lacked the manpower. To transform hundreds of thousands of complex, interest-laden *gobierno* petitions into a single matrix of easy-to-use information would have required vast investments of labor and money. Crown officials thus never truly sought to create from its repositories a domain of perfect, systematic, total knowledge. Instead, they largely maintained their dialogue with vassals, while strategically employing limited, labor-intensive efforts to reorder certain papers in response to acute crises.

That being said, officials could reap certain limited but very important advantages from making its repository of papers into a useful archive, and which might also benefit vassals. Thanks to the council's improved decree registers, ministers could reach more consistent decisions, and their publication of Encinas' compilation of *de oficio* decrees likely settled numerous social conflicts in the Indies which arose from previous contradictory policies. Officials' accumulation of descriptive facts also provided them with certain tools for a limited but significant mastery over petitioners' claims by allowing officials to be somewhat more discerning of harmful bias and outright falsehoods. On the one hand, this also increased officials' decision-making consistency and clear-sightedness about certain key topics and was likely instrumental in, for example, the empire's triumph over British pirates in the 1590s. The Junta of Puerto Rico's clear-eyed evaluation of Caribbean defenses "constituted a possibly sinister step" in the increasingly active nature of state administration, but with vassals at risk from piracy, few protested their improved protection.

This move toward legal consistency increased royal legitimacy, reduced Indies social conflicts, and, crucially, made ministers' work faster and easier. However, paradoxically, legal archives also automated council decision-making, which ceded a substantial amount of free-form human power to a more material universe of shelves, papers, and indices. This meant, on the one hand, reduced labor for ministers and the king. On the other hand, both Crown officials and petitioners lost some agency in this automation process; subjects prompted decrees somewhat less often as ministers located precedent more easily, and both ministers and the king used these archival technologies to actually diminish their own engagements with each case.

Just as the transition from the 1550s to the 1570s had inaugurated substantial changes in the petition-and-response system, the transition after King Philip II's 1598 death would also bring about important shifts in royal practices. Some of these were subtle, like the growing role of Crown attorneys (*fiscales*) in reading and reporting on petitions. By the early-to-mid-1600s, these officials' annotations on petitions were ubiquitous. This meant that the council increasingly accepted that an official with the juridical training useful for litigation could indeed play a growing role in helping ministers "discover" more just solutions. This early-to-mid-1600s rise of expert attorneys like Antonio de León Pinelo and Juan Solórzano y Pereira – who were also the virtuosi of royal archives – also marked a major departure from the reign of King Philip II. This suggests that lawyers were bringing a casuistic process to the council which in the 1500s had been largely missing.

Aside from the very active role played by the *fiscales*, whose protagonism seems to have made them ministers in their own right, the council increasingly took on somewhat machine-like characteristics thanks to the archive. These officials increasingly delegated their agency to both material objects and to repetitive paperwork routines. That the king himself had become a sort of machinist, signing hundreds of decrees a day, was a fact not lost on contemporaries. It was the masters of these routines and material resources whose stature grew most in this period. By the early 1600s, this changing locus of power weakened the participation of council ministers in decision-making, increased the stature of secretaries and scriveners, and set the stage for the emergence of the *privados*, the prime ministers who dominated much of seventeenth-century policy-making and paperwork. Meanwhile, the near-invisible labor of subalterns within the council, including not only doormen, carpenters, and other handymen but secretaries' wives, continued to ensure the maintenance of the empire's growing archival repositories – and transformed the petition-and-response process in subtle but fundamental ways.

These seventeenth-century changes' implications for petitioners are unclear. Perhaps there was a two-way influence in the rise of the *fiscal* and the *privados* and the increasing popularity of vassals' drafting of much longer and more ambitious petitions called *arbitrios*. Thousands of these texts, which often had economic themes, circulated the court from the mid-sixteenth and especially the early seventeenth centuries.[167] For many weary contemporaries of the 1600s, this so-called *arbitrismo* was little more than the tumorous parody of petitioning culture – not Spain's deliverance, but one of its most aggravating symptoms of malaise.[168] In

[167] Corteguera, "Mad *Arbitrista,*" 216–217.

[168] Corteguera, "Mad *Arbitrista,*" 221; Dubet, "L'arbitrisme"; Amadori, "Arbitrismo"; Herzog, "El arbitrismo y América."

a way, just as the mid-to-late-1500s council grappled with too many decrees and other documents, the *arbitrios* too showed signs that petitioning was reaching a rather saturated state of development as well.

The important changes of the 1600s did not arrive overnight and were more subtle than sudden. Moreover, old problems still dogged ministers. While they were on firmer ground than they had been three decades earlier, they had not assembled a sort of master key of statecraft that might allow them to entirely or even mostly supersede vassals' constant minor and major complaints, their lies, categories, and half-truths. New crises and monarchs' need to retain strong connections with its vassals meant that this system was going nowhere fast. The bottom-up nature of Indies legislation survived, weaker but solidly intact, well beyond the reign of King Philip II. The petition-and-response system, far from becoming a thing of the past, entered the turbulent seventeenth century almost as robust and dynamic as it had been in the sixteenth.

6

Creating the Royal Decree

Format, Phraseology, and Petitioners' Transformation of Indies Law

The ministers had at last decided. Pedro Rengifo's cover letter on the great 224-page dossier would undergo a transformation from petition to royal decree. The August 31, 1588 priesthood law unambiguously drew from Rengifo's own petitions. The petition's opening statement read "Pedro Rengifo, natural son of the captain Francisco Rengifo … in the power and voice of all sons Spaniards and Indians they call mestizos *who are born in those provinces."*[1] *The edict's preamble mirrored this phraseology almost exactly: "Pedro Rengifo, natural son that said [his father was] captain Francisco Rengifo … for himself and in the name of all the sons of Spaniards and Indians of [the land] has informed me … "*[2]

The parallels continued. The petition had insisted that the mestizos *were "on the verge of receiving the Sacred Orders to introduce themselves into the service of the Church and parishes" and insisted upon the approval of "the Apostolic Seat."*[3] *The 1588 decree almost entirely echoed this: "said mestizos [are] on the verge of receiving the Sacred Orders and have the support of His Holiness."*[4] *Council ministers had also integrated Pedro's recommendation that* mestiza *nuns no longer be restricted to "lay and not regular" status, responding that these sisters were to henceforth enjoy full rights and privileges, and banning monasteries from enforcing "that the mestiza nuns be lay and not regular*

[1] AGI, Lima 126, 115r. [2] AGI, Lima 580, L.9, 8v–10r. [3] AGI, Lima 126: 115r.
[4] AGI, Lima 580, L.9, 8v–10r Ruan, "Andean activism;" Duve, "El concilio."

nuns."[5] A mestizo *had prompted and phrased imperial legislation establishing the equality between* mestizo *and Spanish men and women.*

Council ministers intended these policy changes to apply to much of the Viceroyalty of Peru. Though the petitioners mainly worked in the Lima--Cuzco corridor, the decree's addresses were to be the "Archbishop of the Metropolitan Church of the City of the Kings [Lima] of the provinces of Peru," and the "Bishops of the Church Cathedrals of the cities of Cuzco, La Plata, San Francisco de Quito and Tucumán."[6] *When a secretary placed the council's draft on King Philip's desk, he signed it in a rush, imbuing it with his volition and transforming the document into law.*

Ministers approved a considerable portion of petitions – the towering decree registers and compilations make this abundantly clear.[7] Establishing exactly how many succeeded would be a major challenge. Certainly, however, the vassal–ruler exchange of proposals and volitions was not an empty discourse. As this chapter will show, moreover, the process through which council officials transformed petitions to decrees not only led to a body of legislation with origins in bottom-up initiatives. Ministers lifted petitions' phraseologies, often verbatim, directly into documents which the monarchs signed as their own.

Royal decrees had, and have today, a mythical power. Then, vassals believed the king to be a Christian of unimpeachable intentions, a fatherly broker of vassals' interests, an always-hearing ear. His decrees might be fallible due to ministers' or vassals' perverse deeds, but his will was pure. Today the myth has reversed almost entirely. For example, according to much historical scholarship, administrators created colonial categories and arrayed them within clear hierarchies, and, in the process, undertook the "training of new (epistemologically obedient) members ... controlling who enters and what knowledge-making is allowed, disavowed, devalued, or celebrated."[8] Those subscribing to this view disagree as to whether this project yielded results on the ground, but nonetheless have seen royal law as an attempt to rule the Indies through a top-down, highly coherent conquest through epistemology, taxonomy, and categorization. The archive – not so much the physical repository but the "epistemological master

[5] AGI, Lima 126, 115r–v and AGI, Lima 580, L.9, 8v–10r.
[6] AGI, Lima 580, L.9, 8v–10r.
[7] This chapter has appeared in a substantially different form as Adrian Masters, "Invisible Architects."
[8] Mignolo, *Darker*, 141; Stoler, *Archival Grain*, 1.

pattern" of colonialism – was not just a cog in this panoptical project.[9] It was the prison itself, the very "law of what can be said."[10] According to this view, colonial European writing, legislation, and codification (among other technologies) became tools to "take control of the people and the land" and thereby engage in "colonizing the imagination of people on both sides of the Atlantic – Amerindians and Europeans."[11]

There is much truth that many Europeans often deliberately sought to suppress and deface preconquest epistemologies, categories, and beliefs. And yet neither Europe nor Spain nor the Habsburgs spoke with one harmonious voice. This chapter argues that the council's woefully understaffed administration was not capable or particularly desirous of exerting much editorial effort in reformulating the phrasing of successful petitions as they became policy. This means that officials tended to insert considerably intact parts of petitioners' phraseology verbatim or near-verbatim into the empire's most important legislative documents. That subjects of all backgrounds could create new institutions and new categories, or modify existing ones, deals a serious blow to the mythology of "I, the King"; even the texts of these documents were often not the works of the Crown, let alone the monarch. This also challenges the historiography's common vision of decrees as the coherent expression of the Crown's will.

The petition-and-response system was a massive dialogue – rife with iniquities, mediation, make-believe, and partiality toward Habsburg values – but a dialogue all the same. Petitioners bombarded ministers with secret interests, alien worldviews, new terms, and odd uses of common categories. Decrees often mirrored these values, and could therefore accommodate deeply contradictory models of Indies realities. Even official royal compilations like the 1596 printed volumes by Encinas were nothing but records of previous communications, which subalterns then arranged thematically in a crucial but rather reduced editorial role. The royal administration's papers, then, were not top-down impositions of clear-eyed monarchs and officials animated by a methodical epistemological plan, nor were its contents the engine of Foucault's mythic Archive of perfect, unified discourse. Both decrees and the council's papers were heteromorphic, polyphonic textual accumulations with many cocreators. Of course, dialogue forced participants to seek certain mutually intelligible statements and values, but petitioners always sought to push this

9 Richards, "Archive"; 104. For a critique of archives as panoptic, see Stoler, *Archival Grain*, 23.

10 Foucault, *Archaeology*, 145.

11 Mignolo, *Darker*, 291 and 309.

communication to the limit in order to benefit their interests. The result of the very rational project of vassal–lord communication was an archive of decrees whose policies, categories, and epistemologies could never have been rational or unified.

The monarch's signature on each decree suppressed any explicit recognition of this polyphony. Contemporaries knew that kings did not create Indies decrees from thin air, but also did not publicly reflect on the problems of legal authorship or coproduction. After all, these texts were coauthored by vassals, ministers, and monarchs together; if one steps into the full social milieu beyond the document world, an almost infinite number of actants are responsible for these decrees and archives. The fiction of legal authorship was a powerful and necessary one, nonetheless, and horrific violence loomed for any vassal hoping to usurp the royal signature to create his own decree.

Gobierno decrees had countless themes. This chapter focuses in large part on vassals' ability to shape institutions on the one hand and legal categories of human difference on the other. Despite the historiography's common view of these categories as mere top-down impositions, a closer look at these categories reveals not a coordinated master plan emanating from the mythic state, but, rather, widespread confusion and cocreation.[12] On the ground, confusion, skepticism, and dialogue were the norm. For instance, in 1587 council officials sent to Guatemala a puzzled 1587 royal decree eliciting officials' advice about whether *mestizos* married to Indigenous women should pay tribute. The very existence of the mystery betrays the reign of confusion which Indies categories of human difference were engendering. An anonymous jurist attempted a rather casuistic answer. There was virtually no normative source he did not throw against the wall; he cited one decree from 1553 and then a contradictory 1557 edict for New Granada. He mentioned a number of jurists who theorized on parentage, a Castilian decree, several legal compilations, and common law (*derecho común y del reyno*). He puzzled over the customs of Indigenous lords and Indies vassals in general, noted ad-hoc administrative practice in New Granada, Quito, Lima, Charcas, Mexico, and Jalisco, and observed his own experience. His response to this issue was simply that "I could not adjust this to what I understanded of justice … I feared I would not succeed."[13] His solution

[12] Loveman, *National Colors*, 43–44. Cope, *Limits*, 24. Sue, *Cosmic Race*, 11; Quijano, "Colonialidad," 342. See also Quijano and Wallerstein, "Americanity," 549–557; Carrera, *Imagining Identity*, 21; Hering Torres, "Purity of Blood," 25; Bonfil Batalla, "Sobre la ideología," no page.

[13] AGNM, Hospital de Jesús L.383, Exp.5.

was to "leave this in the hands of God."[14] And yet this sort of problem of conceptual and epistemic imprecision was no fluke. It was a feature, not an anomaly. The petition-and-response system engendered disorderly concepts and muddled epistemological grids entirely by design.

DECONSTRUCTING AND CONSTRUCTING THE ROYAL DECREE

If petitions acted as ruled–ruler pleas trapped in paper, decrees were the same in reverse: a ruler's written response imitating a spoken reply. Ministers followed a loose but reliable formula when composing these texts, which they used to ensure their speedy and consistent production (see Figure 6.1). Atop each text was a small cross – the same God-invoking salutation which subjects included in their supplications. Just below came the title of the monarch in neat cursive (a).

The body of the decree begins with a formulaic opening: the monarch's addressing of the relevant authorities or persons (the *principios*, b). Other elements in the body divulge considerable clues about the circumstances of the text's production. The text either asserts the ruler's recognition of a petitioner's initiative, or includes the phrase "I have been informed" (c). Next appears a segment which acknowledges and samples the petition in the body of the text (the *relación* or *narración*, d). This segment also would explicitly reference what the vassal requested (the *proposición*, d). This is followed by the monarch's optional explanation of the measure (*división*, e) and his or her determination on the given topic (the *conclusión*, e). The body ends with a date (f).[15]

Figure 6.1 provides a concrete example of a royal decree. The text begins with a small cross and the title of the queen, before naming the Viceroy and High Judges of Mexico as its addressees. It then explicitly recognizes "Juana Velásquez, lay sister ... in the name of the other lay sisters ... of Mexico City" as the petitioners who had inspired the measure. The edict states the women had been educating the children of prominent Indians, but that friars had overstepped their authority as they sought to investigate the school. The sisters requested the sovereign

[14] AGNM, Hospital de Jesús L.383, Exp.5.

[15] I have not found Spanish-language breakdowns of decree sections. For a 1640 typology of decree parts, see González de Torneo, *Práctica de escribanos*, 56r–57r. González correctly noted that officials could also add a warning, or *pena*, about the consequences of disobedience, as an optional step.

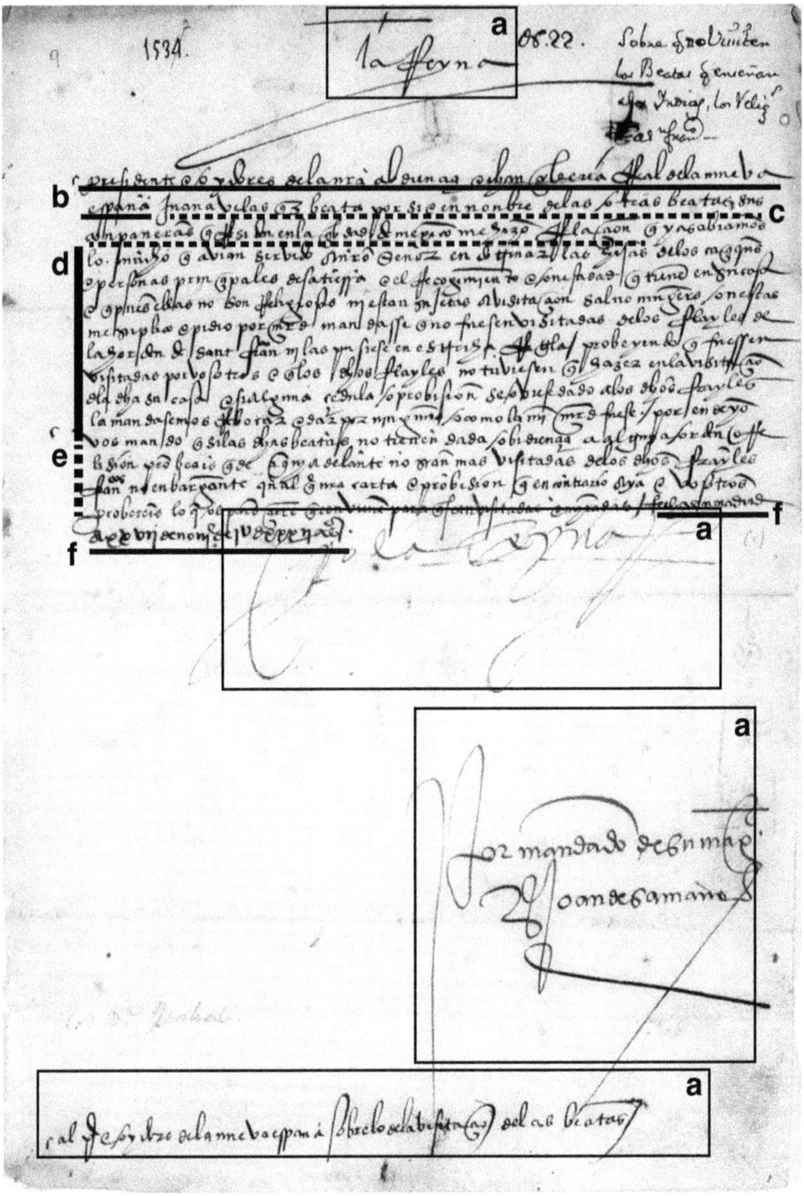

FIGURE 6.1 A 1532 decree signed by Regent Queen Isabella of Portugal, in response to the petition of Spanish lay sisters in Mexico (LOC- HKR, 9).

exempt them from future investigations of this sort in consideration of the fact that they did not belong to any religious order; the viceroy and high court were to ensure that these nuns would receive no further grievances from friars. The date was November 27, 1532; Queen Isabella of Portugal, the ministers, and Secretary Sámano had signed in Madrid. This *gobierno* decree, while structurally formulaic, was remarkable in that it was not only won by a woman, in the name of multiple other women, but also ratified by the queen regent.

As this case demonstrates, historians equipped with a knowledge of decrees' structures can often identify petitioners and pinpoint the measures they introduced. This is easiest when the decree explicitly states the name of those who prompted the measure. For instance, Table 6.1 shows six decrees which credit their contents to different Indian groups. These petitioners created various different institutions and government practices at the local level, and prompted viceregal action. One reform was jurisdictional: delimiting the towns of Tenacuzco and Matepeque in 1550 (row 1). Another restored the preconquest Indigenous municipal government praxes of Verapaz in 1555 (row 2). A third forced Spanish clergymen and friars to no longer enter and disturb the town of Ipiales in 1584 (row 3). Yet another consisted of a cease-and-desist order against Spaniards and Indians attempting to exact tribute from Tlaxcalans in 1589 (row 4). The fifth barred friars from compelling the labor of Chucuitos Indians in 1595 (row 5). The final case states that Potosí officials were to compensate Indians for travel costs in 1596 (row 6). These examples demonstrate how Indian petitioners would use the petition-and-response system to prompt new Indies institutions and shape officials' practices.

Many non-Indigenous individuals and groups also suggested new institutional arrangements. Some were major. On August 30, 1515, ministers agreed with *encomendero* Rodrigo Manzorro's request that the king only grant Indian tribute to married Spaniards.[16] The Santo Domingo municipality won a measure in 1524 which would relocate the new House of Trade courtroom to a building on the Seville plaza, where it would be more available to distribute justice to Indies merchants.[17] In 1551, responding to a *consulta* featuring "accounts from many persons" from Peru, the king established the Charcas High Court.[18] Doctor Muñón,

[16] AGI, Patronato 172, R.5, 135r. [17] AGI, Patronato 172, R.5, 115r.
[18] AGI, Indiferente 737, N.68.

TABLE 6.1 *Six royal decrees* de gobierno *with recognitions of Indian petitioners*

Petitioner(s)	Intitulation of decree	Contents of decree	Province/cit.	Date
Indians of Tenacuzco	"por pte de los indios e gov.or e prinçipales e mazeguales del pueblo . . . "	Conflict, border/border stones (mojones) vs. town of Matepeque; Crown approves	Mexico AGI, Mexico 1089,L.4, 245 r	June 7, 1550
Cacique of Verapaz and cohort	"por parte de vos don Ju.o Apo Batz governador y caçique . . . y de los otros caçiques y pncipales"	Requests restoration of pre-Conquest system of Indian town administration/elections; Crown approves	Guatemala AGI, Mexico 386, L.1, 167v	Aug. 25, 1555
Cacique of Ipiales	"don Pedro de Henao yndio natural della me ha hecho relaçion"	Quito High Court must order clergy, friars who harass Indian men, women to cease, desist; Crown approves	Quito AGI, Quito 211, L.2,132 r	Aug. 22, 1584
Laborers and leaders of Tlaxcala	"por parte de los yndios maçeguales y prinçipales de las quatro caveçeras"	Tlaxcalans do not pay tribute; local Spaniards, Indians can't compell them; Crown approves	Mexico AGI, Mexico 1092,L.12, 178 r	June 21, 1589
Indians of Chucuitos province	"por parte de los yndios de la provincia de Chucuitos se me ha hecho relaçion"	Viceroy must prevent friars from having Indians build elaborate, ornate monasteries	Charcas AGI, Charcas 418, L.2, 55v	Sept. 30, 1595
Indians of Pacaces province	"por parte de los yndios de la pro.va de los pacaces se me ha hecho r.on"	Indians who labor in Potosí mines should receive officials' compensation for travel costs; Viceroy to implement decree	Charcas AGI, Charcas 418,L.2, 64v	Feb. 29, 1596

Oaxaca's *maestrescuela* (cathedral teacher of divinity), won a July 27, 1570 decree granting the province's church officials the authority to obligate its Indians to speak Nahuatl.[19]

Vassals could not only prompt new measures, they could also transform the monarchy's legislative output by employing, and even creating, legal categories (Table 6.2). Their petitions' phrases often entered *verbatim* into Crown policy. For instance, supplicants of many social backgrounds proposed new edicts featuring novel categories of human difference either mostly or entirely absent from Old World legislation to characterize others. Not only Spaniards but subjects identifying themselves previously as Indians, *mestizos*, *mulatos*, Blacks, and others could invent, introduce, cement, or contest legal categories.

For example, King Philip II ratified an edict on July 3, 1581 crediting "the caciques and Indian leaders" of Chimbo for having informed them about certain "Spaniards, mestizos, and mulatos" who were oppressing and aggrieving them (row 4).[20] Similarly, a December 31, 1598 edict ordering abusive "Spaniards, mestizos, blacks, and mulatos" out of the Yucatán's Indian towns, attributing the measure to the request of the "Indians of that province" (row 7).[21] Tlaxcalans successfully proposed decrees circumscribing the status of Greeks, Portuguese, and Levantines, as well as other Indian groups defining Spaniards, *mestizos*, and *mulatos* as "not of their nation" or as permanent outsiders in their communities (row 5).

Nonelite subjects did not simply employ elite Spaniards' categories. They could even introduce rare or entirely new categories in their petitions themselves. The Mexico City *mulatos*' 1570 decree ordered the baptism of "blacks and muzzled blacks" (*bozales*) – that is, those arriving enslaved from Africa (row 2). On another occasion, *mulatos* introduced unique legal terms, such as the Mexico City *mulatos*' edict on Indian *pusteca* merchants, to Indies law; the term derived from the Náhuatl term *pochteca*.[22] The latter category never appeared in other sixteenth-century decrees.

Another method for linking petitions to decrees is to consult a unique resource produced by council officials between 1571 and 1594. President Ovando's reforms introduced several novel bookkeeping practices. One

[19] AGI, México 1090, L.6, 135v–36r. [20] AGI, Quito 211, L.2, 78r.

[21] AGI, México 2999, L.4, 580r–v. [22] Pomar Jiménez, *Pochtecas*, 18–20.

TABLE 6.2 *Seven decrees the Crown attributed to nonelite petitioners, demonstrating how these groups categorized others*

Name/intitulation	Contents of decree	Categories used	Province/cit.	Date
Mex. City mulatos; "por parte de los mulatos vecinos"	Priests must baptize arriving slave men, women; Viceroy, Archbishop must investigate	"negros y negras boçales . . ."	Mexico, Mexico 1090, L.6, 170v	Sept., 24, 1570
Mex. City mulatos; "por parte de los mulatos de esa tierra"	Indians becoming itinerant merchants; must live part-time in towns, farm, pay tax; Viceroy must enforce	"muchos . . . Indios naturales . . . se hazen pustecas . . . tales pustecas . . ." (*pusteca* = Nahuatl *pochteca*)	Mexico, Mexico 1090, L.6, 247 r	April 11, 1571
Naolingo Indians; "en nonbre de los yndios y naturales"	Spaniards and their cohorts hurt Indians and rape women; President and High Court to investigate and quickly solve	"españoles . . . muchos negros y criados suyos"	Guatemala, Guatemala 386, L.1, 261v	March 4, 1559
Indian leaders of Chimbo; "en nombre de los caciques e yndios principales"	Officials must appoint justices to province; says outsiders are criminals; High Court must investigate	"muchos españoles, mestizos, y mulatos" are troublemakers	Quito Quito 211, L.2, 78v	July 3, 1581

(*continued*)

Tlaxcala caciques; “ahora” (four names) “de la prov.a de Tlaxcala me han fecho rela.on”	Vagabonds harming Indians, directs viceroy to expel all non-Indians from Tlaxcala	“españoles vagamundos, entre los yndios . . . levantiscos, griegos, portogueses, ni otras naciones”	Mexico, Mexico 1091, L.11, 203 r	May 19, 1585
Jocotenango Indians; “por pt.e de los indios del pueblo”	Bars non-Indian parishioners from Indian church; President to investigate and enforce	Move “mestiços y mulatos y gente q no es de su naçion” to “parrochia de spanoles”	Guatemala, Guatemala 395, L.6, 386 r	Sept. 2, 1595
Yucatan Indians; “por parte de los Indios desa prov.a”	Bars outsiders from harming local Indians, who are too poor to pay justices for help;	Harassed by “los españoles mestiços negros, y mulatos”	Yucatan, Mexico 2999, L.4	Dec. 31, 1598
	Governor to enforce, report			

of these was the scribes' production of petition registers (*libros de peticiones*), which catalogued incoming requests. Before ministers would begin their deliberations every workday, these scribes were to engross a summary of each petition into a hide-bound inventory, assigning each a number to facilitate ministers' orderly review and retrieval of each letter.[23] Though the ordinances date to September 24, 1571, the incoming Scrivener Juan de Ledesma had already begun one of these twenty-two volumes on March 28, 1571. He would diligently summarize petitions until his death in 1594, at which point officials seem to have abandoned the project.[24]

Petition registers also offer valuable insights on the daily operations of council officials. For example, we can open them to a specific page and immediately gather some of the activities of specific ministers in the sequence in which they occurred. These entries often also provide evidence of vassals introducing novel or modified legal categories. For example, the Indian *caciques* and leaders of Anboca, Chungacaro, Caranama, and Aganeme appeared in these tomes with several proposals; on Saturday November 3, 1576, ministers considered their (successful) proposal to prevent certain *mestizo* and Spanish justices from abusing Indian laborers.[25] In the process they not only used a Latin-derived term – *mestizo* – but included and reformulated categories of Caribbean and Inca origins to fit their case. They self-identified as *caciques* – the Arawak term for leaders in the Caribbean – as well as the Spanish *líderes*, or leaders.[26] They then invoked the category *mitayo*, from the Quechua *mitmaq*, an Inca or even pre-Inca class of part-time, long-distance laborers.[27] The resulting royal decree featured all of these terms, just as they appeared in the petition register.

Table 6.3 shows yet another case located in Ledesma's petition registers: a decree won by don Pedro de Henao, the *cacique* of Laloma, Quito. Here, Cacique Henao used his petition to create another legal category of human difference, the "Barvacoa Indians." He also describes their characteristics as flesh-eating "war Indians," pushing authorities to intervene against their aggressions. This case shows that the many sub-categories of "Indian" were not all the creation of Spaniards or the Crown, but also included the contributions of many self-described Indians as well.

[23] AGI, Indiferente 582, L.1, 4r–v.142–143. [24] Manzorro Guerrero, "Prácticas," 130.
[25] AGI, Indiferente 1085, L.4, 247v; for the decree, see AGI, Quito 211, L.1, 310r–v.
[26] Muñoz Arbeláez, *Costumbres*, 35. [27] Larson, *Cochabamba*, 135.

TABLE 6.3 Cacique *don Pedro Henao of Laloma's entry in the petition registers and 1586 decree*

1. Petition register entry (December 2, 1585) AGI, Indiferente 1088, L.13, 247 r

Don Pedro Henao Caçiq de Laloma en el pueblo de Ypiales en la provinçia de Quito dize que los indios que llaman barvacoas han sido y
son de guerra y tan bravos que jamas se han podido conquistar antes salen de su tierra a saltear y robar y matar los indios comarcanos y especialmte los
de Mallama que son de don Gomez su yierno cacique del pueblo de Mallama hasta llegar a la iglesia del dicho pueblo y rovar los ornam.tos, retablos
ymagines y adereços della y matar en el pueblo y en la dicha iglesia muchos de los indios naturales y mugeres y niños y despues se los comen y han hecho
y hazen otras muchas crueldades y aunque por parte del dho don Gomez se ha requerido a la Audiencia de Quito y al Governador de Popayan y al
Corregidor de pasta (sic) muchas vezes que pongan remedio en lo suso dho no lo han hecho de que han resultado estos inconvinientes y para que se
remedien y los indios comarcanos a los dichos barvacoas no se vengan a destruyr sup.ca se de ç.a para que el audiencia de Quito provea persona que con
gente entre en los dichos indios barvacoas. y los castigue y çesen las crueldades muertes rovos y salteamientos que an hecho y hazen y que pues el Doctor
barros esta aqui y ha de pasar por aquella comarca vaya informando dello para que alla lo provea y remedie dando orden como tambien el Governador
de Popayan y el corregidor de Pasta entren en los dichos indios con la gente armas y otras cosas que para castigarlos fueren necesarias y que siendo
necess.o los dichos don Pedro de henao y su hierno con los Indios a ellos subjetos y los demas comarcanos ayudaran a esta impressa pues estan del
serv.o de N Sa y bien de los dichos indios naturales

Officials' marginal comment: *Esta Relaçion a la aud.a pa q lo bea y pbea*

Rubric on marginal comment: Secretary Antonio de Eraso

2. *Decree copy in Council archives* (January 10, 1586) AGI, Quito 211, L.2, 157 r–157v

† El Rey. Presidente e oidores de la mi Audiençia real que reside en la çiudad de sanct françisco de la provinçia de quito don pedro de henao indio caçiq
de la loma de esa provinçia me ha sido hecha Ron. que los indios della que llaman varvacoas han estado y estan de guerra y salen de su tierra a saltear y
rovar y matan los indios comarcanos en que an hecho y cada dia hazen grandes estragos y crueldades especialmente entre los indios de Mallama de
ques caçique un yerno suyo y aunque de parte del dicho su yerno se ha pedido en esa Audiençia y al Governador de Popayan ques e remedie no se ha

(*continued*)

TABLE 6.3 (*continued*)

hecho ni haze y sino se Remedia con brevedad los dichos indios comarcanos se ventran a acavar y el Remedio. que se podria poner es que vos

enviasedes una persona de confianca e inteligençia con alguna gente que entrase entre los dichos indios varvacoas y los castigue para que cobrasen

temor y escarmiento y si fuere neçesario el y el dicho su yerno con los indios sus subjetos y los comarcanos ayudarian en lo que pudiesen para ello

suplicandome lo mandase proveer como mas conviniese de manera que los dichos daños çesaren e visto por los de mi Conss.o de las Indias [157r–157v]

fue acordado que devia mandar dar esta mi c.a por la qual os mando que veais lo sobredicho y lo proveais como convenga que yo os lo remito y de lo que

se hiziere me avisareis fecha en sanct mattheo a diez de henero de mill y quin.os y ochenta y seis años yo el Rey. Refrendada de Antonio de erasso y

señalada del Conss.o

The surest way to gage the similarity between petitions and decrees is therefore to locate the original petition, match it to its corresponding decree, and submit the two to close textual comparison. Many near-verbatim resemblances reveal themselves. For example, in the early 1560s Nicaragua's Archdeacon Juan Álvarez de Ortega's petition and the March 18, 1564 edict he successfully prompted feature the same phraseology (Table 6.4). He had complained that *encomenderos* had been violently entering Indian towns, along with "mestizos and mestizas, Indian men and women, and blacks." He asked the monarch to force the governor to solve the problem. Sure enough, the resulting decree ordered the governor to act using almost precisely this language, with only one exception, reading "mestizos and mestizas, Indian men and women, and black men *and women* (emphasis mine)." Council officials had added "black women" to the measure, perhaps anticipating that a broader policy would have made the policy easier for local authorities to enforce. The decree featured other minor syntactical changes, but remained largely identical.

In exceptional circumstances, ministers and subalterns might insert an entire petition into a decree. This offers even further evidence of the link between vassals' requests and the law. For instance, when High Judge Cepeda of Charcas wrote a January 13, 1588 letter to the king, council ministers sent a March 20, 1590 decree to the Viceroy of Peru. Among other things, this document requested the viceroy attend to social disorder in lowland Charcas. Cepeda had complained about the area around the small town of Santa Cruz de la Sierra, particularly of the locals, "an

TABLE 6.4 *The Archdeacon's petition chapter and the 1564 decree*

1. ***Petition of Juan Álvarez de Ortega, archdeacon of León, Nicaragua*** **(ca. 1563?)** AGI, Guatemala 168

Capítulo: Otro si los encomenderos de la dha provinçia en tiempo de las sementeras y de la cosecha dellas y en otros tiempos seban a los pueblos de su encomyenda y llevan los mestiços e mestiças yndios e yndias e negros de su serviçio y estan muchos meses de asiento en los dhos pueblos y estos serviçio q llevan como dh es carta para destruyr a los pobres naturales porq tratan y contratan con ellos y los engañan con algunas davidas de poco valor y les sacan lo q tienen que mucho mas vale y les comen sus mantenymyentos y vasta que el encomendero u otro hombre por el vaya a poner en cobro su hazienda sin que den tanta molestia a los dhos naturales porq como testigo de vista de la vexacion que en esto reçiben los dhos naturales por su pobreza dellos e se proveyo de vra Real Audiençia y no se guardo ny cumplio

Official's first marginal comment: *q el g.or se ynforme y guarde lo p.veydo crca desto*
Official's second marginal comment: *fha*
Official's third marginal comment: *proveydo dntro*

2. ***Decree in Council archives*** **(March 18, 1564)** AGI, Guatemala 401, L.4 26v–27 r

Nro governador al.lde myor de la provi de Nicaragua por parte del lic. Ju. Alvarez de Ortega Ar.no de la yglesia cathedral de Leon de la Prov.a me a sido hecha rel.on que los encomenderos dessa tierra en tpo de las sementeras y de la cosecha dellas y en otros tpos se van a los pueblos de su encomienda y llevan los mestizos y mestizas yndios e yndias negros y negras de su serv.o y estan muchos meses de asiento en los dhos pueblos y queste servi.o que llevan tienen y les comen sus mantenim.os y aunque por la gran desorden que nesto ha abido y vexaçion que a los dhos naturales se les hazia se proveyó de Remedio por el presidente e oidores de esa audi.a Real de Guatimala a quello no se guarda ny cumple que los dhos naturales reciven muy gran daño y me fue suppl. lo mandase proveer y remediar de manera que para Adel.te ceßasen semejantes agravios o como la mi mrd. fueße lo qual visto por los del my consejo de las yndias fue acordado que devia mandar dar esta my ca. pa vos e yo túvelo por bien por ende yo vos mando mando que veais lo suso dho y os ynformeis y sepais como y de que manera ha pasado e pasa lo susodho y proveais que se guarde y cumpla o que por nos çerca [26v-27 r] desto esta ordenado y mandado y no fagades ende al / fecha en Varçelona a XVIII de marco de mill e quios y seßenta y quatro años yo el Rey Refr.da de Vargas y se.do del q de yndias

unsettled people, and the *criollos* [Creoles] there, who have been born there with vices and with no discipline [*policía*]."[28] There were also "mestizos … many, free, and brutal." Of course, the decree echoed this language, informing the viceroy of "an unsettled people, and the *criollos* there that have born with vices and without *policía*" and "mestizos … many, free, and brutal."[29] This appears to be among the very first decrees, perhaps even the very first, featuring the term "criollo" in reference to Indies-born Spaniards.

"I Have Been Informed": When Decrees do not Acknowledge Specific Petitioners

The aforementioned decrees all clearly referred back to petitioners. This allows researchers to easily establish which specific subject proposed the initiative, and to reveal vassals' roles in shaping imperial legislation, institutions, and categories. More often, however, ministers left the identity of the letter-writer anonymous in the decree's *exposición*, with a simple "I have been informed," or another similar phrase. Brendecke notes that this statement served a threefold purpose: to emphasize the monarchy's responsiveness to vassals, to underscore that the council had attempted diligence in seeking subjects' reports, and also to warn subjects that these communications may have been faulty and could be invalid in the light of new evidence.[30] In the event that decrees begin with "I have been informed," the only option for historians seeking to identify an edict's petition is to painstakingly comb the archives – including the petition registers – and hope to match a letter to the decree's *exposición* and *disposición*.

Why did council officials only sometimes explicitly name the petitioners who prompted decrees? There is no clear answer. In some cases, ministers likely found the phrase "I have been informed" easier to formulate when rushing their production of a decree. Sometimes officials would be so inconsistent regarding this naming process that they would explicitly name the petitioner in one decree, and then omit this in another copy it issued only days later. For instance, on June 5, 1559 a decree stated "we have been informed" that in Santiago, Chiapas, and San Salvador of Guatemala certain Indians were abused by tax-collecting Spaniards; all Indians involved were henceforth free, and would pay tribute directly to royal authorities.[31]

[28] AGI, Charcas 16 R.27, N.143, 2r. [29] AGI, Charcas 415, L.2, 65r.

[30] Brendecke, *Imperio*, 112–118.

[31] Curiously, the first decree had no addressee; perhaps it was to go to the Indians themselves for them to invoke when necessary.

Twelve days later, council officials issued a very similar decree to the same addressees, now crediting this measure to "the Indians who were held as slaves."[32] These seems to be no political calculus behind this change; it was probably the result of council officials' strained workload.

On certain rare occasions, ministers concealed petitioners' names to protect their identities. Charcas High Court magistrates wrote on July 25, 1579 that they were facing a deluge of grace petitions from so many vassals that they were incapable of responding to them all. They requested the ruler's permission to introduce new and more rigorous practices limiting these petitions, but also noted with a hint of fear that this reform might upset many (armed) subjects. The high judges thus requested that the king issue a new ruling that did not credit them with the initiative.[33]

Another such case came from within the walls of the council itself. In 1572, Secretary Juan López de Velasco was undertaking his task as the royal historian of the Indies when he noted a controversy regarding Diego Fernández's *History of Peru*.[34] This book had angered certain subjects, though Fernández insisted that he could demonstrate the work's veracity. Velasco suggested the sovereign place the book's publication on hold, pending further investigation, and asked that "His Majesty … be served to order that this opinion of mine not come to the attention of any of the involved."[35]

The opposite might occur as well, with vassals expressly requesting ministers mention their names in the decree. Procurators might seek this, for example, to demonstrate to their clients that they had completed their assignments. In one 1591 case, Diego de Carrión requested such a correction after the council had mistakenly credited another agent who acted as his subaltern.[36]

Many decrees do not reveal petitioners' identities at all. This substantially complicates historians' task of determining the petitioner responsible. Intensive archival research and textual analysis can sometimes solve this problem. For example, a November 25, 1578 decree stating "I have been informed" noted that "Indians … were in the company of mulatos, mestizos, and *negros* … they teach them bad customs."[37] This corresponds to a November 7, 1578 petition by Friar Rodrigo de Loaysa, the representative of Peru's Augustinian Order. It stressed "the bad company" that Indians had with "mestizos, mulatos, and *negros* … who

[32] AGI, Guatemala 386, L.1, 295v, 296v, [33] AGI, Santa Fe 16, R.23, N.93.
[34] Fernández, *Primera*. [35] AGI, Patronato 171, N.1, R.9.
[36] AGI, Indiferente 1091, L.20. [37] AGI, Indiferente 427, L.30, 295r–v.

teach them many wickednesses."[38] In a marginal comment next to this proposal, a minister had written his approval of the friar's suggestion, confirming the link between the petition and the decree.

A January 26, 1586 edict for Charcas also follows this pattern. It states that "I have been informed that in those provinces there are many *negros*, mulatos, and mestizos and people of other mixtures ... they are all raised in great vices and laxity."[39] The Peruvian viceroy and high courts were to more diligently Christianize these groups and enroll them in vocational training. On February 1, 1585, Cuzco's Jesuit rector José de Teruel had submitted a petition which noted that "many are the people who are of the *negros*, mulatos, mestizos, and other new mixtures ... they are all raised in great vices and laxity."[40] Sure enough, next to Teruel's warning is minister Licenciado Antonio Gálvez's signature and marginal comment acknowledging that council officials would issue a decree to Indies authorities.

Relaciones, *Consultas*, and Other Intermediary Phraseological Phases

Substantial parts of *gobierno* decrees were verbatim copies of petitions' phraseologies and categories. But what if administrative processes within the council could result in some minor or major changes? Two of these less common practices concern us here: the scribe's production of *relaciones*, and the council's production of *consultas*. As we have seen, *relaciones* were summaries of subjects' written proposals which scribes or other officials produced to help ministers deal with messy, poorly written, or overlong letters. Ministers would sometimes rule not upon the original petition, but these *relaciones*. These therefore presented officials with a moment in which they could have, at least hypothetically, sought to impose upon Indies letters their editorial vision, with their own vocabularies and ideas.

An April 10, 1575 example (Table 6.5) shows that while *relaciones* diverged slightly from petitions, these changes were not necessarily major. The twenty-seventh proposal of the high judges of Santa Fe's April 10, 1575 letter stated that "two mestizo bastard sons of two conquistadors" sought to "be caciques" in nearby Tunja. The judges were opposed to this because of certain "great inconveniences" and because of "the bad inclinations of these mestizos," and asked that the council prohibit that

[38] AGI, Indiferente 1388, "El presentado." [39] AGI, Charcas 415, L.2, 39v.

[40] AGI, Lima 316, "Aunq indino."

TABLE 6.5 *A 1578 petition by the High Court of Santa Fé, its* relación, *and 1576 decree*

1. Petition (High Judges of Santa Fe to King & Council, April 10, 1575) — AGI, Santa Fe, 16, R.19, N.56, 6v

Capítulo 27: dos hijos bastardos mestizos de dos conquistadores pretendieron avra cinco a.os ser caciqs en dos reptmtos del distrito de la ciudad de
tunja y aunq a la sazon uvo contradiciones fueron por esta aborencia metidos en la possession / despues aca de un año a esta parte por el fiscal de v mt
y por los encomenderos de aquellos reptim.os y por la ciudad de tunja se a tratado pleito y del a constado seguirse grandes inconvenientes y danos de q
mestizos sean caçiqs y tenemos entendido q no los ay en todo el piru ni la nueva españa emosles suspendidos en vista el exercicio y uso de los cacicadgos
supplicamos a v mt nos mande avisar de loq mas as es pvido porq realmt pareze q çesaran grandes inconvenientes y q por su mala inclinacion deestos
mestizos es bien prevenir a cosas venideras y por estar supplicado por ambas partes no se inbian los autos de lo q se determinare en revista sera v mt mas
plenam.te avisado

Officials' first marginal comment: *vista y saquese en relacion* — *Rubric of Lic. Alonso Martínez Espadero*

2. *Relación* (likely prepared by scribe Francisco de Burzeña) — AGI, Santa Fe, 16, R.19, N.56, 6v

27. Que abiendo pretendido dos hijos bastardos mestiços de dos conquistadores ser caciquez en dos repartim.os del distrito de la çiudad de Tunja, y
aunq huvo contradiçiones fueron por aquella Au.a metidos en la profesion/ y de un año a esta parte por el fiscal y encomenderos de los repartimientos
y por la ciudad de Tunja se a tratado pleyto y del a constado seguirse grandes ynconvinientes de que mestisos sean caciques / anlo suspendido en vista
el exercicio de los cacicazgos supplican se les avise que haran en ello y por estar supplicado pro ambas partes no se embian los autos y de lo q
determinaren en revista avisaran

Official's first marginal comment on *relación*: *q no los consienten ser caziques ni se hagan de aqui adelante y pa ello se les inbia c.a y inbieseles.*

Officials' second marginal response on petition: *Respondida en la relacion, despachese luego* — Rubric, probably of scribe Francisco de Burzeña

3. *Decree copy in Council archives* (January 18, 1576) — AGI, Santa Fe 528, L.1, 28 r–v/ BNM, Mss/3045, 349v–350v

† El Rey. Presidente e oydores de la nra audiencia Real de la çiudad de santa fee del nuevo reyno de granada por la carta q nos escrevistes en diez de
abril del año passado de setenta y çinco avemos visto como dos hijos mestiços de dos conquistadores pretendian ser caçiques de dos repartimentos de

(*continued*)

TABLE 6.5 (*continued*)

yndios que caen en el destrito de la ciudad de tunja y aunque huvo contradiçion dello fueron metidos en la posesion y q despues que lo an sido a resultado
seguirse algunos ynconvinientes dignos de remedio y haviendose visto en el nro consejo de las yndias fue acordado que devia mandar dar esta mi çedula
por la qual os mando que no consintais ni deys lugar a q ningunos mesticos en esa tierra sea caçiques en los pueblos de yndios della en ninguna forma y si
algunos lo fueren de presente los quiteys y rremobays luego de los dhos [28 r–v] caçicadgos y hareis que se guarden en su election la orden que los dhos
yndios an tenido sin q para agora se haga nobedad fecha en madrid a xviii de hen.o de mill y qui.os y setenta y seis a.os yo el rey por mandado de su
magd Antonio de Erasso señalada de los señ.es del consejo

"mestizos be caciques." The *relación* abstract included the phrases "two mestizo bastard sons of two conquistadors" and "great inconveniences that mestizos be caciques." The final January 18, 1576 decree had undergone several minor phraseological changes, but left the overall phrasing intact. It stated that the high judges had informed the king about "two mestizo sons of two conquistadors" (the term *bastard* was missing), and that the king ruled that due to "some inconveniences" (instead of *great* inconveniences) henceforth "no mestizos in that land be caciques." The mention of "bad inclinations" was also missing. However, the *relación* did not bring these minor changes into effect; it was the ministers' final drafting that produced them.

Historian Caroline Cunill has also analyzed several transformations of certain Yucatan petitions into *relaciones* to *consultas* and decrees. Intriguingly, she has suggested that *relatores* engaged in "significant reductions" of text and "silenced" certain phraseology from petitions – her implication being that this was deliberate. However, she also posited that this may have simply reflected the *relator*'s desire to simplify ministers' labor by editing the text – a far more likely scenario.[41] In any case, *relatores* seem to have played a significant role in decree-phrasing powerful primarily through their ability to subtract parts of the petition from the final decree text. There is no evidence they added categories or assumptions of their own.

[41] Cunill, "Margins," 389. Here we must recall the scandal of the *relator* who manipulated a court case in Chapter 3.

Council ministers and subalterns might transform the contents of petitions somewhat for *relaciones*. However, they did so to a greater extent during the process of the *consulta* in which they elevated proposals to the king.[42] After all, these officials had to create a document which quickly contextualized a case to the monarch. Nonetheless, they did not necessarily rephrase petitions fundamentally during *consultas*, though they substantially abbreviated them. Table 6.6 juxtaposes a 1551 *consulta* between the ministers and the emperor about the possibility of creating certain institutions to help Hispanicize and Christianize young "mestizos" and "mestizas." The case began on January 23, 1550, when a Lima notary recorded the City Council's *poder* grant to two procurators: Dominican friar Tomás de San Martín and Captain Gerónimo de Aliaga. The contract reproduced, verbatim, the petition they were to take to the royal court. This request's phraseology included, among other projects, references to a "walled compound (*emparedamiento*) like a convent, where the *mestizas* can be raised and indoctrinated to the Catholic faith and learn other matters of discipline (*cosas de policía*)."[43] The *mestizo* boys, on the other hand, were to receive an institution where they could be "collected and be indoctrinated until reaching the age at which they can live by themselves." At some point, the agent of the petition became Friar Domingo de Santo Tomás.

The council evidently was not sympathetic to the *mestizo* boys' education, and axed their segment before writing the *consulta* (this was perhaps a measure to punish the infamously rebellious Peruvian conquistadors and their potentially troublesome part-Indigenous sons). Ministers nonetheless asked the emperor if a walled, convent-like enclosure might do the *mestizas* well. An undated *consulta* from sometime in 1551 stated that the Prior of the Dominicans had petitioned about "many mestiza girls, daughters of Christians now deceased," who needed a pension to sustain "a house like a walled compound (*emparedam.to*) in the City of Kings [Lima] where they be gathered and fed and raised in virtue and Christian discipline [*policía*]." Several of the consulta's categories – *mestizas*, *walled compound*, and *discipline* – reveal a very close resemblance to the procurators' January 1550 contract.

Then came the final December 25, 1551 decree. This too closely resembled both the City of Lima's petition contract copy, and the *consulta*. The brief edict featured references to "mestiza girls, daughters of deceased

[42] Schäfer briefly noted the correspondence between *consultas* and decrees; see *Consejo*, 1, 11.

[43] AGNP, Libro del Cabildo de Lima, N.3, 89r-92r.

TABLE 6.6 *A 1550 contract, petition, 1551* consulta, *and resulting 1551 decree*

1. **Contract, Lima City and Friar Tomás de San Martín, January 23, 1550:**	AGNP: Archivo Histórico, L. de Cabildo, N.3, 89 r/92 r
yten ynformar a su mt q como muchos an muerto [en] estos reynos çelosos de su rreal serv.o y an dexado hijo e hijas huerfanos mestizos e por no ab quyen por ellos mire se andan pdidos entre los yndios Su Mt pvea como cristianysymo rrey e señor q es como se funde e hagan en esta ciudad de los rreyes con el socorro de su rreal hazienda un enparedam.oto a modo de monestr.o donde las mestizas se puedan criar y dotrinar en la fe catolica y aprender otras cosas de policia y allí esten rrecogidas con mugeres de buen credito y antiguedad hasta que lleguen a edad que pueden elegir estado y mas se haga una escuela a modo de spytal donde todos los mestizos se puedan rrecogr y ser dotrynados hasta llegan a edad q por si puedan bibr	
2. ***Petition*** **(Friar Domingo de Santo Tomás, June 1, 1550):**	AGI, Lima 313, "Jho Xpo nro senor," 1 r–6v
Capítulo: Tambien ay aca neçessidad de dar orden en los hijos e hijas de los spañoles e indias naturales de esta tierra q son muchos, y como los pobres en esta tierra son mas q los ricos, y no por ser pobres tienen menos hijos ay muchos mestizos y mestizas en ella y muchos de ellos andan como indios entre los indios e sino se da orden como se haga una cassa donde los varones se crien y se les enseñe doctrina y buenas costumbres para q siendo de hedad para ello se pongan a officios y no anden en perjuicio suyo y de la repblica pdidos / y las nyñas se recoxan y no anden destraidas y pdidas, porq empieçan ya ha andarlo asy los unos como los otros porq allende de la general obligaçion que VA. Tiene a pveer a tan grand parte de republica pobre q no ande pdida en pjuicio de la comunidad, paresçe q aca ay otra particular obligaçion lo uno por el mal exemplo q de su mala vida y costumbres a los naturales desta tierra se da: lo qual de offiçio paresçe q hincumbe pveerlo a VraAl. lo otro q muchos nyños e nyñas de estos son hijos de servidores de Vra Al. q en la conquista de estos Reinos y en las alteraciones pasadas perdieron por su serv.o las haziendasy vidas y quedan sus hijos tan sin amparo ni abrigo q no tienen quien les de un poco de maíz q coman quanto más el vestido y la doctrina q tan necesaria les es paresçe que se podrían dar alguna orden en si en las principales ciudades de este reino cómo es en los Reyes, Cuzco, la Villa de Plata, quito, se hiziese una casa de algund recogim.to donde uviesen dos o tres mugeres viejas de buen exemplo que tuviesen de las Niñas de doctrinarlas en las cossas de la fee enseñarles coser, labrar, buenas costumbres, y para los Niños otra cassa como ospital donde oviesen una persona eclesiastica y otra seglar q fuesen de buen enxemplo q el uno tuviese cuidado de enseñarles las cossas de la fee doctrina Xpiana y Principios de leer y el otro de la pvision corporal para lo qual tuviesen las dhas cassas pasadia	

(*continued*)

TABLE 6.6 (*continued*)

para q se les pudiese proveer de lo neçessario. La mayor parte de lo qual agora al prinçipio avra vra. Al demandar proveer de lo necesario la mayor parte de lo qual ahora al principio había vuestra alteza de su caja para q viendo tan grand limosna y buena hobra como en ello se hazia se anymasen algunas personas a ayudar para tan santa y necessaria obra para esta tierra: porq cierto, segund ay los mestizos nyños y nyñas si esto no se haze avra de oy en tres años en estas tierras destos muy grands disoluçiones i perdiçion (5 r)

Official's first marginal comment: *consulta a su mt con pareçer q se haga*

Official's second marginal comment: *vista y respodasse graciano* [Min. Gracián] *a este y cargo y se saque el traslado de margenes y pa las dar a su mt*

3. ***Consulta*** **(no date):** AGI, Indiferente 737, N.66

En los Reynos del peru ay muchas niñas mestizas hijas de christianos ya defuntos, que murieron en servyo de V.M^a que por no tener quien las ampare andan perdidas entre los Indios, Para remedio de las quales dize que seria justo que en la taßa gnal [general] se echaße alga [alguna] pension sobre algun repartimyto para hazer una casa a modo de emparedamyto en la ciudad de los Reyes donde se recogieße y fueßen alimentadas y criadas en virtud y pulicia Chrystiana, Paresce que se escriva al Visorrey, que lo provea con effecto por la via que mejor le pareçiere convenir, por ser cosa del servyo de dios

Emperor Charles' ruling: *Fiat/ fha, deselas algs e asi no prv en todo sobre alg.os repmt*

4. ***Decree*** **(late 1700s copy, December 25, 1551)** AHN, Códices 694: Cedulario de Ayala L.XI, 26 r, N.37

El Rey. Don Antonio de Mendoza, nuestro Visorrey de las provincias del Perú y presidente de la Audiencia Real de de ellas, Yo he sido informado que en esa tierra hay muchas niñas mestizas, hijas de cristianos ya difuntos, que murieron en nuestro servicio, las cuales, por no tener quien las amparase, andan perdidas entre los indios, y que para su remedio convendría que en la tasa general se echase alguna pensión sobre algún repartimiento para hacer una casa a modo de emparedamiento en la ciudad de los Reyes, donde se recogiesen y fuesen alimentadas y criadas en virtud y política cristiana; y porque por ser obra tan pía y de que Nuestro Señor sería servido, holgaríamos que se diese en ello alguna buena orden, os encargamos y mandamos proveéis en esto con efecto, echando alguna pensión por voluntad, sobre algunos repartimientos de indios, o por la vía que mejor os parecerá convenir, que en ello me tendré de vos por servido. Yo el Rey.

Christians," as well as a "house in the fashion of a walled-in compound (*emparedamiento*)," in which they would be "raised in virtue and Christian discipline (*policía*)." The final piece of legislation even featured a reference to the *mestizas* being "lost among the Indians," which the two preceding texts contained as well.

Problems with Phrasing

As this chapter's examples illustrate, many, and sometimes virtually all, of the terms and phrases within imperial legislation arose from petitions themselves. Ministers had two main reasons for clinging so closely to petitions' texts. First, they were pressed for time, and second, they had little information on the Indies. This meant that if they deviated from the smallest detail, such as the spelling of a town's name, major consequences might ensue.

These phrasing-related issues manifested themselves early in the Indies' conquest and settlement. In 1531, the High Court of Mexico noted that ministers had included an unusual town name for a *gracia* edict for Marquis Hernán Cortés. They observed that "there is in it a word (*vocablo*) that says 'Tlan' – in the whole land there is no such name of a town called 'Tlan' – and the said Marquis says that it was an error of the quill and of he who wrote it and that it should say 'Etla.'"[44] The high court requested the council fix this; the outcome is unclear. In 1577, another vassal similarly complained that he received a grace decree for a mining invention, but received a formulaic royal license for an *ingenio*. This term implied a sugar cane mill; he stated that his invention and the mill were "very different" and requested that ministers amend the document.[45]

These two examples related to *gracia* decrees. Vassals might also complain about *gobierno* measures. In 1586, the powerful *encomendero* of Naolingo and Izalco, don Juan de Guzmán, sought to force certain *mestizos* living in these towns to pay tribute as Indians did.[46] The ruler approved his request, but shortly thereafter he complained that "this decree had been approved to be issued to him … and because in its dispatch that has been given to him there is no mention made other than just the town of Izalco, even though in his petition [*relaçion*] he requested that it also have the town of Naolingo."[47] Several months later, Guzmán tersely asked that ministers either rephrase his proposals or at least return his papers. On August 4, 1586, he again complained that he had requested "more privilege [*merced*] than what was given to

[44] AGI, Patronato 184, R.16. [45] AGI, Indiferente 1387, "La villa," 4 October 1577.
[46] AGI, Indiferente 1089, L.15, 75, 35r–35v.
[47] AGI, Guatemala 395, L.6 167r and AGI, Indiferente 1089, L.15, 115v–116r.

him."[48] The following day, council officials issued a decree, but mentioned only the town of Caluco.[49] A week later, it issued yet another edict, in which the council collectively admitted that its officials had not clarified which towns he was to receive tribute from, but had now set the record straight.[50]

Another terminological problem soon emerged. A new decree which Guzmán prompted forbade local *mestizos* from marrying Indians to avoid paying taxes. However, once again, instead of specifying the towns the policy corresponded to, the edict simply stated *mestizos* were to pay tribute in "the towns which [Guzmán] receives tribute from."[51] This was a vague and rushed response, as Guzmán had wished the decree to specifically read that "Spaniards, mestizos, blacks, and mulatos" not live in the two Indian towns and instead relocate to the village of Villa de la Trinidad. Almost eight and a half months after his first petition, council officials resolved these phraseological problems[52] These cases demonstrate that vassals expected, and even demanded, that the language of decrees match their petitions, at least as far as their most central terms and categories were concerned. The deviation of just one category or phrase within a decree could have major social and legal ramifications in the Indies; it was essential that ministers not carelessly add or subtract phraseological elements.

I, the King: The Passage from Draft to Legal Text

Once the council scribes and subalterns had assembled a decree's body, ministers signed the back of the edict and passed their work to the council secretary. This official, likely in coordination with the royal secretary, signed the draft decrees and then delivered bundles of them to the monarch. A brief document, produced by a highly complex labor chain spanning a great part of the globe, finally sat on the king's desk.

Immediately under the body of every decree is the rushed, sometimes nearly illegible handwritten signature of the ruler. The signatures of several other officials also appear: the ministers and secretary or chancellor who were present to sign, and the place from which the secretary or chancellor issued it (Figure 6.1: a).[53] In many cases, council ministers

[48] AGI, Indiferente 1089, L.15, 190v; AGI, Indiferente 1089, L.15, 204v.
[49] AGI, Guatemala 395, L.6, 184v–185r. [50] AGI, Guatemala 395, L.6, 185r–v.
[51] AGI, Guatemala 395, L. 6, 186r-v. [52] AGI, Guatemala 395, L.6, 201r–202r.
[53] Lorenzo Cadarso, *Documento real*, 44.

signed the back of the document with their personal rubrics. These officials' signatures added heft to the decree, but the text remained, until that fateful arrival on the royal desk, a mundane piece of cloth and ink, of no value or heft whatsoever. It was only with the monarch's breezy signature, "I the King," that paper became law.[54] The monarch's will was *ley viva*, the law incarnate, and so from his *voluntad* flowed his authority to create legislation via signature. This rubric imbued the lifeless paper with his intention and, with his intention, he endowed it with his law-creating volition.

This signature here was a mere outer sign of an inner reality, and lacked any magic of its own. A monarch who his contemporaries understood as having sanity and intent could thus invest a decree with his or her "persona ficta."[55] This same principle allowed gout-ridden Philip II to use stamps instead of signing. He declared in 1597 that these instruments were just as "firm, secure, and valid as if they were signed by my own hand, since this is effectively the same, as it is done with my express awareness and *voluntad*."[56] Lest these instruments fall into the wrong hands, he ordered them publicly destroyed upon his death. On the other hand, without royal volition, a monarch's signature was invalid. As Bethany Aram has shown, between 1505 and 1507 debates raged about the mental fitness of Queen Juana. Much of this centered upon her ability to reason; if she was indeed mad, any decrees she ratified would be invalid because they lacked a genuine, intact royal volition.[57]

Violence and the Usurpation of Royal Volition

From a labor standpoint, the signature was a remarkably frail fiction, although it held up so many of the empire's laws. With a little work, anyone might attempt to reproduce this symbol, breaking the brittle act of paper-and-ink make-believe. The temptation was great: one could easily forge this all-sustaining symbolic gesture and furtively claim lawmaking as one's own.

It is here that violence once again patrolled the limits of legal fictions, and officials harshly reasserted the chasm between ruler and ruled. Black markets for privilege decrees granting permission to travel to the New World and for transporting slaves proved one theater in this struggle, even

[54] Real Díaz, *Estudio diplomático*, 5. [55] Vismann, *Files*, 21.
[56] AGS, Patronato, Leg.29, Doc.61, 796v.
[57] Aram, "Juana." For madness and royal volition in Europe, Erwin, *Machtsprüche*, 59.

if here most subjects attempted to change the phrasing of a decree, not the royal signature. Not all were caught. Those who were often received harsh punishments: 100 lashes and exile for a forger of a travel pass; and for a slave license counterfeiter, loss of employment, confiscation of half of his estate, and military service in North Africa.[58]

Some did indeed suffer the consequences. For instance, a young assistant to Council Secretary Luyando was found falsifying travel licenses as well as imitating ministers' signatures on blank sheets of paper. The prosecution argued this was treason and merited bodily mutilation, death, and loss of all earthly possessions. Under torture, the assistant confessed. King Philip condemned him to being paraded on a mule through Madrid with a noose around his neck, having his right hand cut off in the public square, and being exiled from the empire for life. Upon appeals, his exile was reduced to ten years' unpaid labor in the galleys.[59]

A roughly twenty-year old part-Inca scribe working in Seville, Juan Bautista Ramírez of Chachapoyas, mastered a method to use moist cloth to transfer text out of royal documents, but during an attempt to alter a travel license's phraseology damaged, and then hastily reproduced, the royal signature. Juan Bautista and his would-be client were to be paraded through Madrid on donkeys with ropes around their necks, after which they were to hang on the gallows, be torn into four by horses, and to have their body parts displayed on the public roads. While in jail, he made yet another disastrous mistake –again attempting to forge a decree granting himself freedom, royal signatures and all.[60] In consideration of his Inca lineage and his youth, ministers revoked his death sentence, but ordered he receive 200 lashes and perpetual servitude as a galley rower.[61]

These cases demonstrate that the administration's officials were highly invested in maintaining the vassal–ruler divide, and defended the purity of the royal signature as testimony of the royal will. Considerable violence, often of the performative and exemplary sort, was necessary to dissuade subjects from fabricating decrees – and thus minting their own powerful legal documents. No matter how fictive a royal decree might seem to a vassal with skillful penmanship, to forge the phrase and signature "I, the King" was to violate the vassal–ruler bond and commit a heinous

[58] AGI, Justicia 1118A, N.1, R.5. Many thanks to Werner Stangl. See also AGI, Justicia 855, N.10, no folio, "El Licenciado Venegas." AGI, Justicia 878, N.5, 2r–22r. For a counterfeit in Charcas, see Ravi Mumford, "Forgery," and AGI, Escribanía 845B. For travel licenses, Martínez Almira, "Delito."

[59] AGI, Justicia 1183, N.1, R.1.

[60] AGI, Justicia 890, N.1.

[61] AGI, Indiferente 426, L.25, 109r-109v.

crime. Physical violence thus played an essential role in conserving the mystique and exclusivity of royal decrees – preserving the dazzling power which stirred the great logistical chain of the petition-and-response process into action.

Decree Costs and the *de parte/de oficio* Dichotomy

With the royal signature on the decree, council subalterns now began the work of archiving a copy and delivering the original text to the New World. This segment of the labor chain also determined whether a vassal paid for a decree or not, and, if so, how much. During the 1570s, council officials began to label their archived decrees rather inconsistently into two broad categories: *de oficio* and *de partes*.[62] This dichotomy has created a major misconception regarding how imperial legislation arose. Antonia Heredia Herrera argues that the council began dividing legislation into two types during the sixteenth century, definitively so after 1572.[63] The first type of decree, *de partes*, were responses to vassals' written requests for appointments to different careers, and for royal grants for Indian land, travel licenses, book printing, and a host of other privileges the sovereign granted colonists on a case-by-case basis.[64] In short, she argued that petition-prompted decrees were exclusively of the *gracia* sort. The other family of decrees, *de oficio*, originated from within the council and were "dispositions of the state" in the areas of Indies *gobierno* administration.[65] Other scholars, including José Joaquín Real Díaz, Kenneth Andrien, and Angel Hernández García have echoed this dichotomy as well.[66] The implication is that vassals won *gracia* legislation, but could not influence broader Indies *gobierno* legislation.

These descriptions mischaracterize the *parte/oficio* dichotomy. A quick reading of many *de partes* registers reveals that most were indeed *gracia* privileges but that many also had sweeping *gobierno* contents. Moreover, many of the examples in this chapter were *de oficio* but explicitly or implicitly owed to letters by all sorts of Indies vassals. This shows that

[62] For example, Friar Domingo de Santo Tomás wrote in 1562 that *encomenderos* had Indian tribute through "*çédula particular*" decrees and that these privileges were costing the Crown too much; AHNM, Diversos-Colecciones, 24, N.58. See also AGI, Quito 8, R.8, N.22.

[63] Heredia Herrera, "Cedularios," 4.

[64] Heredia Herrera, "Cedularios," 9-12.

[65] Heredia Herrera, "Cedularios," 9.

[66] Real Díaz also divides *de partes* and *de oficio* in this way, see *Estudio diplomático*, 200, 225, 231, as does Andrien, "Legal," 109.

vassals could win either *de partes* or *de oficio* decrees; virtually no legislation of either type simply emerged from within the council. Lastly, decrees like the sweeping 1588 ruling on equality between Spaniards and *mestizos* which Pedro Rengifo won could be *de partes*. In other words, this theory has a second problem: *de partes* is not synonymous with *gracia*, nor is *de oficio* another term for *gobierno*.

This leaves us in need of a new explanation for the existence of these two types of decrees. Both could feature legislation, both could be prompted by petitioners. The origin of this distinction lies in the nitty-gritty of imperial bureaucracy. Secretaries and scribes earned salaries, but also charged for their services. When these officials dispatched decrees to individuals or groups, they did so in return for a fee, or *derecho*.[67] This was a formal part of council work; the king's 1559 appointment of Secretary Eraso, for example, explicitly stated that he would receive both a fixed salary and the right to charge additional *derechos* to compensate him for his work with "the *cartas*, cédulas, and other dispatches that you produce."[68]

In a rare but telling document on the costs of secretarial work, the Council of the Indies' secretary Juan de Luyando explicitly stated that every year he earned a base salary of 100,000 maravedís, along with 100,000 maravedís for the "*derechos* for the provisions and decrees *de partes*," plus 50,000 for reading *procesos* (lawsuits).[69] In the end, Luyando was making 250,000 maravedís a year, largely thanks to the *derechos* from these *de partes* decrees.[70] This wage would help him offset the costs of paper, string, and ink (20,000), decrees that vassals failed to pick up once he had completed them (12,000), "and delivery-related expenses for *de oficio* decrees (100,000)."

Exactly how much *de partes* decrees cost vassals throughout the sixteenth century is hard to say. Imperial paperwork tended to omit these rates, and because of officials' efforts to ensure that the poor received pro bono help, subjects did not often complain and thus lay bare the details. However, one manuscript regarding internal council bureaucracy from 1575–1577 does reveal the base cost of *de partes* and some *de oficio* decrees. This text features 59 different Crown dispatches and their

[67] In a 1540 Peru court case resolution (executoria) in 1540, we see a scribe paying his peers the *derechos* he owed them for issuing decrees without having received Crown permission; see AGI, Patronato 246, N.1, R.11.

[68] AGI, Indiferente 425, L.23, 402r.

[69] AGI, Patronato 171, N.1, R.4.

[70] Of course, this document is merely "what the *derechos* might seem to be worth" according to Luyando, meaning he might have inflated the costs and understated his total earnings.

costs.[71] Ordinary *de partes* decrees cost roughly 150 maravedís. Certain special grace appointments to various Crown positions could cost as cost as much as 300 maravedís, and some judicial documents could cost even more, at 350. *De oficio* decrees appeared on the list as having no cost whatsoever.

The picture that emerges from these prices, and from the general lack of vassals' complaints, was that Indies officials received decrees on Crown business for free, the poor received their *de partes* decrees for free as well, and other subjects seeking *de partes* edicts paid a pittance. Even for those who did have to pay, it was an affordable system: 150 maravedís came out to 4.4 silver reales, which in the 1570s could buy 2 chickens from rural Indians in Tierra Firme.[72] Around 1585 *mitayo* miners in Potosí earned 3.5 reales a day; free workers won 4.[73] According to historian Manuel Fernández Álverez, in sixteenth-century Spain, a digger's daily pay might be some 60 maravedís, and a wage laborer would make 40; 960 grams of bread was 10, a pound of cheese, 14, and a pound of lamb 17.[74] For many subjects that were too well-off to qualify for the administration's poverty exemption, such as priests, friars, merchants, nobles, Crown officials, and the like, this 150 maravedí price was well within reach.

How did this vassal-to-secretary payment work? Procurators in Madrid might pay their clients' fees. For example, the Mexico City resident Diego de Santa Cruz delegated the Madrid procurators Pedro de Arriola, Juan de Larrea, and Juan de la Peña the power to seek certain grace decrees *de parte*, and stipulated that whoever could take the case should pay for the costs of any resulting dispatches.[75] Anyone fortunate enough to be near the council might also pay directly to the doormen or the secretary. Yet not all subjects lived near the court; there is a certain mystery regarding how they paid council officials for *de partes* rulings. Perhaps the local high courts or other Indies institutions charged subjects locally, and paid the council the difference. This would explain why Secretary Luyando did not have all of his *derechos* in hand and had to wait for the royal treasury to pay him directly every year.

[71] AGI, Indiferente 1387, "*Relación.*" [72] Borrego Plá, *Cartagena*, 219.

[73] Larson, *Cochabamba*, 58. [74] Fernández Álvarez, *Siglo XVI*, 456.

[75] For example, the Mexico City resident Diego de Santa Cruz delegated the Madrid procurators Pedro de Arriola, Juan de Larrea, and Juan de la Peña the power to seek certain grace decrees de parte, and stipulated that whoever could take the case should pay for the costs of the provisions or decrees, in AHAHNCM, Alonso, Antonio. México 2-11-1576, Not.1, Vól.9, Leg.15, 635v/636.

Everyday Council Labor: Decision-Making and Humbler Toil

The work underpinning council officials' repetitive daily tasks rarely appears in the archive. The antipatrimonialist reforms of the sixteenth century forbade ministers from treating their duties as family business without the monarch's explicit approval, meaning that while women continued to play reduced roles, they were often "horizontally and vertically segregated into certain occupations and into lower status positions … in the organizational hierarchy."[76] Women's labor was essential for the empire's operations all the same. Officials' wives, sisters, and daughters likely often cared for ministers' clothes and food, and undertook many other tasks at home.

Fragmentary evidence also suggests that the king expected Madrid's female and male homeowners to provide housing for royal officials and Indies justice-seekers, often for years at a time.[77] This required landladies to make financial investments in their properties, and surely to exert great efforts to accommodate their guests. For instance, a circa 1584 report stated that doña Inés de Ribadeneyra and her sisters had petitioned the king "diverse times for the privilege of being free of guests." Doña Ana de Guevara also said her house was in shambles and also requested to be exempt.[78] These homeowners' (often unwilling) contributions were indispensable for ministers conducting their work close to the royal palace.

One type of female worker within the council appeared particularly often in its paperwork: the *barrenderas* (maids or floor-sweepers, sing. *barrendera*). In November 1552, council ministers issued an edict paying a certain unnamed female sweeper 45 reales.[79] In 1558, the council disbursed 32 reales to Luisa de la Cerda for four months' work.[80] Ministers did not mention another barrendera until 23 November 1563, when they delivered another identical payment to María Vázquez, who worked at least until late 1572.[81] Until the 1580s, the barrenderas' pay seems to have been 8 reales per month, which ministers supplemented with 2-ducat Christmas bonuses beginning in the 1570s.[82] On

76 Ramsay and Parker, "Gender," 259; Crompton and Sanderson, *Gendered Jobs*; Hakim, *Occupational Segregation*; Walby, *Patriarchy*.

77 BFZ, CA, E.223-46 (undated but ca. 1586-87).

78 BL, Mss.Add.28345, 88^{r}.

79 AGI, Indiferente 424, L.22, 465^{r}.

80 AGI, Indiferente 425, L.23, 346^{r}, 363^{r}, 392^{v}, 408^{v}, and 426^{r}.

81 AGI, Indiferente 425, L.24, 169^{v}-70^{r}, 181^{v}-82^{r}, 198^{v}, 219^{v}, 248^{r-v}, 262^{v}; Indiferente 426, L.25, 146^{v}, and 215^{r}.

82 See AGI, Indiferente 426, L.26, 18^{v}-19^{r}; Indiferente 426, L.26, 67^{v}; Indiferente 426, L.27, 150^{r}.

December 24, 1571, ministers gave two ducats to María Vazquez "for the care she has had in sweeping the furniture."[83]

The barrendera who seems to have worked best and hardest for the council was "black Damiana" ("la negra Damiana"). In 1585, she petitioned for a dress for her Easter baptism, suggesting that she had converted recently Christianity. She was likely a slave.[84] Damiana commanded a higher salary than her predecessors, taking home at least 14 ducats in 1586, 50 reales and two ducats in 1587, and 8 ducats in 1588.[85] She knew the value of her contributions, petitioning ministers repeatedly and successfully for rewards, stressing her service in keeping the fire burning in the council offices every morning.[86]

Men also undertook humble but essential sorts of labor which impacted the *gobierno* process. Pedro Romero, the doorman of the council in the 1580s, not only regularly obtained reams of paper, string, and ink for ministers' everyday business, He and his assistants also bought and carried bags of coals for heating, brought horologists to fix the clock, had officials' desks and chairs repaired, fixed the windows, acquired and installed curtains, brought food and wine for workers' lunch, built a box to hold the urinals, and replaced the urinal bags regularly.[87] Without these essential contributions, council ministers' work would have been miserable indeed – and perhaps even impossible.

Quantifying Royal Decree-Production

These many actors – kings, secretaries, ministers, assistants, and humbler workers – made the empire's production of many thousands of decrees possible. But exactly how prolific was the petition-and-response system? Taking stock of the council's output of *gobierno* royal decrees is a major challenge. Ministers mixed *gracia* and *gobierno* decrees together in their large manuscript registers, which by 1598 numbered between 300 and 500

[83] AGI, Indiferente 426, L.25, 146^{v}; Indiferente 426, L.26, 145^{r}; Indiferente 426, L.26, 192^{r}; Indiferente 426, L.27, 175^{v}.

[84] AGI, Indiferente 1398, "Damiana"; Indiferente 426, L.27, 125^{r} and 149^{r}.

[85] AGI, Indiferente 426, L.27; 149^{r} and 150^{r}; Indiferente 426, L.27, 165^{v}-166^{r}; Indiferente 426, L.27, 174^{v} and 175^{r}.

[86] AGI, Indiferente 1398, "Damiana," 1585.

[87] AGI, Indiferente 1395, "P. Romero," April 27 1583, "P. Romero," "P. Romero," December 16, 1583, November 11, 1584. See also AGI, Indiferente 1384, "Memoria," April 9, 1579.

tomes.[88] Then comes the terribly challenging task of classifying decrees as *gobierno* and *gracia* – a distinction which was sometimes blurry if the *gobierno* decrees dealt with minutiae or the *gracia* edict had sweeping consequences.

One official in the late 1560s estimated the number of *gobierno* decrees to be as high as 18,000.[89] Officials eventually percolated many *gobierno* edicts into brief principles. By one count, officials whittled these principles from 12,000 to 7,308 in 1635, then to 6,385 in the council's 1681 printed collection of laws, the *Recopilación*.[90] Another count from 1637 stated that by 1618 officials had slated upwards of "11,000 laws" for inclusion within the *Recopilación*.[91] Clearly, then, the monarchy produced tens of thousands of *gobierno* decrees in the sixteenth century, of which many thousands would become fundamental royal policies. Unfortunately, the exact number will likely forever remain elusive.

Just as difficult to quantify are these decrees' themes. Fortunately, an anonymous council official kept an invaluable resource for historians hoping to understand this type of document: a register exclusively of *de oficio* decrees featuring *gracia* and *gobierno* themes. This register enumerated and abstracted the edicts the council sent to royal Indies officials mainly between February 2, 1567 and July 4, 1576.[92] The vast majority went to those in royal employ: ciceroys, presidents, governors, high court justices, *alcaldes de crimen*, and Crown attorneys. Despite the fact that some edicts were addressed to nonofficial individuals and groups such as friars, priests, and city councils, these were to remain in the possession of high courts or other lesser centers of local governance. In other words, these *oficio* edicts generally went to local officials, or to anyone whom council ministers felt should receive a decree free of cost due to a particular case's relationship with imperial affairs.

[88] I have made the very rough calculation of 300 by adding each *registro*'s folios for 1492-1598, using Rubio y Moreno's *Inventario General*, 103-60. Fifteen massive registers (*registros*) of laws are missing, so this count is quite likely several thousand pages too low; see Ibid., 43-44. In 1597, council scribes possessed at least 300 register books, according to a notary's inventory; AGI, Contaduría 7A and 7B and Gómez Gómez, *Sello*, 175. However, Diego de Encinas counted five hundred; see AGI, Indiferente 1416, "Diego de Encinas," May 28, 1598.

[89] La Peña Cámara, "Manuscrito," 52.

[90] García-Gallo, "Legislación," 100; Sánchez Bella, *Nuevos estudios*, 103.

[91] AGI, Indiferente 1651, N.4, October 3, 1637.

[92] This is located in AGI, Indiferente, 1505, L.1. There are two outlying decrees, one from September 14 1565, and another from December 10 1566.

These entries reveal extremely complex topics of *gracia* and mostly *gobierno*. Policies included orders to exile belligerent bishops, investigate monasteries, disburse funds to help Indian orphans, undertake botanical investigations, or expel non-Spanish priests from the Indies, among countless others.[93] This register also shows just how numerous important legislation could be in the empire. This work lists at least 2,506 decrees the Crown sent officials, mainly between February 2, 1567 and July 4, 1576 (Figure 6.2).[94] It spans 3,441 days, meaning that during this period council officials produced approximately 73 *de oficio* edicts every 100 days.[95]

There are risks involved in extrapolating the 1567–1576 register abstracts' lists backward to estimate how much legislation emanated

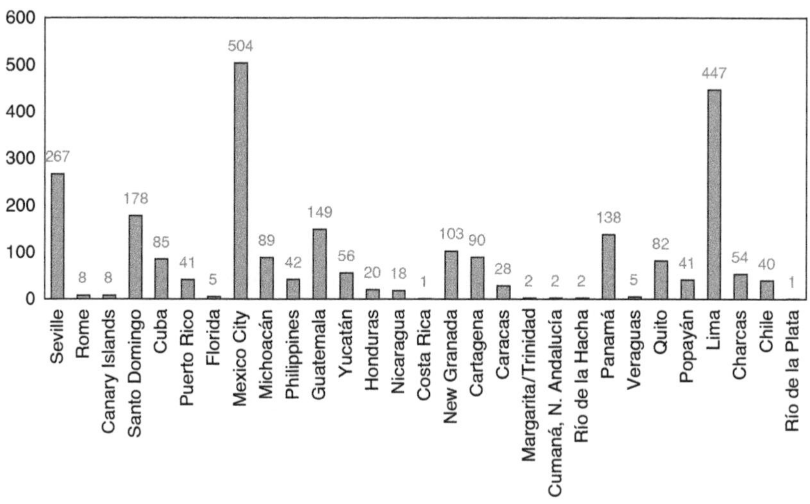

FIGURE 6.2 Destinations of 2,506 de oficio decrees (mostly *gobierno*), early 1567–mid-1576.

[93] AGI, Indiferente 1505, L.1, 131r, 193r, 215r, 62r, 171v, 226v, 250v, in that order.

[94] The council clearly sent these in early 1567 to supplement official records some time after the secretary first engrossed them in the register books. More puzzlingly, the prolific House of Trade *oficio* decrees only comprise May 9, 1571 to December 23 1572, meaning that my count of 2506 is clearly too low. Lastly, various decrees went to multiple officials at once, but Ledesma did not clarify exactly how many council officials issued, meaning once again that the count of 2506 is too low.

[95] The exact number is 72.83.

from the council in earlier decades, because the Indies were unsettled and had uneven development between 1492 and about 1565. However, the conservative forward projection that the council remained equally prolific from February 2, 1567 until the beginning of 1600 suggests that ministers would have issued 8,756 *de oficio* decrees. Likely the number is far higher for these nearly 33 years, as Spanish cities and towns continued to form and expand over time.

This *oficio* register also provides a glimpse of council officials' distribution of these edicts between different Indies provinces. Scrivener Ledesma noted the final destination of these many laws, and may have used the abstract registers to keep track of these deliveries, sorting each by province or city. The High Court of Mexico received just over a fifth (20.1%) of the total. The High Court of Peru was not far behind, with 17.8%. The House of Trade was to implement another 10.7% of these edicts. The next highest were high courts such as Hispaniola (7.1%), Guatemala (5.9%), Panama (5.5%), Nueva Granada and Santa Marta (4.1%), Cartagena Nueva Galicia (Michoacán, 3.6%), Quito (3.3%), and the Cities of Cartagena (3.6%) and Santiago de Cuba (3.4%). All other regions in aggregate only comprise 13.3%. This tome shows that royal decrees had radically different concentrations in different corners of the empire. Costa Rica, Río de la Plata (Asunción), and San Juan de Puerto Rico had one paltry decree apiece. Meanwhile, the High Courts of Mexico and Peru claimed a total of 37.9% of *de oficio* policies. Mexican and Peruvian officials would have been swimming in decrees to implement, while marginal areas might have been wishing that their access to royal justice were stronger. And, of course, this register only records *de oficio* decrees, meaning that the abundant *de partes* edicts – including many with sweeping legislative heft – were not included.

Conclusions

All decrees begin and end with the awe-commanding introduction: "I, the King." This was one of the empire's great fictions: that the monarch was the author of decrees which contained his pure volition and command, his volition alive in a lifeless ink-and-cloth paper rectangle. However, the empire's legislative corpus was neither the will nor the authorship of the monarch alone – it was a polysemic chorus of the volitions, words, and labor of successful petitioners and a whole array of subalterns and others. The empire's *gobierno* laws were therefore not just hyperabundant, but conceptually undisciplined, internally cacophonous, phraseologically dissonant, and ontologically rather nonsensical. Under the guise of a single man's volition they instead contained thousands, and under the pretense of royal magnanimity toward all they concealed as many secret biases and injustices.

The pervasive image of the Spanish Empire as a state determined to impose its will and epistemological-conceptual grid upon vassals through constant, hyperparticular edicts cannot hold when we consider that vassals prompted them and largely even phrased them. Ministers had substantial power – they decided which petitions they would present to the monarch, and had total authority to phrase edicts as they pleased. However, their labor burden was too great and their information-gathering capabilities too limited for them to exercise a strong editorial hand over the petition-and-response process. Royal decrees' concepts and phraseology were thus not a rational, comprehensive, and coherent body of policies but a reflection of petitioners' hodgepodge, bottom-up, conflict-driven agendas.

That is not to say that various sorts of domination were not rife in the petition-and-response process. We have seen that those who sought to exploit and usurp the lawmaking process's many flimsy legal fictions faced gruesome violence. Moreover, subjects themselves might use petitions to lash out at others. Vassals (including local Indies officials) sought policies which bolstered their own interests and projects, often at the expense of others. Augustinians sought to restrict the rights of *mestizos*. Self-described *mulatos* sought to restrict the movement of Indigenous merchants. Tlaxcalans aimed not only at *mestizos* and Spaniards for expulsion but Greeks, Levantines, and *mulatos*. Spanish officials, friars, priests, conquistadors, and occasionally, women would also engage in this agonistic struggle – against their peers, their oppressors, and their social inferiors. Those who petitioned most often – viceroys, high judges, Indies attorneys, prelates, municipal councils, and others – certainly set the majority of these policies through their ability to avail themselves of the advantages of high literacy, superior access to faster communications, and their ability to afford legal agents. Nonetheless, the empire was not theirs alone to define.

Lastly, the agents involved in the toils of lawmaking were not restricted to ministers, secretaries, and monarchs. Both paperwork and humble everyday labor remained essential throughout the sixteenth century, enabling these processes of decree phraseology and production to take place. Edict-drafting was grueling for all involved from start to finish, a great collective production which the monarch signed "I, the King."

Pedro Rengifo's Epilogue

Subjects of Chance

By September 1588, Pedro Rengifo had been living and languishing in Spain for some four years; an illness was partly responsible.[1] He had petitioned for a three-year renewal on his expired travel license and made clear his desire to return to Peru, complaining that his long stay in Madrid had bankrupted him.[2] There is little information about the ordeal of his return, other than that he left with his legislation in hand. The *mestizo* was in Lima by October 24, 1592 at the latest, when he and his wife, Juana Rodríguez de Castro, received yet another power of attorney – this time to petition the Charcas High Court for privileges on a client's behalf.[3] Once home in La Paz he clearly thrived, for between 1597 and 1599 he appears to be lending considerable sums of money and selling llamas, wheat, and wine to local merchants and officials.[4]

As often occurred, implementation of the decree proved difficult. The *mestiza* clause of the 1588 priesthood decree was at least partly successful. The bishops had ordered Lima abbesses include mestizas already by 1584 at the behest of the *mestizo* petitioners Ruíz and González.[5] The Augustinian Antonio de la Calancha would later note that the Convent of Our Lady of the Incarnation had once drafted a constitution barring *mestizas*, but that the arrival of this royal decree had prompted the Abbess to change this practice, without providing details; by 1592 there

[1] AGI, Indiferente 1402, "Léase toda," November 28, 1588.

[2] AGI, Indiferente 1402, "Léase toda," November 28, 1588; His travel license original is in AGI, Indiferente 2097, N.187; the petition register entry is in AGI, Indiferente 1089, L.14, 165v.

[3] Risly Clemence, *Harkness*, vol. 1, 275.

[4] Archivo y Biblioteca Nacionales de Bolivia, Escrituras Públicas 63, 593r–v; 64, 139r–140r; 65, 200r–201v.

[5] AGI, Lima 126, 111v–112v.

were two nuns of the black veil who belonged to the Ampuero-Yupanqui dynasty in Lima's Convent of the Conception.[6]

Mestizo ordination similarly seems to have partially succeeded. In the late 1590s representatives of Quito's Dominican, Augustinian, and Mercedarian Orders complained that the bishop had been diminishing friars' parishes by appointing "many clerics … insufficient and incapable, and many of them mestizos." The bishop defended his actions as conforming with papal and royal decrees.[7] In his spectacular and cantankerous 1615 compendium *Nueva Corónica*, the Peruvian Guaman Poma de Ayala warned the king that *mestizos* in general caused problems for Indians, "and much more so mestizo priests."[8] Indeed, the regions of New Granada, Charcas, and Río de la Plata probably had many part-Indian priests in the late 1590s and 1600s (and beyond).[9] We can thus be satisfied that, in subsequent decades, the great *mestizo* petition succeeded to a certain degree.

The 1588 edict seems to have faded from public view within several decades. Occasional complaints against *mestizo* priests did surface from time to time.[10] This forgetting was another consequence of the fact that Rengifo had requested a *de partes* decree. Ministers handed *de partes* documents to vassals as their private business. *De oficio* laws generally went to Indies officials, who took better care of them. In Madrid, the latter group also received more regular consultations by council officials.

This decree did remain within the council, enjoying salutary neglect for decades. By the 1600s, royal officials' desire to sponsor more coherent archiving began to rouse texts like this from their slumber. Minister Aguiar printed a brief excerpt of the edict in his 1628 collection of pithy decree abstracts, the *Sumario de la Recopilación*, under book 1, title V, section VII.[11] In his seminal 1648 juridical treatise *Política Indiana*, council attorney and minister Juan de Solórzano y Pereira – a true master of its archive – directly cited this decree while defending *mestizos'* access to the priesthood.[12] In his influential 1668 *Itinerario para parochos*, the Bishop of Quito Alonso Peña Montenegro also defended this position citing Rengifo's edict.[13]

[6] *Corónica moralizada*, Book II, 429. [7] AGI, Quito 84, N.7.
[8] KB: GKS 2232 4,° 978/996. [9] Olaechea Labayen, "Aspectos."
[10] For some of these debates, see Hyland, "Illegitimacy."
[11] Aguiar and Acuña, *Sumarios*, 10v. [12] Solórzano and Pereira, *Politica Indiana*.
[13] *Itinerario* L3, Tr.8, §.3, N.2, 368–369.

Even more importantly, the council's 1681 *Recopilación*, the landmark official printed compilation of *de partes* and *de oficio* decrees, excerpted this policy. Suddenly Rengifo's victory was widely available.[14] Interest in the decree spiked. In an April 20, 1687 letter, the Bishop of Arequipa informed the council that there was a vacancy in the cathedral canonry. Officials had recently received three eligible candidates' requests, the strongest nominee being one Juan Núñez Vela de Rivera. His appointment posed only one major problem – he was a *mestizo* of legitimate birth. A minister wrote "bring news of if there is a law that prohibits ... subjects of his nature and quality." The Crown attorney found the 1578 ban and the *Recopilación*'s excerpt defending *mestizo* ordination. Núñez once again wrote on May 3, 1692, stating clearly that he wished to receive the canonry with the title, "mestizo descendant of the Indian gentiles" to thereby inspire his fellow *mestizos* and Indians. The attorney was supportive – the *mestizo* had "all the qualities of the [1588] law."[15]

On January 10, 1690, the part-Indian priest Bernardo Inga encouraged Núñez's further lobbying.[16] Núñez did so once again "in the name and in the voice of all the Indians and mestizos of America."[17] Minister Sierra y Osorio, who had first-hand knowledge of the Indies due to his time in Mexico, set about investigating the council archive. Sierra agreed with Núñez in a lengthy July 28, 1696 memorandum that it was "undoubtable" that they were as capable as Spaniards.[18] The council elevated the issue to the king, who on December 19, 1696 considered its merits. The resulting March 12, 1697 decree, which the monarch ordered dispatched to everywhere in the Indies, approved Núñez's request. The result was a mix of the phraseology of council ministers and that of the attorney and Núñez (a considerably different process from just over a century after Rengifo won the 1588 edict). This ruling, which vassals would later call the *Cédula de honores* or the Decree of Honors, cited Rengifo's victory through its *Recopilación* excerpt as well. It unambiguously stated that noble *mestizos* and Indians were all as honorable as "the noble hidalgos of Castille" and could participate in any institutions or offices previously restricted to only Spaniards.

[14] Council, *Recopilación* B.1, T.VII, L.7, 32.

[15] AGI, Lima 13, "En consulta." We know that he succeeded because on November 5, 1696, the Crown gave him 100 ducats to travel to the Indies and mentioned that he was now Arequipa's canon AGI, Indiferente 444, L.37, 242r.

[16] ADC, Colección Betancur vol.6, no.20. Many thanks to José Carlos de la Puente Luna for generously providing me with an image of this letter.

[17] Muro Orejón, "Igualdad," 366.

[18] Muro Orejón, "Igualdad," 369–372.

Despite local difficulties with implementation, historians regard the *Cédula de honores* as a crucial achievement for Andeans.[19] More members of the Indigenous nobility of Peru began to petition the king and council as a result.[20] By the mid-1700s vassals also began agitating more forcefully for Indian education (with limited success). Beginning in 1783, Indian *caciques* in Peru were becoming priests at a far greater rate than before.[21] Petitioners also followed Rengifo's and Vela's footsteps to the court. In the early 1720s, for instance, a tirelessly litigious Indian from Lima, don Vicente Morachimo, would travel to Madrid and live there for decades, managing to persuade the council to reissue the *cédula de honores* once again in 1725.[22] Thanks to the petitions of one Friar Isidoro Cala of Lima, Charles III reissued this measure in 1766.[23] As historian Peter Villella has shown, the *cédula* also inspired Mexican "cacique-letrados" to request their own equal treatment.[24] Mexico witnessed a surge of Indian applicants to the priesthood in the early 1700s, which resulted in the foundation of various Indian schools and seminaries.[25]

The consequences of the *mestizo* petition of 1582–1588 echoed for centuries. What might have happened if Rengifo had been bitten by a mosquito and died of malaria in Panama, been crushed by the gales of a Caribbean hurricane, been captured by Ottoman forces, or succumbed to illness in Madrid? Conversely, what if the council secretary had categorized Rengifo's decree as *de oficio*, leading to its wider recognition among Indigenous and part-Indian petitioners? How many petitions sank to the bottom of the oceans and the archives, and how many rose to occupy a central place in Indies life, due to causal forces far removed from the simple fiction of the vassal–lord dialogue? The contingencies involved in the making of the law were so great that the exact social nature of the Indies appears, in many ways, to be the subject of chance itself.

[19] Dueñas, *Indians and Mestizos*, 157. [20] Dueñas, *Indians and Mestizos*, 157–158.
[21] Dueñas, *Indians and Mestizos*, 174. [22] Glave, "Memoria."
[23] Navarro, *Denuncia*, 31. [24] Villella, *Indigenous Elites*, 299.
[25] Menegus Bornemann and Aguirre Salvador, *Los indios*, 104–115.

Conclusions

For empires to exist, they must be endlessly created and recreated. Stories of powerful men who shape the world with the stroke of a pen are fictions – and these themselves must also be collectively created by the many. As John Milton wrote in 1651, "a king has not made us, but rather, we the king."[1]

The Spanish New World was not monarchs' or ministers' alone for the defining. Dialogue was the Habsburgs' preferred form of domination over distance; the grislier sorts of Indies violence tended to reside closer to the community level, mostly in the hands of local officials, middling conquistador-lords, religious orders, Indigenous authorities, and petty criminals. Only in the past two centuries have liberal thinkers created new mythologies of Spanish imperial rule which posit the locus of domination and violence to lie within the central state apparatus. It was in the nineteenth and twentieth centuries that the empire became haunted by Napoleonic armies, Prussian bureaus, Stasi operatives, Francoist juntas, Stalinist intelligentsias, and other ostensibly omniscient powers – or by the various sadistic strongmen of Latin America. In reality, monarchs were neither the descendants of Moses, Aeneas, or Hercules (as they would have had it) nor the prefigurations of national-era horrors at home and overseas. Underneath our myths, and those cherished by sixteenth-century subjects, the empire remained rooted largely in a paradoxically fragile but vibrant dialogue, powered by the make-believe and the very real, undertaken not just between vassals and lords but also by the countless actants who

[1] Milton, *Joannis Miltoni*, 3.

facilitated this communication. The legal fiction "I, the King" thus has concealed its cocreated origins: *We, the King.*

The very creation of the phrase "I, the King" required many other fictions big and small, each overlaid upon the other. Each layer of make-believe played an important part. The process began with the legal-magical compression of vassals' volition into paper, including written-words-as-speech, petition-as-ceremonial, and signature-as-will. Petitions might include oaths of translation and notarization, transmission of personhood to legal agents, and compression of fictive group volitions into these intermediaries – all under God's watchful eye. The vassal–lord exchange of volitions, which contemporaries idealized as a direct conversation between two souls before the Lord in a struggle for the salvation of all, had to endure the indignities of intermediaries' constant transformations, compressions, and distortions. The empire's dreadful logistical circumstances badly strained these fictions, though most petitions did reach their destinations (after months or even years).

Far from an idealized dialogue of volitions between vassal and lord, the petition-and-response system was deeply material. Ocean waves, cloth and ink, the bundles of correspondence of the formal and informal courier systems, the oxen hauling ministers and papers through Spain, the decision-making technologies such as marginal annotations and *consultas*, the desks and shelves of council ministers –all were actants which provided material support for the making of petitions and decrees. These material tools and circumstances generally, but never entirely, helped subjects and rulers overcome a similarly daunting array of material obstacles, from hurricanes to dried-out rivers to Moroccan pirates to mosquitos.

For those petitions which did arrive to the court, new obstacles remained. Council ministers, after all, were also flesh-and-blood men and not mere instruments of good government. Crown officials realized, thanks partly to the advertent and inadvertent roles played by influential women at the court, that these officials might usurp monarchs' prerogatives to patrimonial rule. This often endangered Spain and the Indies by contaminating the vassal–lord dialogue with ministers' illicit volitions. Such indiscretions prompted officials to increasingly embrace a new gendered fiction of bureaucratic masculinity which operated against the powerful and enticing, and instead acted in the service of the monarchs and those less fortunate. Men of masculine breasts working in the service of the monarchy were to act as instruments and safeguards of the transfer of vassals' *voluntad* to the king. Here, powerful women subtly but profoundly transformed the petition-and-response system – and decisively shaped evolving ideas of gendered administration in Europe's leading institution of overseas rule.

Subjects and rulers, having collectively safeguarded a robust if imperfect legitimacy for the petition-and-response system, then had to reckon with the unexpected downsides of their success. One of the greatest obstacles, both conceptual and material, was the paralyzing volume of correspondence – a testament to the challenges of the empire's successes in maintaining collective communication. For officials and monarchs, this problem was acute. Petitions passed through the ministers' and monarchs' satisficing process – a series of decision-making technologies which initially prioritized communication with vassals over policy-making coherence. Beginning in the 1560s, however, these decision-making processes increasingly balanced communication with ministers' efforts to recommend to the king legally and descriptively factual and coherent policies. Crown officials' increasingly active capabilities sometimes muddled their promise to dialogue with vassals, but tangibly improved their ability to defend and administer the Indies. Through a final set of fictions, kings imbued decrees with their law-bearing volitions through a signature – a frail ink mark which officials defended with fearsome public violence. *Voluntad* had traveled, improbably, from a subject's heart to the breast of the monarch, and a decree was born.

The legal fictions, everyday routines, and technologies involved in sustaining the petition-and-response system involved massive amounts of labor. The *work* involved in paperwork may not have involved much muscle, but was labor intensive nonetheless. A host of pro-bono and professional intermediaries offered to assist vassals of all stripes in creating petitions, overseeing courier networks, and pressing cases at the royal court. Understaffed ministers and monarchs toiled almost incessantly, describing their trials as "Herculean." Royal secretaries organized everyday papers, coordinated communication, and saw decrees to completion. Subalterns of many sorts played crucial roles. *Relatores* summarized long cases – including some *gobierno* petitions. Scribes and their assistants produced decree registers and drafts, organized compilations, accessed precedent, and managed archives. Secretaries' families – including women – acted as custodians of royal archives in their own homes; indeed, that these documents survive today is partly their doing.

The liberal-era question of the "authorship" of decrees and the "voices" of petitioners, and sixteenth-century fictions of a vassal–lord dialogue of volitions, obscure the many actants involved in shaping the lawmaking process outside of what scholars traditionally consider the domain of law. Much of this work was labor of the hardest sort – such as the toil of Indigenous rangers, canoeists, trailblazers, relay-runners, and oarsmen, largely Afro-descendant muleteers and janitors, the motley sailors and port workers, as well as Iberian couriers, carpenters, and other handymen and women. Indigenous craftsmen also unwittingly played their part, having produced works of such subtle beauty that faraway ministers in Madrid needed to consciously distance themselves and their women from them. Those entrusted with the unsavory task of punishing those who overstepped legality's boundaries also played their part, lacerating malefactors' flesh into imperial legitimacy.

Human beings' constraints in the face of these labor demands had sweeping consequences. The result of the administration's crushing workloads and its officials' desire to maintain communication was that ministers and their subalterns often directly excerpted subjects' petition phraseologies and transplanted them verbatim into royal decrees. The nearly ubiquitous view of the scholarship has been that colonizers have imposed their values, agendas, ontologies, and epistemologies upon the colonized; decrees have served as a paradigmatic example of authorities' grandiose *Wille zur Macht*. This book's account of the petition-and-response system disorders this narrative substantially. While humbler and middling individuals of many backgrounds did not impose their own visions *over* the monarchy, they dialogued with its officials constantly and to great effect. They often shaped imperial categories, in a process ranging from creative innovation, to insertion of Indigenous adaptations, to open negotiation about terms (as in the case of Rengifo and the *mestizos*), to the transformation of these categories' meanings. This, in turn, challenges the notion of the colonial state as the architect of a stable, systematic, rational body of law – including legal categories of human difference. Dialogue and the production of consent were the kings' and ministers' priorities during this crucial century, and categories were almost always merely the outcome.

CURRENTS NOT SAILED

This book has begun, and ended, in media res. It has considered only a small portion of an imperial process: the cocreation of petitions, their transmission, and their reception by the king and his ministers. Its account is thus far from complete. My focus could have been on authorities' slower and more deliberate (but also often partly bottom-up) cocreation of royal ordinances, which had the same heft as decrees but which local officials often implemented more rigorously. However, limited sources have made a sweeping overview of ordinance-making difficult. This story could have also been projected further into the past: for instance, to consider Castilian, Aragonese, Indigenous, Islamic, and Sub-Saharan arrangements before and after 1492. It could have contemplated the changing contexts of the 1600s and beyond, with the rise of kings' prime ministers, the greater presence of Crown attorneys, and the council's ongoing struggles with repositories of social and legal facts. The question of how the petition-and-response system changed into the 1600s and beyond, and what this meant for vassals wrestling not only with normative polyphony but even cacophony, is ripe for future research. An even bolder approach would have linked decrees to our present world – after all, the debates which Rengifo engaged in continue to echo today.

More importantly, perhaps, this work has neglected to tackle the full "life cycle" of each decree as it returned to the Indies by ignoring delivery and implementation. A whole new logistical machinery was needed for each one of these laws to return to the New World, on different ships, upon other currents, carried by new hands, often declared in public by non-Spanish town criers. Then began innumerable fraught social conflicts around implementation – vassals could counter-petition a policy they found unjust, maliciously seek to derail an edict, or take any number of other routes to defend their interests. While this book does not address implementation, however, readers should not assume decrees were never enforced. The trope of vassals constantly and maliciously resisting top-down royal fiats was often untrue. When Indies vassals encountered these policies, it was rarely a simple matter of an "effort made by colonized people to read the archive available to them according to their needs in spite of, and on occasions behind the backs of, the imperial authorities."[2] Indeed, the architects of these policies were often members of these vassals' own communities. Moreover, Pedro Rengifo's story reveals that although subsequent generations of subjects would often encounter difficulties in enforcing *mestizo* equality, the 1588 decree was far from a dead letter.

How actors implemented decrees also brings up important questions about imperial legal culture. New World normativity was complex, and though decrees were extraordinarily common and important, they also

[2] Orquera, "'Race,'" 168. For Indigenous contestations within a *justicia* context see van Deusen, *Global Indios*, and for vassals' manipulation of categories of human difference, see, among others, Lewis, *Hall*; Gharala, *Taxing Blackness*.

interacted with other sources and logics on the ground. Once in the Indies, these texts circulated alongside other nonmonarchical edicts issued by viceroys, high courts, prelates, inquisitors, city councils, and other bodies – a maze of normativities and jurisdictions which, although subordinate to the king's volition, were also essential to determining the shape of Indies society.[3] Moreover, officials, jurists, and theologians might support or oppose a decree based on their interpretations of the rich corpus of normative sources, commentary, and customs, attempting to discern and reconcile justice and the royal volition from these documents.[4] Lastly, decrees' complex penetrations into *justicia* court cases and affairs of *gracia* privilege deserve lengthy reflection.

Certainly, the implementation of human positive law was also always a multiactant process. Declaring, enforcing, interpreting, archiving, and retrieving decrees was never merely the domain of powerful Indies officials. That story – or, better said, those many stories – remain to be told; subjecting the issue of decrees' collective implementation to an actor–network theory would be very complex and highly contingent on local circumstances, better suited to rich case studies. This is a direction I hope to take in the not-too-distant future.

We, the King has focused only on a small set of chain links in the imperial machinery. However, hopefully it has made the case for understanding New World society in a new light. Many have studied the viceregal era through binaries of oppression/revolt and hegemony/resistance.[5] Our understanding of the great mystery of how the Spanish Empire survived over three centuries, in the face of near-impossible obstacles, cannot stand upon those binaries alone. As José Carlos de la Puente Luna notes, "power did not always flow from top to bottom. It could not."[6] By highlighting vassals' and lords' cocreation of empire through an always-unequal but nonetheless transformative dialogue, we can better grasp why so many saw themselves as consenting participants and principled reformers – not merely pawns of a global empire.

[3] For one very thorough and important study of Mexican ecclesiastical ordinance-making, involving a deep analysis of the entire Church hierarchy, petitions, deliberation, theological and juridical reasoning, and extensive debate, see Moutin, *Legislar*, esp. 60, 71–73, 117, 146, and 155; "More than Copy." See also Albi, *Gamboa's World*, 3, 173.

[4] Tau Anzoátegui, "Elaboración," esp. 163–173.

[5] MacKay, *Limits*, 1. Stern, ed., *Resistance*; Jones, *Maya Resistance*; Schroeder, ed., *Native Resistance*.

[6] de la Puente Luna, "That Which Belongs," 21.

This work has also attempted to dial back some of the scholarship's mythological models of state power. Depicting Habsburg rulers as demigods comes at a high cost, creating deeply misleading historical models which not only confuse the past, but disfigure our understanding of the present. We must not trade one pantheon for the next but disentangle, understand, and model how power works, including myth-making itself. To imagine how mythic rulers dominate mortals is easy, but grasping how flesh-and-blood human beings impose rule upon their peers is a mystery of far greater proportions.

The Spanish Indies was one such creation of mere mortals. It was also a string of many fragile little things – paper, ink, make-believe, mules, signatures, shelves, promises, precious pieces of Indigenous goldwork – strung together into something global. Hurricanes, pirates, and crises of trust came crashing down upon this world repeatedly, and yet by the beginning of the seventeenth century the vassal–lord bond remained firmly intact and the Indies were well into the process of maturing into a more stable society – all this thanks to the willing and unwilling labor contributions of countless subjects in the realms of the concrete and the fictional alike.

The society which had emerged in the sixteenth century, and which continues to emerge today, was and is largely a creature of this resilient fragility. Indeed, vassals and royal officials alike managed to form a desire and occasionally a reality of global communication. Subjects and officials struggling more or less rationally to meet their everyday interests created a largely functional network of the most unlikely sort – and with it, a sense of shared affection and kinship with the monarch, albeit generally not a bond of proximity but of longing distance.

With time, however, the pronounced "irrational" or inadvertent outcomes of vassals' local efforts became increasingly problematic for all. Decrees, their categories, and indeed, the administration itself were largely what Anthony Giddens calls "an unintended consequence [of] an aggregate of courses of intentional conduct."[7] The challenge of future centuries was for officials to craft a more cohesive and coherent empire without sacrificing the true origin of its power: dialogue, and the fictions which bestowed this communication with legitimacy in the minds of royal vassals. For subjects seeking changes, meanwhile, the ongoing developments produced by increasing normative cacophony along with local and royal

[7] Giddens, *Constitution*, 13. For two excellent discussions of these debates as regards nonelite and law, see McKinley, *Fractional Freedoms*, 8–11; Premo, "Before," 263–264.

archivalization of these disparate decrees also demanded more creative solutions. Little wonder, then, that Indigenous, Spanish, and other subjects turned increasingly to ambitious, comprehensive, even grandiose, petitions such as Guaman Poma's *Nueva Corónica*, with its hundreds of illustrations and sweeping proposals to create good government in Peru.

What is certain is that from 1492 to 1598, the Indies had entered its young adulthood. We must look to dynamic processes, like communication and action, to explain this fraught, remarkable period. The empire itself was never a finished project; it was a never-ending process of back-and-forth correspondence and labor which could only be repeatedly cocreated by vassals, rulers, and many other actants. Perhaps, then, we should not explore this time and place like academic portraitists, or like taxidermists creating uncannily lifeless objects. We might focus on process instead of essence, petition-writing instead of petitions, on decree-making instead of decrees, race-making instead of race, lawmaking instead of law, state-making instead of the state, empire-making instead of empire.[8]

Documents themselves are not mere testaments of the past. As Robert Darnton memorably wrote, too often we read sources as a "record of what happened instead of as an ingredient in the happening."[9] Petitions, *poderes*, *memoriales*, *consultas*, decrees, inventories, and other such works involved in the petition-and-response system were inanimate yet animated, transforming individuals and society as they crossed land and sea in the satchels and trunks of Indies vassals. The archives may today display these cloth manuscripts like a boreal panorama of endless papers, rows of shelves which "merge into mountains that join together to form entire mountain ranges," and into which historians wander, lost in silent contemplation.[10] But these dormant paper landscapes were once, in the hands of vassals, officials, and monarchs, raucous and transformative.

If we reject the mythologization of power and accept that it has always been cocreated, albeit under violent and unequal circumstances, we can reappraise the past as dynamic and abundant in agency.[11] And perhaps not only the past. In 1924, the Swiss painter Paul Klee warned about approaching one's subject of study as a complete outcome, an entity devoid of agency, change, and movement. He lamented that the painter often explores only "the finished forms which nature places before him."[12] These objects seem unified, harmonious, complete, perhaps even bereft of any vital force. However, Klee's archetypal artist grows curious.

[8] Wilde, "La agencia," 3. [9] Darnton, "Introduction," xiii. [10] Vismann, *Files*, xi.
[11] Laclau, "Politics," 76. [12] Klee, *On Modern Art*, 45.

Were they always this way? By exploring not form but formation, the painter finds "creation itself, as Genesis, rather than by the image of nature, the finished product."[13] The artist now beholds a world of creation and complexity in which dynamism is the constant. Freed from a vision of static objects, he or she does not see inertia but kinesis. Stunned by this vision of vitality and movement, the artist considers: perhaps if "this world at one time looked different ... in the future, [it] will look different again."[14]

[13] Klee, *On Modern Art*, 45. [14] Klee, *On Modern Art*, 46.

Glossary

alcalde(s) mayor(es): regional Indies justice

alcalde(s) de crimen: local justice working for a magistrate and specializing in criminal cases

barrender(o), m. *barrender(a)*, f.: floor-sweeper, janitorial worker

bozal(es): recently enslaved Afro-descendant sent to the Indies

cacique(s) m., *cacica(s),* f.: Indigenous community leader

capítulo: segment of petition, normally roughly one paragraph long, featuring an independent suggestion for reform

casos morales: dialectic, maxim-oriented theological-juridical resolutions of complex moral problems

casuistry: a form of juridical (and less often administrative-legislative) reasoning based on deducing maxims and paradigmatic cases; see *casos morales*

carta de poder: letter granting power of legal representation to a third person, often a *procurador*

cedulario: collection of royal decrees

*cédula(s) real(es) (*also *real(es) cédulas)*: royal decrees

chasqui / chasquero(s): Inca and Spanish-era couriers-by-foot

conciencia real (also *real conciencia*): royal conscience

consulta(s): documents sent by councils to the monarch for resolution; most often for *gracia*, cases but occasionally regarding *justicia* and *gobierno*

consulta(s) a boca: officials' oral consultations with the monarch

correo(s) mayor(es): royal mail officials

conclusión: section of the royal decree featuring the royal determination

corregidor(es): regional Indies justice

de partes: *gobierno* and *gracia* decrees whose processing fees were paid for by vassals

de oficio: *gobierno* and *gracia* decrees paid for by the royal treasury

derecho: justice

Derecho indiano: Indies *derecho* (a twentieth and twenty-first century concept)

división: an optional section of the royal decree, generally following the *proposición*, including the ruler's explanation for a given decision

encomendero(s), encomendera(s): recipients of royal grants of Indian tribute and/or labor

encomienda(s): the jurisdiction of the *encomendero*

emparedamiento(s): walled enclosure resembling a convent or monastery

fiscal(es): Crown attorneys, including those in the council

gobierno: paperwork channel through which petitioners, ministers, and monarchs created administrative-legislative decrees

gracia: paperwork channel through which petitioners, ministers, and monarchs discussed privileges and pardons

guerra: paperwork channel through which royal officials considered military issues

hacienda: paperwork channel through which royal officials considered fiscal-economic issues

junta(s): extraordinary committees gathering various council ministers and (occasionally) nonministers

justicia: paperwork channel through which petitioners, lawyers, and ministers determined litigious justice cases

legajo(s): bundles of council papers, generally petitions and litigation

legislación: sixteenth century term occasionally employed to describe royal power to issue human positive law

ley(es): laws, including royal decrees

***mestizo(s)* m., *mestiza(s)* f.:** term popularized in mid-1500s to describe part-Indigenous men and women; complex semantic overlaps with *mulato*

ministro: minister of the monarch's royal councils

mitayo(s): Indigenous Andean conscript miners

mulato(s), mulata(s): term popularized in preconquest Iberia to describe part-Afro-descendant men and women; complex semantic overlaps with *mestizo* and *zambaigo*

notario(s): notary

navíos de aviso: courier vessels

narración: section of royal decree acknowledging petitioner, very often including verbatim excerpt of petitioner's claims and categories

peticion(es): petition; an alternative was *súplica* or *memorial*

pochteca(s): Nahuatl term for Mesoamerican long-distance merchants

procudaror(es), procuradora(s): legal agents

poder(es): powers of legal representation (see *carta(s) de poder*)

principios: opening lines of the royal decree, including the cross and monarch's address to relevant recipients; includes the phrase *yo he sido informado*

proceso: longer paperwork for *justicia* paperwork, and more rarely for *gracia* and *justicia*

proposición: acknowledgment in royal decrees of what petitioners requested; follows *narración*

Real y Supremo Consejo de Indias: Royal and Supreme Council of the Indies

recopilación: compilation; often of decrees

***relación* (component of decree):** see *narración*

relación / relaciones (summary): a summary of a long petition's statements, often by *capítulos,* prepared by council subalterns, usually *relatores*

relator(es): Royal summarizers, working most often for as court reporters in litigious *justicia* cases, but less often in *gracia* and *gobierno*

solicitador(es): middlemen for cases of *justicia* and less often *gracia*

súplica(s): see *peticiones*

visita: audit, either commissioned by a monarch or other high authority, or undertaken by a powerful local official

visitador(es): official who undertakes the *visita*

voluntad: volition

Yo, el Rey: royal statement on royal decrees, "I, the King." For queens, *Yo, la Reyna*

yo he sido informado/a: monarchs' common phrase on royal decrees, "I have been informed"

zambaigo(s), zambaiga(s) f.:): term popularized in later sixteenth century to describe part- Afro-descendant, part-Indigenous men and women; complex semantic overlaps with *mulato*

Bibliography

ARCHIVAL SOURCES

Archivo y Biblioteca Nacionales de Bolivia:

Escrituras Públicas 63; 64; 65.

Archivo Departamental del Cuzco (ADC):

Colección Betancur vol. 6, no. 20.

Archivo General de Indias (AGI), Seville, Spain:

Charcas:
1; 16; 26; 415; 418.

Chile:
8; 28.

Contaduría:
7A; 7B; 215.

Contratación:
1080, 4325.

Escribanía de Cámara:
845B; 1007B; 1006B.

Guadalajara:
5; 51.

Guatemala:
39; 41; 44B; 386; 394; 395.

Indiferente General (cited in-text as Indiferente):
377; 418; 419; 420; 421; 423; 424; 425; 426; 427; 433; 444; 454; 516; 524; 532; 541; 545; 582; 606; 737; 738; 739; 740; 741; 742; 744; 745; 856; 858; 875; 878; 1084; 1085; 1086; 1087; 1088; 1089; 1090; 1091; 1378; 1379; 1383A; 1384; 1388; 1391; 1392; 1395; 1398; 1400; 1401; 1403; 1404; 1408; 1409; 1412; 1414; 1415; 1416; 1419; 1505; 1588; 1624; 1651; 1866; 1867; 1956; 1961; 2050; 2082; 2092; 2097; 2987; 3058.

Justicia:
434; 855; 878; 890; 931; 942; 1118A; 1164; 1183.

Lima:
13; 31; 33; 92; 93; 108; 118; 120; 121; 123; 122; 126; 134; 135; 270; 274; 316; 565; 567; 580.

Mapas & Planos:
Buenos Aires 12.
Escritura: Cifra, 28.

Mexico:
19; 20; 22; 96; 98; 104; 107; 110; 168; 257; 282; 284; 336A; 357; 358; 364; 367; 369; 1064; 1089; 1090; 1091; 1092; 1391; 2999.

Panama:
1; 13; 14; 33; 233; 236.

Patronato:
1; 9; 16; 25; 26; 27; 28; 29; 33; 34; 37; 48; 90B; 110; 127; 170; 171; 172; 174; 176; 179; 180; 182; 183; 184; 185; 188; 189; 190; 192; 193; 195; 196; 226; 231; 246; 251; 252; 256; 258; 260; 275; 276; 294; 295.

Santa Fe:
1; 16; 17; 18; 37; 56; 83; 85; 187; 226; 233; 234; 987.

Santo Domingo:
73; 193; 201.

Quito:
8; 9; 18; 19; 82; 84; 211.

Archivo General de la Nación, Argentina (AGNA):

Período Colonial: 24-6-25.

Archivo General de la Nación, Perú (AGNP):

Libro del Cabildo de Lima.

Archivo General de la Nación, Colombia:

Colonia: Fondo Visitas SC.62;
Caciques & Indios 63.

Archivo General de la Nación, México (AGNM):

Hospital de Jesús L.383.

Archivo General de Simancas (AGS):

Cámara de Castilla: Diversos de Castilla: 1; 6; 15.
Consejo de Guerra, 171.
Estado: 1.
Patronato: 26; 29; 69; 70.

Acervo Histórico del Archivo Histórico de Notarías de la Ciudad de México (AHAHNCM):

Notario Antonio Alonso, Mexico 2-11-1576, Not.1.

Archivo Histórico Nacional del Ecuador (AHNE):

Corte Suprema, Sección General, Gobierno, Cedularios Caja 1.
Presidencia, Fondos Caja 1, Especiales, Sentencias Caja 607.

Archivo Histórico Nacional, Madrid (AHNM):

Diversos-Colecciones: 22; 23; 24; 43.
Códices: L.691.
Consejos: 21343.

Archivo Histórico de la Universidad de Salamanca (AHUS):

Mss.291.

Archive of the University of Santo Tomás (AUST):

AUST-ASPR, Consultas v.1.

British Library (BL):

Manuscripts (Mss.): Additional (here as Mss.Add.): 8219; 13992; 28340; 28346; 28349; 28357;
28362; 28366; 28381; 33983.

Biblioteca Francisco de Zabálburu (BFZ):

Colección Altamira (CA): Envío (E) 134; 169; 170; 223.

Bibliothèque Nationale de France (BNF):

Espagnol 325.

Biblioteca Nacional de España:

Manuscritos (Mss.): 904; 2814; 2825; 2935; 3035; 5972; 6665; 7677; 9089; 9855; 10509;
10558; 10861.
Invent.: 28851.
Por Doña Iuana Colon, Porcones 833 (19).

Det Kongelige Bibliotek, Danmarks Nationalbibliotek og Københavns Universitetsbibliotek (KB):

GKS 2232 4°.

Hispanic Society of America (HSA):

B2883; 5/III; 7/II; 3/II/45; 9/1/13; 9/IV/5; 9/IV/7; 9/V/2.

Instituto Valencia don Juan (IVDJ):

Colección Altamira (CA): Envío (E): 23; 25; 29; 36; 42; 124.

Nettie Lee Benson Library Collection (NLBLC):

Rare Books and Manuscripts Division: Joaquín García Icazbalceta Collection (JGIC).

New York Public Library (NYPL):

Mss.2570.
Obadiah Rich Microfilm Collection (ORMC): Reel 3, Reel 4.

Real Academia de Historia (RAH):

Colección Juan Bautista Muñoz (CJBM).

Real Biblioteca del Palacio Real (RBPR):

XIV/2995.
XVI/3015.
Papeles tocantes a Indias II-175.

Real Biblioteca de San Lorenzo de El Escorial (BSLE):

&-II-7, 459r–462v.
V-II-4.

Library of Congress:

Hans P. Kraus Collection (HKR):
9; 127; 129; 130; 132; 135; 138; 191.

PRINTED PRIMARY SOURCES

Agia, Miguel. *Tres Pareceres Graves*. Lima: Antonio Ricardo, 1604.
Aguiar y Acuña, Rodrigo de. *Sumarios de la Recopilación General de las Leyes*. Mexico: Francisco Rodríguez Lupercio, 1677 [1628].
Bobadilla, Castillo de, Jerónimo. *Política para corregidores y señores de vassallos, en tiempo de paz, y de guerra*, vol. 1. Madrid: Luis Sánchez, 1597.
Carlos V. *Cómo ser rey. Instrucciones del emperador Carlos V a su hijo Felipe*. Ed. Rachael Ball and Geoffrey Parker. New York: Hispanic Society of America, 2014.
Cieza de León, Pedro de. *Obras completas I*. Ed. Carmelo Sáenz de Santa María. Madrid: Instituto Gonzalo Fernández de Oviedo, 1984.
Council of the Indies. *Ordenanzas Reales del Consejo de las Indias*. Madrid: Francisco Sánchez, 1585.
Recopilación de Leyes de los reynos de las Indias. Madrid: Julián de Paredes, 1681.

Covarrubias Orozco, Sebastián de. *Tesoro de la lengua castallana, o española.* Madrid: Luis Sánchez, 1611.

De Altolaguirre y Duvale, Ángel ed. *Gobernación espiritual y temporal de las Indias.* Madrid: Tipografía de Archivos, 1929.

Díaz del Castillo, Bernal. *Historia verdadera de la conquista de la Nueva España.* Ed. José Antonio Barbón Rodríguez. Mexico: UNAM, 2005.

Furió Ceriol, Fadrique. *El Consejo, I Consejeros del Principe.* Anvers: Viuda de Martín Nuncio, 1559.

Gaspar de Texeda. *Cosa Nueva: Segundo libro de cartas mensageras.* [no press, no year (1553?)].

Guevara, Antonio de. *Libro primero de las epístolas familiares del illustre señor,* Book 1, [no press], 1541.

Hevia Bolaños, Juan de. *Curia Philipica.* Madrid: Ramón Ruíz, 1797 [1603].

Las Casas, Bartolomé de, *Obras Completas 13: Cartas y memoriales,* Ed. Paulino Castañeda, Carlos de Rueda, Carmen Godínez, and Inmaculada de la Corte. Madrid: Alianza Editorial, 1995.

Milton, John. *Joannis Miltoni Angli Defensio pro populo Anglicano.* London: Du Gardianis, 1651.

Ordoñez de Zevallos, Don Pedro. *Historia, y viage del mundo del clérigo agradecido don Pedro de Ordoñez de Zevallos.* Madrid: Juan García Infanzón, 1691 [1614].

Peña Montenegro, Alonso de la. *Itinerario para parochos de indios, su oficio, y obligaciones.* Madrid: Joseph Fernández de Buendía, 1668.

Solórzano y Pereira, Juan de. *Politica Indiana.* Madrid: Diego Díaz de la Carrera, 1648.

Suárez, Fransico. *Tratado de las Leyes y de Dios Legislador Tomo I.* Trans. Jaime Torrubiano Ripoll. Madrid: Hijos de Reus, 1918.

Zurita, Jerónimo. *Historia del Rey don Hernando.* Vol. 1. Zaragoza: Domingo Portonaris, 1580.

SECONDARY SOURCES

Abrams, Philip. "Notes on the Difficulty of Studying the State," *Journal of Historical Sociology* 1:1 (1988), 58–89.

Acker, Joan. "Hierarchies, Jobs, Bodies: A Theory of Gendered Organizations," *Gender and Society* 4:2 (1990), 139–158.

Adorno, Rolena. *Guaman Poma: Writing and Resistance in Colonial Peru,* Second Edition. Austin: University of Texas Press, 2000 [1991].

The Polemics of Possession in Spanish American Narrative. New Haven: Yale University Press, 2007.

Aguilar Moreno, Manuel. "The Indio Ladino as a Cultural Mediator in the Colonial Society," *Estudios de Cultura Náhuatl* 33 (2002), 149–184.

Aiton, Arthur S. and J. Lloyd Mecham. "The Archivo General de Indias," *Hispanic American Historical Review* 4:3 (1921), 553–567.

Albi, Christopher. *Gamboa's World: Justice, Silver Mining, and Imperial Reform in New Spain.* Albuquerque: University of New Mexico Press, 2021.

Alcázar, Cayetano. *Historia del correo en América.* Madrid: Rivadeneyra, 1920.

Alejandre García, Juan Antonio. "Del delito de falsedad testimonial en el Derecho histórico español," *Historia, Instituciones, Documentos* 3 (1976), 9–139.

Amadori, Arrigo. "Arbitrismo y cultura política en América durante el siglo XVII," *Anuario de Estudios Americanos* 71:1 (2014), 15–24.

Amadori, Arrigo and José Manuel Díaz Blanco, "El Consejo de Indias durante el reinado de Felipe IV," *La Corte de Felipe IV (1621–1665) Tomo III*, Vol. 2, ed. José Martínez Millán and Manuel Rivero Rodríguez, pp. 891–958. Madrid: Polifemo, 2017.

Anastasopoulos, Antonios. "Introduction," *Political Initiatives "from the Bottom Up' in the Ottoman Empire*, ed. Antonios Anastasopoulos, pp. 1–12. Rethymno: Crete University Press, 2012.

Anderson, Perry. *El estado absolutista*, 10th ed. Madrid: Siglo XXI, 2007 [1974].

Lineages of the Absolutist State. London: Verso, 2013 [1974].

Andrés Santos, Francisco Javier. "Los proyectos de recopilación del Derecho indiano en época de Felipe IV," *Anuario da Facultade de Dereito da Universidade da Coruña* 11 (2007), 45–70.

Andrews, Kenneth R. *The Last Voyage of Drake and Hawkins*. Cambridge: Cambridge University Press, 1972.

Andrien, Kenneth. "Legal and Administrative Documents," *Guide to Documentary Sources for Andean Studies, 1530–1900*, ed. Joanne Pillsbury, pp. 107–199. Norman: University of Oklahoma Press, 2008.

Aram, Bethany. "Distance and Misinformation in the Conquest of America." *The Limits of Empire: European Imperial Formations in Early Modern World History*, ed. Tonio Andrade and William Reger, pp. 223–236. Farnham: Ashgate, 2012.

"Juana 'the Mad's' signature: The problem of invoking royal authority, 1505–1507," *The Sixteenth Century Journal* XXIX/2 (1998), 333–361.

Araujo, Kathya. "Introducción," in *¿Se acata pero no se cumple?: estudios sobre las normas en América Latina*, ed. Kathya Araujo and Lidia Girola, pp. 7–17. Santiago: Lom, 2009.

Ares Queija, Berta. "El Inca Garcilaso," in *Humanismo, mestizaje y escritura*, ed. Carmen de Mora, Guillermo Serés, and Mercedes Serna, pp. 15–31. Orlando: Iberoamericano, 2010.

Argouse, Aude. "'Otorgo que doy mi poder cumplido'. Apoderamiento y representación voluntaria en la administración de justicia virreinal (Santiago de Chile, 1647–1725)," in *Justicias, agentes y jurisdicciones*, ed. Elisa Caselli, pp. 219–251. Madrid: FCE, 2016.

Armon, Shifra. *Masculine Virtue in Early Modern Spain*. Farnham: Ashgate, 2015.

Arrieta Alberdi, Jon. "Justicia, gobierno y legalidad en la Corona de Aragón del siglo XVII," *Estudis: Revista de historia moderna* 22 (1996), 217–248.

Ashcroft, Bill, Gareth Griffiths, and Helen Tiffin, *The Empire Writes Back: Theory and Practice in Post-Colonial Literatures*. 2nd ed. London: Routledge [1989] 2002.

Ávila, Saint Teresa of. *The Collected Letters of St. Teresa of Avila*. 3 vols. Trans. Kieran Kavanaugh. Washington, DC: ICS Publications, 2001.

Baber, R. Jovita. "Categories, Self-Representation, and the Construction of the Indios," *Journal of Spanish Cultural Studies* 10, no.1 (2009), 27–41.

Bagnall, Roger S. "Women's Petitions in Late Antique Egypt," in *La pétition à Byzance*, ed. Denis Feissel and Jean Gascou, pp. 53–60. Paris: AMCHCB, 2004.

Bahena Pérez, Martha Atzin. "Negociar la ciudad. Procuradores de la gobernación de Guatemala en el Consejo de Indias, 1531–1540," *Nuevo Mundo, Mundos Nuevos* (2020), https://doi.org/10.4000/nuevomundo.79357.

Bakewell, Peter John. *A History of Latin America to 1825*, 3rd edn. West Sussex: Wiley-Blackwell, 2010.

Silver Mining and Society in Colonial Mexico, Zacatecas 1546–1700. Cambridge: Cambridge University Press, 1971.

Banks, Kenneth J. *Chasing Empire Across the Sea: Communications and the State in the French Atlantic, 1713–1763*. Montreal: McGill-Queen's Press, 2002.

Barrero García, Ana María. "La vía ordinaria y la vía reservada en la Administración americana en el siglo XVIII," in *Estructuras, gobierno y agentes de la administración en la América española*, ed. Rogelio Echevarría and Miguel Peláez Posada, pp. 233–250. Valladolid: Casa-Museo Colón, 1984.

Bautista, Juan. *Anales de Juan Bautista*, ed. Luis Reyes García. Mexico: CIESAS, 2001.

Bayle, Constantino. *El Protector de Indios*. Seville: EEHA, 1945.

Becker, Peter and William Clark, "Introduction," in *Little Tools of Knowledge: Historical Essays on Academic and Bureaucratic Practices*, ed. Peter Becker and William Clark, pp. 1–34. Ann Arbor: University of Michigan Press, 2001.

Bedos-Rezak, Brigitte Miriam. "Medieval Identity: A Sign and a Concept," *American Historical Review* 105:5 (2000), 1489–1533.

When Ego Was Imago: Signs of Identity in the Middle Ages. Leiden: Brill, 2011.

Belmessous, Saliba. Ed., *Native Claims: Indigenous Law Against Empire, 1500–1920*. Oxford: Oxford University Press, 2012.

Bendix, Reinhart. *Max Weber: An Intellectual Portrait*. London: Routledge, 1988.

Benítes, María Jesús. "Las cartas de Pedro Sarmiento de Gamboa: la escritura de la súplica," *Telar*, 1:1 (2004), 17–37.

Bernard, Gildas. *Le Secrétariat d'Etat et le Conseil Espagnol des Indes (1700–1808)*. Geneva: CRHP, 1972.

Blair, Ann M. *Too Much to Know: Managing Scholarly Information Before the Modern Age*. New Haven: Yale University Press, 2010.

Blake, Jon Vincent. *Libro de la cámara real ... de Gonzalo Fernández de Oviedo*. Chapel Hill: University of North Carolina, 1975.

Blickle, Peter. "Concepts and Approaches in Recent Scholarship on Statebuilding: A Critical Review," in *Empowering Interactions: Interactions: Political Cultures and the Emergence of the State in Europe 1300–1900*, ed. Wim Blockmans, André Holenstein, and Jon Mathieu, pp. 281–292. Farnham: Ashgate, 2009.

Blockmans, Wim, André Holenstein, and Jon Mathieu, eds. *Empowering Interactions: Interactions: Political Cultures and the Emergence of the State in Europe 1300–1900*. Farnham: Ashgate Publishing, 2009.

Bonfíl Batalla, Guillermo. "Sobre la ideología del mestizaje," in *Decadencia y auge de las identidades*, ed. José Manuel Valenzuela Arce, pp. 79–98. Tijuana: Colegio de la Frontera Norte, 2000.

Boone, Rebecca Ard. *Mercurino di Gattinara and the Creation of the Spanish Empire*. London: Pickering & Chatto, 2014.

Borges Morán, Pedro. *El envío de misioneros a América durante la época española*. Salamanca: Universidad Pontificia, 1977.

"En torno a los comisarios generales de indias entre las órdenes misioneras de América. *Archivo Ibero-Americano* 23: 90–91 (1963), 145–196.

Borrego Plá, María Carmen. *Cartagena de Indias en el Siglo XVI*. Seville: Escuela de Estudios Hispano- Americanos, 1983.

Borreguero Beltrán, Cristina. "Los problemas de comunicación en el gobierno de Felipe II: La relación espacio-tiempo," in *Congreso internacional – las sociedades ibéricas y el mar a finales del siglo XVI*, vol. 2, ed. Ribot García and Ernest Belenguer Cebrià, pp. 403–435. Lisbon: Sociedad Estatal Lissboa, 1998.

Bosch García, Carlos. "Hombres de mar y hombres de tierra en la historia de México," in *España y Nueva España: sus acciones transmarítimas*, ed. Shulamit Goldsmit and Rubén Lozano Herrera, pp. 23–38. México: Universidad Iberoamericana, 1991.

Bourdieu, Pierre. "Men and Machines," in *Advances in Social Theory and Methodology: Toward an Integration of Micro- and Macro-Sociologies*. Vol. 1. ed. Karin Knorr-Cetina and Aaron Victor Cicourel, pp. 304–318. New York: Routledge 2015 [1981].

Brakensiek, Stefan. "New Perspectives on State-Building and the Implementation of Rulership in Early Modern European Monarchies," in *Structures on the Move: Technologies of Governance in Transcultural Encounter*, ed. Antije Flüchter and Susan Richter, pp. 31–41. Berlin: Springer, 2012.

Branche, Jerome C. *Colonialism and Race in Luso-Hispanic Literature*. Columbia: University of Missouri Press, 2006.

Braudel, Fernand. *The Mediterranean and the Mediterranean World in the Age of Philip II*, trans. Siân Reynolds. London: Collins, 1972.

Braun, Harald E. "Conscience, Counsel and Theocracy at the Spanish Habsburg Court," *Contexts of Conscience in Early Modern Europe, 1500–1700*, ed. Harold E. Braun and Edward Vallance, pp. 56–66. Basingstoke: Palgrave Macmillan, 2004.

Bray, Warwick. "Gold-working in Ancient America," *Gold Bulletin* 11 (1978), 136–143.

Brendecke, Arndt. *The Empirical Empire: Spanish Colonial Rule and the Politics of Knowledge*. Berlin: Walter de Gruyter, 2016.

Imperio e información: funciones del saber en el dominio colonial español. Frankfurt: Iberoamericana, 2012.

"Informing the Council: Central Institutions and Local Knowledge in the Spanish Empire," in *Empowering Interactions: Political Cultures and the Emergence of the State in Europe 1300–1900*, ed. Wim Blockmans, André Holenstein, and Jon Mathieu, pp. 235–252. Surrey: Ashgate, 2009.

Brendecke, Arndt, and María Ángeles Martín Romera. "El 'habitus' del oficial real: Ideal, percepción y ejercicio del cargo en la monarquía hispánica (siglos XV–XVIII)." *Studia Historica: Historia Moderna* 39.1 (2017), 23–51.
Brennan, Marie George, "Las Casas and the New Laws," *Revista de historia de América*, 61&62 (1966), 23–41.
Bridikhina, Eugenia. *Theatrum mundi: Entramados del poder en Charcas colonial*. La Paz: IFEA, 2007.
Broussard, Ray F. "Bautista Antonelli: Architect of Caribbean Defense." *The Historian* 50:4 (1988), 507–520.
Brylak, Agnieszka, "Some of Them Just Die Like Horses. Contact-Induced Changes in Peripheral Nahuatl of the Sixteenth-Century Petitions from Santiago de Guatemala," *Journal of Language Contact* 12:2 (2019), 344–377.
Burgos Lejonagoitia, Guillermo. *Gobernar las Indias: Venalidad y méritos en la provisión de cargos americanos, 1701–1746*. Almería: Universidad de Almería, 2014
Burkholder, Mark A. *Biographical Dictionary of Councilors of the Indies, 1717–1808*. Westport: Greenwood Press, 1986.
Burkholder, Mark A., "The Council of the Indies in the Late Eighteenth Century: A New Perspective," *Hispanic American Historical Review* 56:3 (1976), 404–423.
Burns, Kathryn. *Colonial Habits: Convents and the Spiritual Economy of Cuzco, Peru*. Durham: Duke University Press, 1999.
"Dentro de la ciudad letrada – La producción de la escritura pública en el Perú colonial," *Histórica* 29:1 (2005), 43–68.
Into the Archive: Writing and Power in Colonial Peru. Durham: Duke University Press, 2010.
"Notaries, Truth, and Consequences," *American Historical Review* 110:2 (2005), 350–379.
Buyreu Juan, Jordi. "La Princesa Juana y la regencia peninsular," in *La Corona de Aragón de Carlos V a Felipe II: Las instrucciones de los virreyes bajo la regencia de la princesa Juana (1554–1559)*, pp. 39–68. Madrid: Sociedad Estatal para la Conmemoración de los Centenarios de Felipe II y Carlos V, 2000.
Cadenas, Vicente de. *Caminos y derroteros que recorrió el emperador Carlos V: Noticias fundamentales para su historia*. Madrid: Ediciones Hidalguia, 1999.
Callon, Michel and Bruno Latour. "Unscrewing the big Leviathan: How Actors Macro-Structure Reality and how Sociologists Help them to do so," 277–303, *Advances in Social Theory and Methodology: Toward an Integration of Micro- and Macro-Sociologies*, vol. 1, ed. Karin Knorr-Cetina and Aaron Victor Cicourel, pp. 277–303. New York: Routledge 2015 [1981].
Calvino, Italo. *If on a Winter's Night a Traveler*. Trans. William Weaver. New York: Harcourt Brace Jovanovich, 1981.
Calvo, Thomas. *Por los caminos de la Nueva Galicia: Transportes y transportistas en el siglo XVII*. Mexico: Centre Français d'études Mexicaines et Centraméricaines, 1997.

Campos, Javier and Fernández de Sevilla. *Catálogo del fondo manuscrito americano de la Real Biblioteca del Escorial*. Madrid: Estudios Superiores del Escorial, 1993.

Cañeque, Alejandro. "The Emotions of Power: Love, Anger, and Fear, or How to Rule the Spanish Empire," *Emotions and Daily Life in Colonial Mexico*. Ed. Javier Villa-Flores and Sonya Lipsett-Rivera, pp. 89–121. Albuquerque: University of New Mexico Press, 2014.

The King's Living Image: The Culture and Politics of Viceregal Power in Colonial Mexico. New York: Routledge Press, 2004.

Cañizares-Esguerra, Jorge. *How to Write the History of the New World: Histories, Epistemologies, and Identities in the Eighteenth-Century Atlantic World*. Stanford: Stanford University Press, 2001.

Carrera, Magali. *Imagining Identity in New Spain: Race, Lineage, and the Colonial Body in Portraiture and Casta Paintings*. Austin: University of Texas at Austin, 2003.

Carvalho Vilas Boas, Martin de. *Volumen primero del espejo de príncipes*. Milan: Pacifico Poncio, 1598.

Casey, James. *España en la Edad Moderna: una historia social*. Vol. 17. Madrid: Universitat de València, 2001.

Castelló Yturbide, Teresa. *The Art of Featherwork in Mexico*. Mexico: Banamex, 1993.

Castillero Calvo, Alfredo. "Los transportes y las vías de comunicación en Hispanoamérica," in *Consolidación del Orden Colonial*, vol. III. part 1. ed. Alfredo Castillero Calvo and Allan J. Kuethe, pp. 339–398 Madrid: Editorial Trotta, UNESCO, 2000.

Castillo de Bobadilla, Jerónimo. *Política para corregidores y señores de vassallos, en tiempo de paz, y de guerra, Primer tomo*. Madrid: Luis Sánchez, 1597.

Castillo Gómez, Antonio. "Hablen cartas y callen barbas: escritura y sociedad en el siglo de Oro." *Historiar*, 4(2000), 116–127.

Castro, Manuel. "Adriano de Utrecht y el gobierno de las Indias 1515–1522," *Archivo Ibero-Americano* 29:116 (1969), 345–380.

Caswell, Michelle. "Hannah Arendt's World: Bureaucracy, Documentation, and Banal Evil," *Archivaria* 70 (2015), 1–25.

Ceballos, Jorge Díaz. "New World civitas, contested jurisdictions, and inter-cultural conversation in the construction of the Spanish Monarchy," *Colonial Latin American Review*, 27:1 (2018), 30–51.

Poder compartido: Repúblicas urbanas, Monarquía y conversación en Castilla del Oro, 1508–1573. Madrid: Marcial Pons Historia, 2020.

Centurioni, Luca R. and Pearn P. Niiler, 2003. On the Surface Currents of the Caribbean Sea, Geophysical Research Letters, 30, 1279, 1–4.

Cepeda Adán, José. *En torno al concepto del estado en los reyes católicos*. Madrid: CSIC, 2010

Cerezo Martínez, Ricardo. *Las Armadas de Felipe II*. Madrid: Editorial San Martín, 1988.

Céspedes del Castillo, Guillermo. *La avería en el comercio de Indias*. Sevilla: Consejo Superior de Investigaciones Científicas, 1945.

Charles, John. "'More ladino than necessary': Indigenous litigants and the language policy debate in mid- colonial Peru." *Colonial Latin American Review* 16:1 (2007), 23–47

Chaunu, Huguette and Pierre Chaunu, *Séville et l'Atlantique (1504–1650) première partie: Partie statistique*, vol. 1, pt. 1. Paris: SEVPEN, 1956.

Chaunu, Pierre and Huguette Chaunu, *Seville et L'Amerique, xvi.e – xvii.e siècle*. Paris: Flammarion, 1977.

Chuchiak, John F. "'Ah Dzib Cahob yetel lay u katlilob lae': Maya Scribes, Colonial Literacy, and Maya Petitionary Forms in Colonial Yucatán," in *Text and Context: Yucatec Maa Literature in a Diachronic Perspective*, ed. Antje Gusenheimer, Tsubasa Okoshi Harada, and John F. Chuchiak, pp. 159–184. Aachen: Shaker, 2009.

Clemence, Stella Risly. Ed. *The Harkness Collection in the Library of Congress: Calendar of Spanish Manuscripts Concerning Peru, 1531–1651*, vol. 1. Washington: US Government Printing Office, 1932.

The Harkness Collection in the Library of Congress: Calendar of Spanish Manuscripts Concerning Peru, 1531–1651, vol. 2. Washington: US Government Printing Office, 1936.

Cobb, Gwendolin B. "Supply and transportation for the Potosi mines, 1545–1640." *Hispanic American Historical Review* 29:1 (1949), 25–45.

Connolly, Serena. *Lives Behind the Laws: The World of the Codex Hermogenianus*. Bloomington: University of Indiana, 2010.

Consejo de Indias. *Ordenanzas reales del Consejo de Indias*. Madrid: Francisco Sánchez, 1585.

Coolidge, Grace E. *Guardianship, Gender, and the Nobility in Early Modern Spain*. Farnham: Ashgate, 2011.

Cope, Douglas. *Limits of Racial Domination: Plebeian Society in Colonial Mexico City, 1660–1720*. Wisconsin: University of Wisconsin Press, 1994.

Corcoran, Simon. *The Empire of the Tetrarchs: Imperial Pronouncements and Government, AD 284–324*. Oxford: Clarendon, 2000.

Corona Núñez, José. *Estudios de antropología e historia*. Morelia, Universidad Michoacana de San Nicolás de Hidalgo, 1992.

Corteguera, Luis R. "Encuentros imaginados entre súbdito y monarca: historias de perdón y petición en la España de la Edad Moderna," in *Tradición y modernidad en la historia de la cultura política*, ed. Riccardo Forte and Natalia Silva Prada, pp. 23–45. Mexico: UAM Iztapalapa, 2009.

"The Mad *Arbitrista*: Vulgar Men, Municipal Politics and the Rhetoric of Counsel in Early Modern Spain," in *Urban Elections and Decision-Making Processes in Early Modern Cities (1500–1800)*, ed. Rudolf Schlögl, pp. 216–236. Newcastle upon Tyne: Cambridge Scholars, 2009.

Crawford, Sue E. S. and Elinor Ostrom. "A Grammar of Institutions." *American Political Science Review* 89:3 (1995), 582–600.

Crompton, Rosemary, and Kay Sanderson. *Gendered Jobs and Social Change*. London: Unwin Hyman, 1990.

Cunill, Caroline. "De Yucatán a la Corte: defensores de indios, procuradores de los cabildos españoles y proceso legal en el siglo XVI," *Revista Allpanchis* XLVII:85 (2020), 161–196.

"El uso indígena de las probanzas de méritos y servicios: su dimensión política (Yucatán, siglo XVI)." *Signos históricos* 16:32 (2014), 14–47.

"Justicia e interpretación en sociedades plurilingües: el caso de Yucatán en el siglo XVI," *Estudios de Historia Novohispana*, 52 (2015), 18–28.

"La protectoría de indios en América: avances y perspectivas entre historia e historiografía," *Colonial Latin American Review* 28:4 (2019), 478–495.

"Margins of documents, center of power: A case study on the Consejo de Indias' annotated paperwork and the construction of legality in an imperial archive," *Archival Science* 20 (2020), 381–400. "Un mosaico de lenguas: Los intérpretes de la audiencia de México en el siglo XVI," *Historia mexicana* 68:1 (2018), 7–48.

"Philip II and Indigenous Access to Royal Justice: Considering the Process of Decision-Making in the Spanish Empire," *Colonial Latin American Review*, vol. 24/4 (2015), 505–524.

Cutter, Charles. *The Protector de Indios in Colonial New Mexico, 1659–1821*. Albuquerque: University of New Mexico Press, 1986.

Darling, Linda. *A History of Social Justice and Political Power in the Middle East: The Circle of Justice from Mesopotamia to Globalization*. New York: Routledge, 2013.

Darnton, Robert. "Introduction," in *Revolution in Print: The Press in France, 1775–1800*, Robert Darnton and Daniel Roche, pp. xiii–xv. Berkeley: University of California Press, 1989.

De Carlos Morales, Carlos Javier. *Política y finanzas en el siglo xvi. El gobierno del Erario Real y el Consejo de Hacienda de Castilla, 1523–1602*. Madrid: Universidad Autónoma, 1994.

de Pazzis Pi Corrales, Magdalena. *La Armada de los Austrias*. Valencia: Real Sociedad Económica, 2001.

De Vito, Christian G. "New Perspectives on Global Labour History," *International Journal on Strikes and Social Conflicts* 1:3 (2013), 7–31.

Delsalle, Paul. *A History of Archival Practice*, Trans. Margaret Procter. New York: Routledge, 2017 [1998].

Derrida, Jacques. *Archive Fever: A Freudian Impression*, trans. Eric Prenowitz. Chicago: University of Chicago Press, 1995.

"Signature Event Context," *Limited Inc.*, pp. 1–24. Evanston: Northwestern University, 1988 [1972].

Dery, David. "'Papereality' and Learning in Bureaucratic Organizations." *Administration & Society*, 29:6 (1998) 677–689.

Díaz, María Elena. *The Virgin, the King, and the Royal Slaves of El Cobre*. Stanford: Stanford University Press, 2000.

Díaz, Pablo C. "Visigothic Political Institutions," in *The Visigoths from the Migration Period to the Seventh Century: An Ethnographic Perspective*, ed. Peter Heather, pp. 321–355. Woodbridge: Boydell Press, 1999.

Díaz Blanco, José Manuel. "El régimen de despacho en la corte de Felipe III: Un análisis desde el gobierno colonial," *Investigaciones históricas: Época moderna y contemporánea*, 31 (2011), 69–92.

Díaz Ceballos, Jorge, *Poder compartido. Repúblicas urbanas, Monarquía y conversación en Castilla del Oro, 1508-1573*, Madrid, Marcial Pons, 2020.

Diederich, Toni. "Zur Bedeutung des Kreuzes am Anfang von Siegelumschriften," *Graphische Symbole in mittelalterlichen Urkunden*, ed. Peter Rück, pp. 157–166. Sigmaringen: Jan Thorbecke, 1996.

Diego, Jose Luis de. "Evolución histórica del expediente," *Anuario de Historia del Derecho Español*, 68 (1998), 475–490.

Dios, Salustiano de. *El poder del monarca en la obra de los juristas castellanos (1480–1680)*. Cuenca: Universidad de Castilla-La Mancha, 2014, 71–73

Gracia, merced y patronazgo real: la Cámara de Castilla entre 1474–1530. Madrid Centro de estudios constitucionales, 1993.

"Ordenanzas del Consejo Real de Castilla (1385–1490)." *Historia. Instituciones. Documentos* 7 (1980), 269–320.

Dougnac Rodríguez, Antonio. *Manual de historia del derecho indiano*. Mexico City, 1994.

Drelichman, Mauricio and Hans-Joachim Voth, *Lending to the Borrower from Hell: Debt, Taxes, and Default in the Age of Philip II*. Princeton: Princeton University Press, 2014.

Dubet, Anne. "L'arbitrisme: un concept d'historien?, *Cahiers du Centre de Recherches Historiques*, 24, 2000, 1–24.

Dueñas, Alcira. "Indian Colonial Actors in the Lawmaking of the Spanish Empire in Peru," *Ethnohistory* 65:1 (2018) 51–73.

Indians and Mestizos in the "Lettered City:" Reshaping Justice, Social Hierarchy, and Political Culture in Colonial Peru. Boulder: University Press of Colorado, 2017.

Duindam, Jerome. *Myths of Power*. Amsterdam: Amsterdam University Press, 1994.

Duve, Thomas. "El concilio como instancia de autorización: la ordenación sacerdotal de mestizos ante el Tercer Concilio Limense." *Revista de Historia del Derecho* 40 (2010), 1–29.

Dworkoski, Robert John. "*The Council of the Indies in Spain, 1524–1558*," PhD Dissertation, University of Michigan at Ann Arbor, 1979.

Dym, Jordana. *From Sovereign Villages to National States: City, State, and Federation in Central America, 1759–1839*. Albuquerque: University of New Mexico Press, 2006.

"Taking a walk on the wild side: Experiencing the spaces of colonial Latin America." *Colonial Latin American Review* 21:1 (2012), 3–16.

Elliott, John Huxtable. *Imperial Spain, 1469–1716*. London: Penguin, 1990.

Encina, Francisco Antonio. *Resumen de la Historia de Chile*, Vol. 1. Santiago: Zig-Zag, 1961.

Erwin, Holger. *Machtsprüche: Das herrscherliche Gestaltungsrecht »ex plenitudine potestatis« in der Frühen Neuzeit*. Köln: Böhlau, 2009.

Escalante Gonzalbo, Pablo. "Los caminos del México antiguo," in *Rutas de la Nueva España*, ed. Chantal Cramaussel, pp. 27–37. Zamora: El Colegio de Michoacán, 2006.

Escudero, José Antonio. *Felipe II: El rey en su despacho*. Madrid: Editorial Complutense-Colegio Universitario de Segovia, 2002.

Espinosa, Aurelio. *The Empire of the Cities: Emperor Charles V, the Comunero Revolt, and the Transformation of the Spanish System*. Leiden: Brill, 2009.

Ezquerra Revilla, Ignacio. *El Consejo Real bajo Felipe II: Grupos de poder y luchas faccionales*. Madrid: SECC, 2000.

"La Junta de Reformación de 1586: Tapadas, comedias, y vicios cortesanos." *Revista de historia moderna* 30 (2012), 267–282.

"La reforma de las costumbres en tiempo de Felipe II: Las "Juntas de Reformación' (1574–1583)," in *Europa dividida, la monarquía católica de Felipe II*, ed. José Martínez Millán, vol. 3, pp. 179–208. Madrid: Universidad Autónoma de Madrid, 1998.

Fajardo, Luis Eduardo. "La corrupción heredada: pasado colonial, sistema legal y desarrollo económico en Colombia," *Revista de Estudios Sociales*, 12 (2002), 20–28.

Farge, Arlette. *La atracción del archivo*. Valencia: Institució Valenciana D'Estudis i Investigació. 1991 [1989].

Faroqhi, Suraiya. "Political Activity among Ottoman Taxpayers and the Problem of Sultanic Legitimation (1570–1650)." *Journal of the Economic and Social History of the Orient* 35:1 (1992), 1–39;

Fayard, Janine. *Los miembros del Consejo de Castilla (1621–1746)*. Trans. Rufina Rodríguez Sanz. Madrid: Siglo Veintiuno, 1982.

Feissel, Denis. "Petitions aux Empereurs et Formes du Rescrit," in *La pétition à Byzance*, ed. D. Feissel and J. Gascou, pp. 33–49. Paris: AMCHCB, 2004.

Fernández, Diego. *Primera y segunda parte de la historia del Perú*. Seville: Casa de Hernando Díaz, 1571.

Fernández Álvarez, Manuel. *El siglo XVI: economía, sociedad, instituciones*. Madrid: Espasa-Calpe, 1989.

Fernández-Armesto, Felipe. "The Improbable Empire," in *Spain: A History, ed. Raymond Carr*, pp. 116–151. New York: Oxford University Press, 2000.

Feros, Antonio. *El Duque de Lerma: Realeza y privanza en la España de Felipe III*. Madrid: Marcial Pons, 2002.

Fosi, Irene. *Papal Justice: Subjects and Courts in the Papal State*, Trans. Thomas V. Cohen. Washington, DC: Catholic University of America Press, 2011.

Foucault, Michel. *Archaeology of Knowledge*. Trans. A. M. Sheridan Smith. London: Routledge, 2002.

Fraenkel, Béatrice. *La signature: Genèse d'un signe*. Paris: Éditions Gallimard, 1992.

Francisco González de Torneo, *Práctica de escribanos que contiene la judicial, y orden de examinar testigos*. Alcalá: Antonio Vazquez, 1640.

Freyles, Gabriel, ed. *Actas capitulares de la ciudad de La Paz vol.1*. La Paz: Instituto de Investigaciones Históricas y Culturales, 1965.

Friedrich, Markus. *The Birth of the Archive: A History of Knowledge*. Ann Arbor: University of Michigan, 2018.

"Introduction: New Perspectives for the History of Archives," in *Praktiken der Fühen Neuzeit: Akteure, Handlungen, Artefakte*, ed. Arndt Brendecke, pp. 468–472. Cologne: Böhlau, 2015.

Fuentes, Carlos. *The Buried Mirror: Reflections on Spain and the New World*. New York: Mariner Books, 1999 [1992].

Gachard, Louis Prosper. *Relations des ambassadeurs vénitiens sur Charles-Quint et Philippe II*. Brussels: M. Hayez, Imprimeur de la Commission Royale D'Histoire, 1855.

Gamboa, Jorge Augusto. "El primer 'lengua intérprete; de los naturales de la Real Audiencia de Santafé: El mestizo Lucas Bejarano, mediador y protagonista en los tribunales reales (siglo XVI), in *Las lenguas indígenas en los tribunales de América Latina: intérpretes, mediación y justicia (siglos XVI-XXI)*, eds. Caroline Cunill and Luis Miguel Glave Testino, pp. 97–120. Bogotá: ICAH, 2019.

García-Badell Arias, Luis María. "La frustración de Felipe II," in *Felipe II (1598–1998), Europa dividida, la monarquía católica de Felipe II*, ed. José Martínez Millán, pp. 307–339. Madrid: Parteluz, 1998.

García-Baquero González, Antonio. *La Carrera de Indias: Suma de la contratación y océano de negocios*. Seville: Algaida, 1992.

García Bernal, Manuela Cristina. *Campeche y el comercio atlántico yucateco (1561–1625)*. Campeche: Universidad Autónoma de Campeche, 2006

"El afianzamiento de un precario comercio: Los intercambios entre Sevilla y Yucatán (1590–1600)." *Historia Mexicana* 50:2 (2000), 201–269.

García-Gallo, Alfonso. *Leyes y ordenanzas reales de las indias del Mar Océano*. Mexico: Miguel Ángel Porrua, 1985.

"El consejo y los secretarios en el Gobierno de Indias en los siglos XVI y XVII," *Revista Chilena de Historia del Derecho* 11 (1985), 329–353.

"Presentacion," in *Leyes y Ordenanzas Reales de las Indias del Mar Oceano*, ed. Alonso de Zorita, pp. 15–26. Mexico: Miguel Angel Porrua, 1985.

García-Gallo, Concepción. "La legislación indiana de 1636 a 1680 y la Recopilación de 1680." *Anuario de Historia del Derecho Español* 49 (1979), 99–120.

García Pérez, Rafael. *El Consejo de Indias durante los reinados de Carlos III y Carlos IV*. Pamplona: Universidad de Navarra, 1998.

Gardey, Delphine. *Schreiben, rechnen, ablegen: Wie eine Revolution des Bürolebens unsere Gesellschaft verändert hat*. Konstanz: Konstanz University Press, 2018.

Gargurevich, Juan. *La comunicación imposible: información y comunicación en el Perú (siglo XVI)*. Lima: Universidad Nacional Mayor de San Marcos, 2002.

Garrett, David T. "'En lo remoto de estos reynos:' Distance, Jurisdiction, and Royal Government in late Habsburg Cusco." *Colonial Latin American Review* 21:1 (2012), 17–43.

Garriga, Carlos. "La jurisdicción contencioso-administrativa en España. Una historia de sus orígenes," *Cuadernos de Derecho Judicial* 7 (2008), 47–113.

Gaudin, Guillaume. *El imperio de papel de Juan Díez de la Calle: Pensar y gobernar el Nuevo Mundo en el siglo XVII*. Michoacán: Colegio de Michoacán, 2017.

"La démesure des listes du Conseil des Indes au xviie siècle: Le Nouveau Monde vu depuis les bureaux madrilènes," *Mélanges de la Casa de Velázquez* 44:2 (2014), 83–103.

"Un acercamiento a las figuras de agentes de negocios y procuradores de Indias en la Corte," *Nuevo Mundo, Mundos Nuevos* (2017), https://doi.org/10.4000/nuevomundo.71390.

Gerhard, Peter. *Pirates of New Spain, 1575–1742*. Mineola: Dover Publications, 2003.

Getino, Alonso, "Influencia de los Dominicos en las Leyes Nuevas," *Anuario de estudios americanos* 2 (1945), 265–360.

Gharala, Norah L. A., *Taxing Blackness: Free Afromexican Tribute in Bourbon New Spain*. Tuscaloosa: University of Alabama Press, 2019.

Giddens, Anthony. *The Constitution of Society: Outline of the Theory of Structuration*. 1st ed. Cambridge: Polity Press, 1986.

Ginzburg, Carlo and Lucio Biasiori. "Preface," in *A Historical Approach to Casuistry: Norms and Exceptions in a Comparative Perspective*, ed. Carlo Ginzburg and Lucio Biasiori, pp. xi–xix. London: Bloomsbury Academic, 2019.

Glave Testino, Luis Miguel. "La gran vejación: Manuscritos reivindicativos de Incas, Caciques, y Defensores de la Población Indígena," *Revista Andes* 4 (2021), 35–59.

Memoria y memoriales: La formación de una liga indígena en Lima (1722–1732)." *Diálogo Andino- Revista de Historia, Geografía y Cultura Andina* 37 (2011), 5–23.

"*Simachi:* el traductor o lengua en el distrito de la Audiencia de Lima," *Las lenguas indígenas en los tribunales de América Latina: intérpretes, mediación y justicia (siglos XVI–XXI)*, ed. Caroline Cunill and Luis Miguel Glave Testino, pp. 121–166. Bogotá: ICAH, 2019.

Trajinantes: caminos indígenas en la sociedad colonial: siglos XVI-XVII. Lima: Instituto de Apoyo Agrario, 1989.

Goldwert, Marvin. "La lucha por la perpetuidad de las encomiendas en el Perú virreinal, 1550–1600," *Revista Histórica*, 22 (1956), 336–360.

"La lucha por la perpetuidad de las encomiendas en el Perú virreinal, 1550–1600 (continuación)," *Revista Histórica* (1957–1958), 207–245.

Gómez, Thomas. *L'envers de l' Eldorado: économie coloniale et travail indigène dans la Colombie du XVI' siècle*. Toulouse. Association des Publications de l'Université de Toulouse Le Mirail, 1984.

Gómez Canedo, Lino. *La educación de los marginados durante la época colonial*. Mexico: Editorial Porrua, 1982.

Gómez Gómez, Margarita. *Actores del documento: oficiales, archiveros y escribientes de la Secretaría de Estado y del Despacho de Indias*, Madrid, Centro de Estudios Políticos y Constitucionales, 2003.

"El Consejo Real de las Indias: Casa, Corte, y Cancillería," in *Vencer la Distancia en el Imperio Español*, ed. Manuel Rivero Rodríguez and Guillaume Gaudin, pp. 85–117. Madrid: Polifemo, 2020.

El sello y registro de Indias: imagen y representación. Köln: Böhlau. 2008.

"El documento y el sello regio en Indias: su uso como estrategia de poder." *Documenta & Instrumenta* 13 (2015), 89–105.

El sello real en el gobierno de las Indias: Funciones documentales y representativas. Madrid: Universidad Complutense, 2012.

"Escribir la norma: Problemas de recepción, acatamiento y publicación de los documentos reales en las Indias durante el Antiguo Régimen," *Les Cahiers de Framespa* 30 (2019), no pages.

Forma y expedición del documento en la Secretaría de Estado y del Despacho Universal de Indias. Seville: Universidad de Sevilla, 1993.

"La nueva tramitación de los asuntos indianos en el siglo XVIII: de la "vía de Consejo' a la "vía reservada,'" in *El gobierno de un mundo. Virreinatos y Audiencias en la América Hispánica. Congreso internacional*, ed. Feliciano Barrios, pp. 203–250. Cuenca: Universidad de Castilla-La Mancha, 2004.

"La producción de documentos reales durante el antiguo régimen: Espacios, actores y prácticas," in *De scriptura et scriptis: Producir*, ed. María Encarnación Martín López, pp. 305–354. León: Universidad de León, 2020.

"Secretarios del rey y escribanos de cámara en el Consejo de Indias: oficiales de la pluma para el gobierno de la monarquía," *Nuevo Mundo, Mundos Nuevos* (2017), https://doi.org/10.4000/nuevomundo.71367.

"La Secretaría de la Presidencia del Consejo de Indias y su actuación documental," in *Derecho, Instituciones y Procesos Históricos*. José de la Puente Brunke and Jorge Armando Guevara Gil, pp. 493–514. Lima: PUCP, 2008.

"Secretarios y escribanos en el gobierno de las Indias: El caso de Juan de Sámano." *Revista de historia del derecho* 43 (2012), 30–63.

Gonzalbo Aizpuru, Pilar, "La trampa de las castas," *La sociedad novohispana: Estereotipos y realidades*, ed. Solange Alberro and Pilar Gonzalbo Aizpuru, pp. 17–194. Mexico City: Colegio de México, 2013.

González Echevarría, Roberto. *Myth and Archive: A Theory of Latin American Narrative*. Cambridge: Cambridge University Press, 1990.

González Martínez, Nelson Fernández. "Communicating an Empire and Its Many Worlds: Spanish American Mail, Logistics, & Postal Agents, 1492–1620," *Hispanic American Historical Review* 101:4 (2021), 567–596.

"Correos y comunicación escrita en la América colonial: esquemas de distribución de la correspondencia oficial (1514–1768)," *Jahrbuch für Geschichte Lateinamerikas* 52 (2015), 37–64.

Goody, Jack. *The Logic of Writing and the Organization of Society*. Cambridge: Cambridge University Press, 1996 [1986].

Gouveira Monteiro, João. *Aljubarrota 1385: A Batalha Real*. Lisboa: Tribuna da Historia, 2003.

Graubart, Karen. "Hybrid Thinking: Bringing Postcolonial Theory to Colonial Latin American History," in *Postcolonialism Meets Economics*, ed. E. Zein-Elabdin and S. Charusheela, pp. 215–234. London: Routledge, 2005.

Greenberg, Mark. "How Facts Make Law," *Legal Theory* 10 (2004), 157–198.

Guajardo-Fajardo Carmona, María de los Ángeles. *Escribanos en Indias durante la primera mitad del siglo XVI*. Vol. 1, Madrid: Consejo General del Notariado, 1995.

Gurkin Altman, Janet. *Epistolarity: Approaches to a Form*. Columbus: Ohio State University Press, 1982.

Gutiérrez Álvarez, Secundino José. *Las comunicaciones en América: de la senda primitiva al ferrocarril*. Madrid: MAPFRE, 1993.

Guzmán Brito, Alejandro. "La crítica póstuma al Derecho indiano," in *Derecho y administración pública en las Indias hispánicas*, vol. 1, ed. Feliciano Barrios Pintado, pp. 843–858. Cuenca: Universidad de Castilla-La Mancha, 2002.

Hakim, Catherine. *Occupational Segregation*. London: Department of Employment, 1979.

Hanks, William F. *Converting Words: Maya in the Age of the Cross*. Berkeley: University of California Press, 2010.

Intertexts: Writings on Language, Utterance, and Context. Lanham: Rowman & Littlefield, 2000.

Haring, Clarence Henry. *The Spanish Empire in America*. Oxford: Oxford University Press, 1952 [1947].

Head, Randall C. "Mirroring governance: archives, inventories and political knowledge in early modern Switzerland and Europe." *Archival Science* 7 (2008), 317–329.

Headley, John M. *The Emperor and His Chancellor. A Study of the Imperial Chancellery Under Gattinara*. Cambridge: Cambridge University Press, 1983.

Heerma van Voss, Lex. "Introduction," in *Petitions in Social History*, ed. Lex Heerma Van Voss, pp. 1–10. Cambridge: Cambridge University Press, 2001.

Hengerer, Mark. "Wer Regiert im Finanzstaat?" in *Hof und Macht: Dresdener Gespräche II zur Theorie des Hofes*, vol. 1, ed. Reinhard Butz and Jan Hirschbiegel, pp. 87–140. Berlin: LIT, 2007.

Heredia Herrera, Antonia. *Catálogo de las Consultas del Consejo de Indias, Tomo 1*. Madrid: Dirección General de Archivos y Bibliotecas, 1972.

Catálogo de las Consultas del Consejo de Indias, Tomo 2. Madrid: Dirección General de Archivos y Bibliotecas, 1972.

La carta como tipo diplomático indiano," *Anuario De Estudios Americanos* 34 (1977), 65–95.

"Los cedularios de oficio y de partes del consejo de Indias: Sus tipos documentales (Siglo XVII), *Anuario de Estudios Americanos* 29 (1972), 1–60.

Recopilación de estudios de diplomática Indiana. Seville: Publicaciones de la Excma. Diputación Provincial, 1985.

Hering Torres, Max. "Purity of Blood: Problems of Interpretation," *Race and Blood in the Iberian World*. Ed. David Nirenberg, Max S. Hering Torres, and María Elena Martínez, pp. 11–38. Münster: LIT Verlag, 2012.

Hernández Esteve, Esteban. "Pedro Luis de Torregrosa, Primer Contador del Libro de Caxa de Felipe II," *Revista de Historia Económica* III:2 (1985), 221–245.

Herrera, Juan de. *Sumario Y Breve Declaracion delos disenos y estampas de la Fabrica de san Lorencio el Real del Escurial*. Madrid: Viuda de Alonso Gómez, 1589.

Herzog, Tamar. "Colonial Law: Early Modern Normativity in Spanish America," in *A Companion to Early Modern Spanish Imperial Political & Social Thought*, ed. Jörg Alejandro Tellkamp, pp. 105–127, Leiden: Brill, 2020.

Defining Nations: Immigrants and Citizens in Early Modern Spain and Spanish America. New Haven: Yale University Press, 2008.

"El arbitrismo y América," in *La monarquía de Felipe III*, ed. José Martínez Millán, Maria Antonietta Visceglia, v. III, pp. 925–931, Madrid: Fundación Mapfre.

"Identities and Processes of Identification in the Atlantic World," in *The Oxford Handbook of the Atlantic World c.1450-c.1820*, ed. Nicholas Canny and Philip Morgan, pp. 480–495. Oxford: Oxford University Press, 2011.

"Immemorial (and native) customs in early modernity: Europe and the Americas," *Comparative Legal History*, 2021, 1–53.

A Short History of European Law: The Last Two and a Half Millennia. Cambridge, MA: Harvard University Press, 2018.

Upholding Justice: Society, State, and the Penal System in Quito (1650–1750). Ann Arbor: University of Michigan Press, 2004.

Hespanha, António Manuel. *História das instituições: Épocas medieval e moderna*. Coimbra: Livraria Almedina, 1982.

La Gracia del derecho: economía de la cultura en la edad moderna. Madrid: CEC, 1993.

Hill, Roscoe R. *Descriptive Catalogue of the Documents Relating to the History of the United States in the Papeles Procedentes de Cuba*. Washington, DC: Carnegie Institution of Washington 1916.

Hillerkuss, Thomas. *Documentalia del sur de Jalisco: siglo XVI*. Zapopán: Colegio de Jalisco, 1994.

Himmerich y Valencia, Robert, *The Encomenderos of New Spain, 1521–1555*, Austin: University of Texas, 1996 [1991].

Hofmeester, Karin, Jan Lucassen, Leo Lucassen, Rombert Stapel, and Richard Zijdeman, "The Global Collaboratory on the History of Labour Relations, 1500–2000: Background, Set-up, Taxonomy, and Applications," Project description, 2015. https://collab.iisg.nl/web/labourrelations

Holder, Beat. "*Doléances, Requêtes* und *Ordonnances*," in *Gemeinde und Staat im Alten Europa*, ed. Peter Blickle, pp. 23–67. Munich: R. Oldenbourg Verlag, 1998.

Honores, Renzo. "Colonial Legal Polyphony and Legal Arguments, 1550–1640," *Working Paper, International Seminar on the History of the Atlantic World, 1500–1825*. Harvard: Harvard University, 2010.

"Imágenes sociales de la profesión legal en los Andes durante la época de los Austrias," in *Libro de amigos dedicado al profesor Carlos Salinas*, ed. Alejandro Guzmán Brito, pp. 323–356. Valparaíso: Pontificia Universidad Católica, 2018.

"Una sociedad legalista: Abogados, procuradores de causas, y la creación de una cultura legal colonial en Lima y en Potosí, 1540–1670" PhD diss., Florida International University, 2008.

Houston, R. A. *Literacy in Early Modern Europe: Culture and Education, 1500–1800*. London: Longman, 1998.

Huamanchumo de la Cuba, Ofelia. "Tradiciones discursivas en *documentos petitorios* indianos (Perú–Siglo XVI)," in *Actas del VIII Congreso Internacional de Historia de la Lengua Española*, ed. Emilio

Montero Cartelle and Carmen Manzano Rovira, pp. 1935–1947. Santiago de Compostela: Meubook, 2012.

Huerga, Álvaro, *Fray Bartolomé de las Casas – Obras completas 1: Vida y obras*, Madrid Alianza, 1998.

Hyland, Sabine Patricia. "Illegitimacy and Racial Hierarchy in the Peruvian Priesthood: A Seventeenth- Century Dispute." *Catholic Historical Review* 84:3 (1998), 431–454.

Hyslop, John. *The Inka Road System*. New York: Academic Press, 1984.

Iglesias Ferreiros, Aquilino. "La labor legislativa de Alfonso X el Sabio," in *España y Europa: un pasado jurídico común*, ed. Antonio Pérez Martín, pp. 275–599. Murcia: Universidad de Murcia, 1986.

Iglesias Rábade, Luis. "El falso testimonio judicial en el Derecho hispánico y anglo-sajón en el Medievo estudio comparado," *En la España medieval*, 40 (2017), 67–110.

"Estudio comparado del delito de falsedad documental en el derecho hispánico e inglés (siglos xvi-xviii)," *Revista Chilena de Derecho* 45:2 (2018), 311–336.

Infante, Lucas Antón. "*El Consejo de Indias en la monarquía hispánica de Carlos II, 1665–1700.*" Phd Diss. Madrid: Universidad Complutense, 2019.

Irigoin, Alejandra, and Regina Grafe. "Bargaining for Absolutism: A Spanish Path to Nation-State and Empire Building." *Hispanic American Historical Review* 88:2 (2008), 173–209.

Jansen, Sharon L. *The Monstrous Regiment of Women: Female Rulers in Early Modern Europe*. New York: Palgrave MacMillan, 2002.

Jeay, Claude. *Signature et pouvoir au moyen âge*. Paris: École nationale des chartes, 2015

Jiménez de la Espada, Marcos. *El Código Ovandino*. Madrid: Manuel G. Hernández, 1891.

ed. *Relaciones geográficas de Indias, Perú Tomo 3*. Madrid: Hijos de M.G. Hernández, 1897.

Jiménez Núñez, Alfredo. "Sistema político y legislación en la América colonial hispana: Una interpretación desde la antropología cultural," in *Congreso de Historia del Descubrimiento (1492–1556)*, vol. III, pp. 133–164. Madrid: Real Academia de Historia, 1992.

Jiménez Zamora, Isidoro. "La Emperatríz Isabel de Portugal y el Gobierno de la Monarquía Hispánica en tiempos de Carlos V (1526–1539)" PhD diss. UNED, Madrid, 2015.

Jones, Grant D. *Maya Resistance to Spanish Rule: Time and History on a Colonial Frontier*. Albuquerque: University of New Mexico Press, 1989.

Jonsen, Albert R. "Casuistry, Situationism, and Laxism," in *Memoir of an Ex-Radical*, ed. Kenneth Vaux, pp. 10–24, Louisville: Westminster, 1993.

Jonsen, Albert R. and Stephen Toulmin, *The Abuse of Casuistry: A History of Moral Reasoning*. Berkeley: University of California Press, 1989.

Jouve Martín, José Ramón. *Esclavos de la ciudad letrada: Esclavitúd, escritura y colonialismo en Lima (1650–1700)* Lima: Instituto de Estudios Peruanos, 2005.

Kagan, Richard. *Lawsuits and Litigants in Castile, 1500–1700*. Chapel Hill: The University of North Carolina Press, 1981.

Students and Society in Early Modern Spain. Baltimore: Johns Hopkins University Press, 1974.

Kamen, Henry. *Empire: How Spain Became a World Power, 1492–1763*. London: Penguin, 2003.

Philip of Spain. New Haven: Yale University Press, 1998.

Kaufer, David S. and Kathleen M. Carley, *Communication at a Distance*. New Jersey: Lawrence Erlbaum, 1993.

Keen, Benjamin. *The Aztec Image in Western Thought*, New Brunswick: Rutgers University Press, 1971.

Keenan, James F. "*Moral Theology*," in *From Trent to Vatican II*, ed. Raymond F. Bulman, Frederick J. Parrella, pp. 161–179. Oxford: Oxford University Press, 2006.

Kelly-Gadol, Joan. "Did Women Have a Renaissance?" In *Women, History, and Theory: The Essays of Joan Kelly*, pp. 19–50. Chicago: University of Chicago Press, 1986.

Keniston, Hayward. *Francisco de los Cobos, Secretary of the Emperor Charles V*. Pittsburgh: University of Pittsburg Press, 1960.

Ketelaar, Eric. "Archival Temples, Archival Prisons: Modes of Power and Protection," *Archival Science* 2 (2002), 221–238.

King Philip II. *Pragmática en que se da la orden de...cortesías de palabra*. Granada: Hugo de Mena, 1586.

Klee, Paul. *On Modern Art*, trans. Paul Findlay. London: Faber and Faber Ltd., 1969 [1948].

Klein, Ursula. *Experiments, Models, Paper Tools: Cultures of Organic Chemistry in the Nineteenth Century*. Stanford: Stanford University Press, 2002.

Knorr-Cetina, Karin. "Introduction," in *Advances in Social Theory and Methodology: Toward an Integration of Micro- and Macro-Sociologies*, vol.1, ed. Karin Knorr-Cetina and Aaron Victor Cicourel, pp. 1–48. New York: Routledge, 2015 [1981].

Koziol, Geoffrey. "The early history of rites of supplication," in *Suppliques et requétes; le gouvernement par la grace en Occident, XIIe-XVe siècle*, ed. Hélène Millet, pp. 21–36. Rome: École française, 2003.

Kumin, Beat and Andreas Würgler. "Petitions, *Gravamina*, and the Early Modern State: Local Influence on Central Legislation in England and Germany (Hesse)." *Parliaments, Estates and Representation*, 17:1 (1997), 39–60.

Laclau, Ernesto. "Politics and the Limits of Modernity." *Social Text*, no. 21 (1989): 63–82.

Laird, Andrew. "*Nahua Humanism and Ethnohistory: Antonio Valeriano and a letter from the Rulers of Azcapotzalco to Philip II, 1561*," *Estudios de Cultura Nahuatl* 52 (2016), 23–74.

"Nahuas and Caesars: Classical Learning and Bilingualism in Post-Conquest Mexico: An Inventory of Latin Writings by Authors of the Native Nobility," *Classical Philology* 109:2 (2014), 150–169.

Lagomarsino, David. "Furió Ceriol y la "pragmática de las Cortesías' de 1586," *Estudis* 8 (1980), 87–104.

La Peña Cámara, José de. "El manuscrito llamado "Gobernacion espiritual y temporal de las Indias" y su verdadero lugar en la historia de la Recopilacion." *Revista de Historia de América* 12 (1941), 5–72.

La Puente Luna, José Carlos de. *Andean Cosmopolitans: Seeking Justice and Reward at the Spanish Royal Court*. Austin: University of Texas Press, 2018.

"A costa de Su Majestad: indios viajeros y dilemas imperiales en la corte de los Habsburgo," *Allpanchis* 72 (2008), 11–60.

"That Which Belongs to All- Khipus, Community, and Indigenous Legal Activism in the Early Colonial Andes," *The Americas* 72:1 (2015), 19–54

"The Many Tongues of the King: Indigenous Language Interpreters and the Making of the Spanish Empire," *Colonial Latin American Review* 23:2 (2014), 143–170.

Lamb, Ursula S. "The Spanish Cosmographic Juntas of the 16th Century," *Terrae Incognitae*, 6 (1974), 51–64.

Lane, Kris. *Pillaging the Empire: Global Piracy on the High Seas, 1500–1750*. London: Routledge: 1998.

Larson, Brooke. *Cochabamba, 1550–1900, Expanded edition*. Durham: Duke University Press, 1998.

Las Casas, Bartolomé de. *Este es vn tratado*. Seville: Sebastián Trujillo, 1552.

Las Heras Santos, José Luis de. *La justicia penal de los Austrias en la Corona de Castilla*. Salamanca: Ediciones Universidad Salamanca, 1994 [1991].

Lasala Claver, Fernando J. de, and Paulius Rabikauskas. *Il documento medievale e moderno*. Rome: Editrice Pontificia Università Gregoriana, 2003.

Latour, Bruno. *The Making of Law: An Ethnography of the Conseil D'Etat*. Trans. Marina Brilman and Alain Pottage. Cambridge: Polity, 2010 [2002].

"Network Theory: Networks, Societies, Spheres: Reflections of an Actor-network Theorist," *International Journal of Communication* 5 (2011), 796–810.

"On Actor-Network Theory: A Few Clarifications," *Soziale Welt* 47:4 (1996), 369–381.

"On Technical Mediation," *Common Knowledge* 3:2 (1994), 29–64.

"The Powers of Association," in *Power, Action, and Belief*, ed. John Law, pp. 264–280. London: Routledge & Kegan Paul, 1986.

Lázaro de la Escosura, Pilar and Isabel M. Ceballos Aragón, *Archivo General de Indias*. Madrid: Ministerio de Cultura, 2008.

Leddy Phelan, John. "Authority and Flexibility in the Spanish Imperial Bureaucracy," *Administrative Science Quarterly* 5:1 (1960), 47–65.

Lehfeldt, Elizabeth. "Ideal Men: Masculinity and Decline in Seventeenth-Century Spain." *Renaissance Quarterly* 61.2 (2008), 463–494.

Lentz, Mark. "Los intérpretes generales de Yucatán: hombres entre dos mundos," *Estudios de cultura maya* 33 (2009), 135–158.

Lewis, Laura A. *Hall of Mirrors: Power, Witchcraft, and Caste in Colonial Mexico*. Durham: Duke University Press, 2003.

Lichtheim, Miriam. *Ancient Egyptian Literature: A Book of Readings, Volume II: The New Kingdom*. Berkeley: University of California Press [1976] 2006.

Lockhart, James. *The Men of Cajamarca: A Social and Biographical Study of the First Conquerors of Peru*, Austin: University of Texas, 1972.

Spanish Peru, 1532–1560: A Social History, 2nd ed. Madison: University of Wisconsin [1968] 1994.

Lockhart, James, and Enrique Otte. *Letters and People of the Spanish Indies: Sixteenth Century*. Cambridge: Cambridge University Press, 1976.

Lomnitz, Claudio. *Death and the Idea of Mexico*. New York: Zone Books, 2005.

Exits from the Labyrinth: Culture and Ideology in the Mexican National Space. Berkeley: University of California Press, 1992

Lope Blanch, Juan. "La lenta propagación de la lengua española por América," In *Estudios de la historia de la lengua española en América y España*, ed. Milagros Aleza Izquierdo, pp. 89–102. Valencia: Universitat de València, 1999.

Lopez de Gómara, Francisco. *La Historia General de las Indias*. Antwerp: Juan Bellero, 1554.

López Valencia, L. "The Royal and Supreme Council of the Indies: the Supreme Court of New Spain," in *Central Courts in Early Modern Europe and the Americas*, ed. A. M. Godfrey and C. H. van Rhee, pp. 463–516. Berlin: Duncker & Humblot, 2020.

Lorandi, Ana María. *Ni Ley, ni Rey, ni Hombre Virtuoso: Guerra y Sociedad en el Virreynato del Perú siglos XVI y XVII*. Buenos Aires: Universidad de Buenos Aires, 2002.

Lorenzo Cadarso, Pedro Luis. *El documento real en la época de los Austrias, 1516–1700*. Cáceres: Universidad de Extremadura, 2001.

"La correspondencia administrativa en el estado absoluto castellano (ss. XVI–XVII)," *Tiempos modernos* 2:5 (2001), 1–29.

La documentación judicial en la época de los Austrias: estudio archivístico y diplomático. Badajoz: Universidad de Extremadura, 2004.

Lorenzo Pinar, Francisco Javier. *Fiesta religiosa y ocio en Salamanca en el siglo XVII (1600–1650)*. Salamanca: Ediciones Universidad Salamanca, 2010.

Loveman, Mara. *National Colors: Racial Classification and the State in Latin America*. New York & Oxford: Oxford University Press, 2014.

Lovett, A. W. "Juan de Ovando and the Council of Finance (1573–1575)." *The Historical Journal*, 15:1 (1972), 1–21.

Lowry, James, and Heather MacNeil, "Archival thinking: Archaeologies and genealogies," *Archival Science* 21 (2021), 1–8.

Lucassen, Leo. "Working together: new directions in global labour history," *Journal of Global History* 11 (2016), 66–87.

Lucena Salmoral, Manuel, "Crisis de la conciencia nacional: Las dudas de Carlos V," in *La ética en la conquista de América*, ed. Luciano Pereña, pp. 163–198. Madrid: CSIC, 1984.

Ludwig, Ulrike. "Verwaltung als häusliche Praxis," in *Praktiken der Frühen Neuzeit. Akteure – Handlungen – Artefakte*, ed. Arndt Brendecke, pp. 188–198. Köln: Böhlau, 2015.

Lugo, Américo. *Edad media de la Isla Española, Historia de Santo Domingo, T.1*. Santo Domingo: Librería Dominicana, 1952.

Luhmann, Niklas. *Legitimation durch Verfahren*. Frankfurt am Main: Suhrkamp, 1983.

Luján Muñoz, Jorge. *Los escribanos en las Indias occidentales*. Mexico: UNAM, 1982.

Lupher, David A. *Romans in a New World: Classical Models in Sixteenth-Century Spanish America*. Ann Arbor: University of Michigan Press, 2006.

Luque Talaván, Miguel. *Un universo de opiniones: la literatura jurídica indiana*. Madrid: CSIC, 2003.

Lutz, Christopher and Karen Dakin, ed. and trans. *Nuestro Pesar, Nuestra Aflicción: Tunetuliniliz, tucucuca*. Mexico: UNAM, 1996.

Machuca, Paulina. *Intérpretes y trasuntos, siglos XVI-XVII: el caso de Colima de la Nueva España*. Colima: Alacyt, 2009.

Macías Rosendo, Baldomero. *La correspondencia de Benito Arias Montano con el Presidente de Indias Juan de Ovando*. Huelva: Universidad de Huelva, 2008.

MacKay, Ruth. *The Limits of Royal Authority: Resistance and Obedience in Seventeenth-Century Castile*. Cambridge: Cambridge University Press, 1999.

Madrazo, Santos, and Josep Fontana. *El sistema de transportes en España: 1750–1850*. Madrid: Colegio de Ingenieros de Caminos, Canales y Puertos, 1984.

Mangan, Jane E. "Indigenous Women as Mothers in Conquest-Era Peru," in *Women of the Iberian Atlantic*, ed. Sarah E. Owens and Jane E. Mangan, pp. 82–100. Baton Rouge: Louisiana State University Press, 2012.

Transatlantic Obligations: Creating the Bonds of Family in Conquest-Era Peru. Oxford: Oxford University Press, 2016.

Manzano Manzano, Juan. *Historia de las recopilaciones de Indias*, vol. I, *Siglo XVI*. Madrid: Ediciones Cultura Hispánica, 1950.

"Un documento inédito relativo a "como funcionaba el Consejo de Indias,'" *Hispanic American Historical Review* 15:3 (1935), 313–351.

Manzorro Guerrero, Irene. 2013. "Prácticas documentales y de escritura de Juan de Ledesma," in *Funciones y prácticas de la escritura*, ed. Juan Carlos Galende Díaz, pp. 129–133. Madrid: Universidad Complutense de Madrid, 2013.

Mariluz Urquijo, José M. "El concepto de tierra nueva en la fundamentación de la peculiaridad indiana," in *Memoria del IV Congreso Internacional de Historia del Derecho Indiano*, pp. 391–402. Mexico: UNAM, 1976.

Martínez, María Elena. *Genealogical Fictions: Limpieza de Sangre, Religion, and Gender in Colonial Mexico*. Stanford: Stanford University Press, 2008.

Martínez Almira, María Magdalena. "El delito de falsificación de documento público en la emisión de licencias para pasar a Indias durante el siglo XVI," in *Derecho de las Indias Occidentales y su pervivencia en los Derechos patrios de América*, ed. Alejandro Guzmán Brito, pp. 261–291. Valparaíso: Ediciones Universitarias de Valparaíso, 2010.

Martínez Cutillas, Pedro. *Veragua en el siglo XVI: Historia e imagen*. Salamanca: Ediciones Balboa, 2010

Martínez Martín, Carmen. *Vida y Obra del Calceatense Juan de Sámano, Secretario de Carlos V para asuntos indianos*. Logroño, Instituto de Estudios Riojanos, 2014.

Martínez Millán, José and Carlos Morales. "La administración de la Gracia Real: los miembros de la cámara de Castilla (1543–1575)," in *Instituciones y élites de poder en la monarquía hispana durante el siglo XVI*, ed. Jose Martínez Millán, pp. 25–46. Madrid: Universidad Autónoma, 1992.

La Corte de Carlos V: Segunda parte: Los Consejos y los consejeros de Carlos V, vol. III, Madrid: Sociedad Estatal, 2000.

Martínez Vega, María Elisa, and María Dolores Pérez Baltasar. *Madrid y América: 500 años de historia*. Madrid: MAPFRE, 1996.

Masters, Adrian. "Influential Women, New World Riches, and Masculine Anxieties in the Development of the Spanish Council of the Indies, 1524–98." *Renaissance Quarterly* 74:1(2021), 94–136.

"A Thousand Invisible Architects: Vassals, the Petition-and-Response System, and the Creation of Spanish Imperial Caste Legislation," *Hispanic American Historical Review* 98:3 (2018), 377–406.

Matuz, Josef. "Zur Sprache der Urkunden Süleymāns des Prächtigen," *Acta Orientalia Academiae Scientiarum Hungaricae* 26:2/3 (1972), 285–297.

Mayer Lux, Laura and Jaime Vera Vega, "Historia del falso testimonio: Orígenes y antecedentes de su regulación en el Código Penal chileno de 1874," *Revista de Estudios Histórico-Jurídicos* 40 (2018), 341–370.

Mayorga García, Fernando. *Real audiencia de Santafé en los siglos XVI y XVII: Historia, visitas, quejas y castigos*. Bogotá: Imprenta Distrital, 2013

Mazín Gómez, Óscar. *Gestores de la Real Justicia. Procuradores y agentes de las catedrales hispanas nuevas en la corte de Madrid*. Mexico City: El Colegio de México, 2007.

"La corte del rey y los procuradores de la catedral de México en los siglos XVI y XVII," in *Las cortes virreinales de la Monarquía española: América e Italia*, ed. Francesca Cantù, pp. 119–156. Roma: Viella, 2008.

McAlister, Lyle N. *Spain and Portugal in the New World, 1492–1700*, vol. 3. Minneapolis: University of Minnesota Press, 1984.

McDonough, Kelly. "Indigenous Rememberings and Forgettings: Sixteenth-Century Nahua Letters and Petitions to the Spanish Crown," *Native American and Indigenous Studies* 5:1 (2018), 69–99.

McEwan, Cheryl. "Building a Postcolonial Archive? Gender, Collective Memory and Citizenship in Post- apartheid South Africa," *Journal of Southern African Studies* 29 (2003), 739–757.

McGaw, Judith A. "Why Feminine Technologies Matter," in *Gender and Technology: A Reader*, ed. Nina E. Lerman, Ruth Oldenziel, and Arwen P. Mohun, pp. 13–36. Baltimore: Johns Hopkins University Press, 2003.

McKinley, Michelle A. *Fractional Freedoms: Slavery, Intimacy, and Legal Mobilization in Colonial Lima, 1600–1700*. Cambridge: Cambridge University Press, 2016.

McLuhan, Marshall. *Understanding Media*. New York: McGraw-Hill Book Company, 1964.

Medina, J. T. (ed.), *Colección de documentos inéditos para la historia de Chile. Volumes V and VI*. Santiago de Chile: Imprenta Ercilla, 1889.

Menegus Bornemann, Margarita, and Rodolfo Aguirre Salvador. *Los indios, el sacerdocio y la Universidad en Nueva España, siglos XVI-XVIII*. Mexico City: UNAM, 2006.

Mignolo, Walter. "Cartas, crónicas y relaciones del descubrimiento y la conquista," in *Historia de la Literatura Hispanoamericana*, ed. Luis Íñigo Madrigal, pp. 57–109. Madrid: Cátedra. 1982.

The Darker Side of Western Modernity: Global Futures, Decolonial Options. Durham: Duke University Press, 2011.

Mignolo, Walter D. and Catherine E. Walsh, *On Decoloniality: Concepts, Analytics, Praxis*. Durham: Duke University Press, 2018.

Mijares Ramírez, Ivonne. *Escribanos y escrituras públicas en el siglo XVI: El caso de la ciudad de México*. Mexico: UNAM, 1997.

Millar, Fergus. *The Emperor in the Roman World (31 BC- AD 337)*. London: Duckworth, 1977.

Milton, Cynthia E. *The Many Meanings of Poverty: Colonialism, Social Compacts, and Assistance in Eighteenth-Century Ecuador*. Stanford: Stanford University Press, 2007.

Ministerio de Fomento. *Cartas de Indias*. Madrid: Manuel G. Hernández, 1877.

Relaciones geográficas de Indias. Madrid: Manuel G. Hernández, 1885.

Mirow, Matthew C. *Latin American Law: A History of Private Law and Institutions in Spanish America*. Austin: University of Texas Press, 2004.

Mitchell, Silvia. *Queen, Mother, and Stateswoman: Mariana of Austria and the Government of Spain*. University Park: Pennsylvania State University Press, 2019.

Monter, William. *The Rise of Female Kings in Europe, 1300–1800*. New Haven: Yale University Press, 2012.

Mörner, Magnus. "La afortunada gestión de un misionero del Perú en Madrid en 1578," *Anuario de Estudios Americanos*, 19 (1962), 247–275.

Mörner, Magnus. *La Corona Española y los foráneos en los pueblos de indios de América*. Madrid: Agencia Española de Cooperación Internacional, 1999.

Moss Kanter, Rosabeth. *Men and Women of the Corporation*, 2nd ed. New York: Basic, 1993.

Motomura, Akira. "New Data on Minting, Seigniorage, and the Money Supply in Spain (Castile), 1597– 1643," *Explorations in Economic History*, 34:3 (1997), 331–367.

Moutin, Osvaldo Rodolfo. *Legislar en la América hispánica en la temprana edad moderna*. Frankfurt: Max Planck Institute for European Legal History, 2016.

"More than Copy and Paste: The Drafting of the Judicial Order in the Decrees of the Third Mexican Council." *Rechtsgeschichte – Legal History* 24 (2016), 154–170.

Muhs, Brian. *The Ancient Egyptian Economy, 3000–30 BCE*. Cambridge: Cambridge University Press, 2016.

Mumford, Jeremy Ravi. "Forgery and *Tambos*," in *Corruption in the Iberian Empires: Greed, Custom, and Colonial Networks*, ed. Christoph Rosenmüller, pp. 13–27. Albuquerque: University of New Mexico Press, 2017.

Muñoz Arbeláez, Santiago. *Costumbres en disputa: Los muiscas y el imperio español en Ubaque, siglo XVI*. Bogotá: Ediciones Uniandes 2015.

Muro Orejón, Antonio. "El Real y Supremo Consejo de las Indias." *Anuario de Estudios Americanos* 27 (1970), 195–218.

"La igualdad entre indios y españoles: la real cédula de 1697," in *Estudios sobre política indigenista española en América: Terceras Jornadas Americanistas de la Universidad de Valladolid*, pp. 365–386. Valladolid: Universidad de Valladolid, 1975.

Nader, Helen. *Liberty in Absolutist Spain: The Habsburg Sale of Towns, 1516–1700*. Baltimore: Johns Hopkins University Press, 1990.

Navarro Gala, Rosario. *El libro de protocolo del primer notario indígena (Cuzco, siglo XVI): Cuestiones filológicas, discursivas, y de contacto de lenguas*. Madrid: Iberoamereicana, 2015.

Navarro, José María. *Una denuncia profética desde el Perú a mediados del siglo XVIII: el Planctus indorum christianorum in America peruntina*. Lima: PUCP, 2001.

Nemser, Daniel. *Infrastructures of Race: Concentration and Biopolitics in Colonial Mexico*. Austin: University of Texas Press, 2017.

Nieto Soria, José Manuel. *Fundamentos ideológicos del poder real en Castilla (Siglos XIII-XVI)*. Madrid: Eudema, 1988.

Noack, Karoline. "Los caciques ante el notario: Transformaciones culturales en el siglo XVI," in *América bajo los Austrias: economía, cultura y sociedad*, ed. Héctor Noejovich Chernoff, pp. 191–204. Lima: PUCP, 2001.

Nubola, Cecilia. "Supplications between Politics and Justice," in *Petitions in Social History*, ed. Lex Heerma Van Voss, pp, 35–58. Cambridge: Cambridge University Press, 2001.

Nubola, Cecilia, and Andreas Würgler, eds., *Forme della comunicazione politica in Europa nei secoli XV-XVIII: Suppliche, gravamina, lettere*. Bologna: Il Mulino and Duncker & Humblot, 2004.

Olaechea Labayen, Juan Bautista. "Aspectos del Derecho indiano y el mestizaje en el siglo XVII." *Anuario de historia del derecho español*, 47 (1977), 499–522.

"El vocabulario racial de la América española y en especial la voz mestizo," *Boletín de la Real Academia Española* 65:234 (1985), 121–132.

Olivares, Irene. "Politics of Communication: Writing, Gender, and Royal Authority in the Spanish Empire (1556–1665)." PhD diss., University of Kansas, 2016.

Oliveira e Costa, João Paulo. "A correspondência do Extremo Oriente com a Europa," in *O Domínio da Distância*, ed. Maria Emília Madeira Santos and Manuel Lobato, pp. 21–28. Lisboa, Instituto de Investigação Científica Tropical, 2006.

Olko, Justyna. "Alphabetic Writing in the Hands of the Colonial Nahua Nobility," *Contributions in New World Archaeology* 7 (2016), 177–198.

Insignia of Rank in the Nahua World: From the Fifteenth to the Seventeenth Century. Boulder: University of Colorado, 2014.

Orquera, Yolanda Fabiola. "'Race' and "Class' in the Spanish Colonies of America: A Dynamic Social Perception," in *Rereading the Black Legend: The Discourses of Religious and Racial Difference in the Renaissance Empires*, ed. Margaret R. Greer, Walter D. Mignolo, and Maureen Quilligan, pp. 167–187. Chicago: University of Chicago Press, 2007.

Ostrom, Elinor. "Crossing the great divide: Coproduction, synergy, and development," *World Development* 24:6 (1996), 1073–1087.

Ots Capdequi, José María. *Manual de historia del derecho español en las Indias y del derecho propiamente indiano*. Buenos Aires: Editorial Losada, 1945.

Otte, Enrique, ed., *Cartas privadas de emigrantes a Indias, 1540–1616*. Mexico City: Fondo de Cultura Económica, 1996.

Owensby, Brian P. *Empire of Law and Indian Justice in Colonial Mexico*. Stanford: Stanford University Press, 2008.

"Pacto entre rey lejano y súbditos indígenas," *Historia Mexicana*, 61:1 (2011), 59–106.

"The Theater of Conscience in the 'Living Law' of the Indies," in *New Horizons in Spanish Colonial Law: Contribbutions to Transnational Early Modern Legal History*, ed. Thomas Duve and Heikki Pihlajamäki, pp. 125–149. Frankfurt: Max Planck Institute, 2015.

Padron, Ricardo. *The Spacious Word: Cartography, Literature, and Empire in Early Modern Spain*. Chicago: University of Chicago Press, 2004.

Pagden, Anthony. *The Fall of Natural Man: The American Indian and the Origins of Comparative Ethnology*. Cambridge: Cambridge University Press, 1986.

Paquette, Gabriel. "British Impressions of Spain and its Empire in the Age of Enlightenment," in *The Routledge Companion to the Hispanic Enlightenment*, ed. Elizabeth M. Franklin Lewis, Mónica Bolufer Peruga, Catherine M. Jaffe, and Javier Múñoz-Basols, pp. 231–242. New York: Routledge, 2019.

Parker, Geoffrey. *Imprudent King: A New Life of Philip II*. New Haven: Yale University Press, 2014.

Pearson, Michael Naylor. *Coastal Western India: Studies from the Portuguese Records. No. 2*. New Delhi: Concept Publishing Company, 1981.

Pereña, Luciano. "La pretensión a la perpetuidad de las encomiendas del Perú," in *Estudios sobre política indigenista española en América: Terceras Jornadas Americanistas de la Universidad de Valladolid*, vol.2, pp. 427–469. Valladolid, Universidad de Valladolid, 1976.

Pérez Fernández, Isacio O. P. *Cronología documentada de los viajes, estancias, y actuaciones de Fray Bartolomé de las Casas*. Bayamón: Universidad Central de Bayamón, 1984.

Pérez-Mallaína, Pablo E. *Spain's Men of the Sea: Daily Life on the Indies Fleets in the Sixteenth Century*. Trans. Carla Rahn Phillips, Baltimore: Johns Hopkins University Press, 1998.

Pérez-Perdomo, Rogelio. *Latin American Lawyers: A Historical Introduction*. Stanford: Stanford University Press, 2006.

Pérez Ramos, Francisco José. "Un valido de Felipe IV canciller de Indias: el conde-duque de Olivares," *Revista de Humanidades* 22 (2014), 153–185.

Peterson, Mendel. *The Funnel of Gold*. Boston: Brown, & Co, 1975.

Petroski, Karen. *Fiction and the Languages of Law: Understanding Contemporary Legal Discourse*. London: Routledge, 2019.

Pieper, Renate. "Cartas, avisos e impresos: Los medios de comunicación en el imperio de Carlos V," in *Carlos V y la quiebra del humanismo político en Europa (1530–1558)*, ed. José Martínez Millán, pp. 431–441. Madrid: Sociedad Estatal para la Acción Cultural Exterior, 2001.

Pietschmann, Horst. "Burocracia y corrupción en Hispanoamérica colonial: una aproximación tentativa." *Nova Americana* 5 (1982), 11–37.

"Corrupción en las indias españolas: revisión de un debate en la historiografía sobre Hispanoamérica colonial," in *Instituciones y corrupción en la historia*, ed. Manuel González Jiménez, Horst Pietschmann, Francisco Comín, and Joseph Pérez, pp. 31–52. Valladolid: Universidad de Valladolid, 1998.

Pimentel Carbo, Julio. *Caminos y medios de transporte en nuestro primer siglo colonial*. Guayaquil: Universidad de Guayaquil, 1985.

Pomar Jiménez, Julio. *Los pochtecas: el comercio en América Latina desde los Aztecas hasta la independencia*. México: EDAMEX, 1996.

Ponce Leiva, Pilar. "La argamasa que une los reinos: gestión e integración de las Indias en la Monarquía Hispánica, siglo XVII," *Anuario de Estudios Americanos* 74:2 (2017), 461–490.

Poole, Stafford. *Juan de Ovando: Governing the Spanish Empire in the Reign of Phillip II*. Norman: University of Oklahoma Press, 2004.

Pedro Moya de Contreras: Catholic Reform and Royal Power in New Spain, 1571–1591. Norman: University of Oklahoma Press, 2011.

Porras Arboledas, Pedro Andrés, Eloísa Ramírez Vaquero, and Flocel Sabaté i Currul. *La época medieval: administración y gobierno*. Madrid: Ediciones Istmo, 2003.

Portuondo, María M. *Secret Science: Spanish Cosmography and the New World*. Chicago: University of Chicago Press, 2009.

Post, Gaines. "Roman Law and Early Representation in Spain and Italy, 1150–1250," *Speculum* 18:2 (1943), 211–232.

Pratesi, Alessandro. *Genesi e forme del documento medievale*. Rome: Jouvence, 1979.

Premo, Bianca. "Before the Law: Women's Petitions in the Eighteenth-Century Spanish Empire." *Comparative Studies in Society and History*, 53:2 (2011), 261–289.

Children of the Father King: Youth, Authority, and Legal Minority in Colonial Lima. Chapel Hill: University of North Carolina Press, 2005.

The Enlightenment on Trial: Ordinary Litigants and Colonialism in the Spanish Empire. Oxford: Oxford University Press, 2017.

Pugliese La Valle, María Rosa. "Las fuentes del derecho a través de su aplicación judicial en el Virreinato del Río de la Plata, 2da. Parte," in *Derecho y administración pública en las Indias hispánicas*, vol. II. ed. Feliciano Barrios, pp. 1401–1428. Cuenca: Universidad de Castilla-La Mancha, 2002.

Quevedo, Roberto, Margarita Durán, and Alberto Duarte, eds., *Actas Capitulares y documentos del Cabildo de Asunción de Paraguay*. Asunción: Municipalidad de la Ciudad, 2001.

Quijano, Aníbal. "Colonialidad del poder y clasificación social," *Journal of World-Systems Research* 11:2 (2000), 342–386.

Quijano, Aníbal and Immanuel Wallerstein, "Americanity as a Concept: Or the Americas in the Modern World-System," *International Social Science Journal* 1:134 (1992), 549–557.

Quiroz, Alfonso W. *Corrupt Circles: A History of Unbound Graft in Peru*. Baltimore: Johns Hopkins Press, 2008.

Rahn Phillips, Carla. "The growth and composition of trade in the Iberian empires, 1450—1750," in *The Rise of Merchant Empires: Long Distance*

Trade in the Early Modern World, 1350–1750, ed. James D. Tracy, pp. 34–101. Cambridge: Cambridge University Press, 1990.

Raimúndez Ares, Zoraida. "Las "cartas de los caciques' de Yucatán de 1567: nuevas perspectivas. Aportaciones desde la edición crítica y la traducción," *Estudios de cultura maya* 54 (2019), 219–253.

Rama, Angel. *La ciudad letrada*. Montevideo: Arca, 1998.

Ramsay, Karen, and Martin Parker. "Gender, Bureaucracy, and Organizational Culture," *Sociological Review* 39.1 (1992), 253–276.

Rao, Anupama. "Affect, Memory, and Materiality: A Review Essay on Archival Mediation," *Comparative Studies in Society and History* 50:2 (2008), 559–567.

Rappaport, Joanne. *The Disappearing Mestizo: Configuring Difference in the Colonial New Kingdom of Granada*. Durham: Duke University Press, 2014.

Rappaport, Joanne, and Tom Cummins, *Beyond the Lettered City: Indigenous Literacies in the Andes*. Durham: Duke University Press, 2012.

Raup Wagner, Henry and Helen Rand Parish, *The Life and Writings of Bartolomé de las Casas*. Albuquerque: University of New Mexico Press, 1967.

Real Díaz, José Joaquín. "El Consejo de Cámara de Indias: génesis de su fundación," *Anuario de Estudios Americanos* 19 (1962), 725–758.

Estudio diplomático del documento indiano. Sevilla: Escuela de Estudios Hispanoamericanos, 1970.

Reinhardt, Nicole. *Voices of Conscience: Royal Confessors and Political Counsel in Seventeenth-Century Spain and France*. Oxford: Oxford University Press, 2016

Ribard, Dinah. "Le travail intellectuel: Travail et philosophie, XVIIe-XIXe siècle," *Annales. Histoire, Sciences Sociales* 3 (2010), 715–742.

Richards, Thomas. "Archive and Utopia," *Representations* 37 (1992), 104–135.

Rigaudière, Albert. "Issues at Stake in the Development of the State: Devising and Drafting the Law in Fourteenth-Century France" in *Legislation and Justice*, ed. Antonio Padoa-Schiopa, pp. 74–101. Oxford: Clarendon, 1997.

Riquelme, José Araneda. "Comunicando un desastre. Un mapa, diversos mensajeros y las noticias imperiales de una sublevación indígena (Arauco, 1598–1610)," *Razón Crítica* 10 (2021), 121–146.

Rivero Rodríguez, Manuel. "'De todo dí aviso a vuestra señoría por cartas,' Centro, periferia, y poder en la corte de Felipe II," in *Espacios de poder: Corte, ciudades, y villas, siglo XVI-XVIII*, vol. 1, ed. Jesús Bravo, pp. 267–290. Madrid: Jesús Bravo, 2002.

Roberts, Jennifer L. *Transporting Visions: The Movement of Images in Early America*. Berkeley: University of California Press, 2014.

Roche, Daniel. "L'intellectuel au travail," *Annales. Économies, Societés, Civilisations*. 37:3 (1982), 465–480.

Rodrigues, Vitor and Manuel Lobato. "Circulaçao de informaçao no Oriente," in *O Domínio da Distância*, ed. Maria Emília Madeira Santos and Manuel Lobato, pp. 45–52. Lisbon: Instituto de Investigação Científica Tropical, 2006.

Rodríguez, Jaime E. *La independencia de la América Española*. Mexico City: Colegio de México, 1996.

Rodríguez de Diego, José Luis. "Evolución histórica del expediente," *Anuario de Historia del Derecho Español* 68 (1998), 475–490.

Rohr, Zita Eva, and Lisa Benz, "Introduction," in *Queenship, Gender, and Reputation in the Medieval and Early Modern West, 1060–1600*, ed. Zita Eva Rohr and Lisa Benz, xvii–xliv. Cham: Springer, 2016.

Rojas Rabiela, Teresa, Elsa Leticia Rea López, and Constantino Medina Lima, *Vidas y bienes olvidados*, vol. 2. Mexico, DF: CIESAS, 1999.

Römer, Claudia. "Zu Formular Und Sprache Des „Registerbuchs Der Beschwerden." *Wiener Zeitschrift Für Die Kunde Des Morgenlandes* 80 (1990), 167–183.

Ross, Richard J. "Legal Communications and Imperial Governance: British North America and Spanish America Compared," in *Cambridge History of Law in America, Vol.1, Early America (1580–1815)*, ed. Christopher L. Tomlins and Michael Grossberg, pp. 104–143. Cambridge: Cambridge University Press, 2008.

Rotterdam, Erasmus of. *The Education of a Christian Prince*, ed. Lisa Jardine. Cambridge: Cambridge University Press, 2003.

Ruan, Felipe E. "Andean Activism and the Reformulation of Mestizo Agency and Identity in Early Colonial Peru." *Colonial Latin American Review* 21,2 (2012), 209–237.

"The Probanza and Shaping a Contesting Mestizo Record in Early Colonial Peru," *Bulletin of Spanish Studies*, 94:5 (2017), 843–869.

Rubial García, Antonio. "Religiosos viajeros en el mundo hispánico en la época de los Austrias (el caso de Nueva España)," *Historia mexicana* 61:3 (2012), 813–848.

Rubio Mañé, José Ignacio. *El Virreinato II: Expansión y defensa, primera parte*, 2nd ed. México: UNAM, 2005 [1959].

Rubio y Moreno, Luis. *Inventario general de registros cedularios del Archivo General de Indias de Sevilla*. Madrid: Compañía-Iberoamericana de Publicaciones, 1928.

Rück, Peter. "Beiträge zur diplomatischen Semiotik," in *Graphische Symbole in mittelalterlichen Urkunden*, ed. Peter Rück, pp. 13–48. Sigmaringen: Jan Thorbecke, 1996.

Ruiz-Crespo, Alfredo. *Cisneros, cardenal regente – paradigma de una vida*. Madrid: Editorial Gran Capitán, 1945.

Ruiz-Giménez Cortés, Joaquín. "Derecho y diálogo," *Revista de estudios políticos* 109 (1960), pp. 13–50.

Salazar Mir, Adolfo de. *Los expedientes de limpieza de sangre de la Catedral de Sevilla*, vol. 1. Madrid: Hidalguía, 1995

Sánchez, Magdalena S. *The Empress, the Queen, and the Nun: Women and Power at the Court of Philip III of Spain*. Baltimore: Johns Hopkins University Press, 1998.

Sánchez-Arcilla Bernal, José. *Las Ordenanzas de las Audiencias de Indias (1511–1821)*. Madrid, Dykinson, 1992.

Sánchez Bella, Ismael. "Estudio introductorio," in *Sumarios de la Recopilación General de Leyes de las Indias Occidentales* by Rodrigo de Aguiar y Acuña, pp. xxv–lii. Mexico: Universidad Nacional Aotónoma de México, 1994.

"La recopilación de las Indias" de León Pinelo." *Revista Chilena de Historia del Derecho* 14 (1991), 49–52.

Nuevos estudios de Derecho Indiano. Pamplona: Ediciones Universidades de Navarra, 1995.

Sancho Sayón, José, ed. *Colección de documentos inéditos para la historia de España* 94. Madrid: Ginesta Hermanos, 1889.

Sanz, Eufemio Lorenzo. *Los indios de Nueva España y su pugna con las pretensiones encomenderas en la época de los comisarios*. Valladolid: Universidad de Valladolid, 1976.

Sapiro, Gisele. "Les professions intellectuelles entre l'État, l'entrepreneuriat et l'industrie," *Le Mouvement Social* 1:214 (2006), 3–18.

Sarabia Viejo, María Justina. *Don Luís de Velasco, virrey de Nueva España, 1550–1564*. Seville: Escuela de Estudios Hispano-Americanos, 1978.

Sarfatti Larson, Magali. *Spanish Bureaucratic-Patrimonialism in America*. Berkeley: University of California, 1955.

Scardaville, Michael C. "Justice by Paperwork: A Day in the Life of a Court Scribe in Bourbon Mexico City," *Journal of Social History* 36:4 (2003), 979–1007.

Schäfer, Ernesto. "Der Verkehr Spaniens mit und in seinen Amerikanischen Kolonien." *Ibero-amerikanisches Archiv* 11:4 (1937), 435–455.

El Consejo Real y Supremo de las Indias: Su historia, organización y labor administrativa hasta la terminación de la Casa de Austria, vol. 1. Madrid: Marcial Pons Historia, 2003 [1936].

Las Rúbricas del Consejo Real y Supremo de las Indias. Seville: Imprenta Alemana, 1934.

Schmidt-Wiegand, Ruth. "Die rechtshistorische Funktion graphischer Zeichen und Symbole in Urkunde," in *Graphische Symbole in mittelalterlichen Urkunden*, ed. Peter Rück, pp. 67–80. Sigmaringen: Jan Thorbecke, 1996.

Scholes, France V. and Eleanor B. Adams, eds. *Cartas del Licenciado Jerónimo Valderrama y otros documentos sobre su visita al gobierno de Nueva España, 1563–1565*. Mexico City: Editorial Porrúa, 1961.

Schroeder, Susan, ed. *Native Resistance and the Pax Colonial in New Spain*. Lincoln: University of Nebraska Press, 1998.

Schwaller, Robert C. *Géneros de Gente in Early Colonial Mexico: Defining Racial Difference*. Norman: University of Oklahoma Press, 2016.

Schwartz, Stuart B. *Blood and Boundaries: The Limits of Religious and Racial Exclusion in Early Modern Latin America*. Waltham: Brandeis University Press, 2020.

Sea of Storms: A History of Hurricanes in the Greater Caribbean from Columbus to Katrina. Princeton: Princeton University Press, 2015

Schwartz, Joan M. "'Having New Eyes:' Spaces of Archives, Landscapes of Power," *Archivaria* 61 (2006), 1–25.

Schwartz, Joan M., and Terry Cook. "Archives, records, and power: The making of modern memory." *Archival Science* 2:1–2 (2002), 1–19.

Scott, James C. *Seeing like a State: How Certain Schemes to Improve the Human Condition Have Failed*. New Haven: Yale University Press, 1998.

Segal, Robert A. *Myth: A Very Short Introduction*. Oxford: Oxford University Press, 2004.

Sellers-García, Sylvia. *Distance and Documents at the Spanish Empire's Periphery*. Stanford: Stanford University Press, 2013.

Seoane, Maria Isabel. *Buenos Aires Vista por sus Procuradores (1580–1821)* Buenos Aires: IIHD, 1992.

Shaw, James E. "Writing to the Prince: Supplications, Equity and Absolutism in Sixteenth-century Tuscany." *Past & Present* 215:1 (2012), 51–83.

Silverblatt, Irene. "The Black Legend and Global Conspiracies," in *Rereading the Black Legend*, ed. Margaret R. Greer, Walter D. Mignolo, and Maureen Quilligan, pp. 99–116. Chicago: University of Chicago Press, 2007.

Modern Inquisitions: Peru and the Colonial Origins of the Civilized World. Durham: Duke University Press, 2004.

Simon, Herbert A. *Administrative Behavior: A Study of Decision-Making Processes in Administrative Organizations*, 4th ed. New York: Free Press, 1997 [1945].

Slicher van Bath, Bernard. *Hispanoamérica en torno a 1600*. Alicante: Universidad de Alicante, 2009.

Soll, Jacob. *The Reckoning: Financial Accountability and the Rise and Fall of Nations*. New York: Basic Books, 2014

Steele, Ian Kenneth. *The English Atlantic, 1675–1740: An Exploration of Communication and Community*. Oxford: Oxford University Press, 1986.

Stern, Steven J., ed. *Resistance, Rebellion, and Consciousness in the Andean Peasant World,18th to 20th Centuries*. Madison: University of Wisconsin Press, 1987.

Stolcke, Verena. "Los mestizos no nacen, se hacen," Verena Stolcke and Alexandre Coello (eds.), *Identidades ambivalentes en América Latina (siglos XVI-XX)* Barcelona: Edición Bellaterra, 2008.

Stoler, Ann. "Colonial Archives and the Arts of Governance," *Archival Science* 2 (2002), 87–109.

Into the Archive: Epistemic Anxieties and Colonial Common Sense. Princeton: Princeton University Press, 2009.

Stoler, Ann and Ann Laura Stoler. *Along the Archival Grain: Epistemic Anxieties and Colonial Common Sense*. Princeton: Princeton University Press, 2009.

Suárez Fernández, Luis, ed. *El Consejo de Indias en el siglo XVI*. Valladolid: Universidad de Valladolid, 1970;

Suárez Fernández, Luis. *Historia general de España y América, Tomo IX-2*. Madrid: Ediciones RIALP, 1984.

Sue, Christina A. *Land of the Cosmic Race: Race Mixture, Racism, and Blackness in Mexico*. Oxford: Oxford University Press, 2013.

Tanner, Marie. *The Last Descendant of Aeneas: The Habsburgs and the Mythic Image of the Emperor*. New Haven: Yale University, 1993

Tao Anzoátegui, Victor. "Acerca de la elaboración y publicación de la ley en el Derecho Indiano," *Anuario de historia del derecho español*, 80 (2010), 157–182.

Casuismo y Sistema. Indagación histórica sobre el espíritu del Derecho Indiano. Buenos Aires: Instituto de Investigaciones de Historia del Derecho, 1992.

El poder de la costumbre: estudios sobre del derecho consuetudinario en América hispana hasta la emancipación. Buenos Aires: IIHD, 2001.

La ley en América hispana: del descubrimiento a la emancipación. Buenos Aires: Academia Nacional de la Historia, 1992.
Teresa de Mier, José Servando. *Escritos inéditos*. México: Colegio de México, 1944.
Toro Garland, Fernando. "Una carta inédita sobre las "Leyes Nuevas." *Revista Chilena de Historia del Derecho*, 1 (1959), 63–71.
Trundle, Catherine and Chris Kaplonski, "Tracing the Political Lives of Archival Documents," *History and Anthropology* 22:4 (2011), 407–414.
Twinam, Ann. *Public Lives, Private Secrets: Gender, Honor, Sexuality, and Illegitimacy in Colonial Spanish America*. Stanford: Stanford University Press, 1999.
Purchasing Whiteness: Pardos, Mulattos, and the Quest for Social Mobility in the Spanish Indies. Stanford: Stanford University Press, 2015.
Uría Maqua, Juan. *Alonso de Bello (1552–1632): Un indiano perulero de los siglos XVI y XVII*. Oviedo: Universidad de Oviedo, 2005.
Ursinus, Michael. *Grievance Administration (Sikayet) in an Ottoman Province: The Kaymakam of Rumelia's "Record Bok of Complaints" of 1781–1783*. New York: Routledge, 2005.
Vaca de Castro, Cristóbal. "Ordenanzas de tambos [1543]." *Revista Histórica* 3:4 (1908), 427–492.
Vallejo García-Hevia, José María. "El Correo Mayor de las Indias (1514–1768)," in *Derecho y administración pública en las Indias hispánicas*, vol. 2, ed. Feliciano Barrios Pintado, pp. 1785–1810. Toledo: IIHDI, 1998.
Valle Pavón, Guillermina del. "La economía novohispana y los caminos de la Veracruz y Orizaba en el siglo XVI," in *Rutas de la Nueva España*, ed. Chantal Cramaussel pp. 39–62. Zamora: El Colegio de Michoacán, 2006.
Valls I Subirà, Oriol. *La historia del papel en España – Siglos X–XIV*, vol. 1. Madrid: Empresa Nacional de Celulosas, 1978.
Van der Linden, Marcel. *Workers of the World: Essays Toward a Global Labor History*. Leiden: Brill, 2008.
Van Deusen, Nancy E. *Global Indios: The Indigenous Struggle for Justice in Sixteenth-Century Spain*. Durham: Duke University Press, 2015.
"Oralidad y transmisión de conocimientos legales entre indios esclavos y manumisos en la Castilla del siglo XVI" *Historia*, 52:1 (2019), 169–195.
Vassberg, David E. *The Village and the Outside World in Golden Age Castile: Mobility and Migration in Everyday Rural Life*. Cambridge: Cambridge University Press, 2002.
Vermier, Maarten. "Chancellor Jean le Sauvage/ Ioannes Sylvagius: Erasmus' princeps christianus and a prince of Utopia for Thomas More." *Moreana* 53:203–204 (2017) 269–282.
Vernus, Pascal. "The Royal Command (*Wd-Nsw*): A Basic Deed of Executive Power," in *Ancient Egyptian Administration*, ed. Juan Carlos Moreno García, pp. 259–340. Leiden: Brill, 2013.
Vicens Vives, Jaime. "Estructura administrativa estatal en los siglos XVI y XVII," in *Clásicos de historia social de España: una selección crítica*, ed Jesús Izquierdo Martín and Pablo Sánchez León, 117–152. Madrid: Universidad Nacional de Educación a Distancia, 2000.

Vilches, Elvira. *New World Gold: Cultural Anxiety and Monetary Disorder in Early Modern Spain*. Chicago: University of Chicago Press, 2010.

Villarreal Brasca, Amorina. "Consejero de Felipe III en su Real Consejo de Indias: venalidad y corrupción en el servicio a la Monarquía," *Colonial Latin American Review* 26:4 (2017), 463–482.

Villella, Peter B. *Indigenous Elites and Creole Identity in Colonial Mexico, 1500–1800*. Cambridge: Cambridge University Press, 2016.

Viñao Frago, Antonio. "Alfabetización y primeras letras (siglos XVI–XVII)," in *Escribir y leer en el siglo de Cervantes*, ed. Antonio Castillo, pp. 39–84. Alcalá de Henares: Gedisa, 1999.

Vismann, Cornelia. *Files: Law and Media Technology*. Trans. Geoffrey Winthrop-Young. Stanford: Stanford University Press, 2008.

Vitoria, Francisco de. *Relecciones Teologicas Del P. Fray Francisco De Vitoria*, ed. D. Jaime Torrubiano Ripoll. Madrid: Libreria Religiosa Hernandez, 1917.

Walby, Sylvia. *Patriarchy at Work*. Cambridge: Polity, 1986.

Walsham, Alexandra. "The Social History of the Archive: Record-Keeping in Early Modern Europe." *Past and Present* 230, suppl.11 (2016), 9–48.

Warsh, Molly A. *American Baroque: Pearls and the Nature of Empire, 1492–1700*. Williamsburg: Omohundro Institute, 2018.

Wesch, Andreas, "El documento indiano y las tradiciones textuales en los siglos XV y XVI: La clase textual *información*," in *El español de América en el siglo XVI*, ed. Jens Lüdkte, pp. 57–71. Frankfurt: Vervuert, 1994.

Westbrook, Raymond. *Law from the Tigris to the Tiber: The Writings of Raymond Westbrook*, 1st ed. Eisenbrauns, Indiana, 2009.

Wilde, Guillermo. "La agencia indígena y el giro hacia lo global," *Historia Crítica* 69 (2018), 99–114.

Williams, Megan. "Unfolding Diplomatic Paper and Paper Practices in Early Modern Chancellery Archives," in *Praktiken der Frühen Neuzeit. Akteure – Handlungen – Artefakte*, ed. Arndt Brendecke, pp. 496–508. Köln: Böhlau, 2015.

Williams, Patrick. "Philip III and the Restoration of Spanish Government, 1598–1603," *English Historical Review* 88:4 (1973), 751–769

Witz, Anne, and Mike Savage. *Gender and Bureaucracy*. Oxford: Blackwell, 1992.

Würgler, Andreas. "Voices from among the "Silent Masses:' Humble Petitions and Social Conflicts in Early Modern Central Europe," in *Petitions in Social History*, ed. Lex Heerma Van Voss, pp. 11–34. Cambridge: Cambridge University Press, 2001.

Yale, Elizabeth. "The History of Archives: The State of the Discipline." *Book History* 18:1 (2015), 332–359.

Yannakakis, Yanna P. *The Art of Being In-Between: Native Intermediaries, Indian Identity, and Local Rule in Colonial Oaxaca*. Durham: Duke University Press, 2008.

"Indigenous People and Legal Culture in Spanish America," *History Compass*, 11:11 (2013), 931–947.

"Making Law Intelligible: Networks of Translation in Mid-Colonial Oaxaca," in *Indigenous Intellectuals: Knowledge, Power, and Colonial Culture in*

Mexico and the Andes, ed. Gabriela Ramos and Yanna Yannakakis, pp. 79–103. Durham: Duke University Press, 2014.

Ybot León, Antonio. "Juntas de teólogos asesoras del estado para Indias 1512–1550." *Anuario de estudios americanos* 5 (1948), 397–438.

Zaret, David. *Origins of Democratic Culture: Printing, Petitions, and the Public Sphere in Early-Modern England*. Princeton: Princeton University Press, 2000.

Zavala, Silvio A. "La Encomienda Indiana." *Trimestre Económico*, 2:8 (1935), 423–451.

Zemon Davis, Natalie. *Fiction in the Archives: Pardon Tales and Their Tellers in Sixteenth-century France*. Stanford: Stanford University Press, 1987.

The Gift in Sixteenth-Century France. Oxford: Oxford University Press, 2000.

Zúñiga, Nestor. "El camino de Quito a Tierra Firme," *Revista de Indias* 9:33–34 (1948), 891–948.

Index

Other Books in the Series (continued from page ii)

114. *The Mexican Mission: Indigenous Reconstruction and Mendicant Enterprise in New Spain, 1521–1600*, Ryan Dominic Crewe
113. *Corruption and Justice in Colonial Mexico, 1650–1755*, Christoph Rosenmüller
112. *Blacks of the Land: Indian Slavery, Settler Society, and the Portuguese Colonial Enterprise in South America*, Weinstein/Woodard/Montiero
111. *The Street Is Ours: Community, the Car, and the Nature of Public Space in Rio de Janeiro*, Shawn William Miller
110. *Laywomen and the Making of Colonial Catholicism in New Spain, 1630–1790*, Jessica L. Delgado
109. *Urban Slavery in Colonial Mexico: Puebla de los Ángeles, 1531–1706*, Pablo Miguel Sierra Silva
108. *The Mexican Revolution's Wake: The Making of a Political System, 1920–1929*, Sarah Osten
107. *Latin America's Radical Left: Rebellion and Cold War in the Global 1960s*, Aldo Marchesi
106. *Liberalism as Utopia: The Rise and Fall of Legal Rule in Post-Colonial Mexico, 1820–1900*, Timo H. Schaefer
105. *Before Mestizaje: The Frontiers of Race and Caste in Colonial Mexico*, Ben Vinson III
104. *The Lords of Tetzcoco: The Transformation of Indigenous Rule in Postconquest Central Mexico*, Bradley Benton
103. *Theater of a Thousand Wonders: A History of Miraculous Images and Shrines in New Spain*, William B. Taylor
102. *Indian and Slave Royalists in the Age of Revolution*, Marcela Echeverri
101. *Indigenous Elites and Creole Identity in Colonial Mexico, 1500–1800*, Peter Villella
100. *Asian Slaves in Colonial Mexico: From Chinos to Indians*, Tatiana Seijas
99. *Black Saint of the Americas: The Life and Afterlife of Martín de Porres*, Celia Cussen
98. *The Economic History of Latin America since Independence, Third Edition*, Victor Bulmer-Thomas
97. *The British Textile Trade in South American in the Nineteenth Century*, Manuel Llorca-Jaña
96. *Warfare and Shamanism in Amazonia*, Carlos Fausto
95. *Rebellion on the Amazon: The Cabanagem, Race, and Popular Culture in the North of Brazil, 1798–1840*, Mark Harris
94. *A History of the Khipu*, Galen Brokaw
93. *Politics, Markets, and Mexico's "London Debt," 1823–1887*, Richard J. Salvucci
92. *The Political Economy of Argentina in the Twentieth Century*, Roberto Cortés Conde
91. *Bankruptcy of Empire: Mexican Silver and the Wars Between Spain, Britain, and France, 1760–1810*, Carlos Marichal

90. *Shadows of Empire: The Indian Nobility of Cusco, 1750–1825*, David T. Garrett
89. *Chile: The Making of a Republic, 1830–1865: Politics and Ideas*, Simon Collier
88. *Deference and Defiance in Monterrey: Workers, Paternalism, and Revolution in Mexico, 1890–1950*, Michael Snodgrass
87. *Andrés Bello: Scholarship and Nation-Building in Nineteenth-Century Latin America*, Ivan Jaksic
86. *Between Revolution and the Ballot Box: The Origins of the Argentine Radical Party in the 1890s*, Paula Alonso
85. *Slavery and the Demographic and Economic History of Minas Gerais, Brazil, 1720–1888*, Laird W. Bergad
84. *The Independence of Spanish America*, Jaime E. Rodríguez
83. *The Rise of Capitalism on the Pampas: The Estancias of Buenos Aires, 1785–1870*, Samuel Amaral
82. *A History of Chile, 1808–2002, Second Edition*, Simon Collier and William F. Sater
81. *The Revolutionary Mission: American Enterprise in Latin America, 1900–1945*, Thomas F. O'Brien
80. *The Kingdom of Quito, 1690–1830: The State and Regional Development*, Kenneth J. Andrien
79. *The Cuban Slave Market, 1790–1880*, Laird W. Bergad, Fe Iglesias García, and María del Carmen Barcia
78. *Business Interest Groups in Nineteenth-Century Brazil*, Eugene Ridings
77. *The Economic History of Latin America since Independence, Second Edition*, Victor Bulmer-Thomas
76. *Power and Violence in the Colonial City: Oruro from the Mining Renaissance to the Rebellion of Tupac Amaru (1740–1782)*, Oscar Cornblit
75. *Colombia before Independence: Economy, Society and Politics under Bourbon Rule*, Anthony McFarlane
74. *Politics and Urban Growth in Buenos Aires, 1910–1942*, Richard J. Walter
73. *The Central Republic in Mexico, 1835–1846, 'Hombres de Bien' in the Age of Santa Anna*, Michael P. Costeloe
72. *Negotiating Democracy: Politicians and Generals in Uruguay*, Charles Guy Gillespie
71. *Native Society and Disease in Colonial Ecuador*, Suzanne Austin Alchon
70. *The Politics of Memory: Native Historical Interpretation in the Colombian Andes*, Joanne Rappaport
69. *Power and the Ruling Classes in Northeast Brazil, Juazeiro and Petrolina in Transition*, Ronald H. Chilcote
68. *House and Street: The Domestic World of Servants and Masters in Nineteenth-Century*, Rio de Janeiro, Sandra Lauderdale Graham
67. *The Demography of Inequality in Brazil*, Charles H. Wood and José Alberto Magno de Carvalho
66. *The Politics of Coalition Rule in Colombia*, Jonathan Hartlyn

65. *South America and the First World War: The Impact of the War on Brazil, Argentina, Peru and Chile*, Bill Albert
64. *Resistance and Integration: Peronism and the Argentine Working Class, 1946–1976*, Daniel James
63. *The Political Economy of Central America since 1920*, Victor Bulmer-Thomas
62. *A Tropical Belle Epoque: Elite Culture and Society in Turn-of-the-Century Rio de Janeiro*, Jeffrey D. Needell
61. *Ambivalent Conquests: Maya and Spaniard in Yucatan, 1517–1570, Second Edition*, Inga Clendinnen
60. *Latin America and the Comintern, 1919–1943*, Manuel Caballero
59. *Roots of Insurgency: Mexican Regions, 1750–1824*, Brian R. Hamnett
58. *The Agrarian Question and the Peasant Movement in Colombia: Struggles of the National Peasant Association, 1967–1981*, Leon Zamosc
57. *Catholic Colonialism: A Parish History of Guatemala, 1524–1821*, Adriaan C. van Oss
56. *Pre-Revolutionary Caracas: Politics, Economy, and Society 1777–1811*, P. Michael McKinley
55. *The Mexican Revolution, Volume 2: Counter-Revolution and Reconstruction*, Alan Knight
54. *The Mexican Revolution, Volume 1: Porfirians, Liberals, and Peasants*, Alan Knight
53. *The Province of Buenos Aires and Argentine Politics, 1912–1943*, Richard J. Walter
52. *Sugar Plantations in the Formation of Brazilian Society: Bahia, 1550–1835*, Stuart B. Schwartz
51. *Tobacco on the Periphery: A Case Study in Cuban Labour History, 1860–1958*, Jean Stubbs
50. *Housing, the State, and the Poor: Policy and Practice in Three Latin American Cities*, Alan Gilbert and Peter M. Ward
49. *Unions and Politics in Mexico: The Case of the Automobile Industry*, Ian Roxborough
48. *Miners, Peasants and Entrepreneurs: Regional Development in the Central Highlands of Peru*, Norman Long and Bryan Roberts
47. *Capitalist Development and the Peasant Economy in Peru*, Adolfo Figueroa
46. *Early Latin America: A History of Colonial Spanish America and Brazil*, James Lockhart and Stuart B. Schwartz
45. *Brazil's State-Owned Enterprises: A Case Study of the State as Entrepreneur*, Thomas J. Trebat
44. *Law and Politics in Aztec Texcoco*, Jerome A. Offner
43. *Juan Vicente Gómez and the Oil Companies in Venezuela, 1908–1935*, B. S. McBeth
42. *Revolution from Without: Yucatán, Mexico, and the United States, 1880–1924*, Gilbert M. Joseph
41. *Demographic Collapse: Indian Peru, 1520–1620*, Noble David Cook

40. *Oil and Politics in Latin America: Nationalist Movements and State Companies*, George Philip
39. *The Struggle for Land: A Political Economy of the Pioneer Frontier in Brazil from 1930 to the Present Day*, J. Foweraker
38. *Caudillo and Peasant in the Mexican Revolution*, D. A. Brading, ed.
37. *Odious Commerce: Britain, Spain and the Abolition of the Cuban Slave Trade*, David Murray
36. *Coffee in Colombia, 1850–1970: An Economic, Social and Political History*, Marco Palacios
35. *A Socioeconomic History of Argentina, 1776–1860*, Jonathan C. Brown
34. *From Dessalines to Duvalier: Race, Colour and National Independence in Haiti*, David Nicholls
33. *Modernization in a Mexican ejido: A Study in Economic Adaptation*, Billie R. DeWalt.
32. *Haciendas and Ranchos in the Mexican Bajío, Léon, 1700–1860*, D. A. Brading
31. *Foreign Immigrants in Early Bourbon Mexico, 1700–1760*, Charles F. Nunn
30. *The Merchants of Buenos Aires, 1778–1810: Family and Commerce*, Susan Migden Socolow
29. *Drought and Irrigation in North-east Brazil*, Anthony L. Hall
28. *Coronelismo: The Municipality and Representative Government in Brazil*, Victor Nunes Leal
27. *A History of the Bolivian Labour Movement, 1848–1971*, Guillermo Lora
26. *Land and Labour in Latin America: Essays on the Development of Agrarian Capitalism in the Nineteenth and Twentieth Centuries*, Kenneth Duncan and Ian Rutledge, eds.
25. *Allende's Chile: The Political Economy of the Rise and Fall of the Unidad Popular*, Stefan de Vylder
24. *The Cristero Rebellion: The Mexican People Between Church and State, 1926–1929*, Jean A. Meyer
23. *The African Experience in Spanish America, 1502 to the Present Day*, Leslie B. Rout, Jr.
22. *Letters and People of the Spanish Indies: Sixteenth Century*, James Lockhart and Enrique Otte, eds.
21. *Chilean Rural Society from the Spanish Conquest to 1930*, Arnold J. Bauer
20. *Studies in the Colonial History of Spanish America*, Mario Góngora
19. *Politics in Argentina, 1890–1930: The Rise and Fall of Radicalism*, David Rock
18. *Politics, Economics and Society in Argentina in the Revolutionary Period*, Tulio Halperín Donghi
17. *Marriage, Class and Colour in Nineteenth-Century Cuba: A Study of Racial Attitudes and Sexual Values in a Slave Society*, Verena Stolcke
16. *Conflicts and Conspiracies: Brazil and Portugal, 1750–1808*, Kenneth Maxwell
15. *Silver Mining and Society in Colonial Mexico: Zacatecas, 1546–1700*, P. J. Bakewell

14. *A Guide to the Historical Geography of New Spain*, Peter Gerhard
13. *Bolivia: Land, Location and Politics Since 1825*, J. Valerie Fifer, Malcolm Deas, Clifford Smith, and John Street
12. *Politics and Trade in Southern Mexico, 1750–1821*, Brian R. Hamnett
11. *Alienation of Church Wealth in Mexico: Social and Economic Aspects of the Liberal Revolution, 1856–1875*, Jan Bazant
10. *Miners and Merchants in Bourbon Mexico, 1763–1810*, D. A. Brading
9. *An Economic History of Colombia, 1845–1930*, W. P. McGreevey
8. *Economic Development of Latin America: Historical Background and Contemporary Problems*, Celso Furtado and Suzette Macedo
7. *Regional Economic Development: The River Basin Approach in Mexico*, David Barkin and Timothy King
6. *The Abolition of the Brazilian Slave Trade: Britain, Brazil and the Slave Trade Question, 1807–1869*, Leslie Bethell
5. *Parties and Political Change in Bolivia, 1880–1952*, Herbert S. Klein
4. *Britain and the Onset of Modernization in Brazil, 1850–1914*, Richard Graham
3. *The Mexican Revolution, 1910–1914: The Diplomacy of Anglo-American Conflict*, P. A. R. Calvert
2. *Church Wealth in Mexico: A Study of the 'Juzgado de Capellanias' in the Archbishopric of Mexico 1800–1856*, Michael P. Costeloe
1. *Ideas and Politics of Chilean Independence, 1808–1833*, Simon Collier

For EU product safety concerns, contact us at Calle de José Abascal, 56–1°,
28003 Madrid, Spain or eugpsr@cambridge.org.

www.ingramcontent.com/pod-product-compliance
Ingram Content Group UK Ltd.
Pitfield, Milton Keynes, MK11 3LW, UK
UKHW041837191125
465198UK00012B/337